PRAISE FOR
MY COUNTRY TO
DEFEND

"Whatever your opinion on the war, Diego became a soldier from the heart. Diego fought to give the Iraqi people the same blessing he was so privileged to know. An honest and gut-wrenching portrayal of a patriot and the forces that preserve our way of life...I'm honored to be counted with these men."

—Tommy Franks, Retired Four-Star General
and former Commander-In-Chief, U.S. Central Command

"The story of the life and death of Private First Class Diego Rincon will forever inspire everyone who reads it. I am grateful to Amy Dimond for putting into beautiful words one of the country's most moving tales of patriotism."

—Zell Miller, United States Senator

"A. E. Dimond captures the heart of what makes America unique. She lays bare the souls of true heroes and patriots who have paid the ultimate price for their country. *My Country to Defend* is profoundly written, insightful, and altering..."

—Gerald Molen, Oscar-winning producer Schindler's List, extended review

"In search of the American dream, the Rincon Family gave us one of their own to protect and maintain our freedom. Diego's legacy will carry on, and his sacrifice will set an example for new generations of immigrants that are willing to do anything for their love of this country."

—Emilio Estefan, director and producer

"A. E. Dimond tells an amazing story, allowing you to *feel* an immigrant's love of country. It's not just that Iraq was suffering from the hand of tyranny—it's that the whole world is a better place because Diego Rincon was in it. Dimond delivers that understanding of the responsibility that accompanies the freedom."

—Jim Roope, CNN Radio, Los Angeles Correspondent

"Throughout my professional playing career, I heard people compare football to war. Football is *not* war. This book shows war and all of the courage, the nobility, and the honor of young men in the very real thing…When all eyes were on the *battle* field, Diego Rincon and his fellow soldiers rose to something beyond the mortal contests. Diego relinquished his final breath at Al-Najaf. It seems to me that our own air is borrowed now—that we owe it to soldiers like him to live to be worthy of that sacrifice."

—Richmond Flowers, Jr., attorney
and former player in the National Football League

"What moves a person to enlist in the armed services, to stand in harm's way, knowing he or she may be swept away in the tide of battle? A. E. Dimond provides a timely and often poignant look at the life and death of a young Colombian immigrant who put his life on the line in Iraq for his adopted country. *My Country to Defend* is more than a war story; it's a penetrating exploration of one family's enduring faith in America and its future—a faith that transcends shattering heartbreak."

—T. Jeff Williams, co-author of
A Cambodian Oddysey and the Deaths of 25 Journalists,
former foreign correspondent for The Associated Press and CBS News

FROM THE FAMILIES OF THE FALLEN

"I had so many comrades who returned from Vietnam with Purple Hearts in flag-draped coffins. It seemed that when I came home from the war, few people cared that I had served my country, or that others had died doing the same. My son came home with a Purple Heart in a flag-draped coffin and people have cared immensely. One person cared enough to leave everything behind to tell this story. I can't begin to say what it means to me that Amy Dimond made sure Mike's memory would always be alive in the pages of this book."

—Russell Creighton, father of fallen soldier
PFC Michael Russell Creighton-Weldon,
featured in My Country to Defend

"Our son loved his country and he was honored to serve his country. Amy Dimond has gifted our family not only a beautiful tribute to Michael, and to those with whom he served—she's given a voice to all of us who believe that freedom is worth the fight. Patrick Henry said, 'Give me liberty or give me death' and sometimes that may seem like a far-off sentiment. Sometimes that may even seem melodramatic with all of the blessings we enjoy now. It's not some distant patriotism: it was the conviction of our son, laying down his life after the attacks of September 11. It was the conviction of our son, fighting for the Iraqi people so that they could someday be just as blessed."

—Joan Curtin, mother of fallen soldier CPL Michael Curtin,
featured in My Country to Defend

"Monica was born three months after Eugene died, and she will never get to meet her daddy. My oldest daughter, Mya, was only three years old when Eugene went to Iraq. She has many memories of the good times, but my worst fear was that she would forget them as she grew older. Words cannot describe how grateful I am for this tribute that will show my daughters what a special man Eugene was. I know now that my husband will not be forgotten and it helps ease the pain in my heart."

—Brandy Williams, wife of fallen soldier SGT Eugene Williams,
featured in My Country to Defend

MY COUNTRY TO DEFEND

MY COUNTRY TO DEFEND

A. E. Dimond

iUniverse Star
New York Lincoln Shanghai

My Country to Defend

iUniverse Star
an iUniverse, Inc. imprint

For information address:
iUniverse, Inc.
2021 Pine Lake Road, Suite 100
Lincoln, NE 68512
www.iuniverse.com

ISBN: 0-595-33484-9 (pbk)
ISBN: 0-595-66951-4 (cloth)

Printed in the United States of America

To liberty's brave defenders…
and those they leave behind.

A portion of the proceeds from the sale of this book are being donated to Oliver North's Freedom Alliance. The Freedom Alliance raises funding for scholarships for children whose armed forces parents have either died, or been permanently disabled in the line of duty.

MAIN CHARACTERS

PFC Diego Rincon	Colombian immigrant, awarded posthumous American citizenship. Member of the Outlaw Platoon of the 3rd Infantry Division's 2nd Battalion, 7th Infantry Regiment. Earned the Combat Infantryman Badge. Posthumously awarded the Purple Heart, the Bronze Star, the War on Terrorism Expeditionary Medal, the War on Terrorism Service Medal, the Presidential Unit Citation Medal, and the National Defense Medal, Operation Iraqi Freedom
Jorge Rincon	Diego's father, a Colombian immigrant
Yolanda Rincon	Diego's mother, a Colombian immigrant
Fabian Rincon	Diego's older brother, a Colombian immigrant
Adela Rincon	Jorge's mother, a Colombian resident
George Rincon	Diego's younger brother, a United States citizen, born in Georgia

Stephanie Rincon — Diego's younger sister, a United States citizen, born in Georgia. Nicknamed Tí Tí

Kenneth Khamphiphone — High school friend and cheerleader at Salem High School. Worked at Rockdale Gymnastics with Diego

Jerry Smith — Diego's mentor and head of drama at Salem High School

Pastor Mike Leno — Friend and spiritual leader to the Rincon family

1LT Brian Johnson — 3rd ID, 2-7, leader of the Outlaw Platoon. Served five years in the Navy. Joined the Army after receiving a master's degree in international relations. Earned the Combat Infantryman Badge. Awarded three Bronze Star Medals, including one Bronze Star Medal for Valor. Received the Army Accommodation Medal for Valor during the infamous "Thunder Run" into Baghdad. Awarded the Presidential Unit Citation Medal, the National Defense Medal, the War on Terrorism Expeditionary Medal, and the War on Terrorism Service Medal, Operation Iraqi Freedom. Was promoted and served as General Aide de Camp following service in Iraq. Was promoted to captain and given command over E Company 2-19 Infantry at Fort Benning

SSG Chad Urquhart — 3rd ID, 2-7, member of the Outlaw Platoon. Diego's squad leader. Earned the Combat Infantryman Badge. Awarded the Army Accommodation Medal for Valor. Awarded the Presidential Unit Citation Medal, the National Defense Medal, the War on Terrorism Expeditionary Medal, and the War on Terrorism Service Medal, Operation Iraqi Freedom

SGT Ronald Tolbert

3rd ID, 2-7, member of the Outlaw Platoon. Earned the Combat Infantryman Badge. Awarded the Army Accommodation Medal for Valor during the infamous "Thunder Run" into Baghdad. Awarded the Presidential Unit Citation Medal, the National Defense Medal, the War on Terrorism Expeditionary Medal, and the War on Terrorism Service Medal, Operation Iraqi Freedom. Promoted to staff sergeant. A Bradley section leader, 3rd ID

SGT Eugene Williams

3rd ID, 2-7, member of the Outlaw Platoon. Referred to by the soldiers as "Sergeant Wills." Earned the Combat Infantryman Badge. Posthumously awarded the Purple Heart, the Bronze Star, the Presidential Unit Citation Medal, the National Defense Medal, the War on Terrorism Expeditionary Medal, and the War on Terrorism Service Medal, Operation Iraqi Freedom

CPL Michael Curtin

3rd ID, 2-7, member of the Outlaw Platoon. Member of Diego's squad, Bravo team. Referred to by the soldiers as "Jersey." Earned the Combat Infantryman Badge. Posthumously awarded the Purple Heart, the Bronze Star, the Presidential Unit Citation Medal, the National Defense Medal, the War on Terrorism Expeditionary Medal, and the War on Terrorism Service Medal, Operation Iraqi Freedom. Also received the Distinguished Service Medal, awarded by the State of New Jersey

SPC Anthony Farina

3rd ID, 2-7, member of the Outlaw Platoon. Diego's team leader at Fort Stewart. Earned the Combat Infantryman Badge. Awarded the Army Accommodation Medal, the Presidential Unit Citation Medal, the National Defense Medal, the War on Terrorism Expeditionary Medal, and the War on Terrorism Service Medal, Operation Iraqi Freedom. Promoted to sergeant. Entered Special Forces following his return from Iraq

SPC Patrick Sawicki 3rd ID, 2-7, member of the Outlaw Platoon. Referred to by the soldiers as "Patty Cake." Graduated from Radford University. Earned the Combat Infantryman Badge. Awarded the Army Accommodation Medal, the Presidential Unit Citation Medal, the National Defense Medal, the War on Terrorism Expeditionary Medal, and the War on Terrorism Service Medal, Operation Iraqi Freedom. Promoted to sergeant and began service with the CID (Criminal Investigation Command). Returned to the 2-7's Alpha Company for his second deployment to Iraq

PFC Robbie Brooks 3rd ID, 2-7, member of the Outlaw Platoon. Earned the Combat Infantryman Badge. Awarded the Army Accommodation Medal, the Presidential Unit Citation Medal, the National Defense Medal, the War on Terrorism Expeditionary Medal, and the War on Terrorism Service Medal, Operation Iraqi Freedom. Promoted to specialist. Honorably discharged in 2004 to attend college

PFC Allen Black 3rd ID, 2-7, member of the Outlaw Platoon. Member of Diego's squad, Alpha team. Earned the Combat Infantryman Badge. Awarded the Army Accommodation Medal, the Presidential Unit Citation Medal, the National Defense Medal, the War on Terrorism Expeditionary Medal, and the War on Terrorism Service Medal, Operation Iraqi Freedom

PFC Adrian Cavazos 3rd ID, 2-7, member of the Outlaw Platoon. Member of Diego's squad, Alpha team. Referred to by the soldiers as "Cvos." Earned the Combat Infantryman Badge. Awarded the Army Accommodation Medal for Valor, the Presidential Unit Citation Medal, the National Defense Medal, the War on Terrorism Expeditionary Medal, and the War on Terrorism Service Medal, Operation Iraqi Freedom. Promoted to specialist and then corporal

PFC Michael Russell
Creighton-Weldon

3rd ID, 2-7, member of the Outlaw Platoon. Member of Diego's squad, Bravo team. Referred to by the soldiers as "Big Mike." Earned the Combat Infantryman Badge. Posthumously awarded the Purple Heart, the Bronze Star, the Presidential Unit Citation Medal, the National Defense Medal, the War on Terrorism Expeditionary Medal, and the War on Terrorism Service Medal, Operation Iraqi Freedom

PFC Erwin Rendon

3rd ID, 2-7, member of the Outlaw Platoon. Earned the Combat Infantryman Badge. Awarded the Purple Heart, the Army Accommodation Medal, the Presidential Unit Citation Medal, the National Defense Medal, the War on Terrorism Expeditionary Medal, and the War on Terrorism Service Medal, Operation Iraqi Freedom

PFC Paolo Ronquillo

3rd ID, 2-7, member of the Outlaw Platoon. Referred to by the soldiers as "Ronny Q." Earned the Combat Infantryman Badge. Awarded the Army Accommodation Medal, the Presidential Unit Citation Medal, the National Defense Medal, the War on Terrorism Expeditionary Medal, and the War on Terrorism Service Medal, Operation Iraqi Freedom

EDITOR'S NOTES: The names of the children of Jorge's former employee, found in "The Immigrant," have been fictionalized to protect their identities. The grandmother of those same children is a composite character.

Military personnel in the "Main Characters" section are listed by order of rank, and then subsequently listed in alphabetical order. Ranks listed before individual names are those earned at the time of the soldiers' January, 2003 deployment for Operation Iraqi Freedom. Promotions are duly noted in main character descriptions and were current at the time of printing.

Taken from Paragraph 2-6, Army Regulation 600-8-22 (Military Awards), February 25, 1995: The Combat Infantryman Badge (CIB) was established by the War Department on 27 October, 1943. Lieutenant General Lesley J. McNair, then the Army Ground Forces commanding general, was instrumental in its creation...Then Secretary of War Henry Stinson said, "It is high time we recognize in a personal way the skill and heroism of the American infantry"...Of all soldiers, it was recognized that the infantryman continuously operated under the worst conditions and performed a mission which was not assigned to any other soldier or unit...[many] factors led to the establishment of the CIB, an award which would provide special recognition of the unique role of the Army infantryman, the only soldier whose daily mission is to close with and destroy the enemy and to seize and hold terrain. The CIB is also commonly referred to as the Combat Infantry Badge.

PROLOGUE
ON BEHALF OF
DIEGO RINCON

When you feel the warmth of the sun on your face, think of me.

Sidling up to home plate, savoring the expectation of some sweet-spot crack of the bat, about to propel so much childlike innocence into center field—these were the small things that lent me breath and took it away in such measured strokes; moment by moment, the small things, really, for which I lived and I died.

I was born a Colombian, but it was the United States of America that stole my heart, a pile of Atlanta Braves baseball cards and a turbocharged engine in a yellow Mustang convertible the only temporal traces of an existence so cherished and so short. I won a chance at freedom like some once-in-a-lifetime lottery and I never forgot the responsibility that accompanied the rights.

I shouldered it with an M16 assault rifle to my grave.

Remember me as audacious and spontaneous and steadfast. And then remember me as human: a nineteen-year-old with fears and misgivings and sorrows. That I struggled with the brutalities of combat and my own mortality— that I *struggled* is what made my final morning so heroic. I was not unafraid: I was homesick and scared and longing for a better day, far from the throes of war, and still I rose to all that was expected of me as a citizen soldier when citizenship was still but a dream. That was my characteristic will and my optimism—that was my heart overcoming the natural feet of clay that might have caused a lesser man to shrink.

Remember me with affection: someone so full of sunshine that those whose lives I touched have been forever shadowed by my passing. And then remember me as young always, catapulting to dizzying heights—a never-ending series of gravity defying back handsprings and carefree cartwheels and a smile so dazzling I lit up stages and gymnasiums and even a mess tent in the middle of a blinding sandstorm. I could have grown old like some men, worthy to sit on a porch in the afternoon, reminiscing of glory days with musty irreverence and content. That is the privilege afforded longer lives, the twilight of a fuller day.

Remember my family and their arduous journey to bring me to a country where we would not live in fear of bombs and civil unrest; where we would not live in a moral poverty so stark it could hollow a man's soul as well as his gut. My parents sacrificed so for all my little boy dreams and they'd never even heard of Al-Najaf, Iraq until a terrorist attack took my life there.

These days my mom sits quietly on my bed holding my pillow with the lingering scent and the memories so poignant, so overwhelmingly painful that it is hard for her to get up in the morning.

Remember that I used to love the tartness of her fresh pineapple juice on my tongue, and that I used to pull the top down on my convertible just to feel the air washing over my face, the heat of the Georgia sun trickling down my neck. Remember that the sweet taste in my mouth and the treasured breath in my nostrils that only liberty brought are still yours—to be on a long stretch of highway with nothing behind you but patriot dreams and nothing ahead of you but more of the same, God and His people willing. These are the things for which I fought and sacrificed with my seared flesh and my honor. These are the things for which my brothers on the battlefield have continued to pay the debt—so much blood and infinite grief shed for your right to live and be blessed now.

Remember that I would do it all over again:

I have come to know the sweet face of Jesus, of His redeeming love, and I have come to understand in my own way what it is to lay down the most precious gift of life for humanity's sake.

I was a soldier once: the red, white, and blue of my soul's desire still waving undaunted beneath so many bright rays of promise and every sure beam of hope. Freedom was the color of my sunlight in the only country I ever wanted to call home.

Yours now, shining so brilliantly in the liberated sky overhead.

THE
IMMIGRANT

And how stands the city on this winter night…after 200 years, two centuries, she still stands strong and true on the granite ridge, and her glow has held steady no matter what storm. And she's still a beacon, still a magnet for all who must have freedom, for all the pilgrims from all the lost places who are hurtling through the darkness, toward home."

—*Ronald Wilson Reagan*

CHAPTER 1

Jorge Rincon caught a bird's-eye view of the ticket counter in his reckless descent. He scanned it frantically then lost sight of it, making the sign of the cross again. The check-in line was enormous, crawling with old people, bent over people, then children crying and clinging to their mothers, and a pair of lovers in a final embrace off to one side. There were too many people and a clammy, nauseating desperation began to heighten his terror.

He was tall—for a Colombian very tall—and he used his size, the brute force of his bodyguard training, to push headlong past the swarm on the escalator.

If they knew, the people gawking at him, murmuring in discontent over his brusqueness…

If they only knew the kind of despair that had tossed him to and fro each night in such misery; the kind of famine that Jorge had tried and tried to feed and could never fully satisfy—the expectation of finally filling the void only to have it snatched from him at the very last second.

But of course they did know, and perhaps they envied him for the very last shred of hope that was driving him like a madman through the airport terminal. A madman, distraught and blinded by fear, hurling toward a ticket counter, indifferent to fate.

"Padre nuestro que estás en los cielos, santificado sea tu nombre…" *Hallowed be thy name.* The Lord's prayer rose, fervent, to his lips. "…sea hecha tu voluntad en la tierra así como en el cielo."

He was mumbling, his shirt was wet with perspiration. He was on the brink of tears.

Thy will be done. He had whispered it, hoarse. *On earth as it is in heaven.*

+>==<+

It took nearly five years to earn the equivalent of 3,000 U.S. dollars in Colombia. The man who actually held it in his hands, felt its stiffness and weight—actually got to smell the relentless fatigue that scented such hard-earned wages—that was a man rare in Jorge's country.

Unless, of course, he was willing to work overtime, to arrive home every night with such weariness that he could feel his bones sink into the sustaining marrow; was willing to take a bullet for his dreams.

Then a man could sell everything once so tediously accumulated for a rock bottom price, and touch a life's work in the form of bills in a week.

Some birds flail at their cages so fiercely that they do physical damage to the very wings that would hasten their flight. In their endless obsession to flee, the wildest will continue to bat at what confines them, oblivious to the small round of daylight that has inexplicably opened before them.

Jorge was not so indiscriminate. He felt true emptiness as he closed the door of his Bogotá apartment, years of deliberation and trial and so much systematic sacrifice that had allowed for a release, finally. The laughter of his two small sons had rung hollow that morning in the dullness that a gutted home assumes. All that he had—all that he had ever been in Colombia—was carefully counted, meticulously folded into a plain, brown wallet that fit unassumingly in the back pocket of his trousers. It was the wallet's contents that served as the means to the end, and there was nothing foreboding in that as he swung Diego into his arms, light as a feather in the sudden joy that accompanies a long-awaited journey.

+>==<+

To attribute Jorge's happiness solely to the escape of hardship would be to thrust upon his native country a terrible injustice. Even the most punishing of national crucibles have their virtues, inasmuch as all sovereignties consist of human nature. Everything has its opposite, and there is often found on a hillside, encrusted in hardened shale, a sego lily that has grown to grace the stone. The existence of hope and faith and boundless charity against the backdrop of such perpetual misery and corruption made the realization of goodness supreme in Colombia's citizens. Some of the country's finest chose to stay, to battle for reform; and others chose to go to improve their lot. Both would have a hard time of it, with only that which they saw in their children's eyes sustaining them.

Jorge was wise enough to see that a country was defined by what flickered in the eyes of its youth—that their perception of what lay ahead of them, coupled with their resilience to reach for it or overcome it, was ultimately what shaped a forward destiny.

For his part, Jorge overlooked one of Colombia's premier military compounds as a young boy. It was the sole view from his backyard, the reflection of his country's continual upheaval and strife. The naked brooding of a seven-year-old taking it all in was frequently mirrored in the glass of his backroom window at night. He was awakened from a shadowy sleep each morning at five by the sounding of a trumpet, followed by the hurried footsteps of men—always the fierce-looking, exact regiments of men tramping, grunting, and barking in the dimness before sunup. The deafening volleys of gunfire from the range were forever with him, and Jorge skipped school often enough to watch the soldiers' splendid formations in the afternoon. There were 700 of them during the camp's heyday, training with the artillery and the cavalry—archaic cavalries with horses, the likes of which hadn't been seen since World War I. The Colombian army could round up young men at the point of an assault rifle any time more forces were needed.

In Jorge's day, it seemed that forces were needed much of the time.

The proximity of Jorge's family to such a daily and imminent threat could only be ascribed to one thing: Colombia had a crude lottery system that ensured its defenses and the fate of a young man of age hung in the balance of colors: red in the valor that preserved Colombia's borders at any cost of bloodshed; green in the Andes Mountains' overhangs that sheltered the insurgents; and white in rare salvation. The young man who reached blindly into a box for one of these colored ping pong balls drew out an eternal sort of fortune. Only his grasp on a white ball secured his liberation from military service and the disaster of fighting a more capable opponent in the jungle. Every youth prayed for the deliverance; but, in truth, a bullfighter had more chance of winning a portal with no charging enemy in its tunnel.

Jorge's mother chose to work and live at the edge of such a coliseum because, as many bullfighters were prone to admit, hunger had bigger horns.

The woman was a terribly hard worker and savvy—separated from her husband and compelled to provide for the entire household. Jorge's father operated a grocery—an enclosed fruit and vegetable stand, really, and it lay a small distance from the military camp. Jorge's father was a serious man with a dry sense of humor, respected and liked for the conversation that rose so easily near his roadside industry.

Jorge's mother opened a restaurant at the front of her new home with no more capital than was required to feed an extended family. She tiled the floor in bright checkerboards, situated six metal tables of four for intimacy and then two long wooden tables for cafeteria-style gatherings. It was the kind of sociality that encouraged heavier meals, the kind of arrangement that turned a profit. She cooked what suited the local tastes—the flat potato-like pancakes known as arepas; the culinary art of empanadas, and carne asada, and a savory broth known as caldo. She made 100 tamales every morning and, because they alone required three hours of preparation, she arose very early. From four o'clock in the morning until the last customer left—often as late as two o'clock the following morning—Jorge's mother cooked and washed dishes and served and entertained. As business at the new restaurant grew there were a hundred people at lunchtime filling the front entrance and spilling into the street. Jorge's mother hired young waitresses who drew the soldiers from the nearby camp which, in turn, gave her pretty employees incentive. There was always simmering, always grilling, always the aroma of food where Jorge lived, and it was a blessing—that ever-present ability to ward off one of Colombia's harshest adversaries.

Jorge was tended by the benevolence of his mother's patrons on many occasions. There was an older man who came early to eat his breakfast before taking the long bus ride to the city center. He interrupted his meal to place the child on his lap and appreciate the small treasures Jorge liked to glean from the nearby trash heaps. There was a mother of two who allowed Jorge to eat his dinner at her table, allowed him the pretense of belonging. Jorge was never without food and never without the kindheartedness that characterized Colombia's common people, but he was rarely found having the companionship of a family meal either. He looked upon togetherness—a mother and father together, attentive to their children—with the same yearning pangs in his gut that his mother tried so hard to appease. He attempted to help her at times, to be part of the bustle, but he was too small. He fumbled with the forks and knives and he seemed to always be intolerably underfoot. His mother had stopped long enough to give birth to him apparently at the previous establishment she had run.

So far as Jorge knew, it was the only thing that could have closed a restaurant in Bogotá.

It was his birthday and his mother cooked an egg for him, presented it to him as his gift; it was Christmas and there was a celebration of more food, steaming cups of hot chocolate on the tables and music—always music in Colombia. Jorge tugged at his mother's skirts, tried to find someone to play with him, and then resigned himself to watching the forlorn exercises of men at the military camp outside—men for whom there might never be any holiday cheer or presents either. There was all around Jorge a feast of the richest order in a land where banquets were scarce. It was the crumbs of his mother's time that the child wanted, ached for until it embittered him.

It was not her fault, of course, that life was grueling and hard. It was not her fault that the lowland heat and the constant flames in the kitchen created a sweat that only yielded more hunger and more sweat. In the earliest, most obscure way that children know things are not as they should be, he couldn't quite grasp the complexity of the problem or figure out a way to fix it. In his loneliness he sought entertainment in the never-ending watch guard on the army, and he sought his spare playmates in the street. He acted out, not because he thought misbehavior would garner the right kind of attention—he acted out because a certain kind of neglect had trained him to disbelieve one critical law of nature: that for every action, there was not only an equal and opposite reaction, but any reaction at all.

Jorge truly believed the guard at the edge of the compound would remain stone-faced as he taunted him, goading him as the lesser of all the ranks in the Colombian army. He failed to take into account the misery of a young soldier, compelled to take up arms against an enemy no less disenchanted than Jorge. He failed to take into account the crestfallen face of a boy who had once reached into a Pandora's box and drawn a green ball of two options: a death sentence in the jungle on the one hand, and imprisonment in the lowland on the other. The guard looked invincible enough before Jorge began sniping at him and the small boy failed to think of others—he didn't perceive a soldier so like his mother, trapped and carrying grave and hidden wounds.

The guard turned on him with such pent-up ferocity that Jorge was taken aback.

Of course, Jorge's fascination with the military was undeterred if not heightened by such small incidents. He maintained a kind of wistfulness for the hard edge and the order and predictability that characterized the various forces. There was remarkable beauty in the military police who marched abreast with such dignity, such gallantry. Their symmetry, their exactness—their sheer dependability at attention—these were the things that inspired him. There was often a fine line between the awesome and the fearsome that seven-year-olds had difficulty discerning, even when that line was breached. Not long after his encounter with the guard, a convoy of trucks thundered through the streets at midnight and an ominously intimate scene followed. The swiftness, the agility that Jorge had admired from afar spilled from the camouflage canopies and his older brother was among the first to be captured. The military police met little resistance from the able-bodied men who surrendered themselves to the trucks.

All about the streets was a despairing resignation, the stunned silence of teenagers who were suddenly faced with the notion that all their time had been borrowed up to that point. As the MPs prepared to move on to the next neighborhood and the next assault, a lone figure emerged from the dwellings.

The twin doors of a particular home with a fledgling business in front yawned as wide as a barn entrance.

To see the silhouette of Jorge's mother squaring her shoulders to the glaring headlights and the heavily armed militants was to see the army implausibly begin to bend as steel. There was an exchange of words, muffled to Jorge's ears by the idling trucks, and then the police released his older brother.

He was seventeen years old—prime for the guard—and he was released because his mother had said so.

Jorge's mother had dressed down the enemy without raising a hand and her youngest son would have liked after that for her to hug him once. He would have liked it if she had reassured him of the isolation of such events and her power to always prevent the personal catastrophes. Jorge would have liked it very much if she had eased the transition in his mind from the orderly magnificence and the elegant reserve of those marching men to the random barbarity of the previous night. No one spoke of the incident the following day at the restaurant. He hung around just to be sure.

In the void of explanation, Jorge helped himself to his mother's hidden deposit of cash for the first time. He didn't really steal her money to rent a bicycle so much as he saved her the trouble of getting it herself in such preoccupation. She would not have liked that he did it, but in the grotesqueness of the prior night Jorge had come to a hazy sort of determination: it was every man for himself.

His impression was underscored by the fact that he had, not long ago, found a stash of coins in an ordinary, red towel. It had been buried in the refuse at the end of the street, accidentally thrown away by three young boys who had cleaned the idle buses. It was a significant accumulation of fares and it was, by far, the grandest treasure Jorge had ever happened upon in his daily digs through the trash. He had taken it to his mother, such an exorbitant amount of money, with so much anticipation.

His mother had promptly placed notices everywhere that a large sum of money had been found.

She hadn't rested until its rightful owner returned weeks later, the man describing the towel and the amount of money in great detail—leaving the restaurant relieved to the verge of tears. Jorge's mother was restrained like that. So consummate in her judgment, in her honesty, and in her affections.

Jorge was left to his own reasoning on yet another day and it was precisely that which proved to be his next, spiraling downfall.

⊬⇒⇐⊣

Colombia's buses resembled the crawling of ants—the burgeoning, straining creatures of public transportation that carried excessive loads on their backs. In the mountains, the buses were older, dilapidated, and trembling under an uphill struggle and the weight of human cargo. People spilled out the side doors and hung from the windows, even rode on the tops of the vehicles. Those who were transported inside often stood or sat on the floor in the empty crevices, shielded from daylight by the hordes of riders. They were continually jounced as they breathed the stifling, pungent odor of tremendous effort—men returning from the blaze of the fields mingled with children in soiled cloth diapers. At each makeshift bus stop, the lower rear door was opened and the occupants dipped and drained from the interior with eyes blinking against the sun. To emerge from one of these buses was to take a relieved and sizable gulp of air at a more hospitable elevation.

The Bogotá buses were newer and cleaner, transporting the city's working class in a great arc that stretched from Tunjuelito to Quirigua. A handful of them were left unlocked and allowed to rest, exactly across the street from the restaurant and the military base.

It was there, at the head of one of the buses, that Jorge most liked to occupy his time.

He was a fantastic driver in his imagination, which was made keener by the absence of genuine and human interaction. He scaled the Andes with grace and ease. He raced, practically flew, along what he supposed were the virgin white sands that laced the Caribbean. There were gleaming sands of opal that shimmered in the sun and that was his favorite fantasy—a small glimpse of paradise as he let the tropical breeze and the waves carry him far from the dull dirt roads and the barrage of the firing range.

For some reason, Jorge had always been enamored with a sea no one ever really got to visit.

He pushed at the clutch and he pulled at the stick shift with such fluidity it was practically a blur to the naked eye. He made great rumbling noises, a tribute to a fine-tuned engine really, and he screeched and he honked and he spun on a dime. And then, curiously enough, he thrust the stick shift into neutral gear and the great hulk of his imaginings took on actual motion. The bus lumbered from its incline and rolled without restraint as Jorge frantically pumped the clutch.

There was a quick snap and grate, the jar of an obstructing wooden lamppost as the fender caved to it, and the bus came to an abrupt halt.

Jorge jumped out of the bus quickly and looked upon the damage. It was a fine mess, a gloriously awful predicament.

He wasn't as sorry as he was stunned, and so it came as a surprise—even to him—when he started from his appraisal and began to run. Perhaps it was the crack of the rifles nearby, but there was an instinctive coil, a compelling urge to race toward his father's grocery. His father was composed; his father was amiable; his father had always been reasonable. He arrived with the panting and panic of a child in search of a mediator, in search of some redemption. There was a church some twenty-five blocks from Jorge's home where the townspeople assembled to pay their homage, where men and women crawled on their hands and knees to a sure altar of salvation. His offering was not so elegant, but Jorge had run for over a mile with the prolonged sweat of fear and dread. He welcomed the base humility and the euphoric relief that always accompanied the confession of terrible misdeeds. His admission of guilt was so extravagant in its detail—so that his father could plainly see the inexperience.

It was not the result of ill intentions, the continued offenses of an errant child.

For a moment he felt the anticipated sag in his shoulders and the sweet savor of his relief. His father's mouth was set in a grim, straight line. That's what Jorge saw just before he struck him—hard. It was an open-handed slap across the face that stung the child most with its shocking reproof. Jorge bowed his head and an onlooker thought the resignation in his eyes was one of mere anger and disappointment.

Catastrophic disillusionment had a habit of disguising itself in such small measures like that.

Jorge kicked at the dogs that strayed in his path home; he kicked at the rocks and the aluminum cans and then he kicked at the dust. Jorge kicked and swung with such fury and futility at the air that his shoulders tensed and ached. He wanted to cry and, in the damming of the torrent that young boys force upon themselves, he felt his body quivering under the weight. There were no outlets for his rage, no constructive release for what was going to churn inside of him for a very long time. He braced himself for an awful beating when he returned to the restaurant—there were no theatrics and no attempts at understanding in his explanation. Indeed there was a flatness in his tone as he told his mother: the damage to the bus amounted to 120 pesos. In Colombia, the average monthly salary was a tenth of that sum. He had created a nearly insurmountable calamity.

His mother turned away without reprimanding him; she went quietly back into the restaurant and retrieved the cash from the register. She had the money on hand to pay all of her youngest son's debts, and she never brought the matter up again. Jorge attended mass that Sunday and they entered a large and plain church that was filled to its 300-occupant capacity. The priest was clothed in an ornate white vestment, trimmed in elaborate gold braid. There was no organ, no musical instrument whatsoever to accompany the grave melodies that arose a capella to the chapel's vaulted spaces. The praises and chants rolled off the walls in such decorous reverence that there seemed to be an other-worldliness quality to the service.

It was not the presence of patron saints or archangels or anything quite so glorious. There was just a haunting echo of pale-faced ghosts—of men and women who had gone before and men and women who would come afterward with no particular achievement but existence. Their voices echoed a dull despair from the rafters, a complete lack of exaltation. It was the stagnant steep of tradition as thick as the mists that shrouded Bogotá and the ghosts' lives, their deaths, and their dreams—to Jorge they all availed nothing—and in time he, too, would amount to nothing.

There were usually more people than space in the pews and that accounted for the boy's bleak outlook, originating from his seat on the floor. He was isolated from the grand entrance of the priest, and his eyes were fixed on hundreds of lowly feet. It had always been hard to think lofty and holy thoughts from such a state of body and mind—on this day, though, he was even more impervious to the virtuous Virgin Mary and the risen Son who hung from a cross beyond Jorge's vision. What he knew was that his mother had finally saved him. His mother alone had borne the cross of his vile conduct. In that sudden sweep of generosity had come a new dimension of perspective that grew to the most punishing of paradoxes.

She loved him after all—his mother actually loved him—and she had paid no small price to redeem him.

Jorge was so abundantly amazed in her ability to atone, in the deliverance that had come through such selfless labor and resolve and sacrifice, that he was ashamed. The detachment and the constant unsettledness of business and the sheer fixated grind—day after day, it had all been for him. The distance between them actually widened for his recognition of that; she, being lifted up, and he being more abased than ever. Whatever quick dissolution of his long-held resentment, whatever the startling revelation that led to a newfound regard for his mother, Jorge had to face a more sizable, inner demon.

He had few redeeming qualities; and he had no will to be good.

Perhaps if he had not been forbidden to read the Bible, if he had not been told he would become crazy like the Protestants for doing so—he might have gleaned a more abundant interpretation from a passage in Luke being expounded upon by the priest:

And the publican, standing afar off, who would not lift up so much as his eyes unto heaven. He smote upon his breast in utter shame.

He cried: God be merciful to me a sinner.

Perhaps he might have seen in that parable that the lowest of them all had gone home justified that day.

Jorge, in his misery, did not hear a sermon and he was filled with no desire to acknowledge God. His awe came full circle to a true and dreadful fear of Him, of His endless punishments and His will and His fury. He surely had the omnipotence to deliver, but God had no natural affections to save someone like him. The child could see no further than a wall of wretched legs and so he saw no further than the flesh and a continual hopelessness and damnation.

His mother knew none of this, was mystified by her youngest child's increased rebellion from that day forward—succumbed to the idea that nothing could penetrate his hostility. If she had had the luxury of time to read to her son, she might have been struck by the assertion of E.B. White.

It was a book made famous in the United States first and she might have seen that her child was clinging—seen that she alone mattered in the way that children's first impressions of God and humanity are borne of the mercy and love and devotion of their caretakers. There was not just a pig and a spider in the famous barn of *Charlotte's Web*. There was a swing which hung from a beam which sailed from the doorway, so high that a child had to summon all her nerve to climb on it and then take a deep breath before zooming toward the clouds.

"Mothers for miles around worried about Zuckerman's swing. They feared some child would fall off. But no child ever did."

"Children," White had written, "almost always hang onto things tighter than their mothers think they will."

CHAPTER 2

Jorge's distress was suddenly equaled only by his panic. Hearing his anguish and his pleadings, his mother, too, began to weep. The professor of the children's home assigned to escort Jorge to his classroom was trying, haplessly, to soothe them both.

"It's a good place for children." It came out rather strenuously. "He'll have all that he needs. The little ones are so cared for and he'll have lots of friends. The teachers will keep an eye on him."

The professor's last declaration was made quite intentionally to remind Jorge's mother of all the past sins and grievances.

Jorge had quite recently stolen his older sister's money for her First Communion from the priest—the *priest*, of all people. Prior to that not-so-rectifiable sin, he had also acquired the habit of disappearing for long stretches, skipping school to play near the river and squandering his days in his obsession with the military. Jorge also had some morbid fascination with the slaughter house, and the last time he had gone there, more than a few head of cattle had broken through the pens. It was not so unlike the Running of the Bulls in Pamplona—a virtual stampede through the passages of Bogotá. Jorge had narrowly escaped and there seemed to be something missing in him that his mother was at a loss to fill. It had mounted steadily to an equal lack of conscience—another year like the past one and he was going to surely end up dead on the streets or in juvenile detention.

She had registered Jorge that morning in the garden area reserved for families and wealthy benefactors. The school relied on the charity of what appeared to be kind, albeit ancient women. They smelled of medicine; they clapped gnarled hands in delight when the children performed for them. They were comely but not too ostentatious for afternoon visits, always appropriate and reserved. For them, the school's trees were pruned and shaped and the flowers opened their buds expectantly. For them, the fountain gurgled, its waters glistening and appreciative in the midday sun. El Amparo de Niños was a lovely place, really, and Jorge's new professor seemed kind enough. These were the things on which Jorge's mother tried to dwell—her child was hysterical, sobbing, brokenhearted, begging her not to abandon him.

She began to cry again, sufficiently uncontrolled to heighten Jorge's anxiety even further. The professor touched Jorge's mother ever so gently on the shoulder, entreating her with such patience and such restraint. "He'll be fine," he reiterated. "We take such good care of the little ones."

He smiled tenderly at Jorge.

Jorge's mother was worn down by the time she wrenched herself from her child and made her way to the bus stop. It was a forty-mile journey back to the restaurant near Tunjuelito, and she needed the precious time to compose herself. The professor closed the door and took Jorge by the arm as he led him away from the front entrance. They entered a small round—a patio overlooking the manicured gardens and the bubbling fountain and a church.

For a moment, Jorge wondered why there were no children inside the waiting area. He had the sudden, prickling sensation that he was in a dungeon—a shrill kind of siren that sounded in his head and lurched something nauseating in his stomach. He couldn't see the thick adobe walls and the barbed wire that was strung the entire distance of the complex. He had yet to make his way to the inner corridor that was oddly hushed for all of its childish inhabitants. The school just gave the impression of a monastery where all must have taken a vow of silence. What he sensed was a foreboding of something cold and extremely hardened ahead.

He heard the distinct echo of footsteps, hurried and obliged. *If someone had to attend to the children then so be it*, their clip seemed loathe to resonate. The professor took a step back so as to get a good, long look at Jorge. The boy was in tears and cowering.

He was weak enough to have hung onto his mother, a complete lack of discipline accounting for his immodest show of emotion and the petty behavior that had forced his enrollment. The professor swung his leg back with all his might and unleashed his disapproval upon him. He dropkicked him as if he were a soccer ball—the startling spring of being put into play without so much fanfare as a game. Because of his size Jorge didn't sail as most eight-year-olds, but landed a short distance with a rather unimpressive thud. He curled up in a protective ball, gulping and inhaling sharply.

And then he simply crumpled into great ragged sobs, the agony of the smallest of children betrayed and utterly alone.

+≻━:━≺+

Unfamiliarity heightens the intensity of bad experiences, making the first hours the most terrifying. Jorge was perceived as a true threat by the school administrators though he had always been careful to skirt the real trouble. He was escorted to the third floor, deemed the most punishing, and all that would become routine in the months ahead perched like pebbles in his throat. The children on the floor ranged in age from six years old to fourteen, and they seemed oblivious to the distinct and pungent smell of urine in the dormitory bay. It was the area designated for bedwetters—the school wasted none of its scant means on replacing the mattresses.

His mother had bought him brand new underwear—freshly laundered, snow white underwear. They had made him feel extraordinarily clean and he bit his lip hard, trying not to touch the mattress. He pulled the sheet to his head and scrunched the edge of it over his eyes and his nose, attempting to suffocate the odor. It all reeked of incontinence, an intolerable singe from his lips all the way to his throat. His eyes began to water and burn, first from the smell and then from the hot tears that spilled onto his face.

The physical sting was met by his tortured thoughts—a wonder that swirled around and around in his head as he tried to determine what awful crime he had committed. He hadn't killed anyone, hadn't beaten anyone; his little mind worked and worked at the dilemma.

Before summer's end, he had awakened outside, lying in a basket in the near pitch blackness of a deserted street. Circling him like vultures had been a set of doves and they had not been the sedate creatures of his Biblical interpretations. They had shrieked and plummeted toward him, decrying a certain objection and then ultimate condemnation. He had been locked out of the house, and he had lain in the basket with the bewilderment and trembling of doom.

In the welcome absolution of dawn, he had been let back inside the restaurant and his bafflement had been met by a quite simple explanation on the part of his sisters: the devil had carried him away and he hadn't had any reason to question such fair judgment.

The more he was forced to think about it, the more he decided he must have been a very bad boy.

He awoke the next morning and found himself in a strange place, overcome by the denial that followed his disorientation. The harsh call to order left him with the same sunken hollowness the young men at the military camp must have known on their first full day of imprisonment. In his tendencies toward survival, Jorge hung back at breakfast, trying to get a handle on things and ascertain character. There was the professor who had kicked him—he was going to avoid him by scarcely looking up. There were established gangs inside the walls, a brutal sort of pecking order among the older boys. And then there were the little ones who were never going to experience anything like a real childhood.

They weren't orphans per se, which spared them that other most traumatic facility, but they were abandoned just the same. Nobody was ever going to claim them on the weekends or come to visit, and that made a good many of them meek enough so that they picked on no one.

The dining hall resembled a soup kitchen and it was that culinary disaster which dismayed Jorge most. He didn't have the stomach for gray broths and gray porridges and all the spoiled leftovers that came from the nearby vendors. What wasn't sold at the open air markets was delivered to the children's home—the benevolent old ladies saw to that. The food was dry when it should have been moist, and soggy and sticky when it should have been dry. It stuck in Jorge's throat in an ever-increasing lump until, by the third afternoon, the ache in his belly convinced him to clamor for scraps like the other children. He was given meat for dinner that evening, attached to a bone, and he held onto it throughout the night as he had been admonished by the younger children. He gnawed at it, sucked on it, and finally snapped it in half to dig with an eager finger at the coveted marrow. To get a bone at meal time—that was the expectancy on the faces of so many little boys as they waited in an interminably long line for their food.

There was one female on staff and he sneaked an apple for her—a premeditation that won him praise and an initial show of kindness. The object of his affection was a very good teacher and he tried hard to do his studies just right. Children who did poorly were sent to the guardians whose sole labor in life was punishment. They stood in a menacing line with bullwhips and, when the crack of discipline was over, the most unfortunate were sent into solitary confinement. There was a room constructed of concrete blocks with two small windows that stood behind the dormitories, obscured from the view of the sweet old ladies and visiting parents. By all survivor accounts, it was ice cold in confinement and one stayed long enough to wonder if he was ever going to be let out. For his good behavior, Jorge earned a seat by a window in the classroom that overlooked the front entrance and the patio. He watched the strained faces of parents and children, all the comings and goings day after day of boys held against their will. He began to classify their expressions in his gloom—those who were sad, those who were scared, or those who were indifferent. The older kids and the indigenous children were the ones who most often wore signs of resignation.

His mother retrieved him on the weekend and there was the initial elation of seeing her face and of climbing on the bus—of devouring tamales and empanadas and ravenously chewing at chicken, and asking for more, and never minding the bone. It was very like the feeling he'd had once at a passion play his family had attended in the heart of Bogotá. His mother had let go of his hand, and he'd been jostled away from her in the masses and the pressing of hundreds of people. A soldier had found him and he had taken his hand and stayed with him until he was reunited with his mother. He had been a soldier in camouflage who had been grossly out of place among the refined pillars of Good Friday. It was very much like that feeling—of being lost and then found again, no matter the instrument of the rescue—right up until the time he had to climb on the bus to return to the school again.

He slithered between the sheets with the raw and renewed angst of children surrounding him, unable to control anything, least of all their bodily functions. He felt sorry for the others at the same time he had to tolerate them in the greater pity for himself. The youngest ones cried themselves to sleep and the oldest of them barked for silence. He was going to have to put up with them all for an indefinite amount of time, just as he was going to have to put up with the stench and the food. No matter how good he had been on the weekend at his family's house, he had been unable to change the course of the bus that carried him back.

He was unable to change his fate through an ever-recurring calendar of dismal Mondays through Fridays. He began to mark time again with each swing of the door at the front entrance—mark time in a steady grasp on what it was to be crushingly indebted.

Jorge's mother dropped him off at the front entrance on a Sunday, at the end of April in springtime. She was accompanied by Jorge's oldest brother who worked at a commercial bakery where the aroma of fresh baked bread and cakes and cookies always wafted. Jorge's brother swore to stop by with postre and pastel that week—any number of desserts and sweet cakes. It was just a rash promise made to cheer a little boy momentarily—Jorge promised to share his wealth with all of his classmates, and he eased gingerly into his bed on the third floor that evening. The acid stench was made bearable by the anticipation of a treat so sugared and iced and soft that the dream seemed to melt on his tongue.

His brother didn't come the next day, or the day after that, or even three days after that. Every morning, Jorge found a reason to trust he might get a taste of some minimal sweetness and then the sun set and he had to struggle with the bitterness in his mouth all over again. At the end of the week he brightened to think that his brother might just need a reminder—if he told his mother over the weekend, perhaps she would take care of it all. The children filed out one by one on Friday, but nobody came to retrieve Jorge.

He wanted to go outside to wait for his mother; perhaps she had forgotten how to get to the beautiful garden by the church with its gurgling fountain. Perhaps she had forgotten exactly where the bus stopped and needed someone to wave from the road. The school administration didn't allow a child to wait outside, of course, and that added to the growing worry—being locked inside the compound with its stale walls and its concrete barriers and all the little boys for whom no one came. Hour after hour he waited with the abandoned children with his chin resting in his hands, his heart leaping with expectation every time it appeared an adult might be summoning him to leave. He rolled into a ball in his bed on Sunday night, and he dug clenched fists into his eyes, the pain so sharp in his chest that his breath came in fitful stops and starts. He clamped a hand over his mouth, tried to cover the hurt, squeezing extraordinarily hard with small fingers drenched in tears.

No one came for him the next weekend—or the weekend after that. He wondered if something dreadful had happened: maybe his mother was dead or someone was sick, or maybe they had all just given up on a boy like him. There was only the smallest sliver of hope as the school administration relocated him to the second floor. There, he was able to slide between clean coverlets and hide from a newer, even crueler blanket of desolation.

His mother showed up, quite unexpectedly, on the fourth weekend with no explanation for the delay. She brought with her a set of miniature army jeeps— each was khaki and plastic, but one was slightly larger than the other two. They all fit into the palm of his hand and he held them with great wonder and excitement. It took a great deal of time away from the restaurant to go to places where luxuries like that were sold. It was really quite something to have not one, but three little army jeeps. Jorge treasured them and drove them in circles at night, cleaning them and hugging them to him. He finally placed them for safekeeping under his pillow and dreamed of soldiering all night.

He woke up on Tuesday, just two nights later, and found that the trucks were gone. He searched the pillow and the sheets and the mattress and the floor before class and at the peril of being late for formations. He stewed and he fretted through all of his lessons. When the day was nearly done, he spotted a scrawny six-year-old boy on the patio, playing with one larger truck and two khaki ones. There were three teenage boys surrounding the scrawny one and, judging by their threatening stance, he was never going to reclaim his toys. It was a terrible helplessness that began to pound in Jorge's head and choke at his throat, some foe before him that was always bigger and stronger.

That evening, two teenage boys scaled the adobe wall as the remainder of the children settled in for formations. The professors had been distracted—so intent on identifying the child who talked or squirmed or created a small stir that they lost track of the really big disturbance. The teenagers mounted the wall, straddled the barbed wire and pumped their arms heavenward in praise of St. Jude—just before they dropped out of sight and began to run through the adjacent pasture with all of their might.

For the next five months, Jorge was consumed with a day and night study of some similar means to escape.

+═══+

Jorge had few friends and so it seemed odd that a fifteen-year-old had sought him as a confidante.

"I'm getting out of here." The boy was one of the abandoned ones and he had a nine-year-old brother.

"Yo quiero ir con ustedes." Jorge's reply commanded so much fierceness in his response that it was not a request to escape with them. They were in the thing together immediately—that was clear to any number of flies on the wall that sought refuge in the eerie glow.

The only way out was the way the teenagers had chosen—it was the corner of the adobe barrier that had to be scaled. Others had tried different parts of the wall and slid and climbed, and slid again in such desperation that it knotted the stomachs of any decent human being who stood at attention and witnessed the catastrophe. The faces of failed attempts were always distorted as the guards approached with their bullwhips. There was acute terror in the eyes of little boys who tried to claw one last time at the slippery slope of stone, just before they were snatched at the collar and dragged. They kicked and screamed in their collapse and the pall that settled over the compound after each instance was devastating.

It wasn't merely the idea that they were always going to be held captive—it was the idea that just for exhibiting a desire to be free they were going to be captive in a way worse than before.

They were whipped and beaten and placed in solitary confinement for days on end, and then they were banished indefinitely to the third floor with its endless suffocation of free will. There but for the grace of God go I, a young child who had played it safe could tell himself, but there was really no grace in hanging back forever either. The remaining boys saw all the harsh penalties and still ached for the kind of release that had driven the attempted flight in the first place.

Jorge chose to focus on those teenage boys and their triumphant ascent and their jubilant, outstretched arms.

┼╾┈╼┼

There was a sixteen-year-old who joined them at the wall, just before formations. There wasn't anything distinguishable about him—just a young man with nothing to lose anymore; a young man who spoke very little and showed no sort of attachment to those who conspired with him. Each boy took his turn, thrusting his hands in his pockets and walking nonchalantly past the corner—eyeing the footholds and the jagged wire and the blue sky overhead that stretched to an unimaginable beyond.

At night, in hushed whispers in the dormitory, they each shared the conclusion that the first nine feet would be the most difficult. Adobe was made from sun-dried bricks of clay and the wall was worn the smoothest at the bottom.

For three weeks, they kept an ever-present watch on the guards and the professors and made an unassuming circle around the compound. It was difficult to concentrate in school, but Jorge tried very hard, feeling that someone, somewhere, was on to him. He was jumpy and calculated and resolute, his emotions seesawing the entire time he was awake and making it nearly impossible to sleep. They determined the order in which they would leap to the wall, the sixteen-year-old having clear seniority and so assuming the first position. At fifteen, Alfonzo would have been next but for the liability of a little brother. Jorge claimed the second spot, and Alfonzo took the last position, knowing he would have to push Luis to the top.

It was Alfonzo who faced the harshest demons: if his little brother did not make it over the wall, they would both be subjected to the whippings and the confinement and the third floor. If Luis made it over and Alfonzo did not, the child would be no better off in a world where there was nothing and no one to which he could run. The boys had no family, no shelter, and no food—perhaps they would starve in their triumph.

Alfonzo mulled this, and decided any life was better than the children's home so long as Luis and he were together.

The long-awaited morning in September dawned exceptionally beautiful; the sky was brilliant—cobalt and flawless. The other children gathered for formations like children do when duties and discipline overshadow perfect weather. Jorge felt the yearning to be free under the glorious sun stronger than he felt the uneasiness of his next move. That feeling endured right up until the moment he broke ever so quietly away from the group to take his position at the wall.

The sixteen-year-old had will and size on his side. Even so, the fluidity with which he climbed was a torturous exercise in patience. Jorge had the pronounced feeling of vulnerability, exposed to the guards in his conspiracy and still not able to even touch the instrument of his escape until the sixteen-year-old had scaled it.

The first nine feet were the hardest for sure. Jorge realized that in the form of proof as he seized his opportunity. He had always envied the neighborhood children who acquired heroic costumes for Halloween—Superman and Spider-Man so superior to the homely disguises he made himself. He felt that keen envy again, for some Herculean strength that might overcome his inadequacies and propel him to the top of the wall. He dug a left foot and then a right foot and then a left in a steady wedge and leverage of the corner that continually threatened to fail him. The toeholds which had seemed so clear from the ground became invisible to his scraping fingernails and dangling feet. Each time he slipped, he could sense Alfonzo jumping up and down in angst. He gritted his teeth and he felt the quake in his arms from the fear and the dread and the sheer, epic effort.

They had constructed the wall high enough so that it caused a young boy to give out just below a hand's grasp from the top.

Jorge pulled one last measure of reserve from the pounding and the adrenaline, and there was some relieved gasp when he pulled the full weight of his body onto the ledge. He saw the pasture below in great rolling waves of green and then he saw in some quick acknowledgment the child who was being pushed from below by his brother. Luis appeared to be the size of a mouse from where Jorge was balanced for a time. The child was no more than a church mouse, and as Jorge precariously tried to overpower the sharp barbs and the last wiry constraint, it struck him—they were so inconsequential in such a great big world with such ferocious guards. What would it matter to the professors and the benevolent old ladies if a child that small just wanted to be free?

There was commotion inside the compound—Jorge heard it as he leaped to a ground that swallowed him whole. He scrambled back from the wall, still heaving from the exertion, his eyes wide with expectancy as he looked for Luis to break the perimeter. There was no small swell when he saw the tiny figure emerge, a straining, crawling silhouette against such an even-tempered blue. In the distant, tinny way a newly released boy hears the cries of his fellow inmate, Jorge heard Alfonzo yell to Luis to jump to the side of the pasture. The little boy perched on the ledge, trying to encourage his brother's climb, hoping to lend a hand to Alfonzo when he reached the top. Luis obeyed his brother's urging as the guardians neared the barrier with their curt, harsh footsteps and their anxious bullwhips.

Jorge attempted to break the little boy's fall—there was too much noise in the compound. He was witness to the trepidation and pain in the smaller child's eyes. Luis was actually older than Jorge by a year, but he seemed terribly young and alone in the vastness of the field.

He waited beside Jorge with a terrible apprehension for Alfonzo to appear on a stark horizon.

In time—mere seconds that were relative to great escapes and heightened anxiety—Jorge sensed that Alfonzo was doomed. The guards had hold of his ankles because he'd spent his strength pushing his little brother. They had seized him at the point where boys almost always gave out regardless. Jorge knew it as he studied Luis and pitied him as he calculated the length of pasture to be crossed before they could all reach the main road. The sixteen-year-old broke from the group with no word; Jorge was reluctant to wait any longer.

All boys appeared devout enough when they streamed into the Catholic church that flanked the courtyard and the blooming flowers and the jubilant fountain. Whether Luis was religious or not, whether he was imploring the heavens for mercy or simply maintaining a vigilant watch on the ledge, the little boy's eyes never wavered from an upward gaze. He stood with such firmness, such a fierce clench in the fists at his side, that Jorge, too, was compelled to turn his full attention to the wall. For that, he didn't see the child as he suddenly began to talk to the stone, began to will all his nine-year-old might to the other side. For that, Jorge did not see the spark of elation that suddenly lit the child's face.

It was the sound of extreme effort—the screamed will of a death charge as Alfonzo made it to the top.

He hurdled the barbs and sailed with such glorious strength in his limbs that it seemed a great eagle had just discovered its wings. For the rest of his life, Jorge would remember the warmth of the sun on their cheeks in that moment and the taste of uninhibited liberty as the young boys cheered. Alfonzo did not stop to catch his breath, though he'd made twice the effort of them all. He grabbed Luis by the arm in the easy spin he took from the ground and he ran like the wind with his younger brother's legs churning to keep up. The three boys made a beeline for the railroad tracks, for traction on the wooden boards that marked the path to a road where buses could carry them far away from their captors. So many years later, Jorge would wonder what eventually became of Luis and Alfonzo.

On that stunning, picture-perfect morning he only looked upon the pair as any young boy might when some great thing has been shared between warriors. They arrived at the stop with no money and sneaked onto an outbound bus by pushing their way in when everyone else was coming off. They were thought to be very rude children, panting and proud in their ascent. There were a few stolen glances and then Jorge bade them goodbye at Los Molinos—at a junction.

He never saw them again except in his mind—the protective arm of an older brother draped over the younger as they turned and walked away to the mountains, walked away to the rest of their lives. Jorge waved and then he trudged on, alone for three hours, in an arduous journey back to Tunjuelito.

Perhaps it was the excitement of the day or the relief of the smell of carne asada wafting on such a casual breeze, but Jorge fought sobbing when he finally entered the restaurant. His siblings were working, and they looked at him with a strange mingle of confusion and consternation. His youngest sister had forgiven him the most readily for the money he had taken for her First Communion. He still felt oddly out of place as she gaped at him, as if he was a stranger in his own home. He wanted his mother and he feared her reaction and he began to call for her, seek her out in every part of the house. His siblings' surprise was no match for his mother's shock when he finally found her, washing dishes. The shoulders of his mother dropped as she saw the quivering and the hurt, heard the jumble out of Jorge's mouth. He could feel as he pressed his cheek next to hers that she wept and then he collapsed.

He had exhaled it all when she promised him fiercely that he would never have to return to the school.

CHAPTER 3

Government officials and municipal workers from all parts of Bogotá crowded the streets for an unprecedented display of pomp and circumstance. The locals were dressed in their Sunday best, and there was going to be a huge party. In solemn accord, the officials christened the neighborhood—the family restaurant and the bus stop and all the roadways that flanked the military base. The area was given the name of the barrio of Abraham Lincoln, and it was really something, quite a symbol of optimism, to be given American esteem like that. Neil Armstrong landed on the moon not long afterward, exceeding every human imagining. His voice resounded to earth in that clarion call: "That's one small step for a man, one giant leap for mankind."

Armstrong believed "that a successful lunar landing could, might, inspire men around the world to believe that impossible goals were possible, that the hope for solutions to humanity's problems was not a joke." The Americans' achievement was the topic of conversation at every table in the restaurant that night. Secretly, Jorge's mother aspired to change her youngest child's disposition in her own prayer to Santa Rita—the patron saint of impossible dreams. She had mulled the idea of moving the family to the township of Funza, a one-hour bus ride from Bogotá, believing in part that she could keep Jorge away from the mischief and the dangers of the inner city. When she resolved to make the move, her youngest son was the most distressed that he would have to sacrifice his overlook on the military.

Jorge's mother allowed one last, longing survey of the base before she helped him pack up his belongings. He stood at a crossroads at the end of the street, the kind of melancholy overcoming him that characterized life's most altering events. The barrio of Abraham Lincoln had been his faithful companion and Jorge

24

suddenly felt less fortunate somehow—leaving a neighborhood treasured enough to have finally been paid American homage. *The Jetsons, the Flintstones,* and *Sesame Street*—they were all scheduled to play on the only television set in the neighborhood as the Rincon family piled into the car. Growing up in Tunjuelito, Jorge had taken portions of his mother's tips to pay for the occasional viewing. There was a family next door who owned a television and charged for any admission into their living room. Mostly Jorge had learned how to sneak alongside the window and catch glimpses of his favorite shows from outside. Wiley Coyote and the Road Runner didn't really need translation, which meant they didn't really need sound either.

It wasn't just that he might miss the antics of el Pato Lucas, a crazy duck that bore the name of Daffy in the United States. It was that he might miss the front row seat he had had for a while on a whole different solar system. That man, dressed in a spacesuit who had planted a red, white, and blue flag on a place that embodied the remotest of dreams. That country that saw mortal threats like the Soviet Union do something unreachable and then not only reached the unreachable stars, but surpassed them. Jorge had paid every last centavo just to sit in his neighbor's house and see that kind of resolve and ambition up close.

The car picked up speed and a sad face peered from its window on the blurring barrio. It was the expression of a child who remembered how they had owned their very own television set once, and remembered that the blessing had only lasted for two days.

The reception had been terrible and the noise had been a nuisance to his mother. She had traded it in for a gas stove.

Jorge stared at the last visible signs of his home, wondering if the stove was coming to Funza.

<hr />

Jorge's mother knew how to make a living. That was one thing certain. The family moved into a residence that was alleged to have been a brothel in some bygone day. The children surmised that it had to have been some place unusual to account for the elongated floor plan—there were three large entertaining areas and row after row of bedrooms bordering the commons.

Whatever its previous dishonor, Jorge's mother scrubbed the checkerboard tiles and painted the walls and the trim in promising colors until the place took on respectability. The comforting aromas of home-cooked meals began to drift onto the street again and, soon enough, business was booming, every patio filled with tables and satisfied customers.

In Funza, as had been the case in Tunjuelito, there was labor and simmering and stewing—the savor of caldo and a fresh renewal of resentment on Jorge's part, coupled with the boredom of a child with little to ground him. He found some consolation in another neighbor with another television set who charged for the price of admission. He stole glances through the window at el Pato Lucas and watched a dogfight in some other miserable jungle across the ocean—some place called Vietnam.

As summer approached, Jorge's mother bought him a basket to carry on his arm, filled it to the brim with empanadas and sent him five miles down the road each mid-day to the ICA. It was a Colombian bureau of agricultural affairs that had been established by the Americans in the early 1960s. His mother had struck a deal with Jorge that allowed him to keep 20 percent of the profits from the empanadas he sold to each of the employees. The ICA was lush and sprawling and pristine; Jorge was content just to be outside, making money.

The workers liked to reach into Jorge's basket without permission—to take two empanadas and claim only one. He had to argue with them strenuously, resort to all kinds of tricks to manage the recovery of his price. No matter how the empanadas disappeared, Jorge would have to account for them later to his mother. He would have to pay her out of his own pocket for the workers' impropriety. That was how she taught prudence.

The ICA was nothing more than a magnificent abundance of produce and cultivos—fields that stretched so far it took him three hours to cross them in by foot. Jorge helped himself to strawberries and goose eggs and molasses as often as no one was looking to make up for his occasional losses. He returned home each weekday afternoon with the profits, just before his mother lined all the children up again to hand out their next assignments. Her strict charges to Jorge to buy meat or bread were always accompanied by cold, hard cash. If she asked him to buy two pesos' worth of bread, Jorge shorted her a couple of loaves and pocketed the rest. Between the wages he earned at the ICA and the smaller windfall from his errands, he was able to make his way to the neighbor's house to catch an episode of *The Flintstones*. The days wore on mundanely enough and life in the new barrio was nearly tolerable if not for the unpredictability that always came at nightfall.

For some inexplicable reason in Colombia—unlike in America—people were driven crazy by the realization of that brilliant white orb of a moon.

There were bars on the window of the restaurant, just as there were bars on every window in the barrio. Dinner was ordinarily served in their new neighborhood around six o'clock but, in the restaurant business, people came and went at all hours. The harder they worked for meager wages, the more their discontent grew to desperation. It was only intoxication that seemed to numb their frustration and many overstayed their welcome in drunkenness. Jorge's mother had rarely turned out anyone, and that accounted for years of earning a lot of money and perpetual insomnia—really, the only problem with exterior restraints like window bars was that they just kept what was outside from getting in. They failed to shield against what had been welcomed in the name of business, and they failed miserably for a woman who was known to be single with only children as guardians. More often than not, it was Jorge's mother who had to break up the knife fights, try to sober the men who had become surly and bear up the men who had become despondent. And then on one unseemly night, Jorge was witness to a skirmish on the patio adjacent to the lunch counter that infuriated him more than most.

He stood on the threshold between their private quarters and profitability and he saw that none of the customers intervened. There was a local, a regular customer who was violently drunk, assaulting his mother over liquor charges.

Jorge felt the keen flush of violation on behalf of his mother, and he felt the fury rise in the face of childish helplessness—the woman who had talked down the military in the dead of night in Tunjuelito was no match for a drunk lacking reason in Funza. Jorge's rage led him to a sudden grasp on the only weapon in sight as he seized a nearby wine bottle at the neck. He rose to the fullest extent of his height and, with all his might, brought the bottle down as hard as his throwing arm would allow. Surprise and momentum sided with Jorge, the awful downward thrust of the glass shattering the bottle and breaking across the top of the man's head. Torrents of blood streamed from his skull and began to soak the man's shirt.

The remaining patrons stared at the child, incredulous, as his mother sat the man down at the table. Blood began to pool in his hands, and Jorge met the assailant's anger with a newfound defiance. He was tired of the insults, of people always trying to take advantage of his family, of the continual fights and the late hours and the constant racket. He was tired of being victimized, and he dared anyone to oppose him as his mother poured coffee on the man's wounds as was the custom—in Colombia coffee beans were the balm for everything, one of the few things they had in abundance.

The man with the insulting tone and the insidious threats left, and then he had the audacity to still frequent the restaurant. He returned to the family business the following week, meek and overly courteous. The other patrons seemed to be just as guarded, appearing to defer to Jorge from then on. His mother gave him a .32 caliber pistol and the child began to keep it loaded and holstered for lack of a better place in the back waistband of his pants. The gun couldn't spit bullets for love nor money—that was Jorge's closely held secret. He just kept it in the holster and he pulled it out to let people know he might be armed and dangerous.

He resigned his post temporarily as the man of the house when he accidentally broke all of his mother's bone china. He was wiser, though, in Funza than he had been in Tunjuelito—he didn't resort to the edgier streets where the insurgents wreaked nightly mayhem and violent carnage on the weekends. There were rarely blankets or leftover articles of clothing in the garbage on the rougher streets. They left a child quite miserable and very cold and alone in the gray of dawn. He made his way to a makeshift warehouse: an enormous tent where the builders of a local factory were known to keep tools and machinery. He swore a guard to confidence, one of dozens of men who ate at his mother's restaurant every morning—and, out of pity, the guard brought the boy the only food that he could scrounge.

For nearly a week, Jorge ate pumpkin in every dish imaginable—pumpkin soup and pumpkin pie and pumpkin bread. He ate mashed pumpkin, followed by baked pumpkin, until he began to feel a reflexive gag in his throat at the smell of it. Jorge's mother asked everyone who entered the restaurant, every passerby on the street, if they had seen an eleven-year-old boy. The guard never let on that the child was hiding at the warehouse. Those kinds of things were best left to families to work out.

Besides, he knew, if he fed Jorge pumpkin long enough, the boy would soon long for the culinary luxuries of home.

When Jorge finally returned to the restaurant, his mother was so relieved to see him that she not only didn't scold him, she nearly fussed over him—it might have been a turning point in their relationship had he not turned his back on such on outward show of affection.

+〓·〓+

Jorge's mother sensed more trouble, and she might have grounded him after such a horrid week of worry. She had resorted to taking every last stitch of her son's clothing and hiding it all in a trunk of late. She provided Jorge with his youngest sister's dress to wear and he was too ashamed to leave his bedroom. The growing problem with Jorge was his size—he hadn't achieved the growth spurt that characterized teenage years, and still he towered over many high school kids.

His ability to pack a weapon and pose a threat to grown men gave him an added sense of invincibility.

Jorge's mother had been sweeping the front patio of the restaurant and she tried to wedge the broom handle between Jorge and the door. When she found that act futile, she attempted to push the door shut, and Jorge wrestled past her easily. She began to plead with him, with all the fervor that flowed from her foreboding.

"No se vaya. No se vaya." *Don't go. Jorge, please don't go.*

Jorge heard her cry that one last time and, for many years, he would feel the anguished touch of his mother's hand on his arm. He would hear the desperation in her voice as he walked with his friends to a car parked outside the restaurant. The party of eight had no intention of staying in Las Tres Esquinas as Jorge had been prone to reassure her. The town square at the northern end of Funza was just as deserted as Jorge's barrio when they approached it, and that offered no fun at all. Jorge sat in the backseat of a black, 1948 Studebaker, squirming under an older, but smaller boy that rested on his legs. The group was headed toward the nation's capitol, in search of a better time.

The car did slow momentarily at Las Tres Esquinas, skirting the corner where Jorge's family lived. The night crowd was winding down at the restaurant and Jorge spied an acquaintance at the bus stop with a route to the heart of Bogotá. It was midnight and the last bus to the city had left at 11:30 p.m. Jorge understood the boy to be stranded and he yelled at the driver to stop.

"¿Que haces tú? ¿Quieres ir con nosotros?" Jorge called from the window.

"I'm waiting for a ride to Fontibón," the acquaintance yelled back.

He was the thirteen-year-old friend of a friend who was dating a girl in Funza, and Fontibón was a small barrio near Bogotá.

"We'll take you there. It's on our way," the adult driver of the Studebaker motioned to the boy. It was pure luck that the acquaintance had found a ride, and then a good time all at once.

There were five people crammed into the back, so he happily took a spot on the lap of an eighteen-year-old in the front seat on the passenger side. The men joked and laughed with the boys in the back hunched over the front seat. They strained to hear and strained to be heard in the raucousness of escape. Jorge's vision was blocked, but not so impaired that he didn't see a pair of headlights on some kind of SUV barreling toward them as they sped along. The road to Fontibón was a single lane highway and they were halfway between Las Tres Esquinas and Bogotá. Jorge could not make out the color or make of the vehicle—or the state of its driver. For a split second, only God saw a green Land Rover with a man at the wheel, drunk and swerving toward them.

Parts of Jorge's life flashed before him as the SUV neared, and in every single scene he heard his mother call to him. *No se vaya. Don't come near the stove. Don't sleep in the streets. Don't steal from the priest. Don't go.* Jorge suddenly saw with abrupt and unusual clarity that his mother had had his best interests at heart all along.

The vehicles collided at sixty-five miles per hour—not a pure head-on collision, but a mismatched grind in which the drivers' side engines took the full impact. The Land Rover had a wide enough base and was taller, but the Studebaker was older and heavy. There were screams and something bashed Jorge's head as both vehicles flipped on their sides and momentarily careened in opposite directions on the single lane highway. Some kind of grassy embankment repelled the Studebaker back to the center lane as it threatened to spill its occupants off the highway. It spun on its top in tight loop-de-loops, at breathtaking speed toward the front of the Land Rover. The SUV sucked at the car like a magnet. On and on, the Studebaker coiled, twisting its occupants in such force they were bound to the steel as if they had been welded to it. When the two vehicles finally came to a standstill, the car and its occupants were at a grotesque ninety-degree angle to the SUV. There were bodies lying at unnatural angles everywhere; blood splattered on the inside of the car and moans that were most ghastly for their weakness. The back of Jorge's head had been concussed by a portable radio, but it was the radio that had saved him. He had chosen to sit near a malfunctioning radio, and he been crated by the bodies on top and in front of him.

He crawled through the mass of his friends and broken glass, on his elbows until he could raise himself up on the highway. He saw as he emerged the body of the driver of the SUV, his head jutted against the tire of his own vehicle. Somehow in its merciless whirling the Studebaker had missed the man's torso entirely. Blood puddled from a multitude of wounds and Jorge stood in a fog to flag down the next vehicle for help.

The acquaintance was sobbing, his legs crumpled under the dashboard and pressed to the glove compartment. No motorists were inclined to stop and help and Jorge worked to pull the boy from the wreckage. It was an extraction made harder by the sideways angle through the shattered window and the inversion of the car. The boys with only minor injuries tried to administer first aid and pull the remaining friends from the vehicle because no emergency crews were ever going to arrive on the scene.

In the less populous areas of Colombia, that kind of help was reserved for the rich or the dead.

The driver had taken the full brunt of the steering column in his chest. Only three other boys had made it out with Jorge. They began to jump up and down, waving desperately at the oncoming traffic for help. One car slowed and then sped off to the nearest police station to try to get some assistance for the injured. The driver of the Studebaker was over six feet tall and weighed nearly 300 pounds. He was the only one still trapped inside the car; essentially, because the steering column had embedded in his body, wedging him to the seat.

The boys on the highway were hoarse from yelling at oncoming traffic; their tongues were swollen in their mouths like cotton in the growing shock and panic. The brother-in-law of the Studebaker's driver was nearly in tears, making one last attempt to yank the driver from the car. He bent the steering column, forced it so far toward the dashboard, that the remaining boys were able to drag the driver's body to the middle of the road. The driver was unconscious, the lack of oxygen already sapping his brain so that he was never going to be the same when he awoke.

The boys took turns talking to him, trying to comfort an unconscious man, because it somehow consoled them.

It didn't matter to those who eventually stopped the nature of the injuries. No one thought about severed limbs or the need to stabilize critical injuries. They raced the casualties to the hospital as fast as they could, and Jorge held the thirteen-year-old's hand in the back of the police car as he continued to scream— he was writhing in the wake of two broken legs and a jouncing car with no significant treatment. Jorge stayed like that—with the friend of a friend who was dating a girl from Funza—while the doctors set the breaks. He stayed like that until six o'clock in the morning, holding the acquaintance's hand until the boy's family finally arrived.

Every passenger survived, including the driver of the SUV, but Jorge remained shaken by the portions of his life that had passed before him. Even the most rebellious of boys knows when he's been given a second chance, and Jorge tried to make it up to his mother. The acquaintance had lost his wallet somehow in the accident and wanted to sue Jorge for damages. The sheriff arrived at the restaurant to serve papers to an eleven-year-old, but told Jorge he could forget the whole matter for a nominal fee.

Jorge retrieved 200 pesos—months and months of selling empanadas at the ICA—and he begrudgingly paid off the sheriff.

Jorge's mother stepped quietly into her youngest son's bedroom following his first experience with blackmail and she told him to pack his belongings. "Next week," she informed him flatly, "you're going to the SENA."

She turned on her heel with little flourish.

At eleven, Jorge was three years younger than the minimum required age for enrollment at the Servicio Nacional de Aprendizaje. The SENA was an agricultural school, distinguished by proud brick dormitories and classrooms that lay seven miles from the ICA. Colombia was the world's largest producer of emeralds, but really it was the verdant plantations, the rich soil that yielded her fruits in such abundance that made the country's borders appear jeweled. The curriculum was more than respectable and the young men who attended were subject to a discipline comparable to the military.

The school and the bureau had a cooperative relationship in which students graduated through three levels of classes, and then earned their practical experiences in the fields and the investigation center. Jorge's mother had a regular patron who was the brother of an administrative head and that's how things went in Colombia. The patron was more than happy to assist Jorge's mother, more than happy to recommend that the child be a full-time resident of the school— a 24-hour-a-day lockdown, Monday through Friday, which relieved a substantial burden.

Jorge's age was not called into question by the faculty or the students, his size and his assuredness making him appear to be much older. He felt the same lurch in his stomach as he entered the facility that he had known at El Amparo de Niños. He stood at attention, and was issued his books and sent forward in a rigid formation to class. The men who addressed him there, who tutored him almost immediately, were very stern stuff coupled with academic distinction. That they demanded extreme respect was a reciprocal courtesy inasmuch as the students obeyed their rules. The strictness, the order, the practical challenges of daily study all complemented a boy surprisingly ready to learn and eager for usable skills. Jorge spent the first eighteen months studying mechanized agriculture—learning how to start and own a farm; learning how to estimate profits based on crop yield and how to handle crop failure. He learned how to buy and repair equipment and, by his thirteenth birthday, Jorge operated heavy equipment—John Deere and Massey Ferguson and Ford branded equipment that did a hundred times the labor of men. He drove tractors and combines, and he learned to till and fertilize and plant and harvest in season. On some occasions the boys were asked to circle the great cultivos of ICA all day long, doing nothing but blowing through plastic whistles to scare the scavenging birds away. It all had purpose and every night he showered with over 200 boys in stalls that rained ice cold water on their sweat-drenched bodies. Jorge ate well and slept hard and arose each day with a sense of pending accomplishment—learning how to reap what he sowed.

It was there, at the SENA, that the prayers sent aloft to Santa Rita finally, truly took hold.

It was a six-hour bus ride to the savannah, a trip made unbearably hot by the sticky, tropical climate and the lack of ventilation. The class had been sent to study agriculture for two weeks in an alternate environment. There were boys who came from the mountains and boys who came from the lowlands and each needed a legitimate chance of success wherever they settled. By the weekend, all of them were ready to shed the shirts and pants that pasted their armpits and thighs in dark, wet patches. They fled the rice patties and cocoa farms in a one-day break to the Coello River. They discarded their wilted clothing on the banks, stretching young and taut muscles. It was the middle of July and a group of seven boys that included Jorge waded to an inlet two feet deep. They reveled in the luxury of chilling water until they saw the second group—it hadn't taken long for more than a dozen of his schoolmates to locate a boulder farther downstream.

The larger group consisted of natives who had been raised on the coast, near the Pacific Ocean. Their skin wasn't just bronzed, it was black as ebony—generations of indigenous cultures deepened by the sun and the sand that had always beckoned them in waves to their shorelines. They began to leap from the boulder, glorious swan dives that made Jorge's companions feel infantile, submerged in a child's wading pool. The first group scrambled onto the bank with Jorge and a friend he called Oruga in the lead, bound for greater honor and release at the mammoth swell below.

They were powerful swimmers—the black boys had the kind of mastery over the waters that made elongated strokes and fishtail splashes look easy. Not one of the boys in the first group knew how to swim, but they were lured by the seeming effortlessness of the second. One by one the boys dived in, led by Jorge and Oruga.

Jorge surfaced momentarily, gasping at air because he had been plunged much deeper than he had anticipated. It had been a chilling, dark sinking and he tried to steady himself as he had seen the ocean natives do. He was carried in futile breaststrokes farther downstream in a rising panic where the waters began to churn exceptionally hard. He felt his legs bat as uselessly as putty at the rushing current that enveloped him. His arms flailed, his head bobbed up and down; water taunted at his chin and then filled his mouth and his lungs. He was sucked under twice before he felt himself tumble in the tow, felt himself being wrapped in the thrashing spin that a spider threads against a fly. It was an ill-omened twirling, the same as the car spin, and it was precisely that sensation that led him to believe he was dead after his first full two minutes underwater. It was ominously quiet where he lay; the churning having stopped and a strange ability to see his body in the threads of the spider. He was wrapped in the white sheet customary for Colombian burials—he was enclosed like a mummy and mourners passed by him, shaking their heads in sympathy as they peered through the viewing glass of the coffin. His eyes were wide open and the glass came in waves, and he thought that it should have been cause for alarm to the passersby. A little girl stood over him, and then a little boy, and then an old lady—all of them peered curiously at his dead, frozen face from some suspended view.

In a few of the villages, embalming fluid was overlooked because of its price, the morticians stuffing cotton in the noses of the dead with an astringent to stanch the smell. Jorge felt the suffocation in his nose, felt every breath of life sucked out of all of his tissue. He tried to scream and nothing seemed to escape his impacted chest. He experienced his funeral in rich, vivid, petrifying colors and he prayed that he could yet live, just before a great blank was drawn over his face and his memory.

The casket had been closed—that was all Jorge knew as he grasped precariously at a large rock, suspended oddly enough on a sand bar in the middle of the river. He didn't know how he had gotten there, how he had escaped the blackness, but he felt the sun on his face and he heard someone shouting to him from the riverbank. He had a soft foothold on the bar and his confusion succumbed to terror again as he felt the sand give way beneath him. His strength was spent and he could hold onto the rock no longer and he struggled, pointlessly, again.

Just as he felt the water drawing him in, felt his hands sliding from their last stranglehold on the stone and his feet sinking into a warm, sickening abyss, he saw his teacher. Walter was a strong man who grasped at Jorge's hand, latched onto him like a tugboat and pulled him safely to the bank.

He was a professor from Uruguay and he cradled Jorge as he spewed water and gulped great breaths of the sticky savannah into his burning lungs. Jorge saw a strange mixture of relief and dread on Walter's face—a strained look that did not disappear even when it became clear that Jorge had survived.

Oruga meant "caterpillar," and his swollen body was recovered from the cocoon of the river two days later. After hours of calling for him, thinking he would surely surface, his classmates knew the outcome; and still they were unprepared for the sobriety of the moment. It was a graphic scene and the professors were uncharacteristically subdued and Jorge concluded that they felt wholly responsible for the tragedy. The boys had been foolish—wanting to show off, Jorge thought—and they had gotten in over their heads; that was all. Oruga's face was pale and his lips were bruised a deep and ugly purple. Jorge tried to remember him the way he had looked before he went into the water. He tried to see him in flashes of his shortened life and it all made him reflect on his own life which had been spared—grasping at the rock in the middle of the river, lying on the bank with a fighting chance, he had come to understand one thing:

No one but God could have ever saved him and somehow that changed everything.

He couldn't understand why he was alive and Oruga was dead—he only knew that God had looked upon him. God had actually looked upon him—Jorge— and that surely meant that He cared. In the mournful swell that shadowed the river and the carefree sun, something enlarged in his mind and his heart that made him want to be better, to shrug off all the old habits and do something noble. If God had shown the interest years before to place that rock precisely where Jorge would drift downstream in the grip of death, precisely where he could be reached by his professor and lifted from his grave—then Jorge had been wrong all along and he must have some purpose in some grand designed ordained by the heavens. He filed onto the bus with the rest of his classmates, saddened and pensive and altered. The professors had taken up a collection to rent a hearse to get Oruga's body back to his parents in a faraway village—it was that or the body would have to be taken back on the bus in the heat and the sweat and the grief.

It appeared they had all been punished enough that week: there surrounded Jorge a kindness and a concern that he had not expected. In that mixture of emotions and compassion, he was as anxious as a fourteen-year-old ever could ever be to see home and the face of his mother.

She looked at him rather blankly as he told her of his ordeal. He had awakened her at two in the morning because he wanted her to pull him close. He wanted her to tell him that she could not have borne the loss if he had drowned, and that she'd give him a hundred chances if needed.

She turned out the light and drifted off to sleep, and Jorge tried to do the same. It was hard to shut his eyes under a weight like that—a vice on his heart that felt as if someone was sitting on his chest. All the near misses were harbored inside, and it was futile to think his mother and he might ever really connect. It had happened for years that his father had asked him what compelled him to such a peculiar habit of constantly staring at the sky, and Jorge had nearly always shrugged self-consciously.

It was hard to explain that he'd long thought there had been a terrible mistake; that in his unsophisticated view he thought an angel had become sore with him and kicked him down to earth. He'd never felt he belonged in mortality—that he'd fought death so fiercely in the river had come as the greatest surprise to himself.

Alone in his room, struggling with all that it meant, Jorge prayed for the first time in so many years. If he was going to be forced to stay, if in fact God had a mission for him, then he only asked for one thing.

He wanted that someday, someone might truly have the heart to love him back.

CHAPTER 4

La Curva del Diablo was an obscure path, aptly named for the devil. No matter how brightly the sun shone, the severe bend in the road was always dark and ominous. It hid its torment in thick foliage until it straightened abruptly, until it was entirely too late. Childhood was forged on a number of paths and this one was Yolanda Reyes' lot. It was the only road home in a five-mile journey she was compelled to take from school each day.

There was a mansion on the top of the hill that shaded the road, and its occupants saw the same scene week after week—a tiny, pretty girl who, no matter how quickly she walked, never escaped the boys who awaited her, taunting and chasing her at the curve. It was clear that she was morbidly afraid at the beginning of the school year, the way she approached the bend with such foreboding. By the end of the first grade, she still cried to herself, but she had learned to just start her run at the outset, to get the thing over with as quickly as possible.

Yolanda was a child prone to acceptance; the faithful companion to Colombia's inevitability.

She lived in a one-bedroom house in the state of Santander that was moderately sturdy and plain. It was small, but it was a house and that was more than many in her region could have claimed. Her father was a farmer who grew yucca and potatoes and a cousin to yucca known as arracacha. At varying seasons, he raised bananas and avocados and coffee and Yolanda gathered it all with the oranges, the sweet limes, and the guava to sell for a profit. Everyone congregated in town on

Sundays to buy the local produce—the horses carting swaying loads of fruits and vegetables on their backs and stumbling in their lather along the rock-strewn paths.

Yolanda's father did not own a horse and that made the trip more demanding.

The crops were traditionally sold in the open-air markets and, when the sales were final, Yolanda's father disappeared. The family ate because Yolanda's mother cooked all day at a nearby restaurant, and because the children kept back some of the produce each week. Yolanda's father had a preference for Bavaria, a nationally produced beer, and he spent his earnings on a lot of it. Only Yolanda was too small to escape his violent temper when he eventually made his way home. Her mother took the brunt of his anger while Yolanda hid outside, cowering and covering her eyes until it was over. There were enormous stretches between his appearances and her mother's midnight flights to the neighbors when the nights turned extreme and ugly. In those lapses, Yolanda sought friendship with the chickens and the dogs that scoured the front yard and she created an imaginary friend. When her loneliness grew the most acute, she wandered to the outskirts of Puente Nacional just to speak and to be spoken to.

Hers was often a lone figure on the streets, an even more resigned profile walking from town than it was on the Curva del Diablo.

Yolanda's father came home early one day, in the middle of the afternoon. The child was busy picking oranges and guava and making plans with her imaginary friend. Her father called her over to the two milk cows to help him bathe the animals in a remedy for ticks. He poured a fine powder into a bucket that rose in a gray vapor, then he hauled some water to make a wash. He stirred the mix with his hand because he had neither the patience nor the inclination to find a stick. When he finished, he sat down on the ground. He looked rather strangely at Yolanda.

It wasn't just the peculiar expression he wore—it was that Yolanda's father had rarely even glanced at her; and he'd never really seen her, ever. "Get me a glass of water," he said to her faintly and Yolanda ran toward the house.

She absorbed herself in the beauty of the flowers when she reached it and she did not fetch what was asked.

"Where is your father?" her mother frowned when she returned home very late from the restaurant.

Yolanda shrugged and motioned to the backyard. "Está durmiendo, Mamita."

"He is sleeping, Mommy," she replied, for he had lain like that all day long. What was a six-year-old to think but that her father was insufferably lazy, and a drunk.

Yolanda's mother knelt on the grass, weeping, and began to rock back and forth. The neighbors brought the body into the house, laid it in the laundry room where only a long, wooden table was present for ironing clothes. They placed four candles on the table, one candle for each corner and began to pray with rosary beads. Yolanda looked upon the corpse, the profile of fine, chiseled features so breathtakingly handsome if only they'd been tempered in kindness. One brother was already in the military, occupied; the oldest was attending college, working in Bogotá to pay for tuition. Out of a family of seven, only the young man from Bogotá had made the bus trip from the capitol city to pay his respects and Yolanda wondered why Manuel had even bothered.

She studied her brother throughout the service, determined they were very much alike in that respect. It was impossible to understand their mother's grief, to imagine anything but indifference for the stranger on the table.

Manuel took Yolanda in his arms after the burial, and he told her she was a very smart girl—he was going to take care of her, make certain she had the best education and opportunities. He was studying to become a reputable, commercial artist and he was going to take extraordinary measures to move the family to the city, pay for books and school uniforms and try to care even for the one who was about to be released from the military, agitated and floundering. It was one of the few times that anyone had held Yolanda and she was drawn extremely close to him for that.

It was a chance to get his family away from impending poverty that compelled Manuel to take them in. He rented a small Bogotá apartment, filled with six people and then nine after Marcos returned from the military, married and with a child. Yolanda paid attention in school, worked very hard at her studies and felt no sort of attachment to the students when she was uprooted seven years later. Manuel moved them all to a larger house in Mosquera, the friendly neighbor to Funza. Once they settled, Yolanda remained as diligent as she had been in Bogotá and Santander—a child who had once played in a river where there were natural stepping stones, polished as smooth as glass from the endless current. That was the way Manuel liked to look at her as he watched his sister from a distance, delicate and graceful in an ever upward climb that was bound for greater heights.

Her lack of companionship had developed a protective sheath that made Yolanda a loner still. But she had substance; she had style; and she had a beautiful gown the color of pale lime that Manuel bought for her coming-out party on her fifteenth birthday.

Yolanda was a young woman of enormous potential and her detachment only made her all the more intriguing. It was a beautiful quinceañera—one of the few times Manuel was able to enjoy his family's company in the midst of fourteen-hour workdays.

+≍+

If Yolanda had had any expectations at all, they were that she would stay in Mosquera her entire life. She would haul water by bucketfuls from a pond in the backyard and boil it on the stove for the occasional luxury of a warm bath. Her anticipations included scrubbing the clothes by hand week after week, hanging the homespun dresses on the line only to see the rain retard her efforts. Such was the life of many rural Colombian women and if there were storms, there were also great rays of sunshine that broke through the clouds in majestic relief afterwards.

Manuel had been true to his word, had provided for her materially, and that was the way to look at things.

It was Yolanda's exquisite beauty that bore such patience, the sweetness when longsuffering was not even her intent—her temperament grounded Jorge and it made him want to bow and soar all at once. He caught a glimpse of her at a high school soccer match, and in that slow motion kind of reverie that tends to take hold in love at first sight, he simply reasoned that someone had to be with her. Someone had to spoil her, protect her, befriend her—someone had to win her over.

He tried to sweep her away to the tune of salsa and tango and *Saturday Night Fever* on Colombia's version of *American Bandstand*. He was sixteen years old, had graduated from the SENA, endured night school and found his way to a real man's job at the city bank. It was the late '70s and Jorge was a fantastic dancer, having earned a spot on television for which he needed a captivating partner. John Travolta and the Bee Gees were the rage in Bogotá, though few there believed Travolta would amount to a serious actor.

It was only Jorge who impersonated his every move, who thought quite passionately that some people just needed a little more time and a legitimate chance to shine.

For all of her natural agility and charm on the dance floor, Yolanda was not easily moved by her heart. Jorge twisted and turned, tried to bend himself to the smallest of her indulgences, but she returned very few of his advances. He saw that she had grown up extremely poor—an older brother her only guardian, away from the home for long periods and doing his best to provide for so many—and then he saw that she was a model of restraint; like his mother, out of sheer survival perhaps, but ultimately elusive nonetheless. She had other suitors: men with more means, more education, more good looks and, more importantly, cars. All Jorge offered was an outstretched hand when he parked his bicycle near the porch.

He always saved some delicacy he was given at the bank each day—a truffle, a petit four, some individually wrapped gourmet sweet that he had cradled all the way home. It was hard to carry fragility like that in Colombia, but Jorge was willing to try anything to win Yolanda's favor.

He bought all of the bread and chicken and corn flour so that her family would not think he was taking advantage of them when he arrived at their house for dinner each night. And then on many days he waited for Yolanda after school, walked her home as much for compassion's sake as for being in love. He believed Yolanda to be his equal as well as his complement; the two of them very much like olive trees having been left to the hardened soil of the same vineyard. Jorge had set his roots deep and grown wild while Yolanda had been tamed by the opposition to flourish. If ever they were grafted, entwined, the strength of one would shelter the other. Jorge never wanted Yolanda to be alone on difficult paths again, something dark and startling awaiting her.

He made some tremendous leap and asked her to be his girlfriend with remarkably raw disclosure. In Colombia, the formality of courtship made a man lay all of his intentions in a clumsiness not so unlike his flailing in the Coello River. If Yolanda agreed, Jorge was required to ask further permission from Manuel. He dared not hope Yolanda might condescend to say yes, and he dared not think of a tomorrow without her.

He tossed and turned at nights, waiting for Yolanda's response; thrashed about his bed as if he was in over his head again. His self-doubt at times was matched only by Yolanda's sinking supposition that all men might bring upon her the misery of her father.

Jorge knew his heart and he prayed his heart and somehow God smiled upon him. It was so easy to care for Yolanda after that, to seek heaven and earth for her when he was floating so high above the clouds already.

It wasn't a youthful infatuation, though Manuel judged it so. It was the purest, most genuine love Jorge had ever known. He took such elaborate measures to be sure Yolanda would never be sorry she had chosen him. Had he thought for one minute she might ever have cause for heartache, might ever have cause to suffer anything that could so exceed what her father had inflicted—Jorge would have left her well enough alone. He cared for her that much.

Manuel was polite, cordial, even a gentleman when Jorge asked for Yolanda's hand in marriage. He had planned on college for Yolanda, coupled with a contract with a modeling agency, and he thought she was far too young to settle. Manuel simply hid the birth certificate so that she could not readily obtain the license. Yolanda's sister made a twelve-hour journey by bus to Santander to retrieve a copy of the certificate, arriving at the house just in time.

The wedding ceremony was a modest one in a Catholic church at the edge of Mosquera, a small crowning achievement that Jorge's mother hosted. She offered the restaurant for a reception afterward, offered one of the rooms off the commons area for their honeymoon. She could see that Yolanda made Jorge strive to be a good provider and that was the most a mother could hope for a son.

There were always the forks in the roads that, once taken, paved entire lifetimes. Yolanda had met Jorge at just such a crossroad, a turning point following his near death experience and a most unusual journey. He had sold his television set and his radio quite recently to spend a week on the Caribbean. Like Manuel, Jorge's mother was a scrapper—a saver—and it seemed a most ridiculous lark. Sometimes the greatest learning experiences were masked like that, even the willing adventurer not quite knowing the impact such a trip would have on the development of character. Jorge went with a friend and they boarded a train, and they were able to upgrade to first class right away. It was glorious to know such license, the way the servers approached them, asking with such deference, such politeness, if anyone fancied wine. At each stop, the local vendors tapped at the windows and offered their best selections to the boys on vaulted, overflowing trays. Jorge sat back with content as the train lumbered on, absorbed in a prized copy of *El Hueco*. It was the story of a group of illegal immigrants who had slipped through the United States borders to freedom. He was 80 percent through the book, enough to covet their emancipation when it was stolen from him as he napped. The end of the book didn't really matter because he had already envisioned some kind of alternate heritage.

Jorge had just committed something significant to memory and heart.

The boys arrived on the coast near Santa Marta, saw that hotel rooms were out of the question and slept their first night on the beach. They awoke in the dawn on their backs, watching as the sky warmed to daylight, and turned from a faint gray to a smoky slate and then turquoise. Jorge had taught himself to swim by then, and he dived in the surf, unabashed. He had never seen water that shimmered like blue topaz, and he became gluttonous on the roar of the changing tide and the allure of fresh shrimp and guava.

On the outskirts of Santa Marta was San Pedro Alejandrino, a site with particular significance to Colombians: it was the death place of Simón Bolívar, a chance to catch a midnight glimpse of the life altering, heroic paths he had trod.

Jorge was not so like his father except in that one thing: they both revered Simón Bolívar. The conqueror was known to many Latinos as the Great Liberator, the George Washington of South America. He was far more legendary than a phoenix, for his truest risings had been born of more improbabilities than mere ash. His parents had died young and he had been left a small fortune, privately tutored and refined as a child. But Bolívar had been a restless youth in Venezuela, leaning to the Age of Enlightenment as his gallant and foremost north star. It was the contrast in him, the pure discontent that had ultimately shaped his and a continent's fortune.

He had taken to Europe young where he was further inspired and defined by the meditations of vigilantes like Jean-Jacques Rousseau. In his mid-twenties, Bolívar had made his passage back to his homeland through the colonies of North America. He had been deeply impressed by the newly secured liberation of the United States from England and joined the patriot swell for the same kind of freedom in Venezuela. He charged with the revolt against Spain, under the command of an associate from their foe's mother country. Francisco de Miranda and the revolutionaries were soundly defeated by the Spaniards in 1812, forcing Bolívar to retreat in his first attempt at loftier pursuits. It was in exile that he wrote the Cartagena Manifesto entreaty for independence—so inspired by his own expressions that he returned to Venezuela in 1813 to retake Caracas. For a season, he received a conqueror's welcome as the country's newest dictator.

He suffered a severe defeat in 1814 in his homeland and was forced back to New Granada, which later became part of Colombia. Determined to advance his cause of liberation anyway, he took command of the Colombian forces and seized Bogotá from the Spaniards in furious retribution. Royalist armies compelled him to a self-imposed exile in Jamaica in 1815 and it was there that he wrote a series of unyielding letters that reflected the musings of Rousseau, representing Bolívar's unparalleled vision for Latin American sovereignty. He returned to Venezuela with confederate forces in 1817 and, after an astounding victory, was elected as the Presidential heir at the age of thirty-four.

It was a turbulent road to the ultimate independence of all of Spanish South America, but by 1819, Bolívar and his insurgents had conquered the Spaniards in Boyacá. They lashed in fury at the enemy, driving across the Andes Mountains, and creating the Republic of Colombia. Bolívar became the country's president and freed Ecuador, Peru, and Bolivia in short order, the last nation founded and named in his honor. By pen or by sword, Bolívar's life was always marked by such stark hills and valleys; a king or a fugitive depending upon the conquests of his forces. In the end, he triumphed over his contemporary, Napoleon Bonaparte, by five times the land mass conquered in Europe—his battles were won with small bands of troops that so often numbered in the hundreds. He had never remarried after his wife had died young, but the last love of his life, Manuela Saenz, had fought at his side throughout any number of intrigues and resistance. She had risen to the rank of a colonel in Bolívar's army and stood by him as he relinquished his power to the bitterness of internal factions—she had remained at his side until he had died a broken man on the coast.

It was said that Bolívar was penniless at the end of his life and that he resigned his presidency in a failure to create political unity. Historians agreed that his health also failed miserably at the time of his resignation and that he died just seven months later from tuberculosis. Really, his demise might just as well have been attributed to the fact that Bolívar was more warrior than politician—and yet none of that mattered so many years later to South Americans who still had their illusions intact.

There was an indebted mantra to which Jorge and his friend subscribed as they stole from the estate and sang in lyrical attest to the swell of the seaside night:

It mattered not where Bolívar had been born, nor even where Bolívar had died.
It mattered only to the realization of human potential where Bolívar had fought.

Jorge lay under the stars of Santa Marta with the full weight of moonlight upon him and the impression of greatness and nobility's thirst for freedom. It was a pity to him that a man like Bolívar should not have known his worth while he had yet been alive. There was one particular assertion by Rousseau that seemed to have lit such fire in Bolívar's breast and it made Jorge's pound in rhythm to the Atlantic surf. It was the declaration that civil association was "the most voluntary of all acts"—that "every man being born free and his own master, no one, under any pretext whatsoever, can make any man subject without his consent. To decide that the son of a slave is born a slave is to decide that he is not born a man."

The depth of Jorge's meditations went unnoticed by his friend and any number of late night visitors to the beach. He stared at heaven's expanse, his ideas taking on lasting form, best articulated in an address Bolívar had made to the Congress of Angostura in 1819. Bolívar had insisted that liberty was subject to failure if man's happiness was not founded in the practice of virtue. Correct morals under the auspices of law had a more powerful effect than force—he had maintained that throughout his career. Ignorance was the cause of slavery, wherein excessive license was traded for liberty, sedition confused with patriotism and retribution mistaken for justice. Jorge agreed with Bolívar in all of his zealous cases except for one: Bolívar had insisted on a tighter reign than the governance of democracy.

The headiness of self-actualization remained until Jorge's third day on the beach.

Along with the ocean-side swells and the white tails of sunrise came the exaggerated cost of a resort town. Jorge and his friend bought their last high-priced meal, and became utterly, hopelessly destitute. It was the famine of means that always seemed to blur their vision and they succumbed to it, gradually drained by the sun and the tropical breeze. They had no fare for the return trip to Funza and, in the course of a week, suffered hunger so severe they wished to claw at the sand. They crept along the shorelines and the improvised boardwalks with the ravages of street dogs.

For a few glorious days he had been a young man of privilege and grandiose dreams, and then he was a beggar, staggering across the beaches. Jorge was too proud to solicit much so he sneaked onto an outbound train. Such deceit was a problem for him because he had grown a conscience since his epiphany at the river. He tried to feign sleep when the coachman passed, but the man shook him, undeterred on the question of a ticket. Jorge was let off at the next stop and it was there that he faced his most disheartening irony. How was it, he considered, that he was besieged in his hunger and frustration, and that the North Americans had achieved such enormous significance? To the South they were all paupers and he might remain a pauper—die, like Bolívar, a broken man. He coaxed his way onto a bus seat, vacated by an old lady, and then he stood for five hours when the old lady returned. The trip was so ultimately discouraging that he only wanted to go home at some point, but he had not left the beach without consequence.

He had stood at the waters' edge, thinking that someday he would return to the Caribbean as triumphant as Bolívar—thinking with some fierce resolution that when he came back, he would never be hungry or in want again.

Yolanda did not pass judgment on Jorge's trip as he recounted it; not for the impetuous nature that had instigated it in the first place or squandered the money in a matter of three days. For one thing, she rather admired the youthful impulsiveness that she alone could balance in her moderation; and, for another thing, she would have surely starved with him in the end.

She only wanted to know what the ocean breeze felt like on one's face; what it was to be filled on crab so decorously chilled on ice—what it was to squint at hues of blue and green and a sun so strong that one went temporarily blind in the brilliance.

Yolanda was not adventurous, not so enthusiastic as Jorge. What she offered was a profound appreciation and support of his passions.

Someone had to actually do the fighting and Bolívar had been that valiant man in the trenches. "Do you see it, Yolanda? ¿Me entiendes, amor?"

She did understand, and she also took note that Bolívar was still only the second most influential leader in her husband's life.

+>==—=<+

Jorge's greatest hero was a visionary who was willing to extend his battles to every continent beneath the expanse of the Almighty. It was not a stretch for

Jorge to emulate the thought processes of one who held so doggedly to his ideals no matter how improbable they seemed. They were the revisionists who not only believed in fate, but believed in a fate that required the strife that rested squarely on their shoulders. It was just a little over the one-year anniversary of the assassination attempt on that most admirable, remarkable man.

Their first child was almost eight months old and, though Fabian was old enough to sit on his own, Jorge coddled him on his lap, wanting him to be a witness to such a momentous occasion. Yolanda sat beside him, four months along with their second child with a hand embracing her stomach, protective. Jorge was compelled to hold Fabian tighter, whisper in his ear while the footage of such magnitude trickled into their home.

The President of the United States—Ronald Wilson Reagan—was paying a personal visit to Colombia.

Violence was such a fixture in his homeland that Jorge should not have been as stunned by the shots that had rung out in the North the previous year. It was just that an attempt at assassinating a man like Ronald Reagan was an attempt at killing the epitome of hope. They had translated his first words into Spanish after Reagan underwent surgery to remove that offensive bullet. He had forgotten to duck and that self-deprecating humor had caused Jorge to laugh in tears of relief. Reagan had that sunny disposition, that easy command of his words and faculties; and then he had had the lion-like resolve to issue ultimatums in stalemate arms negotiations. He possessed that warmth—and the audacity to stare down the Cold Warriors, to fight for the common man and force the totalitarians to blink. Jorge feared for the President's life in a land as rocked by upheaval as Colombia. He uttered any number of "Our Fathers" as he saw Reagan descend from Air Force One and began to tenderly caress his baby's hand.

"As God is our witness, we are something very special and something very good to have a man like that visit our country," he exhorted Fabian.

He held his breath as his son grasped his finger, as Reagan moved toward the Colombian delegation. Yolanda saw that he subconsciously rocked their son, that the President's mere presence buoyed her husband and stirred him to more than tears. Jorge could not put his finger on the exact nature of Reagan's charisma; he just discerned virtue in the President as he had seen it in Yolanda. He thought Reagan had an ordinariness about him and then he thought he seemed larger than life. He had observed enough leaders in his lifetime who could govern the masses, but he had never seen one who could inspire such individual greatness among them. Reagan had been known to express "that the most meaningful words in the Constitution are three in number, contained in the phrase, *we the people*." That made him more of a truster than Bolívar and more like Jorge to an extent: men who believed the heights to which mankind could aspire when life, liberty and the pursuit of happiness were given a precious, honest chance. "We have every right to dream heroic dreams," Reagan had told his countrymen at his 1981 Presidential inauguration. It had been an assertion made despite the U.S. alone having fallen victim to inflation and the hostage crisis of Iran and every manner of malaise.

Reagan had been emboldened with the mantle of destiny, and Jorge had felt vindicated somehow. "We are a nation under God," Reagan had avowed, "and I believe God intended for us to be free."

Jorge stood a little taller, walked a little brisker as Reagan concluded his swing through Latin America. The President's words and his extension of friendship were so cherished that it would become an extreme puzzlement to Jorge years later—how Reagan had returned unscathed from Colombia only to face the gravest wounds among his own fellow citizens in a second term. A man who had been able to bring such optimism by mere footsteps on Colombian soil should have been exceptionally esteemed in his homeland.

Perhaps some of the Americans were as blind to true love and devotion as Yolanda's brother had once been, thinking Reagan's sunny nature was only born of naïveté. Or perhaps they were just that inexperienced—having never been truly oppressed since Bolívar had passed on their sacred ground, had labored under that greatest banner of liberation.

As it was, in December of 1982, Jorge resolved his continued battle in the smallest corner of his universe: like Reagan he would have to build on the hardships with a brick and mortar resolve.

CHAPTER 5

Jorge held Yolanda's hand and wiped at her forehead, and did his best to console her as Diego tore his way into the world on a cold and rainy Saturday afternoon. Their child seemed to be stunned by the abrupt entrance, weakly gaping at air like a fish that had lost the energy to flail after fighting the hook for so long. He remained just as limp while the local doctor cradled him, trying to start his lungs. If there were complications the provisional medical staff was at a loss to help.

They were hours from the capitol and its more advanced medical centers, alone in a clinic on a floor above a small town pharmacy. The conditions were primitive and Yolanda lay spent on the bed, desperate for a cry from the tiny, bloodied form that was still bound to her by the umbilical cord.

Diego finally took in the excruciating rush of a first breath and then he only wailed briefly.

It wasn't that anything had gone wrong necessarily—it was that Diego was never going to be much of a crier.

The couple's second son was unquestionably skinny, a trait made more prominent by the thick tufts of black hair that swallowed his head. Yolanda swathed him tight, held his contentedness to her face, nuzzling him. He instinctively suckled the finger that caressed the small pout of his lip and she wondered, as all mothers do in the face of such purity and innocence, what lay ahead for him. The future had never seemed bleaker for Colombian citizens, the distressful state of their country only increasing with time.

Their president, Belisario Betancur, was attempting negotiations with multiple insurgent groups only to be point-blank refused. The country was soon to be traumatized by a sixteen-year-old's leveling of the minister of justice, Rodrigo Lara Bonilla, with a sub-machine gun. Children from the most poverty-stricken areas had already joined the cartel-connected gangs in reckless throngs. President Betancur had no choice but to enact a frantic treaty of extradition with the United States with so many of the drug traffickers fleeing north anyway.

The battle lines had become unequivocally drawn between the young and aspiring assassins hired by the drug cartels and any sense of lawfulness and order.

It should have worried Yolanda that the front lines had been blurred by the more traditional and ruthless warfare of the streets: teenagers so angry and bent on revolt that they chose to end their own lives in the destruction if necessary. It should have worried her that under the extremity of these circumstances—the sheer randomness and kamikaze nature of the attacks—it had become impossible for the government to guarantee the most primitive safety of its citizens. The truth was Yolanda had grown accustomed to the violence and the poverty, to the cardboard box dwellings of the country's lowliest class and to the vacant stares of the orphans that shared their streets. It wasn't a sense of inhumanity that caused her to turn aside; it was a long held sense of resignation to her station and theirs.

Diego gazed at her with the veiled eyes of a newborn and it was impossible to imagine the gangs or the guerillas or any sort of homicide that was the number one cause of death in Colombia. She simply didn't want him to ever be hungry or cold or afraid and, most of all, she didn't want him to ever be as lonely as she had once been.

Jorge saw his tiny family in the bath of twilight through a window above the pharmacy; saw that Yolanda's virtue as a wife was exceeded by only that one most noble thing even her protective brother could not have anticipated: it was motherhood that had gradually brought Yolanda full circle, made her glow as expectantly as the springtime sun.

Yolanda had not thought of her father in years—not until she saw the variations in Diego's eyes. They had that striking penetration, but they seemed to lighten more in color with each passing month. Her youngest son's face had that prominence, a strength in his features, all softened by what peered back at her and so many locks that had eventually straightened to frame his forehead. His skin was golden brown and Yolanda saw that a natural glow highlighted his cheekbones and brow when he awoke every morning. There was a keen sense of optimism that bore such a remarkable resemblance to gratitude that it compelled her to make Diego's smile sparkle all the more.

His laughter spilled from the front door as Jorge returned from the city, set down his load from the market. It was an overjoyed, contagious giggle that made his father's heart swell in an unexpected release. There were signs of development that marked the milestones and Diego had finally achieved that depth—where he had once been deterred in his want of something because it had simply been placed out of eyesight—Diego had grown up enough to perceive the hidden things, to have faith in what was just around the corner.

His mother was crouched behind the wall that adjoined the kitchen, and Diego stumbled toward her with outstretched hands. He stopped just short of actually seeing her, some sly grin of expectation on his face. He cocked his head to one side, listed behind the wall, waiting for her sudden appearance.

"Where's my Dieguito?" she called too loudly and her son pulled on his shirt anxiously, squatting like a frog.

The child's mother seemed to be lost, confused; it was apparent Diego had to rescue her.

"Wight here! I'm wight here!" he pounded on his chest as he sprang forward, fearless and bracing himself for the attack.

Yolanda jumped out at him, threw her arms around him and swung him just before she tickled him mercilessly. Jorge appeared at the door without warning and that made Diego squeal in delight some more.

He ducked his head and he wiggled away from his mother and she came after him just as he had hoped. Fabian was so much bigger and faster that he ran over his younger brother in his desperation, trying to avoid the chaos. Diego got up and tripped over his brother again and again in the confines of such a small kitchen. They expired in a heap together, screaming with joy when their mother captured them both.

Fabian turned his head from so much kissing, but Diego wrapped his arms around her tight. He buried his face in her neck and shook with great gales of laughter as she pulled back from him, blowing raspberries on the skinniest of two-year-old tummies.

Diego had faith in what was just around the corner and it was that childlike trust to which Jorge completely lost himself at nightfall. He saw himself so clearly in both of his sons and, despite their sheer innocence and playfulness, the reflection made Jorge forget who he was. He ached to be the unfailing companion to his boys, the ever presence that he had lacked as a child. He changed jobs frequently, trying to maintain precious time with his family, and all the while he felt increasingly inferior to his mother. There were two sides to caretaking, and it was the nature of Colombia to make one choose between attentiveness and food. He saw it all with utter clairvoyance and it made him want to beg forgiveness of her in the rawest form of penance possible.

Jorge lay in the bedroom with Yolanda, one arm stretched pensively across his face. He was troubled and his wife sensed it; she had waited for him to speak ever since they'd tucked the children in bed.

"They'll come after them both, Yoli. He said it quietly. It was just a place to begin.

It was the fact that the leftist M-19 rebels had stormed the Palace of Justice that month—even if Jorge seemed accustomed to bloodshed. When he was a student at the ICA, men had overrun the school and taken the lives of workers there.

But this was different—an urban bloodbath at the Supreme Court with the military trying to intervene. The hostage crisis had left more than 100 people dead in their capitol; there was nothing that resembled a refuge anymore.

The convoys of trucks and the glaring headlights and the barking, grunting men of his youth—they had begun to plague him the day Fabian was born, always marching through his head and stealing the future of his loins. He could pinpoint the exact moment he had lost his ardor for the Colombian army, but he was powerless to stop its sway. It was still well enough for a man to fight at times, but a son needed something truly noble to fight for. That was the real source of his disquiet when he searched the depths of his heart: their scarlet sins kept flowing through the streets, something always staining their dreams.

Yolanda knew as well as Jorge did that he was never going to make enough money to buy the fake military cards to avoid the service. It was quite possible that their children would die in the brutality of a jungle against the slaves of drug lords long before they had a chance to become men.

The alternative, of course, was to struggle, to battle, to live and be failed by the empty promises of one's country—was that the breath of life God had instilled in his children and for what? "For what?" Jorge implored her.

"God will take care of it," Yolanda tried to deflect it and her perceived calm only animated him more.

He rose and sat upright and draped himself, anguished, over his knees. "I work and I work, Yolanda. And for what? For what?" he grasped to the dark.

Yolanda lay very still, knowing his anger was not directed toward her, knowing he did not beg her answer just then. Jorge spoke in such eloquent diatribes that Yolanda had learned to listen and sometimes even marvel at the beauty of it. If one had not been so personally attached to his arguments, she could have seen how her husband might have been a brilliant trial attorney, a professor, or even a politician like his brother. Jorge wasn't an orator who talked in circles like some men were prone to do when they became impassioned.

He built his case line upon line, in great, swelling repetitions that emphasized the former.

The great communicator, she thought, though Jorge's was a rhetorical frustration that pleaded the age-old subject matter. Yolanda could imagine the answers coming to him in a whirlwind someday, in a great booming voice like unto Job. *Where wast thou when I laid the foundations of the earth? declare if thou hast understanding.* His justifications for living, for striving, did not even demand extravagance: Jorge was only consumed with the never-ending thought that he and all the rest were consumable. He worked and he worked so that Yolanda could work, precariously transporting their children to daycare in a basket on a bicycle. They worked and they worked so that they might have the most meager of roofs over their heads, the most meager portions of food on their table. They worked and they worked and they might just die working on the streets someday, after all of it, from gunshot wounds to the head for what pennies they'd guarded in their pockets. They strived to send their children to school, to pay for Diego's medicine so that he might draw an easier breath—all so that he might relinquish it for a military that felt no particular loyalty to his brother or him. He was going to be picked up by a barbarous convoy and dumped in a barbarous battlefield, to die alongside Fabian in barbarous, unmarked graves in the Andes.

"Why are we here in this place—in *this* place—why are we here?" *Tell me that.*

"Tell me, Yolanda, why are we here?" Jorge's eyes glowed black and fiery; smoldering coals in the dimness. His hands were so tormented, running through his hair and trembling under such insurmountable adversity. His older brother had warned him of feelings that ran so strong—they were unpatriotic, disloyal to Colombia, he said.

Jorge thought quite to the contrary—thought so much of his fellowmen that it wounded him to see the benign acceptance of underachievement in life, and in death. "Give me a place where I can work with my own two hands for something lasting, something worthy.

"Give me a place where my children can be free; to run and to play, to be boys and make plans and have dreams and live—really live to be gallant old men.

"Give me a place where *I* feel like a man, Yolanda; where ambition and loyalty and faith have their rewards.

"Give me that place, and I will die a patriot's death if I have to, baby." *Just give me that place.*

He did not break down and cry in front of his wife, though it seemed he was poised to do so. It was only her tears that could bring him to that and she remained in his arms very quiet. He had pulled her to him fiercely, needing her warmth and her calm like a second skin to settle the churning. Hers was a tranquility that softened him, made him speak lower in the deadness of night.

"Can you imagine Fabian coming back from the Army, baby? Can you imagine something like that?"

His observation was not disjointed at all; Yolanda made the connection as intimate partners were able to. A murmur of protest passed her lips, made her wearily rub the bridge of her nose. Jorge was haunted by the midnight raids and the Uzzi spitfire while Yolanda was equally afraid of making men into hollowed-out shells. Neither of them could account for why Fabian seemed to take things harder, why there was some agitation that stirred inside of him. Yolanda only had her brother as a frame of reference, the way he'd returned in the beginning, so disconnected and irritable. Jorge was entitled to think that a thing like the Colombian Army would destroy Fabian, steal his last measure of buoyancy.

"Fabian's a good boy, you know. He's just grumpy. That's all," she conceded.

Jorge had to laugh a little. That was the effect she had on him in the void that was sheer exhaustion. Fabian had a lot of his father's traits and the boy loved Diego so much; that was probably his trial and his saving grace. His little brother was so content, so jubilant, so sunny, that it only made Fabian seem like perpetual rain. They had been born so close together that one of them had been destined to overshadow the other in such stifled surroundings.

Jorge curled around Yolanda but she refused to yield to sleep on that kind of end to the night. She stole from the bed and padded to her sons' bedside for one final glimpse.

In a ten-by-ten room lay that small brush of accomplishment that she needed to paint her world anew. A mother, too, could feel just as inadequate as Jorge did—overwhelmed in the face of such challenges.

She knew there were fundamental differences between Jorge and her as she listened to their boys' steady breathing and pulled disheveled sheets over them, shielding. She sat on the edge of the bed, studying their faces in the blank draw of midnight. Diego's lips parted in the untroubled slumber his temperament knew, his serenity soothing her and making her ache. She had the notion to draw him to her, cuddle him in the crook of her arm and bathe his forehead in kisses. They were growing up so fast, but she allowed both her boys to sleep, allowed for the sweet exhales that blew as soft as a lullaby. She slid down the wall and it was not a sigh of resignation that escaped her that time for Yolanda had found her strength and contentment.

It was like looking upon her own heart as it beat, she thought, sending lifeblood to all of her senses—knowing with such absolute certainty exactly why she'd been born.

+⊱═⊰+

Jorge didn't mean to be ungrateful—not when he had been gifted such beautiful boys and a wife with such goodness as Yolanda. Every morning he struggled to overcome his discontent and count his blessings because his mother had been most generous, giving them an apartment near the restaurant when Jorge could no longer afford rent. He tried to bear up under his wife's unquestioning gaze and the unconditional love of his children. He simply felt vulnerable as he watched Diego scrapping and physically waning with something undiagnosed. He saw early on that Fabian had a tendency for rebellion in their continual vice of poverty.

It all accumulated with the injustice that Jorge had to take so many trips to the airport for his employer.

He watched from the gates, saw hundreds of carriers, lifting off toward heaven, so privileged in their steady ascent. He didn't want to stow away, didn't want the dishonor of the illegal aliens in *El Hueco*, and that was his greatest punishment—he needed so badly to make an honorable go of things that his dream was always precluded by a phrase that signaled he was truly wanted there: "Welcome to the United States of America," someone was kind enough to extend a hand to him, and Jorge was equally dignified in his response.

With inexplicable longing, Jorge grasped at the outskirts of his affliction, symbolized in the wrought iron gates of the American Embassy in Bogotá. He had felt like a man wrongly imprisoned for some time, but he was trapped suddenly in a way he'd not known since El Amparo de Niños. The festering swelled the most on afternoons when he was compelled to make the two-hour journey by bus to the heart of the capitol. He was burdened with suitcases under each arm, the only means he had to carry groceries from the open markets back to Funza and back to their one-bedroom home. Fabian would be bedded in a crude crib when he returned and at least he was sheltered from the concrete walls and the cold, hard floor. But there was no insulation and Yolanda would have swaddled Diego, sick, in all the blankets she had, wrapping a scarf around her own head before lying down to sleep with him in her arms for warmth.

It was a sin, Jorge thought every time he envisioned them—a tragic sin to have to cover such sweetness. The lack of progress hid the virtuous expressions of childhood and the soft black tendrils of hair that curled so effortlessly through his fingers when he cupped his wife's face in his hands.

The bus began to creep along the Avenida Boyacá and no passenger feigned interest in the passing landscape on another repressive close of day. Someone might have asked him how long he had harbored such feelings, and Jorge would have said it had all started the day he was born. He set his jaw in some lonely determination that only a man who still believed in the unattainable knew. It was an ache that pinpricked his nerves, made him suddenly wish to find any passage to crawl out of his own skin. Colombia was his flesh and blood, but it was a hard thing to be obliged to a country that could never fully house his soul.

The view on the American Embassy had opened his world and closed it, all at the same time that afternoon. It was very much like the skewed room in which Alice in Wonderland had once found herself. Was Jorge getting bigger, or was his corner shrinking by the minute?

His mother was still up, of course, when he passed by the restaurant in the silk cape that was Colombian fog. His weariness was unexpectedly met by a steaming bowl of caldo and an advertisement she had clipped from the newspaper. She handed it to him discreetly, patting his arm as he read it with sudden interest. The restaurant was still full, patrons demanding and drunk as his mother beckoned him to the privacy of the kitchen

"Can you imagine a job like that, Jorge?" she whispered, her dark eyes almost flickering, illuminated. "I'll drive you into the city. You'll have a better chance if you apply in person, don't you think?"

Jorge fingered the clipping and glanced intently at her for it was not a rhetorical question. It had been a long time since he'd taken a trip like that into Bogotá and some faint kind of tenderness passed over him.

His aunt with eleven children had constantly hoarded for him, tucked extra money into her blouse. She had actually motioned Jorge into the house once, giving him all the change she'd had for a bus fare downtown. He had been young but he had needed work in the worst way and she had thrust the money in his pocket at the first sign of his vehement protests. "A few skipped meals are a small price to pay for your hope. Go on," she had insisted gently.

Had he gotten the job?

Of course not, though she had watched and prayed and waited for him all day long. He had rounded the corner of her neighborhood, his head hung low, and she had said never mind all that.

It was the art of child rearing, it was so obvious now, that had prompted such wisdom, such charity.

All she had ever wanted to instill in a boy was that he had to keep on battling.

"We'll go tomorrow," Jorge rose to his full height, giving an appreciative nod to his mother. The light was soft and he studied her face, the lines near her eyes, on her forehead. She was so tall, so sure of herself, and he wondered that she had always been that stoic and practical. When had she learned to save him like that, cast her line to him without ever making him feel less of a man?

It was a short walk back to his apartment, but he idled in his preoccupation, strangely jubilant and renewed. It was an anecdote worth the recall that hurried him along suddenly, made him even smile to himself.

Don't you dare leave this house. Don't even think of leaving this house, his mother had been prone to threaten him.

And then, naturally, he had left the house because that was the kind of kid he had always been.

He had danced with his friends until the wee hours of the morning, knowing full well his mother's stamina. She had opened two restaurants by the time he was sixteen and his only concern had been to crawl into bed before she did.

He had encountered a street gang on his way home that night that had mistaken him for an older boy. They had beaten him senselessly, bloodied his nose with a chain before abandoning him in his gore on the street. He had limped to the house, doubled over at times, and his greatest fear had still been the reprisal of his mother. He had ransacked the house with a great deal of care when he returned, cautiously overthrowing furniture and dumping any contents he dared from the drawers. He had defended the household with such courage, of course, that he had been forced to stage a great struggle. He had made certain he dripped blood on the tiles in all the right places, oozing the carnage from his nose near the door. He had laid face down, appearing unconscious, but waiting—and waiting and waiting.

He had waited so long that the blood had eventually dried and he wondered that no one had come to his rescue. The tiles had been ice cold. *Where could they have gone?* He had grown more frustrated and pathetic by the minute. He had been relieved to tears by the time he had finally heard them—his mother's clipped footsteps as he had sprawled himself dismally back on the floor.

What pity he was going to evoke with such wounds. It had been such a terrible battle. His mother had taken one long look at Jorge and the room, and not one blood curdling scream had escaped her.

What have you done? What on earth have you done? She had shaken her head in contempt. And then she had retired to her bed unruffled, not even the least bit sympathetic.

He had never been able to get anything past his mother—nor his wife for that matter, he thought. He paused in the doorway, caught in his self-absorption as he looked upon Yolanda sleeping. She had waited up for him most of the night, the soft glow of the lamp her only company. The children were already tucked in bed. She was so beautiful, so serene as he bent to kiss her.

"Do you see this nose, baby?" he whispered softly, the trials making him more enamored with her than the day he'd first said it. *I got hit by a chain. That's why it looks like this. You understand, don't you, baby?*

She did, of course; that's why he had taken her home, to meet his family immediately. In his mind he saw her reach out a gracious hand, to his mother, his sisters, and his brother. She had been so graceful, so enchanting, so demure—he would have been lost without her. He carried her to bed, brushed her face with his lips and gently lay down beside her.

Of course I understand. A sly smile in his flashback; she was only sixteen years old and so captivating. Only Yolanda could disarm him as she had that night: that touch of satire in a temperament so sweet.

I've met them all—it's so clear to me now—they were hit by the very same chain.

He laughed out loud and she didn't stir, and it was the only disappointment he was sure they would ever know in their lifetimes.

He wanted so very much to see the light flicker, to see her eyes dance before daybreak. He had to content himself to simply look upon her. *I love you, baby*, he whispered. He settled and then slept, his face buried wearily in the soft nape of her neck.

CHAPTER 6

There were three stacks of applications in the front office where Jorge applied for the position—500 applications from which only two men would be chosen. Jorge chewed at his thumbnail as he placed his own papers on top, willing some small light of his aunt's confidence to shine upon his credentials. It was a rather impossible wish to be chosen from so many stacks of desperation: one had to lean on the kind of expectations the women in his life never surrendered.

Jorge's mother waited patiently in her car outside, the militant embodiment of General George S. Patton. *In war nothing is impossible, provided you use audacity.*

The human resources director pressed Jorge so hard for his qualifications that he had to be brutally honest. He had two small boys, a family of his own that he desperately needed to care for—he could understand completely the paternal instincts of both CEOs.

"You must be available whenever they call you. You must be very good with the children."

Jorge vigorously assured the director he would be devoted and dependable. A man was nothing without his honor and his family.

He was so shameless in his appeal, the naked exposure of need so overt it would have made other men cringe. The human resources director remained too aloof, too professional, so that Jorge found it necessary to put him off guard.

"I want to be the chauffeur for the family with the Mercedes-Benz, not the Chevrolet Monza," he shifted boldly.

The director's head snapped up, his response to Jorge's brazen declaration immediate and flat.

"We have already assigned a driver to that particular family and vehicle. No."

They had made a decision on one candidate and Jorge saw the stakes double, eyeing the pile of applications. One man out of 499; the odds were even worse than before. He pushed his papers forward a bit, so that they overhung the stack with as much impudence as he dared. "I want to drive the Mercedes-Benz," he said firmly, squaring his shoulders to the director.

The man studied him intently, from head to toe it seemed, but there was no significant break in his demeanor. "Thank you, Señor Rincon. We will be making a decision by Friday. We'll call you if you get the job."

They had liked his looks, his honest face that could suddenly turn quite imposing. And then they had liked that he brashly took up space, a must when the only thing between children and a bloodbath on the streets was their driver. Jorge twirled Yolanda in his arms and then hugged his boys until they squirmed against him, cheerfully rebelling. They were moving to Bogotá, halfway up a ladder of sprawling affluence to the north.

Fabian hid his little brother under a pile of stuffed animals as his mother packed up their dishes. "Lay very still," he whispered, too loudly. "Don't move and she won't be able to find you."

Yolanda smiled to herself, tiptoeing toward the door jam. A small set of eyes peeked out between Mickey Mouse and the tail of a dinosaur.

"Hmmm, let's see, Jorge, where did I pack those knives?" she began to drum her fingers.

She rummaged through a drawer, pulled out a meat cleaver in triumph, unnaturally animated in her find. "Just look at all those stuffed animals on the bed, baby. I don't know how we'll fit everything in the car."

The pile began to quiver, threatening to topple as Diego fought a new fit of giggles.

"Shhst!" Fabian's warning was so dire Yolanda projected her voice again toward the bedroom.

"I guess we'll just have to cut Diego's legs off. There simply isn't enough room."

Diego's eyes grew round and panicked just before he burst through his cover.

"Wight here! I'm wight here! I can fit!" he bounced, anxious and then laughing in his spring.

<hr />

Their company car was indeed packed as they journeyed past the conquered mountains of Bolívar—past the erosion on the hillsides so painfully evident at midday. Colombia's people appeared tempered and submissive to the insurgent blood that continued to ferment their rich soil. It was surreal, the feeling Jorge had that he'd just somehow been exalted above the despondency. Their new home was, by Colombian standards, an exceptional highrise, resembling the function over form look of a dormitory. There was some metropolitan architecture that embraced its surroundings, taking on the natural contours and graces of its neighbors. His home was not so stylish and still it seemed to bludgeon the lowlands with aspiring condescension. They took an elevator, the lift catching Fabian's caution in a strange swell of dissension—it was the gradual intermediary between enormous wealth, that offhanded sidling up to the rich.

Jorge bought Yolanda a denim skirt and a tangerine colored blouse, something trendy in a small celebration—and then he bought her a washing machine for their new apartment so that her hands would no longer bear the rawness of scrubbing. The owner of the Fortune 500-like company had taken on the extra expense, the extra burden, of giving Jorge all the necessary social amenities. It was refinement they worked on so that he could act the irreproachable escort of the family in all their public outings.

Jorge was not offended by the grooming—it was a sign that the owner had a long-term commitment. He sent Jorge to the local country clubs to get tennis lessons; to get massages and facials, and then manicures. Jorge was emboldened by what he saw as he viewed his reflection in the most fashionable shops in the city: he was being fitted for fine-woven Armani and Versace, the tailor hand-altering his suits. He selected crisp button-down shirts with heavy starch collars that were to be dry cleaned at company expense. His Luis Vuitton shoes were professionally polished to a shine as brilliant as his gold-studded cuff links.

He was hardly recognizable: the imported silk ties and even his socks so exquisitely chosen. He smiled in great earnest and that was the ultimate transformation as he modeled before Yolanda, pleased. His whole countenance was lit—for a moment she saw a hint of Diego's exuberance. Jorge had shrugged off the cloak of brooding he had worn since a child in the cacophony of their streets.

Bogotá had always been speckled with patchworks of laundry, be it garish or simple or proud. Yolanda hung her boys' stiff white dress shirts from the balcony to dry, the staple of their new school uniforms. A passerby could discern a lot about households by the mere view of what was publicly displayed: the Rincon laundry was composed and modest, the up and coming influence of newer money and prestige.

Jorge dropped off his children at an elite private school and the image of them made his eyes watery. It was the morning sun in his face and then it was joy, seeing them grasp so boldly at opportunity. Fabian took Diego by the hand and the two of them marched confident, little gentlemen in navy blue blazers and grey wool trousers. Diego twirled back toward his father, once, waving to him with all his might. Fabian smiled broadly and then they were off, running to the building. Diego's feet on the pavement were haphazard in a child ever willing to go along.

The owner's penthouse was impressive, a friendliness exuding from the windows that revealed its inner tranquility. He was greeted by the owner's wife and three little boys at the door, the intimidation of extreme luxury suddenly dissipating. The children were gracious and prodded to politeness, all the while longing to get back to their playtime. Jorge's intuition led him to their inner sanctuary, some magical and absorbing setting like Peter Pan's adventures in Never Land. The littlest one was Diego's age, his eyes bright and beckoning, discerning as he took Jorge's hand. He wanted to play a game with him, instantly drawn to his new driver's kindness and approachability.

They toured the split levels and the plush foyers with chandeliers that were so ornate they could have overhung grand ballrooms. The flowers opened soft petals on the verandas and the ferns swayed in the breeze like great, Spanish fans. The owner's wife was an aficionada of art, pausing at each oil painting to explain the variations in light and texture. She shared Jorge's love for contemporary music, the soulful agility from urban pop to sultry ballads playing out on a superb sound system in the formal dining room. She had an exceptional ear for talent, Jorge thought, putting in a cassette tape of an aspiring American vocalist with an earth shattering range. "You Give Good Love" was not her debut single, but it had made Whitney Houston a household name, made her a diva as far south as Colombia.

The sliding doors yawned in wide pleasure as he eased onto the balcony to embrace the focal points of the city. The sky had turned overcast in the afternoon, subduing the private golf greens and the soft shimmer at the lake's abrupt edge. The course and the waters were overshadowed by weeping willows, stirred by such painstaking wealth. The owner stepped outside with Jorge, drew in a much needed breath, seeming to settle in his home. It was reasonable to assume that he carried a burden worthy of his corporate command.

"Does it suit you here?" It was just a slight formality, the result of breeding and manners.

"Yes, of course," Jorge reassured him. "You have such a beautiful family; such an exceptionally beautiful home."

He considered the owner and he was taken by the notion that he carried himself a great deal like Prince Charles. One had that sense that he would never be rash, the Prince of Wales so collected and regal. The CEO was thoughtful, though somewhat aloof, with reasonable attention to details.

"Tell me, Jorge, what are your hopes—your aspirations, your plans?"

There was a long, studied pause. Would he sound so ungrateful if he really said it out loud? The owner's eyes were still focused intently on the lake, the ripple effects from the boats.

"Yo quiero ir a los Estados Unidos—con mi familia." It came out like a prayer.

The United States—did he know what it took to get that kind of money and permission?

Jorge expected the retort, perhaps even laughter, but the owner simply nodded his head. It was the first time it had been uttered to a man of such magnitude—someone who had stick-built his fortune and fame.

"The $5,000 might be easier to acquire than the visas," the owner said quietly.

That was just for a vacation—to take the children to Disneyland.

"Well, a man must have his dreams."

The pair retired to the interior of the penthouse and Jorge saw that it was a panoramic snapshot on the disparity: the haves and have nots divided by the fault line of the owner's spacious building. On the one side, the picture windows offered that breathtaking view, the body of Los Lagartos—and on the other was a lofty outlook on a kind of middle-class poverty, so wanting from below. It occurred to Jorge that failure and the overcoming of failure were ever present in the owner's mind, straddling both worlds in complete transparency, awaking each day to the perspective.

Sergio! Mauricio! Enrique Miguel! Jorge called them from oldest to youngest. He was terse like a drill sergeant and they warmed to the game, lining up in the foyer with eagerness.

"Come," the owner's wife beckoned them, "we are going to the museum! We are going to study modern art!"

There were no groans, no hesitation, in the friendly insistence that bordered her firm command. They had the day off, to meet their new driver, and they followed her, charmed—the Pied Piper. Jorge took the driver's seat, put the key in the ignition and was surprised to feel a small hand.

It was Enrique who had taken his seat beside him, placing his newfound affection on Jorge's leg. His smile was as soft and pure as a cherub; he looked up at his driver with adoration.

Jorge smiled in return, took the little hand in his as he raced the motor repeatedly. It was a good first day; there was nothing lacking—except a Mercedes-Benz.

+⇒⇐+

Something set Fabian off, near the end of the school day; it was hard to know exactly what. The children were lined up, marching like tiny toy soldiers, and then he broke violently from the ranks.

"Diego! No!" Fabian cried, twisting his little brother's blazer in his attempt to pull him back from the others. The bus driver looked up in surprise and saw awful panic on the older child's face. Diego, too, was confused by the outburst but he was pliable and willing to concede. If his brother didn't want to board the bus, it was nothing to him: he abandoned it in a playful leap.

He sat on the curb as Fabian stewed, that perpetual study in contrasts: his older brother was anxious and glowering, and Diego appeared unflustered. The youngest smiled brightly—what else could he do—Fabian was just unpredictable.

"You're missing the bus," a teacher tried to scoot them, but Fabian jerked back from her, warning.

"Don't touch me," he hissed, wagging a vicious finger.

The teacher took a wary step back.

She seemed kind enough; Diego looked up, expectant and anxious to make peace. "We can't take the bus," he smiled amiably and shrugged—his job to point out the obvious.

She took Diego by the hand, leading him back to the schoolyard and his older brother was compelled to follow.

Fabian sulked for an hour in the superintendent's office while Diego made paper airplanes. They were well-behaved children, the secretary thought, except the younger one was outgoing and friendly. She had found their father's number on the inside of their lunch boxes—maybe now they could get the older one to talk. Jorge had rushed from the penthouse and, when he arrived, he was panicked, cradling a face in each hand.

Diego brightened and Fabian sagged so that Jorge stroked his older son's cheekbone with his thumb.

"¿Que pasó, mis hijos? *What's the matter, boys?*

And then Fabian came close to hyperventilating.

"They...t-t-tr-tried...to...kidnap...us," he began to sob. It was hard to understand him.

"Who? Who tried to kidnap you?" Jorge's hand cupped him tighter, a reflexive lurch in his stomach.

"They...h-h-had...a...big bus...and they tried t-to...t-take us away... Outside...the...schoooooool...Papi."

Diego's legs stopped swinging happily, dangled awkwardly for a moment from his seat.

"It's a school bus, Fabian. It takes you home," Jorge felt a strong sense of relief in his gaffe.

He should have explained it; it had never occurred to him. He looked apologetically at his sons.

"Oh, Fabian," he laughed suddenly, ruffling his son's hair and then Diego began to laugh, too.

No more walking for miles or baskets in bicycles. Fabian grappled with the luxury.

"Oh Fabian," Diego threw his arms around his brother. He had stopped frowning, had shrugged off the gloom.

Diego just liked the sound of it—*oh Fabian*—it was that simple and the storm clouds just blew away.

"I'm terribly sorry," Jorge turned to the superintendent. "It seems we had a misunderstanding."

"We'll see the boys tomorrow." *These things sometimes happened.* Jorge apologized again.

Diego hop-scotched to the car and then he fell all over himself. *"Oh Fabian,"* he was tickled inside out. The secretary watched curiously from the superintendent's window, so endeared to the little one.

"I don't know what to make of it," she told the superintendent. He had locked his desk drawer for the day. "They're new of course, but they're such different temperaments. It *is* rather funny, don't you think?"

The superintendent had a look of disquiet: Fabian seemed threatening and angry.

"They're both very bright," the secretary protested. "It's possible he's just mistrustful."

But a child that young, with such strong emotions—it was really quite fortunate they had money. There were telltale signs, the superintendent thought; sufficient to give him pause. Fabian's behavior was not so atypical; just a mirror on the lack of control thrust on so many of the children. It was the vice of Bogotá, hardened in the anarchy that might give rise to the bottled up frustrations later. They had bridged a social gap, but the child was straining: his coping skills were painfully low. The superintendent knew a great deal about child development and this was a boy who was confused.

"He's in a critical stage—where reasoning develops—where realities and rationale are formed. We have to keep an eye on him," he locked the office door. "I'll speak with the teachers tomorrow."

+≻═══≺+

It was true they had been saved from the deprivation, given extravagances the children hadn't even known they'd been missing. But Fabian had been right to be extraordinarily cautious: human ransom was the number one cash crop in Bogotá. He seemed to sense the inherent dangers that had actually intensified with means. There was some justification for Fabian's erratic behavior: he was street-smart beyond his years. A number of stray bullets in Colombia stayed lodged in the flesh like detonators: so much harshness that exploded skin deep, manifesting itself without warning.

Jorge breathed easier, and then suddenly he didn't in the empathetic toll chronic illness exacted. That it happened to Diego, limiting such cheerfulness, such virtue, was the most trying assailant of them all. The vibrancy that had played in his earliest expressions gave way to the most severe languish and pallor—first red in the exertion and then blue in the breathlessness, as if someone laid an anvil on his chest.

There was a sickening smell from the gray river behind their highrise and Yolanda began to attribute its lifeless drift to Diego's flares. He coughed so hard at nights that he gasped and choked, a low, rattling whistle sounding from his chest each time he arched his back. Always the sound was followed by a gurgling that blocked all passages of air from his lungs. His attempts to overcome the constriction were so forceful that Yolanda could see his skin fold into the gaps in his ribs. There were two sunken holes emerging with each try, one near his trachea and the other just below his diaphragm. The demon that plagued him, squeezed the life from his rail thin frame, came with no noise and no form.

Yolanda's mother gave her any number of home remedies that included a mix of aloe and egg whites. She poured bucketful after bucketful of water for boiling, trying to create enough prolonged steam for his relief. She ironed t-shirts as hot as she dared, tugging them over his head every thirty minutes. She saw that he was exhausted when he raised his arms, but the added heat supposedly helped.

There was something in her child's toleration of it all that that pierced her heart to the center. He was so trusting that Yolanda wanted to breathe for him, will all of her life to his lungs. He looked scared at times, but he never looked desperate and there was some extraordinary unfairness in that restraint. He was just a little kid—a very little kid whose growth seemed to be stunted by an inordinate amount of torture. Yolanda rocked him, night after nerve-racking night, sponging at the scarlet flecks on his lips.

Diego was asmático—a severe asthmatic, choking on his own blood in the city.

Jorge was exhausted on many occasions, by the nightly vigils and the worry. The morbidity rate was higher in the urban areas—that coupled with the lack of good medical care. His burden was a private one as he took his seat. It was lunchtime and he'd accompanied the owner. It was an occasional occurrence that irked some investors, like having to acknowledge the maid.

Jorge leaned back, unbuttoned his suit coat. A glass of sparkling water would be fine. He tried to remain as inconspicuous as possible, knowing his proper place.

"I'd like you to go with us. We're headed to the coast."

Jorge straightened at the owner's request.

"Which coast?" his heart pounded.

It was the tone of his voice. The owner looked up from his menu.

"Santa Marta," he said casually. "It's a beautiful resort. The death place of Simón Bolívar."

It was the lack of sleep, having been up all night with Diego that made Jorge's feelings so transparent. The vulnerability, the wonder was so prevalent that he had to lower his head. He would not be a guest; he was the driver, of course, but it felt like a personal favor from God.

The owner's mother appeared with a flourish, just as they finished dessert. She was dressed the only way she knew how, which was like fashionable, movable art. Her hair was feathered in the soft trend of the times and her calf-length dress was royal, blue velvet. She had seen Princess Diana in a gown that same color on her most recent visit to Portugal. The difference, of course, was the striking black hair but it still made a lovely statement. Her shoes had been dyed to match the dress, and her accessories blended the sapphires with black onyx.

She had come from a fundraiser, was aching for amusement. "Let's be off!" she waved at Jorge breezily. She was overdressed for any other occasion, so svelte in the mid-afternoon.

They picked up the children, and she took a seat in the front. They were going to El Museo del Oro. He had to remind her—it was always so unorthodox.

"Why do you sit here, señora?"

"It's safer, Jorge. I want the children in the back," and then he was caught in the middle. There were conflicting realities: possible gunshots from the side, and the safe distance a proper chauffeur should assume.

"It doesn't bother you—what the executives say?"

"Well, it's their problem. Not yours and not mine."

He had earned such a salary—he made as much money as some of the vice presidents it seemed. He was just the driver; but the grandmother made no apologies for the deference she shared with her son.

The woman was so open, so broad-minded, and so complex that Jorge liked to press her. The Gold Museum was a cavern of wealth: the affluence so heavy that it made Jorge heady. The work was exquisite, the repository of centuries of hand-crafted metals and artistry.

"What do you think—of wealth like this—of the loss of such civilization?"

She didn't answer him directly, just handed him a folio, an excerpt from Albrech Dürer: *Then I saw the things that had been brought back from the New Land of Gold for the King…more beautiful than any fairytale. Never in my life had I come across anything that had filled my heart with such joy…I saw strange art treasures, exquisitely made, and I marveled at the subtle skills of these men from distant lands.*

I do not have enough words to describe the things that were set before my eyes.

It had been written before the arrival of the European conquistadores, before the artisans had been enslaved by the Spaniards. It was their love of art, articulated elegantly in the words of a master artist.

"There was greatness here once," the grandmother charged and in her voice there was an unusual hint of longing. They moved on slowly to the Gallery of Gold to one of the greatest treasures of El Banco de La República.

It was a Muisca piece which resembled a raft, adding credence to the El Dorado legend.

The children knew the story, but they liked it so much when their grandmother became the narrator of her passions. "*You* tell it to us," Mauricio tugged at her and she waxed dramatic again.

"Hundreds of years ago this land—the Caribbean—was showered with endless beauty. There were gold mines, plantations, mountains, and plateaus—with fruits as pure as the Garden of Eden. The people were rich, and the land that we live on was a paradise full of achievement. The rivers flowed clear, and in their beds was the sparkle, the wealth you see all around you."

Her voice was melodic; the boys were spellbound with the enchantment that had characterized their heritage. She quoted the textbooks of her time and she wanted them enamored, so that they would truly feel it—the full, crushing blow of oppression.

"Then came explorers and some of them were greedy. They wanted the gold for themselves. They brought sickness with them. They made the native people slaves until none of the Indians were left…

"The white man had come. The tribesmen thought it was Quetzalcoatl—the fair god who was humanity's savior. The traditions were lost—but we have this one—the Legend of El Dorado."

Jorge listened in wonder, to the lilt and the compassion. Why would she care when she now knew no want? Her grandsons stared at the raft; it was a familiar story and in their childishness he still thought he saw sadness.

The raft had left its shores before Columbus' great ships: the Santa María, the Pinta, and the Niña. The great king had been covered in balsam gum so that it had made his entire body an adhesive. The tribesmen had been ordained to blow gold powder dust over him, until he appeared to stand like a golden statue. He had been a servant of the people, and the king had led them down to the waters of Lake Guatavitá. He had boarded a raft and there he'd been paddled to the center of the lake by his noblemen. He had stood in his majesty, on the tip of the raft, and then he had dived into the water, supreme. The lake had been pierced by his regal reflection, just before he had sunk to the deep. The waters had washed away his golden coat, cleansed the people of all of their sins.

Was there a moral to the story? Jorge had never been quite sure, though some thought it symbolized Colombia. If anything, he thought there had been rich potential once and it lay just below the surface, swallowed whole.

He had known the owner's family for nearly a year, and there would always come the aloofness in his station. He weighed the professional distance and his need to expound, and he pulled aside the family security guard. The guard nearly always escorted them; the guard nearly always appeared grave; but the guard was a very good sounding board. "Have you ever wondered what it would be like if the American Revolution had fought its way south? It's all the difference between conquerors and liberators—the state of affairs in our country."

The security guard's smile was that of the devil's advocate. He liked geopolitical discussions.

"And that's the paradox—if they'd exceeded their borders—they would have been conquerors, no?"

A thousand times Jorge had wished for intervention; that George Washington had not been content with mere colonies. It was the raft that was the symbol of that never ending folly that propelled them from that which entrapped them. They had not been conquerors—those Founding Fathers—and it had blessed and cursed the continent so. The security guard was right so that he had to search for meaning; he had to search his own soul.

He had begun to read the Bible, and his childhood priest had been right—it could drive a man truly mad. Joshua had suffered the Exodus and then he had suffered much greater, being forced to wander for forty years. He had been one of twelve spies sent to the land of Canaan to provide an accounting of its inhabitants. He had offered it up—his best report—that God would deliver His children. Ten other spies had disputed his claim, their doubts overcoming their faith. The children of Israel had adhered to the negative and, for that, they had been driven to and fro. Joshua had been punished with the unbelievers, the promised land just beyond his reach.

They were all in a great wilderness—how long must he wander, the promised land just beyond his reach?

For all of his worldliness, for all of his acquired sophistication, the security guard had a simple kind of faith. He was a composite of Colombia: a mere veneer of the rich, overlaying the soul of the poor.

"It's not enough—that you have a good income? That's more than most in Colombia."

"More than twenty-five years, clinging to hope. I cannot help what I feel."

"You could go to Europe," the security guard mulled. "There's enlightenment there, too, you know."

"It doesn't interest me," Jorge was alternately deflated. "It's like a mistress when you've been blessed with true love."

"But it's so cultured there, so refined, "he urged. "Trust me. You would fall in love with their depth."

"Yes, Europe is old. I want something modern—not so weighted by all the past offenses."

"This infatuation you have with the United States. It's so dull there—you'd know it if you'd been."

Oh, how could he explain it? The thrill that enveloped him when he had heard of Reagan's speech at Brandenburg Gate.

"...for we believe that freedom and security go together, that the advance of human liberty can only strengthen the cause...

"General Secretary Gorbachev, if you seek peace...*Mr. Gorbachev, tear down this wall!*"

"I admire your spirit, but don't you see it? They're just men and there's the fallacy, that's all."

One man with courage makes a majority.

The security guard's head fell back.

It was Andrew Jackson, Jorge was quick to point out, and the guard continued to laugh in his utter defeat.

"I think you should be a politician—like your brother—anything, except you cannot be President."

They need to change that law. They will change it for me. You will see, my brother. You will see.

"No, you cannot be President in the United States of America. You'll be lucky if you ever get to vote." He raised a solemn hand, before Jorge could speak again. Before another impassioned speech. "You'll make it there. I'm sure that you will. Only do not take a raft when you go.

"Do yourself a big favor. Go when you're wanted. A plane and a visa are so much more noble."

Jorge wanted to interrupt—he was poised to do so—except for the earnestness in the guard's eyes. "Put something dignified in your suitcase, Jorge. Place it on top of your clothes."

He suddenly understood. When he arrived at Immigration—they would search his luggage first thing.

"Put something dignified on the top of your clothes, Jorge. Give them a sense of your means."

Jorge and the owner traveled alone to Santa Marta and it was hard to imagine the boy he'd once been: begging for scraps, so skinny in his want, and sleeping near the swell of the ocean. Jorge thought upon him like a character in a book whose ending was promising, but not quite fulfilling. There was a saying, he had learned, at El Museo del Oro—that the most willing adventurers found fortune.

Some of them made it by the blow of a miner's pick and some by the flash of a sword. To emerge triumphant required such perseverance, overcoming each fear in waves.

You hear it behind you,
The rushing wings of a thousand gulls,
Ominous and thunderous.

It coils like the cobra,
White fangs in its spray,
So turn to face it from protected inlets.

It will gasp with you,
And mount its icy hold,
Crush, and then plummet in churning gray.

In its sink to the shallow,
To a brooding grave,
It will claw at the shoreline then sigh in defeat.

You will rise to overcome it,
Above the shine of its ebb tide,
Stand on warm, dry sand in the sun.

It was progress, that was all, a grateful farewell to the bitterest of his seasons in the tide. Santa Marta was named for the patron saint of servants, the sister of Mary and Lazarus. Jorge re-committed himself to a greater good—not for the gold fever of his youth.

In the illusory nature of the pearl-agitating sands, he saw his treasure for Fabian and Diego.

CHAPTER 7

His youngest son was listless, lying on the couch with the same labored breathing his father carried home. Jorge was pale. He felt like he had a stick in his throat as he rubbed a hand over his mouth.

"You're sure you were followed? All the way here?"

Yolanda's question came out frantic, in a whisper.

"It's the third time this week. The same car. The same driver. The same. The same. The same."

I have to get the gun. The gun at my mother's house. "You'll have to stay here with Diego." It was another asthma attack, the second in so many days, and Jorge felt helplessly torn.

Yolanda nodded, helped him with his jacket before he disappeared into the black of their district. It might have been funny, that eagerness for arms—accompanied by his swagger and bravado. It had forced a nickname the locals had maintained through all of his teenager years. Pecos Bill had been escorted by a not so intimidating mutt; they had liked to call him Fifi. It might have been funny in another life, another country, but the stakes were always too high.

Jorge and Fifi had once made the rounds of the neighborhood every night and the dog had not been of the street variety: he'd been well fed and groomed, a fixture at the family restaurant that passersby petted and patrons allowed scraps from the table. He had been a good dog and a good companion and, if it hadn't been for the malady that had come upon him—well, it had been bad for business;

the customers had lost their appetites—other than that he'd have died an old mutt.

Jorge's mother had commanded him to put the dog out of his misery, and the eleven-year-old child had faced up to it like a scene from *Old Yeller*. The dog had sensed something terribly amiss, cowered on the corner of the street.

Jorge's mother was unaware of the malfunctions of the gun and her youngest son had always hoped it would work. He had cocked the pistol and involuntarily squeezed his eyes shut as he'd pulled the trigger on his friend.

They had both recoiled at the dead click in the chamber, worse than the anticipated snarl of the gunfire. Jorge had clenched his teeth, cocked the pistol again and fired in the trembling of grief.

The gun was obviously perpetually jammed, and so Jorge had taken the bullets out of the chamber. One by one he had filled the compartments, and then spun the chamber for good measure and tried again.

He had put the pistol directly to the mutt's head and cried softly when the gun had clicked, unspent. The dog had begun to make a low, pleading whine and Jorge had covered his eyes. He had turned away and aimed the pistol in the general direction of the dog. Twenty times he had fired like that. And twenty times there had come a mere click, and the dog had lain on the sidewalk in agony.

Eventually Pecos Bill had sat down on the curb, dejected, and his mother had had to call his cousin. He had been bound for the military; he had finished the job with the very same pistol Jorge owned. The dog had shaken violently in the throes of death when the chamber had finally relinquished its bullet. It was exactly in that moment that Jorge had lost his enamor for the Colombian army.

Ten years later, the pistol still wouldn't discharge and Jorge cursed softly to his mother. It was two o'clock in the morning. His children were in bed; he never saw them awake anymore.

"I fired it in the alley. Nothing, Mother. What am I going to do?"

It should have been comical—they should have laughed at old times—except bodyguards had to be formidable.

He knew nothing about protective services; he'd just been called to the house—well past the middle of the night. The informant had been an acquaintance of the owner of sorts: he had known of their plot; they had staked out the museums, all the restaurants.

"They want Enrique. He's the baby, of course. They know all of your vulnerabilities."

It had sent such shivers up and down his spine that they had deadened his nerves and his brain. His hands had gone numb and then they had trembled, the sweat even torrents behind his ears. How long had they watched them? Had them all in their crosshairs? That sweet little boy in their sights?

He had met with security. He was somewhat of a marksman. The owner trusted him, that was enough. "You're now a bodyguard." As if he'd been knighted, a tap on the shoulder and some implausible duty accompanying him.

His blood pressure was high. He was liable to stroke. He had to get hold of himself.

I'll carry the gun. I'll pose an imminent threat. I love that little boy, don't you know?

He would do anything—anything—lay down his life, when a child's safety was at stake.

"Jorge, be careful," his mother said quietly. "You have two boys of your own."

He carried the pistol for three long months and the other bodyguard beside him owned an Uzzi. He needed a weapon—a real man's weapon—and he finally confessed his misfortune.

"Do you see this fork?" Jorge jabbed it toward the owner. "I could do more damage with this fork. I could fork him to death." The owner grew wide-eyed and turned to the security guard.

"Get Mr. Rincon a gun!" he commanded, and there was an unusual scramble after the bark.

He applied for a .38 Special, a Smith & Wesson, and carried it to the firing range daily. He tucked it inside an undercover holster, one that allowed him to pull his handgun vertical. The bodyguard worked with him, made him a good shot, until Jorge could have pulled the trigger in his sleep. And then he rather liked the idea of playing Clint Eastwood in his own homespun version of *Pale Rider*.

He experienced the oddity of passing that old school frequently, El Amparro de Niños, in his travels. It knotted his stomach to see the adobe walls and the abandoned church and that long, threatening driveway. He had vowed for a while to help the school when he had enough money saved—maybe make certain the children had clean laundry and an abundance of food to eat. He had had a strange reaction when he'd inquired about it and learned they'd shut the place down.

It was enormous relief, coupled with profound sadness for the children who surely lived then on the streets.

The other bodyguard had surrendered the driver's seat of the Chevrolet Monza once they had passed the school. The violence of their landscape, the obliged exposure had drawn them fiercely together. They enlarged themselves, their physical presence, in that surety that gave the illusion of boundaries. In fact, there were no safe zones in the mental crowding to which Jorge succumbed every day. There was a fragile woman, elderly and bent, but was she really an old woman? There was a taxi cab that appeared to be on its last leg, but perhaps it was more reliable than it seemed. Perhaps the extortionists were crouched in the back, ready to spring on command. Were they just around the corner, or tailing the Monza? Would they drive a truck or an SUV? When Bonilla had been slaughtered, the teenager had pulled his machine gun in a drive-by shooting. Sometimes they used motorcycles. There were no logical patterns and no formal training; Jorge had no real concept of profiling.

If forced to narrow it down to two characteristics, the assailant would be a man, probably between the ages of sixteen and forty-five. Money would play into it, but it could have been the thrill; it could have been envy or rage at the disparity. The child was just a pawn and in that inhumanity came the only sure thing—they were depraved. They might harm the child or they might be quite kind to him, so long as the ransom was promising. It was an art, not a science, this game Jorge played, and it exhausted him to sheer paranoia.

He had a gift, a sense made more acute by the obsessive reeling in his brain. It was enhanced visual recall that would be his companion, then and for the rest of his life. He passed a fruit and vegetable stand and he saw another woman, exactly what she wore and what she carried. A half hour later, as they circled the barrios, he saw the same woman, walking home. She had eaten the banana. She had bought five bananas and then she only cradled four. There was a red Toyota truck, and the driver had a scar above his lip and Jorge had seen him three times in two hours. The second bodyguard was relieved of his duty at the end of the day, and Jorge found himself alone.

A motorcycle edged to the passenger side of the Monza, dangerously close to the trunk. Jorge sped forward, slowed, and then sped again, and the driver of the motorcycle wasn't shaken. Jorge shimmied right slightly in an attempt to repel him. There were two men and each of them wore blue jeans. The second passenger on the bike wore a black leather jacket and something bulged in his pocket.

There was one rule of engagement of which Jorge was aware: shoot and ask questions later. Jorge drew his gun and it was a harrowing instinct and still so methodical that it frightened him. He didn't want to kill them, or even disable them, but he elongated his aim toward their gas tank. He anticipated the explosion, like a scene from *Miami Vice*, the drug dealers perishing in a ball of flames. There was a firecracker pop and he swerved left from the heat, and the certain collision of traffic. But there were no theatrics, no angry outbursts, just a pause that resembled blank puzzlement. A lowly stream of gasoline spurted from the motorcycle tank and the driver slowed and pulled away. The trickle was so miniscule that Jorge imagined the second passenger putting a finger to the hole to plug it. He imagined they would drive to the nearest gas station and ask the attendant for some duct tape. *We have a slight problem here. You know Colombia. An overzealous world out there. He tried to shoot us, or maybe it was a nail gun. See here, this small hammer hole, right here?*

Jorge cursed Don Johnson and he cursed Pecos Bill and then he cursed himself in disgust.

It was the strangest thing, all those pent-up suspicions and the constant whirling anger, the defensiveness. And then all the fight just dribbled out from him, like that slow trickle of gasoline with the same amount of wonder. He saw his life pass before him—not the way that it once had in that deadly skid in the old Studebaker. What he saw was the future, more threats and more insults, and maybe a real shooting here and there. Maybe someday the tank would explode and maybe he'd go up in flames, too. It was a heartless prospect, and no amount of standing or money could fill it—that was the greatest offense of them all.

He caught a glimpse of two men in dark suits and dark glasses with gleaming, Rolex watches. They walked too briskly with their heads held high and a constant scan of the street. They had only left the bank, one of them with a briefcase in his hand and a fidgety sort of snap plaguing his other fingers. The second bodyguard called their kind "el majico," Pablo Escobar's magic. They made money show up and men disappear in some mystical underworld at their feet. A shudder so overcame Jorge that he looked away, a blind impulse to step on the gas.

He parked the car and made out his sons' heads, bobbing above a rollick of waves. There was always a hard lip at the edge of a pool like the one where Fabian and Diego swam. Fabian was the type of child who liked to test the water, feel the chill of it lapping at him for a while. If a little boy curled his toes around it at just the right place, he could still feel the brink of solid ground. Diego, on the other hand, jumped in with complete abandonment, splashing until he adjusted to the cold. There was a three-year-old girl, wading in a pink halter top. Her mother held a beach towel with an imprint of dolphins. Jorge took one last survey of the pool before he knelt, before he feigned joviality to his boys. His feet were perched on the verge of the water and it was a small reflection on his mental state. He could feel his toes curling around the last steel of his sanity. He could feel the actual precipice of his mind.

"Los Estados Unidos?" *You're going to the United States?* Jorge felt his heart skip and the accompanying lightheadedness.

"Yes," the owner said, "there's a world congress I'll be attending."

"You might need my services then."

It came out with more eagerness than Jorge intended and the owner regarded him, calculating. One boat on the lake carved a figure eight in the water; Jorge was as transparent as their penthouse view. The owner sliced an envelope with the flick of a jeweled letter opener, and he snapped its contents curtly. Jorge shifted slightly, his brow was perspiring—funny, because his mouth felt bone dry.

There were so few people who had the luxury of selfishness in Bogotá—just that driver of the boat and the owner. Jorge had carried a passport since he was seventeen years old and every four years he'd renewed it.

"For what?" his mother had asked him repeatedly. "Where do you possibly think you'll be going?"

Ten years he had carried the weight and the yearning—in ten years there had never been a stamp.

"I think it would be wise to take a bodyguard."

A man really could jump out of his own skin.

Jorge sat in economy class two weeks later and the plane touched down with great ease. It had been such a superlative effort to get off the ground that Jorge was amazed at that streak of simplicity. The vice president had returned from the embassy in Bogotá, empty-handed and deflated just before Jorge's attempt. "They'll not give you a visa. They'll turn you away. Just like the rest of us. Don't bother."

Step this way, Señor Rincon. Right this way, Señor Rincon. We'll give you a six-month visa—is that suitable?

He had imagined it like that, willed that same light at the embassy window that he had cast on the stacks of the driver applications. Sometimes he just saw things, had strange premonitions, and he had been sure he would not be rejected. The man at the window had been formal and abrupt and he'd peered at Jorge for some time. Jorge had stood erect, the result of the recent breeding, the tennis classes, the opera, the country club. There had been a shuffle and a stamp and Jorge had willed it again—was it a light, or a prayer, or just fortitude? His papers had been spit back at him in a judgment decreed, the inalterable verdict on his life. His hand had trembled so that he had thought he was mistaken.

But, no, the visa had been valid for five years.

There had been a bomb threat, just as the flight attendants had done a cross check of the cabin over the intercom. The owner had settled into a copy of *El Tiempo*, had lazed into the privilege of first class. Jorge supposed that in heaven there might be some equality, those subtle advantages rightly twisted. The first would be last and the last would be first because the owner was ten persons ahead of him. The explosion would most likely come from the rear and take Jorge in just a flash before the owner. Yes, Jorge would see God first—a little thing like that—you just never knew who'd die in front of you.

It was Colombia in the 1980s so that a bomb threat was handled like an elementary school fire drill. It had been real, all right, down to the panic and the swaying of fainter ladies and the heroics. But it hadn't been long before the plane was re-boarded, and the trip had gone on with an unusual familiarity among the passengers. *That man behind us—he pushed my little girl down to try to get out of the plane first. But that man over there, the white-haired gentleman, he stayed in his seat the whole time. He thought to himself that he'd lived a good life and the youngsters—they ought to have their chance.* And then the plane had touched down, on the Miami International tarmac, and it was so unceremonious except for the fact that they were all still alive.

Jorge stood at the carousel to collect his luggage, straining to see the owner's Luis Vuitton bags.

"Con permiso…perdón." *Excuse me, sir.* A stately man stepped forward to claim his own baggage.

Jorge obliged politely.

"Gracias," the man said.

"De nada." *It's nothing,* said Jorge.

It wasn't nothing. Jorge nearly gasped as the man turned away from him, plain-clothed and unaccompanied. It was Alfonso López Michelson, with no fanfare and no barriers, a former president of Colombia. Jorge stared openly as the leader looked about, then purposefully strolled to the automatic doors. It was like getting a pair of glasses, when the world had been fuzzy for so long—when he'd always had that hunch something had been missing. His vision was corrected in Miami, Florida so that he saw distinct blades of grass and leaves on trees in all their shapes. Everything came into sharp focus in a way he couldn't have imagined before, only seeing those vague clumps of colors.

America was like heaven, the great equalizer, where the president was just like himself. The security guard had been intolerably wrong—there was nothing boring about a country that ignored the caste rules like that.

He flew to Atlanta and then to Orlando and back to Miami again. He talked abstractedly to Yolanda by phone about Disneyland and Stone Mountain and *Gone with the Wind.* In the United States, the stuff of civil wars was made into bestselling books and major motion pictures. It wasn't true, of course, that bloody histories could be so easily, so gloriously dismissed. The real point was that his namesake, the president of his old barrio, had graced their soil and had eventually united them.

"What constitutes the bulwark of our own liberty and independence?" Lincoln had asked of his countrymen. "It is not our frowning battlements, our bristling sea coasts, the guns of our war steamers, or the strength of our gallant and disciplined army. These are not our reliance against a resumption of tyranny in our fair land. All of them may be turned against our liberties, without making us stronger or weaker for the struggle. Our reliance is in the *love of liberty* which God has planted in our bosoms. Our defense is in the preservation of the spirit which prizes liberty as the heritage of all men, in all lands, every where. Destroy this spirit, and you have planted the seeds of despotism around your own doors."

There were no bars on the windows, on the antebellum polish that so elegantly emerged from sprawling woods. There was no self-pity in the rain that soaked the red soil and laced the foliage in dripping dew in Georgia. There was an assertion of prominence that rolled with the countryside, nothing daunting or imperial or forged—just a genuineness of dignity, of that reliance in the love of liberty, of that easy charm that came with confidence.

His room charges included the numerous calls to Colombia: all told they were $462.35. He had a sinking feeling as he checked out of the Beverly Hills Inn, so much money and no one had warned him about that. He clutched the bill to him, like some grand souvenir, though, because even that somehow felt gilded. There were no bomb threats, no mishaps; the plane left on time, soaring into a cobalt blue. America grew smaller, faded to a distant dream, and he felt the snap of his own heart. He ached for Yolanda, for the bright, hopeful eyes of his boys who awaited him back in Colombia. There was a cold, drab rain as he landed in Bogotá, and there he felt the most acute letdown of his life. That kind of pain had only been so humanly articulated once when Lincoln had been defeated by Senator Stephen Douglas.

The result of the election was "somewhat like that boy in Kentucky, who stubbed his toe while running to see his sweetheart. The boy said he was too big to cry, and far too badly hurt to laugh."

He made his way wearily back to their apartment, with the bars on the windows and the sick, flowing river. On the evening news there came the drumbeat of his despair: the drug lords had formally declared open war on the government.

CHAPTER 8

It was the desperation, the unrequited feeling that drove him to rummage through the closet. It was an exquisite dress for the afternoon, black and understatedly elegant. It was four sizes too big because the owner's wife was not as petite as Yolanda. Diego wore the Mickey Mouse ears that his father had brought him and he gazed at his mother inquisitively. The significance of the moment was lost on both Jorge's children; they just thought their mother was stunning.

"I can pin it at the waist, but I don't think I can hem it without doing permanent damage to the fabric." Yolanda felt too young, as if she was playing dress-up and might get caught any minute.

"What did the owner's wife say—when you borrowed the dress?"

Jorge diverted his eyes. "The boys should wear suits."

"I see," she said quietly.

Yolanda had always been an honest but dutiful wife.

The American embassy rose auspiciously from all of its more common neighbors. It sat like a pearl in an otherwise colorless shell, though on some days it had seemed hopelessly impenetrable. It was the way Jorge saw reality since he'd gotten his figurative glasses, since he'd achieved his vision in Miami. His reality had been altered and, while everyone else was circumventing, Jorge thought that he could simply transform it. He had found he could stand in a certain place and sidle up to the former president of Colombia. He had found that he could peer through that bulletproof window and unmask the Wizard of Oz. He was just a little man, after all, with a desk job that required stamping, and he turned knobs on a whim behind a fabricated affront. Jorge had walked into the embassy with Yolanda slightly hugging him so that the dress did not appear to be ill-fitted. They had walked in a cluster, slower than usual—it was hard for Yolanda not to shuffle her feet when she wore such oversized shoes.

Jorge chitchatted idly, not so forced at first, because of his altered reality. It was an appeasing sort of day, not too hot, not too cold—the stuff of porridge and fairy tales. He had an exceptional letter of recommendation from his prestigious boss, which certainly helped his cause. If he maintained that very special, positive outlook, all the stars would have to align. Not too hot, not too cold, not too hard, not too soft, and everything would fall into place. It took some time to comprehend the lack of energy, the stale air and the vacancy in the eyes.

He turned casually enough to a couple beside him, inquired of their upcoming journey. It was their fourth attempt to secure a visa; they made it a point to try every two years. And then to the left of him, the number four man in the line, had been turned down just the day before.

"It's random," he said. "So I thought I'd try again. Another day of Russian roulette."

Jorge hugged Yolanda tighter and touched his sons' heads in the absent way that extreme duress does. The man in front of him had quite a story—yes, he'd been to the United States, just like Jorge. He'd been to New York and he'd fallen in love; his fiancé was waiting for him there.

"How far have you come?" There was a distinct sort of accent.

"Medellín," the man looked down.

It was a costly trip, a burden of a journey, but a man would do anything for love. It was the third time he had applied and he had waited one year for another interview at the embassy. Diego pulled respectfully at his father's hand, well-behaved but bored with the hollowness. The embassy was too strait-laced, its angles too severe and it echoed of so much exhaustion.

"How much longer, Papi?"

His father couldn't say. *Perhaps the rest of his life.* His eyes grew dull, the lackluster of lead, something empty and distracted overcoming him.

The man from Medellín approached the window and made quite a passionate pitch. At least it sounded passionate; Jorge could see the transparency as if he could bore through the back of the man's head. More than the ardor and the reasonable explanations, though, Jorge could predict the knob turn of the wizard. "Lo siento, señor," it was not clipped enough. It was not said with enough movement at the forefront of the mouth. The wizard was a gringo and he had that lapse of enunciation that originated in the throat and fell nasal. The man from Medellín recoiled slightly, as if he'd been shot and hadn't realized it yet. He tried to pull himself up, tried to rectify his posture, but he couldn't lift the decline in his muscles. He attempted a wan smile at Jorge's children, some show of kindness for the family's earlier expressions of support. He shuffled out of the embassy though his shoes fit him well, though he'd put on his Sunday best for the interview.

Jorge had set aside his golf clubs to take to the States—because he'd done quite well on the first hole he'd played. It was that easiness in his swing because there had been no expectations when a man was just starting out. *See here. Your first hole? Well don't worry about that. Golf takes years to master.* And then the ball had sailed into a glorious arc as he'd teed off the first time with his woods.

It was beginner's luck, not the same as natural talent, perhaps not even deserved or fair.

He presented his visa, that gift, that charm, that had been won when there had been less to lose. The gringo had piercing blue eyes that matched his sternness and Jorge made no impassioned pleas. It was pride that kept him from blurting the truth, from spilling the despair of his life. The gringo didn't read the letter of recommendation and Jorge felt something much larger, much greater than panic.

Yolanda's hand had turned ice cold in his and somehow that strain surprised him. Cold was nervous and Yolanda was rarely nervous, not in the fatalistic view that she took. *If God wants us in the United States, then God will provide a way. If not, if we're turned down, it was never meant to be, Jorge. Then you must let the thing go.*

The gringo looked up once. Perhaps it was the deference. Diego's face was upturned. Unencumbered by rejection, the purity of his youth, he offered that haphazard smile. It wasn't the beaming kind that overtook his face, just an involuntary shrug of his friendliness. He stretched forth his hands, and then he twisted his mouth in the habit he had on monotony. *Not sure what we're doing here. Your guess is as good as mine. But I hope you have a nice day.*

Yolanda Rincon. There was a loud stamp and a snap as the passport was overturned.

Fabian Rincon. A stamp and a snap.

Diego Rincon. A stamp.

It would have been heartless to dance or cry out in front of the resounding defeat that surrounded them. Yolanda walked ahead of Jorge, hiding the skirt from the wizard and any delayed misgivings. She took small, dainty steps and gingerly exited and then her shoes fell off in his embrace. Fabian and Diego began to jump up and down in an exultance they didn't comprehend.

He had been given five years to make a go of things and the most peculiar thought struck him as he swung the car door for Yolanda. It was a prayer he'd uttered once that had gone so unheeded, that selfish, unseeing prayer. *I want the Mercedes-Benz*—and it would have made all the difference; that particular executive was anything but lenient. He would have never appointed his driver to be his trusted bodyguard—the driver had never even ventured outside Bogotá.

It was a beautiful car, that Chevrolet Monza, and it was a beautiful, watched-over world. God had planted a car like he'd planted a rock in the middle of a river once. God in His infinite mercy.

+≈≈≈+

It wasn't true that everyone south of the border wanted to immigrate to the United States. Among Jorge's siblings, those who would remain in Colombia represented exactly half of the family. Jorge's sister, Elsa, held the hands of her children and they appeared melancholy, left out. Diego hugged Anna Maria spontaneously, and her big, brown eyes blinked back greater understanding. If Diego sensed the permanence of such an adventure, his own expression never changed. He wore dark sunglasses, not intentionally trying but still coming off very cool. There was the courageous sort of laughter that carried such genuineness because it was tinged in so much finality. There was often laughter like that, at funerals and at airports, and it fell heavy at the boarding gate.

"You'll come to America. You'll live down the street from us." Elsa gleaned something hopeful and smiled. It was Fanny who had to act more resolute. *You know I'd never leave Colombia.*

Like her mother, she had a good head for business; Fanny had done well for herself.

"Who'll steal your offerings from the priest when I leave?" She laid a gentle hand on Jorge's arm.

"Yo tengo sed." *Papi, I'm thirsty.*

Jorge reached for his wallet.

He carried large bills, the conversion rate was abysmal, and still it was the largest sum of his life. He had sold his couch and his refrigerator and his suits; the Armani and Versace all gone. They had sold the dishes and Yolanda's wedding dress and managed to keep Mickey Mouse. It had amounted to $3000 in U.S. currency—by the owner's estimation not enough for a mere vacation to Disneyland.

God will provide, Jorge. Yolanda in her faithfulness, Yolanda in her steadfast support.

He touched his hand to the right back pocket of his trousers and then, puzzled, he felt the left side. He shoved his hands in his jacket pockets and unzipped his coat in haste. He checked the interior and then he checked his pants again and then he turned a half circle, nauseous. He frantically started the body search all over again, as if the thing might appear in his socks.

He opened his briefcase and rummaged the contents. He knelt by the chairs to look under them. It was there, nearly prostate, that he began his beseeching, a prayer with unprecedented feeling.

"Papi, let's go." Fabian tugged at him and Jorge inexplicably bolted. His eyes had that look, that extreme anxiety of Fifi, just before Jorge's cousin had shot him. He felt a kind of dampness, the sort of uncontrollable sweat that plagued a man just before he threw up. He lost the ability to swallow, a nearly incoherent whisper that a passerby surmised was the Lord's prayer.

For Thine is the kingdom and the power and the glory, forever and ever...amen.

It was such a small mistake; it could have happened to anyone amid all the preoccupations. And maybe someday, if he got another job, in another ten years, he'd have that kind of money again. It had been a stroke of luck, really, such incomprehensible luck that he'd gotten the visas after all. The owner had been happy for him because there'd been a downturn, because the outlook just hadn't been good. He'd been prospecting buyers, at the world congress in Atlanta—and if he lost his fortune, he'd have less need for a bodyguard. *God is watching out for you, Jorge Rincon. He really seems to favor you of late.* He could try to renew the visas. It would only be another five years. Perhaps if they lived with his mother again. Perhaps if they scrimped and toiled and deprived themselves, and if Diego's asthma went away.

Jorge's hands lost all sensation, and he cupped one of them over his mouth to keep himself, finally, from vomiting.

I was born a Colombian and I'll die a Colombian. It's what his mother had always said. He could not imagine sneaking his family through Mexico, through the Rio Grande, through the denial of the desert.

He had been bound for America on a DC-10, something big and elegant and right.

There was a woman with a red scarf, and he'd held the door open for her earlier, and she looked at him in wonder. She looked at Jorge as if she'd seen a ghost and it was true, perhaps, that she had. He was a shell of the man who'd walked into the airport with all of his dreams intact. There was a young father at a newsstand and his shoes were still scuffed, but his child had abandoned his tantrum. There were hordes of people, broad daylight in Colombia, and the wallet and its lifeblood were gone. It was just that total visual recall that made him think that he still saw it, sitting at the check-in counter.

He no longer ran, no longer drew attention to himself, lest anyone else see the mirage. It was perched rather obviously in front of all of those people, perpendicular and bulging. It had no marks of the good breeding, of any of the retained luxuries, that plain brown, unassuming wallet. It lay perfectly aligned because Jorge was a neat freak, everything centered and painstaking. Even in its homeliness it seemed to be flashing a neon-like presence, a brilliant white, beacon-like light. And then he understood it as he reached for it, snatched it, that angelic brightness that had preserved it just for him. *God is watching out for you, Jorge Rincon. He really seems to favor you of late.*

As if there had been some impenetrable fortress, a shroud over the wallet so that no one could see it but Jorge.

He opened it discreetly, his heart was in his brain; he could feel his heart pounding in his temples. Every crisp, new bill, all those large denominations, with no one's fingerprints but his. It was only right, his blood and his sweat and his very genetic code in those earnings. They were virgin and pure, and he felt a re-birth of his soul as he slowly ascended on the escalator. He'd been saved again, and he pulled Yolanda to himself, and Fabian wanted a drink so that he ruffled his head in the relief and the giddiness.

I'd have to break a $100 bill. The first $100 and you can wait for a soda on the plane.

His legs still shook a bit as he stood before her; maybe it was the near catastrophe or just standing in her presence. His mother's face was unreadable, something mixed, as she hugged him goodbye at the gate. It was his father who broke, the old man he'd become, cupping Diego's face in gnarled hands. All the insurmountable history lay between Jorge and him, that practicality of his father. Every day for two years he had helped him care for his invalid grandfather in Funza. He had changed his diapers and turned the mattress and bathed him and made his favorite soups. The grandfather had been terrifying, the hollowed-out eyes and the terseness and the smells and the flailing. Jorge had just been a boy and his grandfather had yelled at him; the soup had never been quite right. Jorge's father had added more salt or warmed it or cooled it, adhering to all the demands. Jorge's father had not shielded his son from the punishment. He had been gruff and more attentive to the invalid.

Someday you'll understand. He's my father, Jorge. Someday you will understand.

Jorge faced the sensibility, the watery eyes and the phantom look of poor health. And he did understand, more clearly than he had thought, the sum total of the life he would miss. It was Fanny who would read to him, calm all the nightmares, lay down beside him as he died. It was Fanny only who would achieve the intimacy that came when the roles were reversed. When the child nurtured, the child comforted, and the child helped the parent through that milestone. It was the most somber of moments with a strange lack of regret because that was the natural course. Children were supposed to outlive their parents, the fruits of a long, useful life.

Jorge's father hugged him in the brusque kind of motion that had characterized all of his days. He seemed to tremble—from the grief or the years—Jorge never really knew. His father waved to the children and then he bowed his head and that was the image that seared. Jorge would never see him again except in his mind, at that terminal, shattered in his farewell.

Fabian drank soda and ate a small bag of peanuts and then there came a series of announcements. The Continental Divide was the virile backbone of the United States of America land mass. It separated the westward-flowing waters from the eastern-bound streams, sea to shining sea. It followed the Sierra Madre Occidental and sometimes designated the entire Rocky Mountain spine. There it was called the Great Divide, an almost impenetrable barrier to early explorers. Once the Atlantic and Pacific were separated by this great, illusory wall, the eastern seaboard was further divided. The line was drawn through the Appalachian Mountains, most distinctly from Georgia to Virginia. Atlanta's Peachtree Street sat atop the second divide, the Southern midtown of commerce and bustle and leisure. It was ostensibly modern, given its earlier charms, once captured like Norman Rockwell in turn-of-the-twentieth-century-like paintings. That was all Yolanda envisioned—the illustration in her mind as it had been depicted ninety years before.

Diego lay on Jorge's lap, sound asleep as they finally approached the border. The divide was something like the wall at El Amparo de Niños, an enormous swell of achievement. Jorge was an explorer, a pioneer, a conqueror, a liberator all in one. He caressed his tiny son's face. He felt the softness of his skin and the inherent trust in the relaxed drape Diego had on his knees. He felt a joyous leap and he felt the weight of it—the enormous responsibility. Where would they sleep? How would they eat? His sons' lives were in his hands. Their entire futures, a new destiny set, and he couldn't answer the questions to their most basic needs.

By faith, it had been set forth in the eleventh chapter of Hebrews, Moses' people had crossed over on dry ground. There had been two walls of water, the Red Sea held back on either side by the hand of God. The United States of America was that vast and sacred passageway, preserved by its flank of two oceans. Tears steamed down Jorge's face in the awe and the emotion of a man in a miracle.

He didn't know it yet—the butterfly effect that was about to spring humanity. It was his one small step, and then the rest would collapse two months later, the Berlin Wall and the Soviet Union. The walls rose and they fell, the plane ascended then descended, and Jorge took his own place in history. He had wandered in the wilderness for twenty-six years and then, too, the walls of Jericho were tumbling down.

"Please stay seated, with your seat belts fastened. We'll be reaching the terminal shortly."

They didn't understand a word the flight attendant said. Jorge tightened and loosened his grip on Diego. They were at a standstill, and then there was a chime overhead and then the symphony-like sound of release. Hundreds of seat belts, clicked then unclicked; they were free to move about the cabin. They were free. They were all free. They were gloriously free. All the cabin pressure rushed out as the aircraft doors opened. The great walls of water lay beneath their jet stream, closing past them on the sanctuary of their harbor. Jorge passed through the aisle in a state, impressionistic and dreamlike, and then Customs and Immigration stood before him. The angel at heaven's gate looked just like a Ken doll, and Jorge spoke for the entire family. They were the only words he really knew. *Hello. Colombia. My family.*

The man at Immigration was Barbie's Ken, so tan and so blond with eyes the color of sapphires. He smiled at the children, a broad, beaming grin, seeming to understand the significance. Jorge had stopped crying; there was too much elation. He held his breath waiting for the words.

"Welcome to the United States of America," Ken said, and then Jorge's view on Immigration became impossibly blurred.

Diego began to hop up and down like a sprinter, warming up for a great race. The Ken doll smiled and Jorge clutched his carry-on luggage. The tennis rackets were on top of his clothes. He nodded his thanks, his voice caught in a lump that inhibited all sound from his throat. They were wanted, they were welcome; and it surpassed his understanding, and that's all he had needed to know.

He had arrived in the promised land with his wife and his children. He had come with his dignity in tow.

THE PATRIOT

In America, our origins matter less than our destination, and that is what democracy is all about.

—*Ronald Wilson Reagan*

FOREWORD
WITH FABIAN RINCON

It's not that I never missed Colombia, it's that Colombia never missed me.

I was a troublemaker there, not a real menace but enough of a nuisance to put all the teachers on notice at my elementary school; and, to this day, I don't really know why. My father had had that same reputation as a kid, but I didn't share many of his frustrations. I didn't share any of the apologies he was allowed for all of his bad behavior. I'd never slept on the streets with newspapers my only warmth, never grubbed through the gutters or searched for food in the trash that peppered the stench and the filth of the outlying ghettos.

I don't want to give the impression my father's family was overcome by poverty—my dad was just so rebellious in his native country. There was something always agitating inside him, fighting against whatever it was that had seemed to gnaw at him from the time he was born.

He was aggravated as a kid, or so I hear, and he resorted to the streets a lot.

I remember how it all started; how my dad began to sell our things when I was just seven years old. How all of our possessions piled up one day and then dwindled to a miniscule mound of nothingness. My father's impassioned outbursts came to pivot solely around America, this place around which everything seemed to rotate. It was like the sun, but far more removed and foreign. At least the sun radiated some kind of warmth.

We were all going on a very long, hopefully cool kind of field trip—that is what I thought.

Up to that point, Diego's life had been measured in bouts of sickness and so, not surprisingly, he slept the entire flight from Bogotá to Miami. He stirred just as the plane made its final descent and that moment marked one of our few similarities:

We crossed the border, and it seemed to me that we both woke up in America.

He yawned and stretched on my father's lap in the friendly blue and yellow sweat suit he wore. We didn't have the luxury of window seats; we were all crammed into the middle section of a DC-10; all in this remarkable undertaking together, taking our cue from my father's high spirits. It wasn't long before Diego began to jump up and down, trying to get the smallest sliver of a peek at our new life through those funny bubbled windows commercial jets have. The sky was fading in and out, topsy-turvy, as he strained for it.

I was the more introspective one, continuing to leaf through the pages of a book my dad had bought for us a few weeks earlier. I mulled its pictures and its bilingual captions, one set of images and phrases striking me more than the rest.

There was a boy and a ball. A niño and a pelota, and the children who spoke English seemed happy.

Now supposedly it's easier to learn a second language when you're a child, that's what "they" all claim. Whoever they are, I maintain there's a reason adults call those years formative, and that throwing a new kind of personality into the mix just complicates things.

When you're a toddler and learning to speak for the very first time, there are so many exclamations and pleasurable smiles, so much sense of accomplishment for a little word like "niño." You forget the effort, all the stops and starts and the headlong stumbling over vocabulary. You point and you clap for yourself, especially if a word like galleta actually brings some sweet taste to your mouth, some cookie kind of reward for your trials. Nothing like that happens when your accent is strong and you're older, trying to start all over.

You suddenly feel very isolated from the rest of the world and very, very juvenile. You talk like a baby at an age when the last thing you want to be accused of is being a baby.

I clutched that bridge of a book to me as we made our way through the Miami International Airport to a connecting flight bound for Atlanta. Even Diego was subdued by so many people swarming the terminals, speaking some kind of indecipherable code. I pushed innocently enough at the glass door before me, the one leading outside that allowed my first intake of really pure, really land-of-the-free-oxygen.

And then the most peculiar look crossed my face as I swung back toward my parents. I had the wide, shocked eyes of a child who, poised to freefall from a diving platform, suddenly sees the chasm between the diving board and the water as profound as the Grand Canyon. I was so startled that my mother and father pushed with great intrigue past me and then it hit them too.

It was a stifling, suffocating, scorching heat we had never known in the high elevations outside Bogotá. My parents laughed so hard at my reaction that I chose to believe there was no harm in allowing my head to explode in an oven.

The United States of America was as hot as the devil. That was my first impression. But I was about to learn that heat, like all things relative to democracy, could remain intensely stimulating, or it could be tamed and civilized at will in such a strange land with solutions. Some little luxury as small as the air conditioning in our first car ride through Georgia brought this stunned, swelling kind of feeling in my stomach. I can't explain it to people who have never lacked much, but that cool breath of deliverance was like a wind beneath sails.

It was direction—suddenly, inexplicably born when I hadn't even known our course was stagnant.

I remember looking at paved roads—not just single-lane highways—but whole arteries of roads, crisscrossed and jumbled and always leading somewhere out of the entanglement called Spaghetti Junction on Atlanta's elaborate freeway system. In Colombia the government had often started projects that, for one reason or another, workers were never able to finish. That meant there were a lot of potholes in dirt roads that were never patched up; manholes for electrical lines and sewer systems and waterways that never came to be—all these little loopholes on expectation and improvement dotting the landscape.

I wasn't able to articulate it then, but I saw there was something even more magnificent than direction in the United States:

There was a *choice* in direction in all those interstate outlets and all of them were paved in something called progress.

I can't pinpoint the hour exactly—the epiphany I had that led me to believe I'd just come home. But I knew the same feeling washed over Diego as quickly as it overcame me. Even with the inherent challenges of moving to a new country and adopting a new culture, we always knew that America was where we belonged. And maybe it was that which caused Diego to shrug off any assumptions that could have ever been made about birthright, even birth order.

I was always so much taller, so much bigger, not all that much older, but older—and when we took on our first day of public school, it was never more apparent who had just come into his own. It became obvious right away who was really going to act the part of the big brother for the rest of our lives. He didn't charge into the elementary school that morning like some extroverts might have done in their habit of taking over.

He sort of eased into the building with me at his side, scoping out the joint in a way.

We'd been taught one phrase for survival and it was simply this: *I don't speak English*. We held onto that and we held onto each other, the only familiarities, in the hallway. A teacher found us, meandering through the school, unsure of where our classrooms were. Her eyes were so kind and I had been so afraid and overwhelmed by all the changes.

"I don't speak English," I blurted out and then my shoulders began to shake uncontrollably. There was some characteristic kind of compassion and protectiveness, some utter confidence that caused Diego to throw his arms around me.

My little, six-year-old brother buoying me with that wiry fierceness he would always possess. "No llores, Fabian. No llores." *Don't cry.* He implored the teacher to help with all the sweetness his upturned face could communicate.

That was the essence of Diego: his strength and his adaptability and his sheer talent to perform and persuade—and then, of course, his inattention to what he couldn't do.

Diego was never one to burst out with something like, "I don't speak English." The more I think about it, Diego simply used to smile, and none of him needed translation after that.

We went on to learn one word in our language class right away that, despite being small, our teacher emphasized was important. We still lacked the skills to really try to sound it out, and of course so many words didn't work like that in English anyway. "T" and "h" didn't make much sense together, so the teacher gave that one to Diego and me as a freebie.

The word was "the," and Diego and I practiced it, trying to say it like the first "d" in "verdad."

I was the studied one and he was the theatric one, and we eventually learned things like dramatic irony—when the audience members know something the characters don't, acting out all those scenes. We learned that first word: *the* boy, *the* battle, *the* tried and *the* true; *the* triumph and then, of course, *the* end.

Always *the end* when our heroic stories were finished because that was the luxury of childhood.

Life had a much more sympathetic way of warning us when we were kids that there were ends.

CHAPTER 1

There was a huddle of adults in the elementary school hall; there were low voices, some debate, and sideways glances. One teacher smiled encouragingly at Fabian and Diego and took them by the hand to her classroom.

"This is kindergarten," she said and, for a moment, there was a breakthrough—the boys spoke in tongues. And then Fabian recognized the words; the kindergarten teacher spoke Spanish and an enormous hurt left his eyes.

It was just for the day, until they got their bearings; the teachers allowed for the paired acclimation. Diego was advanced to the first grade before Fabian because he appeared to be more secure. It was Diego's social skills—the little girls liked him and he was invited to a birthday party right away. He sat happily at his desk, fingering a glittery card, Papa Smurf, and his great expectations. It meant nothing to him that he couldn't decipher the words or the buzz that clouded his world: there was going to be cake and ice cream and presents; he was going to be part of their noise.

Second grade was a disaster the minute Fabian arrived, all the curious stares and the code talkers. He devised a plan to go to the bathroom and escape academics altogether. He'd go back to kindergarten where they had snacks and naps and he'd live out his life as a five-year-old. He crossed his legs and he hopped and he pleaded, trying not to be too obscene. His teacher understood, but she foiled his plans with a personal escort to the boys' room.

Fabian stood at the urinal, glowering and idle because he had no real business there.

Diego was not as talented as his brother at charades, and down the hall he had to draw a picture. He was good at art, and he used a thick, purple crayon to illustrate the toilet. He put water in the bowl, and he gave it a handle and a lid for the sake of refinement. He had to add the dignity—the boy he had sketched was graphic enough to illustrate dire need. It was the first time he had ever felt the red flush at his cheeks, the utter humiliation.

His displeasure faded as he passed Fabian in the hallway. He waved energetically at his brother. Fabian's mouth was downturned and he raised a sulking hand. The older child returned to his classroom in annoyance. Diego wasn't the least bit phased by America. Diego was never put out. Fabian slouched in his seat, and he tapped his pencil furiously at the blank sheet of paper before him. There was some kind of announcement, something that brought wild cheering, and Fabian breathed a long sigh. He waited for the translation, for the delayed briefing of the kindergarten teacher, and then he sat up abruptly.

There was a contest and the winners got homemade cookies at the end of the week for achieving a good amount of work.

It startled the teacher, the sudden change in disposition, or at least the frenzy of activity. Fabian was still argumentative, but it was channeled to a productivity that surpassed every student in the class. He worked feverishly and meticulously, the perfectionist tendencies of his father, spurred by this newest, most enlightening concept. It was a virtue called incentive; and, in his rise to the occasion, the teacher saw the lawyer he would become.

Fabian would always be bright; he would always be questioning so that many ideas would require a debate. His language skills would increase to a superb articulation of thought, even at a very young age. That's what Fabian was—he was an advanced kind of thinker who would just need the small recognitions. That's why it would come as a shock when he took an IQ test with Diego, and the results of their scores were identical.

It would come as such a shock because of incentive and what the two boys latched onto so early. Fabian grasped reading and writing and arithmetic to excel in those things both noble and scholarly. Diego tolerated the formalities as a means to an end—the joy of his movement through life. He learned subject and verb and correct conjugation to make friends and to be in the middle of things. He had sociable motivations, to be the life of the party, to span and to bridge and to connect. Fabian would need Diego for a very long while to give him that added sense of belonging: Diego would push and propel and he would make things happen; and, being an extension of his brother—Fabian would reap the rewards of the good company and laughter that Diego always set into motion.

It would be a blessing, of course, to have such a brother who was outgoing and athletic and charming. It would be a blessing to have a brother who was so likable he was invited, immediately, to a birthday party. Diego with his magnetism and his easy smile, picking up chicks at a tender age. It would be acceptable, certainly, to be just a little jealous of your brother because it was almost like being proud of yourself.

They returned to their apartment, and they played in wonder with a touchtone phone, giggling in their discovery of speed dial. Fabian clamped a hand over Diego's mouth when the first number yielded a response.

"Hang up," Fabian hissed and Diego dropped the phone and the boys clambered to the top of a closet. They curled in the fetal position, their eyes wide in terror through all of the banging and sirens.

Dialing 911 was like witchcraft in a way, all those people appearing in costumes at the door.

They had settled in Georgia because their father liked the landscape, and because he had thrown a sort of dart at a map. Jorge had looked up his own surname in the telephone book and he'd found a man with his exact name. The family had moved to Georgia because someone else had had their name and another Colombian family had given them a room in their home. The randomness of their world overcame both of the boys that evening on a borrowed mattress that lay on the floor.

Diego couldn't sleep, staring at the ceiling, an unusual seriousness to his face.

"Fabian, do you think Jesus will take us away soon?"

Fabian rolled to his side, propped his chin on his elbow.

"You mean like kidnap us?"

Diego nodded, an expression not lost in the dark.

"I think it'll be here." His whisper was loud. "Like a thief in the night. Like what it says in the Bible."

His voice carried some kind of awe, and Fabian gripped the covers with a tiny flutter in his stomach. Fabian hadn't thought of it that way. It was certainly possible. It was a beautiful, but very strange land.

Diego passed gas—another voluntary talent—and the boys forgot all about Jesus in their giggles.

They had left all of their belongings and their mistakes and their judgments the minute the wheels had touched down on American soil. Everything they had owned, even their individuality, had been washed away in that baptism. All their father's carnal insecurities had been cleansed from his soul and Jorge had been reborn. To get a fresh start was the most liberating thing, the most religious experience of his life—and then Jorge couldn't recognize his hands, all the manicures gone, the chapping and the calluses of a terrible start.

He could make out the classifieds, but the phone calls were useless when no one could really understand him. He walked the streets in pursuit of "help wanted" signs, hoping to persuade in person. He looked for security jobs until the money dwindled, until the most menial tasks seemed above him. He asked to wash dishes and even the restaurants required more language skills than he had. He went to McDonald's and he ordered Coca-Cola, which was still Coca-Cola in Spanish. It was the Happy Meal that threw him—they were far too specific, the drinks, the toys, the McNuggets sauce. He shook his head as he tried to figure change, and there was a long string of cars behind him. He just handed over bills, wads of bills, hoping the attendant was honest.

He took whatever the server gave him in coins and food and then, sometimes, compassion. Diego hated onions. His son picked off the onions of a hamburger that wasn't McNuggets.

They tried Taco Bell, a chicken quesadilla. *Hold the tomatoes and onions for Diego.* They tried Pizza Hut. *Hold the mushrooms and onions for my little boy, Diego.* Extra pineapple. The kid loved pineapple and guava juice and rice. *I'd like that thing at Weinerschnitzel, that long thing in the bread and please hold the onions for Diego.* Jorge looked up the words in a Spanish-English dictionary and he puzzled at "perro caliente." A dog that was hot. A heated sort of dog or a dog that was in heat, and why?

The family left the drive-through, all the money going out and so little means coming in. Diego was content with little things like no onions and he studied Fabian with expectation. Fabian always did the explaining of the downhearted looks that sometimes crossed their parents' faces. They had entered a building, another strange building, and they were going to clean and get money.

"It's not a good job. This is a really bad place." And, in sympathy, Diego ducked his head.

Estudiantes. Students it seemed. They had left without expecting their deposit. Yolanda was silent as she began to sweep—cockroaches, hair, and mouse droppings. There was a moment's hesitation as she tackled the toilet and scrubbed behind the tank. The rag wasn't black; it was coated in the undetectable as she pulled back to rinse it in the sink. She turned her head and held the rag by the corner; the water pressure was too low. She tried to touch it as little as possible, but at last she had to wring it. She covered her mouth with her forearm to stifle it, the nausea, the smell, the revulsion. Diego watched her kneel and scrub again. His expression became darkened and sad. He wheezed slightly in the disquiet, in the dampness and gloom that pervaded even with the blinds opened. The sunlight was unwelcome for what it revealed, for the dust particles and all the obscenities. Diego coughed harder and Yolanda scoured faster and she looked up once and met his eyes.

"Don't worry, baby. I'll be done soon."

Diego put his arms around her.

He squeezed her hard and she couldn't squeeze back, trying to hold her hands at a safe distance. She covered him in kisses from his head to his neck and once on the belly for good measure. "Try not to touch anything." Diego nodded, and he remained at her side for hours.

He had an asthma attack in the middle of the night that drained him to near lifelessness on the couch. Yolanda rocked him through all the spasmodic fits and the strangulation and heaving. His body quaked as she entered the emergency room.

"¡Asmático!" she tapped her own chest.

Does he have any allergies? Did he swallow poison? She couldn't answer the barrage.

Do you have any insurance? Yolanda stared helplessly as they led her son through the ER. There was too much paperwork, and they didn't understand his temperament—Diego rarely complained.

There was an emergency room bill, the cost of breathing treatments so that more apartments had to be cleaned. Jorge accepted the degradation, the smut and the impurity on his hands and knees with Yolanda.

Yes, Mr. Landlord. We do good job, señor. The former tenant had aid—no problem. Aid was like help, right? The poor man had died and his aid had kept the apartment in good shape.

Diego wrote later in adamant defense of his father—but more in defense of himself. He was small when he immigrated so that he forgot the toil, the strife, the indignity, all the heartache. Diego believed in the Protestant work ethic, in high school, in hindsight, in the journals he kept. *Not everyone has to go to college to get ahead in life…I'm not saying "don't go to college," because you can learn a lot from it. But if your parents own a farm out in the country and you're going to take over when they pass away, then your parents can teach you everything you need to know about farming without going to college. There are hundreds of people in the world who make a lot of money in different types of jobs…*

I know a friend who is not American [and he quit high school] when he was in the 12th grade. He did not go to college and now he owns his own company and makes $130,000 a year. His "friend" and Yolanda arched their backs, sweat trickling down their noses, and bent over and scrubbed some more.

It was the accumulation of chemicals, the harshest anti-bacterials that Yolanda used when she cleaned. It peeled her skin to that epidermal layer that shined before her hands broke and bled. The rags became dirty, and then they became red smears in all that painstaking effort. The chemicals burned mercilessly and she held her hands under the cold running water at the sink. She would have to sanitize the sink last where the man had had the aid; she didn't want her blood to contaminate what they had cleaned and then, too, it was just so unseemly. The landlord had been clear: everything sterile down to the light switch panels.

A nearby tenant glanced at them warily on her way to retrieve her mail. And then another gawked openly at the family through the open front door, her suspicion turning to horror.

Fabian and Diego played in the front room, and there were animated whispers among the neighbors. Jorge thought the ladies were prejudiced and the thought unnerved him, all those tenants staring at the Hispanics. It was Yolanda who understood it because she helped the boys with their schoolwork and the language had come so much faster.

"What are they thinking? The children will catch it!" She caught it in bits and pieces.

The maintenance man had been delighted to find such hard workers, someone at last to clean up. They had come from Colombia he said—perhaps accustomed to the revolting—they hadn't seemed to mind.

"They were desperate for work and no one else would have touched it. You know, it's been a week since he died. The landlord's going to have a really hard time now renting a place like that out."

The neighbors were sympathetic. At least the man was gone. God rest his soul, someone offered. They'd never known anyone before with AIDS. It had been such a lingering, heinous death.

Yolanda stood quietly, biting her lower lip. She closed her eyes on the rawness and the sting.

Jorge took his wife's hands, made her hold them out, so that he saw for the first time the beating. The astringents were so strong that they'd smoothed away her fingerprints; his clean start had swiped her identity.

He gathered the rags and the bottles and buckets and he hurled them into a trash bin.

"Never again, Yolanda. Never again. As God is my witness, never."

The promise itself was only half rash: Yolanda cleaned nicer apartments.

Jorge met a Cuban, just an ordinary businessman, who had come to the country in poverty. He was a real estate developer with an above average income and an above average home in the suburbs. He'd just made a promise once—he'd vowed when he was successful, he'd return the favor someday.

"If you're willing to work hard, Jorge, you can have the American dream. I tell you, there's money to be made in this country."

Some Cubans were like the New Yorkers of whom Jorge had heard—they took time to warm up. But when they befriended you, it was with unprecedented loyalty; Cubans befriended for life.

Jorge and the Cuban entered a bank in Fairborn, a community south of Atlanta. It was morning and clear and springtime and the Cuban was a patron of the local branch. "You'll be co-signing with Mr. Rincon?" The Cuban nodded his assent.

"$2,500. Is that correct?"

"Yes." They were given some papers.

The branch was too quiet, just the scrawl of their pens scratching out Jorge's indigence.

"What kind of business are you starting, Mr. Rincon?"

"Carpet cleaning. I'll come by tomorrow."

The assistant laughed and the Cuban smiled to himself; he was a sedate and methodical man. Jorge wished for a smooth process that wouldn't delay him—an important person with such a tight schedule. The assistant reviewed the terms and conditions of the loan, and for some reason Jorge began to squirm. There was a beige Mercedes-Benz parked near the bank, and a tall man emerged from the driver's side. He carried a briefcase in one hand and a fidgety sort of snap plaguing his fingers as he walked. He was dressed in blue jeans with a black leather coat and something twitchy in his eyes. He seemed to scan the tellers and settled on one and he kept a bandana and a terseness. Jorge was just paranoid. Just those bodyguard instincts and he tried to focus on the papers.

He filled in his social security number and pulled out his passport and visa for verification. The teller was hurried and she emerged with a box. *Focus, Jorge, focus.*

The Cuban's signature was audacious and illegible, the power strokes of a self-made man. Jorge's writing was neat and precise, each letter measured and clean. He shuffled the papers and the tall man walked out, and only then did the teller scream. It had a movie kind of quality, the high-pitched terror, and then she collapsed into tears at her window. She had tripped the alarm and, in a matter of minutes, the branch was locked down. There were sirens. The Cuban was shaken and so was the branch assistant and Jorge sat in a stupor.

The bank had been robbed. The FBI was coming. All he'd wanted was carpet cleaning equipment.

And then it struck him comically—a Cuban and a Colombian asking for money in the middle of a Georgia crime scene.

"Do you have a good lawyer? We might be in trouble."

The Cuban, too, began to laugh.

The teller was hysterical, and hysteria was counter to a reliable physical description. That was Jorge's strength, and he cooperated fully with the men in uniform who detained him. The Cuban glanced at his watch and shifted in his chair; the questioning took a long time. The police combed the branch. They dusted for fingerprints with a handful of witnesses remaining.

"La culpa es mía." *This is my fault.* In Spanish, Jorge was really quite a card. He missed having an audience sometimes: he missed himself in the way that a foreign language limited personality.

"I was in the DAS building in Bogotá, Colombia, el Departemento Administrativo de Seguridad. It was the state security headquarters. I had to get clearance to come to this country and I left my family in the car. I had to get papers and then suddenly there's a bomb threat. Can you imagine how I felt in that moment? Bomb threats aren't hoaxes—not in my country—and my family is in the parking lot.

"I found the closest exit and I ran like the wind. I tell you I've never run like that before. People were screaming, the scene was chaos, and I had to get to my family. I reached the car and the bomb hadn't detonated, and I still had to get my boys out of there. It was the Indy 500 in my Chevrolet Monza. And you know what happened after that?"

The Cuban knew the outcome—the DAS building had become a ball of flames just a few months later, in November. Not the day Jorge was there or even the next, but a few months later, after the Rincons had arrived in the United States.

Terrorists were patient. They bided their time and someone else had perished in the explosion.

"The first time I try to come to the United States, there's a bomb threat on the plane, you understand? Then more than a hundred people are killed when the drug traffickers put a bomb in one of the next jetliners. The plane takes off and—poof—they're gone from the exact same airport. The exact same month as the DAS building. It follows me, hermano, everywhere I go. I cannot escape the violence.

"All these explosions, all these catastrophes—one of these days it's going to catch up to me."

Jorge tried to make light of it in the exaggerated mannerisms, gloss over the powerlessness that had so long accompanied him. "Do you think it's a bad time to ask the status of my loan application?" He covered his mouth with his hand.

The Cuban cracked up, too, the same delirium of anxiety. An FBI agent looked at the men warily.

"I get the money now?" he asked the branch manager, and the manager's face wore something unreadable. There was a pause in his expression, a strange twitch in his left eye like the face of an old stopwatch when the hand stuck. A tick at the ten second mark, a tic in disbelief and then his mouth formed a word. It was "sure." Maybe he felt generous, maybe he was just tired, or maybe it was another $2,500 and who cared?

The bank cut a check and they opened an account and the branch manager shook Jorge's hand.

Jorge picked up Fabian and Diego from school and they drove to McDonald's for Happy Meals. *A Coca-Cola please, Sprites for the children, Chicken McNuggets, one sweet and sour, one barbecue.*

"Will that be everything?"

"Yes, that's it."

"Pay the total at the window."

Jorge pumped his fist in Olympic-like triumph. *"We has the American dream!"*

"Only in this country, Yolanda." Jorge said it often, always when he was out of breath. Carpet cleaning equipment was unusually cumbersome, and so was the work it entailed. The tank was enormous and the hoses stretched for yards and he'd left flyers on every car. *I clean carpets. I do very good job.* He mentioned it in every conversation—in the line at the grocery store, pumping gas at the service station, at PTA meetings and soccer games. He had convinced the manager of a nearby apartment complex to let him clean rooms for his rent. He had cleaned so many apartments he was three months ahead on payments and he would always stay three months ahead. He priced himself higher and did flawless work and then raised his prices again. If he was going to be a carpet cleaner, he would be the best carpet cleaner, not the cheapest, the rock bottom, or the drudge.

He was shameless in his appeals without invoking shame, the discomfort that might have come with hard selling. It was because Jorge possessed a boyish charm—the same charisma that Diego had inherited. It was the type of sincerity that came with a performer, and not necessarily the pretenses of an actor. He was the freckled boy who got pats on the head at the ICA and yet business was business in his tone.

I worked hard on these tamales, they're the very best tamales, and don't even think of stealing my tamales.

Manual labor made him humble, as it was prone to do. But it also gave him time to think. He dreamed of a house in the suburbs for Yolanda, a six-figure income perhaps. All that was required was hard work and will—clean enough carpets and the American dream was for the taking. The Cuban had been right: there was money to be made doing jobs no one else really liked.

The phone rang one night, and Fabian and Diego's father was more upset than he'd been at the sight of the fire engines. It was hard to understand that adults made mistakes, too, that the misunderstandings came in all shapes and sizes.

"Tell me what's wrong. I can fix it," which was a truth because Jorge had enormous pride. He'd distributed all those flyers with a grammatical error and it made him feel weak in the knees. He'd studied every word, scrutinized the dictionary to make a good first impression. It affected him so that his face turned bright red and he stammered intolerably on the phone.

"If you're going to do business and live in this country, you ought to learn some English."

The line clicked dead, and Jorge sat for some time, slumped in a chair in the kitchen.

Diego went to him, climbed on his knee, and kissed him squarely on the mouth. Jorge's tears flowed harder, and it was that exceptional emotion that left a lasting imprint of tenderness. Diego was free-spirited and life was such a joyous game, but even the most fun games had rules: sticks and stones broke a lot of bones and words were even worse for what they wounded.

It was a fierce protectiveness borne in Diego on the night that a man made his father feel small.

Jorge rubbed his son's arm in the faint glow of light that spilled from the front room to the kitchen. He noticed it again, the slight bow in his son's elbow, the subtle crook in the skinniness of those arms. Diego had a patch of long, sporadic hairs at that bow, and then nowhere else that he could see. Jorge stared at that arm that was like no other arm, the uniqueness, the eccentric pattern. He scooted him to bed with a tight hug and a swat on his behind as Diego jumped from his lap in pleasure. Jorge was rarely going to rely on another man's friendship—not with friends such as those.

CHAPTER 2

There were times when Jorge looked around and wondered where all those people had gone—the Americans he had seen on Colombian television, with their estates and their convertibles and their swimming pools.

"We saw so many rich people," he said in disbelief, in his notion of life, liberty, and the pursuit of happiness. It was because in safety, in peaceful times, Jorge had the basics covered enough to dream big.

He had bought into the sentiment of Archibald Macleish in a series of essays that had appeared in the 1960s. "There are those," he had written, "I know, who will reply that the liberation of humanity, the freedom of man and mind, is nothing but a dream.

"They are right. It is. It is the American dream." That's what *Life* magazine and *The New York Times* had printed and so it was true. Jorge tried to eat those words—drink them and sleep them—and when he awoke there was still such immense hunger.

For a Colombian, Jorge had never been truly poor. That had been Yolanda's lot. She still had family in the mountains who grew their own food, whose sole transportation was a burro. It was all very relative and perhaps even selfish, but Jorge had not come so far—there were certain economic laws to which he had to adhere. He just had to clean more carpets with his boys.

The last time Yolanda had driven Diego to the hospital, his head had been in her swollen lap. She had been eight months pregnant in 1993, and grown so enormous she could hardly scrub apartments on her hands and knees. By then, Diego had grown too big to be carried into the ER. The doctor had suggested he take up gymnastics or swimming, and Diego had always taken to leaping. He was wiry and flexible and strong for his size, having never been encumbered by weight. His hands bore such grip strength already from their livelihood that his muscles gave no protest to the assault.

Diego was a natural, not because he was so fearless, but because he was determined and able.

They really hadn't planned to have more children, despite Diego's constant entreaties. "Kids are expensive," Fabian had lectured him. They had fast been approaching their teens then. Jorge's carpet cleaning business had suddenly turned a corner, and still Fabian had been consumed with the economy. They had reached profitability, and Diego had sighed and resorted to the bathroom where he'd stumbled onto that most interesting stash.

He had found his mother's birth control pills and then he had hid them—because God helped those who helped themselves, it seemed.

"Go wash your hands. Dinner is ready."

Diego braced his little brother's back in the family room and rolled him once in a sloppy back flip. George stood like a drunken sailor and Diego propelled him again. He weaved in caution and then in perplexity as he fell in his dizziness to the floor.

George had Fabian's prudence and Diego's outgoingness and he smiled at his brother's delight.

"Diego! I told you to go wash your hands. Come to dinner *now!*"

"Señora," he called. *Yes ma'am, I'll be there.* It was a deeper than Deep South respect.

"Diego, how many times do I have to call you?"

"Señora." *Yes ma'am. I am here now.*

Diego had silently wished for another small mishap and so it had happened that Yolanda became pregnant again. She had gone into labor with their fourth child on April 13, 1997 in an audacious move on her part. So far as the men knew, the Masters Tournament was won on the back nine, and always on a Sunday in April. She had paced the halls, and Diego had appeared torn as he had taken his turn beside her.

Tiger Woods was up. He had strained for a peek and had been thankfully relieved as Jorge had come toward them both, hedging.

Yolanda had taken Jorge's hand in hers. "Oh!" he had cried, losing her grip.

Woods hadn't bogeyed once; it had been the most phenomenal performance her husband had ever seen.

"Did you catch that, Yolanda?" *He's on his way to a tournament record, a 12-shot victory over Tom Kite.* "He's only been in the pros since you got pregnant. Can you believe that, baby?"

Yolanda hadn't believed it. She really hadn't. *Please, God, send me a girl.*

The men had become misty-eyed holding Stephanie—because Woods had stepped forward to try on his first green jacket. "Look at her arms. They're just like Diego's. They even have the little hairs." Fabian had laughed on what had been his birthday, too. They had cut a cake that had come from a mother with foresight.

"Can I hold her? Can I hold her?" Diego's eyes had sparkled, and then suddenly clouded in fear. "What if I break her? Look at her fingers. Oh my gosh. They're so little...

"She's smiling at me."

"That's just gas."

"*No*, she's smiling at me..."

April 13 had been a spectacular day, in Augusta and in Conyers; God always smiled heavily on Georgia.

Diego took his seat by his baby sister's high chair. "C'mon, girl, say 'Stephanie' for me."

She waved a spoon in his general direction. "Tee Tee," she repeated in earnest.

Diego laughed. "Steph...uh...nee. Try it."

There was a pause and then "tee tee" again.

Diego collapsed in mock despair and Stephanie warmed to the theatrics.

She pounded her spoon on the tray for him. She expressed her adoration much like she would eventually sing—there was never so much emotion in the eyes and a great deal of focus on the mechanics. Stephanie seemed nonchalant; Stephanie seemed sedate; and then she opened her mouth and there came a top-of-the-lungs belt that was startling.

"I guess we'll just have to call her Tí Tí," Diego finally resigned.

"If that's what she wants, we gotta roll with it." George was practical for a five-year-old.

The phone began to ring in the middle of dinner, and Jorge rose to answer it. Yolanda sighed. *They always called during dinner.*

"Everybody wants me, Yoli.

"Visa. MasterCard. Publisher's Clearinghouse...they all want to talk to *me*."

Fabian threw his napkin on the kitchen table as the phone conversation progressed.

"Guess what we're doing tonight, Diego?"

His brother's chin dropped abruptly to his chest and it stayed there for full effect.

We're coming right now. Don't you worry. We'll do the best job for you.

Jorge had two employees, slave labor really. Each of them rose from the table dutifully.

"I'm really sorry, baby. I'll watch the little ones for you as soon as I get home."

Yolanda handed Jorge the van keys without looking up. "I'll clean the apartment later."

+⊱═⊰+

His two oldest sons helped haul the hoses and move the furniture and spray for stains. They edged the carpets with the most miniscule of attachments, and their attention to details earned tips. *My, you're hard workers. My, what sweet boys.* Always the accolades and tips. There was no allowance, some sparse after school entertainment: mostly homework and then work work and then bedtime. They were expected to contribute, to pay their fair share for their roof and the food on their table. It was partly their doing that the roofs were improving; they finally had a real house. They took the change and the small bills, all the tokens, and they respectfully turned them over to their father. It went into a family pool— their dream, too—their peace, their prosperity, their full partnership.

There was such disparity among Jorge's customers: not a stick of furniture in some houses. It was those people who lived like Jorge and Yolanda had when they'd first arrived in America. And then Jorge cleaned mansions for Major League Baseball players and his sons tried to be casual in their awe. Diego had a pile of Atlanta Braves baseball cards that he kept safeguarded under the bathroom sink. They pulled into the driveway of a rambler with a well-kept yard, nothing extraordinary except for the smell. The sewer had backed up and the carpets were drenched in puddles of human waste.

Diego pulled a face, squinted his eyes shut, and tried not to breathe too deeply. Fabian blew out his cheeks as he stepped into the hallway, his rubber boots steeped in feces. "Pops, I was thinking. You could go to college. Become an accountant or something."

The machine roared to life, and the last attempt at humor was sucked into the dirtiest of jobs.

They moved to dry ground, deodorized the family room, and the hose stretched from the garage through the kitchen. Fabian sat down with his head on his arm, methodically guiding the extension. It took three hours, and Jorge turned off the vacuum and his clothes were saturated in grime and perspiration.

It required a lot of stamina to clean as hard as he did, the lifting and the bending and the standing. The hose still slithered in a forward motion, and Jorge peeked through the kitchen. Fabian was feeding the equipment mechanically; Fabian was working in his sleep.

Jorge stood in the doorway, and it was a strange sort of smile, filled in admiration and sadness for the hardship. *Someday, Fabian, you will have that law degree. No more cleaning carpets for you.* Diego took pleasure in waking his brother. He licked his finger and stuck it in his ear. Fabian mumbled his irritation as they loaded the equipment back into the van in the darkness.

"Have you ever noticed how dark your skin is? Have you ever wondered about that? You were adopted, Diego. Your mom got you from Africa."

"And you're jealous of me for that, Powder."

There was no animosity. It was just a comeback; a superficial one at that. Diego didn't have the temperament for maliciousness; only that oddity of possessive pronouns lay between them.

My dad wants you to come into the house. Your mom's calling you for dinner. There had never been joint ownership: *our* mom, *our* dad. Why did they talk like that?

"Jealous of you for what? *I'm* the worker bee." Even Fabian heard the edge.

"I work too."

"At the things you like." The boys were so clearly defined.

They were polar opposites, the black and the white of their father's own mixed personality. Diego was gregarious—so predictable in his easy laugh—that the flicker went unnoticed.

Only for a second there had seemed to be a pinpoint of hurt in the younger brother's eyes.

I have been having a very good day because I was not doing too good in math class. We got our grades for the last quiz and homework check. I was very surprised because I got a 95 on my quiz and a 100 on my homework. I really needed that grade and I still need to stay after school and get help because my grades are not good enough. I still have a couple of weeks to bring my grades up...if I don't, I will be in major trouble with my parents...

The men were exhausted when they arrived at home, and Diego fell asleep on the couch. *This is what I like to do in my free time. I'm just kidding. I have no free time.*

Diego had volunteered to help his mother, but he faded as she changed her clothes. He was a full-time student with a full-time job and some stolen pleasures in between. He liked being busy—there was some part of him that thrived on the chaos as if he had to cram his whole life into each moment. Yolanda stole quietly to the van to clean the apartment on Salem Road at midnight.

"Diego should go with you."

"He's got no more to give, Jorge."

"You spoil him too much, baby."

"How could he be spoiled if he doesn't *act* spoiled."

Jorge waved her off. *There was always more to give.* Jorge had the demanding work ethic of his mother in that regard.

It was a ten-minute trip by car through thin traffic, and Yolanda yawned as she parked the van near a street light. It wasn't a bad neighborhood; she was just so tired and needed the visual cue and maybe an assault on her senses. She rummaged for supplies, for the key from the landlord and let herself inside. At times the weariness took her by surprise—their full ten years in America.

She scrub brushed the toilets and shined the faucets and cleaned her way toward the kitchen. She sponged the baseboards and wiped down the doorknobs and soaked the light fixtures in the sink. She stretched her back and wiped at her forehead, trying to work out the kinks through her fatigue. There was a knock at the door, so frantic in its pound that she dropped the sponge in her fright. She looked around the room for any defense, and her heart raced as she edged from the kitchen. The curtains were drawn and she moved slyly to the peephole.

"Mom, open up! It's Diego!"

She unlatched the door and he rushed through it to encircle her. "I'm sorry, Mom. I'm so sorry."

His face was pale and his shirt clung in sweaty patches.

"Baby, what are you doing here? I'm okay. Don't worry."

He was panting hard from his five-mile run. *What if something had happened to you?* His eyes continued to search hers in tender panic. It all accounted for the spoiling and the partiality. Her children were obedient; in part, because she was strict. But some kids just came to earth good. Some kids just had a natural glow about them that brought so much joy to the soul.

"I'm sorry, Mom. I wouldn't let you down." Diego wasn't made to disappoint. The sincerity pricked her; the loyalty touched her, and then some wonder welled in her eyes.

It was the gratitude that lay between them, the battles they'd fought together for one extraordinary chance. Maybe they had all had to band together so much that it seemed the clock had turned backward. A return to those old-fashioned family values, to the industry, the intimacy and the respect. They ate dinner together and they worked together and they prayed and played—together. Diego was a child from a farm in the 1930s. A "yes sir" and a poster boy. He'd known deprivation, and he'd known he had it in him to turn the thing around. He was like the kid who had been raised in the Depression who could rise to the occasion of World War II. It restored something in Yolanda to see the virtue, to see the All-American goodness that stood before her. Yolanda would scrub toilets for the rest of her life if only for the small concessions. The countless breathing treatments, so many hospital trips and the cleaning that had paid for medication. Diego stood breathless, but he wasn't wheezing: even that demon of asthma was gone.

He paused the next morning outside Fabian's room. He listened at the door and then slowly opened it. It was six o'clock and Diego liked to run in the early morning hours, before the heat overcame him. The light streamed on the covers. He stepped into the hallway to get a head start and took off with the bounce of a high jumper. It was a perfect vault into the middle of Fabian's bed.

"*Wake up!!*" he screamed as he landed.

"Aaaaaggggghhhhhhhhhh!!!!!" Fabian thrashed, his heart was embedded in his skull.

Diego collapsed in a fit of laughter. Fabian pushed him end over end.

He couldn't get his bearings. *Why him? Why his brother? Why that cheerfulness in the morning?*

"You said you'd go running."

"Get out of my room!" *Why cheerfulness all of the time?*

Just once, couldn't he brood? Maybe act gloomy? *Why* was he paired with such exuberance? He muffled Diego's protests with a pillow over his head and fell into a coma alone.

Diego showered after his run, and it was then that Fabian stalked him. He threw him to his parents' bed and they rolled on the mattress, all of the frustration matched with the newly acquired skill. Diego was a wrestler; he enjoyed the spirit of the thing and the elusive spring of his body. He'd taken up the sport at Salem High School and there had come the foreshadowing of his competitiveness. One of his last opponents had come from a neighboring school, and Diego had thrown every move he'd known. He'd glanced at the score table and seen no progress and grown more discouraged by the minute. There had been some confusion—the scorers were novices—and they'd corrected the tally all at once. When Diego had looked up, he'd led by four points and he'd suddenly come to life. Diego had pinned his opponent immediately. All he'd needed was a little good feedback.

He put Fabian in a headlock and Fabian tried to resist. It had turned into some kind of freestyle. Diego was at his best when Diego could improvise and play up to an imaginary crowd. He made up the rules as he went along—because the sport existed for him. Not the other way around and certainly not for the spectators, except to express their encouragement. He transitioned to the showmanship, the

World Wrestling Federation, and he slammed from an airborne position. There was a terrible thud, an unlikely snap and Fabian instinctively curled.

There came a vague notion that something was wrong, but he couldn't pinpoint the pain. He felt all the blood drop to his toes. He felt himself turn green. He rolled to protectiveness, expecting the onslaught, but even Diego had heard it. He stared at Fabian, at a stunned standstill; Diego looked sicker than his brother.

"I think my hand's broken." Diego darted from the room. There were panic-stricken steps to his dad's office. When he reappeared, he held scotch tape.

"Hold still. I think we can fix this."

Diego the trainer. Diego the medic. *We'll get you back into the game, son.*

Yolanda had that sense that most mothers do. The house had suddenly grown quiet. She stood in the doorway in her disbelief, in her wonder at the boyhood ingenuity. Sometimes they just floored her and sometimes they just tickled her; at the moment she was not amused.

Fabian didn't always relish his straight man role, which is why he resorted to the dark humor. He was like his father in the ironies that plagued them, the mishaps that were made to be funny. The family returned from the hospital and Fabian felt sleepy and the trauma had drained all his color. He looked in the mirror and he was ghastly white, so much so that it blanched all his acne. Fabian got pimples and Diego didn't, and it was more abundance in his brother's favor. The acne was camouflaged, and Fabian wished with all his heart that the clarity was a permanent fix.

"Here, Diego," he waxed something less than dramatic, "just break my other hand."

CHAPTER 3

Kenneth Khamphiphone rang the doorbell and was met by a stern sort of friendliness. The Rincon home on Greenfield Way had both a warmth and sterility to which all their friends had grown accustomed. The son of a carpet cleaner, Fabian had to say it: "Remember to take off your shoes." Not adhering to that plea would have been a little like showing up in cut-offs at a black-tie affair. The shirts were optional because Diego liked to show off his pectoral muscles—and no shoes actually won service. Yolanda fed them at all hours of the day so long as they showed that deference to the carpets.

Kenneth pulled a face. "Hey, check out Steph's hair. It's practically down to her back now."

"Yeah, what's up with that, Mom?" Fabian asked. "Are we waiting to see if Geraldo calls?"

Stephanie took her cue from her mother's mixed amusement. It broke the seriousness of her face. Stephanie's natural expression continued to bear some thoughtful mildness that broke abruptly when she smiled. She crouched on the floor in renewed detachment as George tried to wriggle from the vice grip. Diego was strong and George was little and he couldn't budge an inch. She resorted to the position of referee, with limited officiating business.

"Help me, Stephanie!" George cried out and his sister looked at him blankly.

"I'm the coach." The price of tea in China.

Kenneth burst into loud laughter.

111

Diego counted to three and George surrendered. He slapped his hand on the carpet, hard.

"Can you touch it like that?"

"You're going to be late!"

Diego stood up abruptly.

People to see, places to go. Diego the social calendar. When he left it was with speed in a 2000 V6, the Mustang convertible of choice.

It was candy apple red, and he shared it with Fabian, the reward for dragging all those hoses. They still worked with their father after school and on weekends; and if the talk had bothered Diego, he hadn't let on. A handful of students had speculated that his father, being from Colombia, of course...

Naturally, they were drug dealers. Naturally, that explained it—Diego with such a nice car.

They had achieved that coveted, six-figure income in 1999. Diego had mounted fog lights, enlisted his mom's help for hours on end in the garage. Some of his efforts to upgrade came naturally; and, if they didn't, he downloaded instructions off the Internet. He installed the stereo, and he washed the car himself. No one else touched his baby.

Diego sang loudly, not quite on key. It was about the pleasure within. Diego didn't have to do something well to still shine in that way that he had. If he fell all over himself asking out a girl, it was inherently part of his charm. He wasn't nearly as smooth as he thought he was, but who could argue with the results?

They stopped at a grocery store. "I need a bag of orange juice."

It was Kenneth's second odd look of the day.

"I promised I'd bring something over to rehearsals."

"Orange juice doesn't come in bags."

"I'm not buying juice. I need a bag of orange juice." It came down to the slow pronunciation. All the linguists in the CIA could have never picked up on the actual origins of his accent. Diego paid for a bag of oranges and began his distracted singing to the radio again.

If I were to skip school today (and not get written up), I would sleep in for a couple of hours because I hate to wake up early every day to go to school. Then I would go out and have a real nice breakfast somewhere and try to go with my friends that happened to skip school that same day. I would then hang out with them at someone's house. We would most likely go swimming or play tennis in somebody's neighborhood. We might go out and have lunch in some restaurant and even take a ride up to the mall to go shopping. I would most likely get voted to drive my car down there. Just because it would be cool to drive with the top down. We would get a lot of attention if we took the Mustang. Who knows, maybe we would pick up some chicks. That

would be fun. Then I would come home and get something to eat and take a shower.
After that, I would go to sleep and be ready for school.

There was a certain amount of manliness to which Leslie Stewart had to appeal as Diego entered the school for rehearsals. She had to cement a marriage between his needs and the artistry—an act of impressive diplomacy. Someday they'd perform *Grease*, and Diego would have every reason he wanted to take off his shirt. *Man of La Mancha* was a stretch when he had to wear make-up—she had found a way around that, too.

"Diego," she had said, "you can't possibly apply it by yourself. You better get some girl to help you."

They had powdered his nose and gotten excited over his eyelashes. *Why do the men get the long eyelashes?*

"I can't believe you go through this every day." Diego had been genuinely shocked.

"We have to, Diego. So you'll think we're pretty. That and we have to stay skinny."

It had spawned a whole new journal entry. Diego the women's activist.

Girls always look at Teen *magazine or* Seventeen *and see all the skinny girls on the covers and wish that someday they could look like them. It makes them feel bad about themselves and want to change the way they look and even the way they act. What I think is that people should not pay attention to what they read in magazines…They should stop worrying about that and worry about more important things.*

Jerry Smith was direct, and Ms. Stewart was clever in accommodating the many layers of Diego. "We need to show you something in *Amadeus*. We need to explain to you the presentation of the calf."

The musical version of Wolfgang Amadeus Mozart's life featured men in tights and high shoes in the 18th century. He didn't balk outright because Diego was a good sport. He didn't even have to have the lead. He just wanted parts that made him look masculine, basking in the harshness of the stage lights. The calf was critical, anatomically speaking, during Mozart's time, during the Restoration era.

"The tights accentuate the muscular flow, and you need to turn your leg like this: slightly outward, flexed but with the hips straight; it's the angle that shows off the leg. This is *so* important. I can't stress this *enough* because men were judged by their presentation. It was a sign of strength and exceptionally good breeding. *Every* man wanted the best calf."

Diego's head took on striking nobility, a certain snobbery flaring in his nostrils as he straightened. He puffed his chest because surely that would matter in the overall exude of testosterone. He flexed his calf, the trim workings of the gym and countless hours of tumbling. He turned to Kenneth and challenged him haughtily. "*I*...will have...the best calf."

Jerry Smith had been the head of drama for over ten years, and he had immediately perceived the stage presence. Not a particular polish, not the assumption of a character's soul, but something from which the eye didn't wander. When Diego entered a room, he took up space without really taking charge. Diego had pull so that he never had to force himself; Diego had a certain magic.

It was an eclectic following—some kids called them lowlifes, the ones who did drugs or were scorned. The socially awkward and the captain of the football team; everyone gravitated toward Diego. He took offense if the misfits were teased; he hated mean-spirited taunts. He liked to laugh, but only if the joke was something that solidified friendship. Diego got jealous, but it was nothing personal: they settled the thing over the girl, man-to-man. The boy was an odd mixture, partly high strung and partly as fluid as water. Mr. Smith had high expectations, and he pushed Diego hard, appealing to the energetic part of him. In the making of *Grease*, he would choreograph an extraordinary scene that would cater to Diego's athleticism.

They would use real tires and hurl them like hula hoops with the excessive burden of weight. It would be *practically* impossible and that's why he would exhort him to do it—over and over again.

"Is this good enough?"

"Nope. Try again."

"Is this good enough?"

"Not yet."

Diego would remain cheerful and Jerry Smith would remain uncompromising until Diego felt the swell of accomplishment.

It was a brief exchange Mr. Smith witnessed before rehearsals that occurred between Alex and Diego. Alex and Carlos and Anna Maria—Diego's cousins from Colombia, apparently. Mr. Smith saw Diego put his arm around Anna Maria. Elsa's family had immigrated to Conyers, Georgia, too. Anna Maria seemed sad about that. She wore the resignation that had been Fabian's lot in second grade.

"You need to stick it out," Diego had told her. "You'll see. It gets better here." It was the blend of his tone, the lack of characteristic compassion, and an omission that struck Mr. Smith.

The first day of school...I did not understand a single word. I had a really long day...I tried to tell the teacher that I had to use the bathroom but I did not know how. I started to ask her in Spanish but she did not understand me at all. I really had to go but she said that she was going to get the Spanish teacher to come and talk to me. I could not wait. I finally took a piece of paper and started to draw a person using the bathroom. She finally let me go and that was one of the saddest days I have ever had.

Anna Maria nodded her head—his cousin had grown up to be stunning with doe brown eyes. They were rounded in softness and dignity and depression, and she had lowered her head in the charge. She adored Diego, and she smiled something complex, a gratitude not suitable to the moment.

"It must be hard to start all over, Diego—new friends, a new language, a new life."

It was offered in kindness, and Diego whirled, a spark of rebellion in his eyes. He wasn't rude—he couldn't break that much character, especially not toward Mr. Smith. He was just more than insistent, a chip on his shoulder. Diego shouldered the accountability.

"My family made it. Anybody can make it here if they're willing to try hard enough."

Ms. Stewart shared a knowing look with Mr. Smith.

The many layers of Diego.

Diego was willing to take a supporting role. Diego was willing to present his calf. He'd give any number of yells to the football team, and he didn't mind that most cheerleaders were girls. That was the point—when it came right down to it. All those dancing, enchanting girls.

"I'm telling you, Kenneth. We'll all be chick magnets. They'll have to spend hours with us practicing."

There was a sardonic reply. He wished Diego had thought of practicing more diligently with him.

They took the floor and faced all of their peers. Tryouts were serious business. The pair was flanked by David Swafford and Josh Kinnebrew and, for some reason, Diego couldn't stop laughing. He went through the motions, which he had managed to perfect, but he wasn't sure yet they were synchronized. He looked to Josh and then he followed Kenneth's suit and then he cracked up in reverse.

You just laugh at the most inappropriate times, Rincon. Kenneth wanted to swallow his tongue. He looked up to see that even the teachers were amused. Diego was like laughing gas.

He had written to an alien in his high school journal. *Dear Mr. UFO.* He would have gotten docked half the score for turning it in late, except for that last-page explanation. Diego had had food poisoning—so had the whole family—so a teacher could sympathize, couldn't she? He had actually never asked for the slack outright; he had just written the sad tale and made it so graphic.

It couldn't even be characterized as passive aggressive behavior; Diego owned his own brand of persuasion.

He stammered away with such innocence and charm, and then he stood on his head if needed. Literally, Diego performed tricks at the mall if the store manager would give him a discount. It was all for the joy of being and for extracting as much from the moment as possible. Sometimes Kenneth was astounded and sometimes he was chagrined. In this case, he felt his side splitting open.

Kenneth laughed until he was sick. He sputtered through the cheer and then the judges had the audacity to ask. "Were they able to perform stunts?" *No, not really. But Diego here's willing to try.*

"It might be funny to just throw Josh up there." Three of the four friends were wrestlers. They were nearly the same weights, the same heights, the same builds, and it was going to be a magnificent feat. They tossed him up, and the coaches applauded the strength and the originality. They turned over the head cheerleader like a sacrificial lamb, and the boys decided on a low stunt.

She was a captain and soon to graduate and she took it rather well when Diego dropped her face first, between the mats.

"Oh my gosh," Kenneth stood with his jaw slack, horrified, and Diego continued to laugh.

"It's okay. Really. You don't know what you're doing." She was a captain because she was cool. The four boys became cheerleaders due to some grace from on high—the potential to entertain. Diego had relied on his play to the crowd and the one trick he always kept up his sleeve.

When Diego did back handsprings, something breathed life into him, a beauty that sailed and inspired.

That uncanny enlargement of body and spirit was the stage presence Jerry Smith had sensed. It was so expansive that it radiated outward, extended until it was all-inclusive. When Diego's mood darkened, it had the effect of an inner hush on the world. It was like a Summer Olympic Games flame being extinguished after so much pageantry and pomp and performance and excellence. It left one hollow to see the fire smothered—some things were just born to be ignited.

This weekend I went to Rockdale gymnastics for open workout. It was Kenneth and I that went…One of the coaches there said that when he saw us walk in, he thought that we could not tumble. Then we got in a line and started to tumble and he got impressed. He offered me a job so I went back at 6 that night and helped them out. It was fun. All we did was take care of small kids and jump on the trampoline. I got to practice my tumbling, which is going to help me out for cheerleading... There are a lot of little kids that come to the gym... They also give us free pizza every night.

Life should have been good and life would have been good if only Diego had been graded on that—graded on life for making friends and for acrobatics and contributing. If only someone had cared about the jubilance, the peacemaking, the struggle, the winning and winning *over*. Mr. Smith was an academic and still there were times when he wished that Diego could just be given an "A."

Of course it *mattered*, the isosceles triangle and all of the sum of its angles. Of course it mattered terribly, the reflections of a man on his youth in *A Separate Peace*. A man's reckoning with war and the object of his tainted memories— Diego, after all, was Phineas. But in the study of the character, they missed the character and the character was the thing. All the scholastics were the means to an end, and Diego had already achieved ends that some people never realized.

And then, like Diego, he couldn't allow the self-pity. "Diego, you have to try."

"I'm just not smart."

"That's not true. You're very bright and you don't apply yourself."

"I'm just not motivated." There was a truth. And therein lay the explanation.

It was a terribly rich irony for the commercial he'd made—kids against drunk driving. *Don't drink and drive. Don't drink at all. Sometimes bad things can happen.* Think before you drive. Think and you *will* drive. *Think* and you can have back your Mustang. He was in a commercial, with his car—he never drank—and still he couldn't drive. There was an enormous graciousness in Diego, even in failure; Diego was still always accountable. He'd been amply warned and he deserved the follow-through. Diego didn't blame his parents.

"They told me this would happen. They told me they'd take the car away. I didn't get my grades up anyway. I have no one here but myself to blame. I just don't know what to do about it."

There was so much more at stake. Diego didn't think that far ahead, but Jerry Smith did and it was punishing.

"Diego, you known you have so much potential. You just need to find some meaning. I don't want to see you back here, in summer school. And I don't want to see you flipping hamburgers."

I just don't know what I want to be.

Except that I want to *be* happy.

I'm always doing something for school or I'm working. This is what my schedule looks like. My week starts on Monday when I have to get up at 6:15 so I can make it to school by 6:50. I work out in the morning for cheerleading. Then I go to my classes for the day. I have all seven classes so I never get to leave school early. Monday after school I do not have cheerleading but instead I have rehearsal for the play. That goes on from 4 p.m. to 8 p.m. By the time I make it home I just have enough time to take a shower and do my homework...Friday is a long day. I do the same things I do during the week. But I have play practice after school. Every other Friday I have to go to a football game. When I do not have a game I go to work from 6 to 11. Then on Saturday I have to go to Rockdale Gymnastics 10 a.m. to 2 p.m. Then I go home and have to go back at night to work. I then get off around 11:30...Sunday I have to go to work with my dad. My dad cleans carpets and I go help him. I don't get back till 8 or 9. Then the week starts over again.

It was a demanding schedule, and his parents had considered a drop of one or two activities. They finally revoked the car because taking away the extra curricular activities would have been a life ultimately without oxygen.

Diego was petrified. Mr. Smith sensed that—Diego without pleasure in his life.

Kenneth and Diego sauntered into the gym. They were right on time and starving. Rockdale Gymnastics was a family-owned business, more than fifteen years old. It sat on Old Covington Highway, and it was an athlete's paradise—a rock climbing wall, dance and karate. It was the gymnastics apparatuses that hooked Diego—and then the kids and the pizza didn't hurt. Every Friday was Parents Night Out, and it was a glorious babysitting job. A free-for-all at the behest of the gymnastics coach, a man of so many faces. Joe Ashley had a way of catering to adults that still let the kids act like kids. Of all the dimensions Diego saw in his boss, Diego settled on Joe Cool.

"Diego! Diego! Show us some tumbling!" He was mobbed like a rock star when he arrived. From the corner of the gym came the shrillest voice in a body that never seemed to grow.

"Deee-ay-gooooo!!!!!" she screamed. Kenneth jumped out of his skin. No matter how many times he heard it. It was such a set of pipes for such a small girl.

"Listen, woman, you sound like a *siren!*" She gazed up at Diego with childish adoration. Diego was handsome and ripped and funny. Even the little ones swooned.

He pulled off his shirt and rolled his shoulders and wrestled a few of the boys. He spied a stability ball and belly-flopped on it, never minding its chuck. It threw him sideways and the children were in an uproar, copycatting his every move. There was one boy and he was better than Diego was at back handsprings and so Diego challenged him.

"Are you serious?" Kenneth asked him. "He's just a kid. Why are you competing with a kid?"

Diego could have given credit—said something brilliant about age and no boundaries, no limits. He grinned and then shrugged, that telling glint. *I don't like him being better than me.* He couldn't outdo him, but he came awfully close; the kid forcing Diego to his personal best. When he'd had enough, Diego wore his perspiration like glitter, something magical and showy.

They jumped on trampolines and ate more pizza and helped the children with tumbling. At least Kenneth and Josh tried; Diego just laughed when the kids went end over end.

How do you do that? He had no idea. Diego couldn't coach. He wore the perplexity of someone so gifted he didn't comprehend biomechanics. No one had ever said, "Arch your back" or "do a round off first." Gymnastics was just a sort of pick-up game—he had seen a jump ball and moved in.

The children went home in a genuine chorus of "see you next week" and "thanks." Little kids smiling, parents smiling, and Diego waving back.

"You work on that volume, girl," he said to the siren and she beamed and called back to him, loudly.

He shook his head and fell blissfully to the mat. "I can't *believe* we get paid for this."

In the quiet and the reverie came a golden moment: they had the gym all to themselves.

Let's climb to the rafters.

Of course, the rafters. The rafters were like a mountain in a way.

We climb to the rafters because they're there. Because they're smug and they deserve to be conquered. Kenneth eyed the height and he eyed their equipment and then it all took on a life of its own. They stacked up mats—every mat in the building for Josh because he had proven his usefulness.

We just throw Josh up and we come out smelling like a rose. Josh and our glorious heights. The mats were thin and the edges were flimsy but it was such an astounding night. Diego looked upward and whenever he did that, he almost seemed angelic, aspiring. *Go, Josh, go.* It was so unlike him, watching someone else's ascent. Josh reached the pinnacle and it *felt* like Mt. Everest, minus the sherpas and the depletion of oxygen.

Diego and Kenneth appeared to be smaller below, only shrunken because of his accomplishment. "Do something up there!" And the gym echoed the moment. *Do something for us...up...there...*

Over fifteen years of dust—it nearly gave Josh an attack—he slated them for time immortalized. *Diego...Kenneth...Josh.* He blew hard on his finger with each scrupulous swoop of a letter. The dust balls drifted like dandelion down, carried away on a mysterious current. He turned in his triumph; he smiled in his glory, and waved to the complete admiration.

It had the eerie foreboding of an avalanche, a split second feeling of uneasiness just before he grasped it.

The mats collapsed in a landslide, a fold that inverted somehow like an accordion. There was a scramble above and a scramble below, and mats swishing and fingernails scraping. Josh hung from a rafter and, objectively speaking, he was the superior gymnast of the three. He had more agility, more schooling and finesse in all of the stunts that he pulled. It was his saving grace because Diego began to laugh, out loud, just rolling in the predicament. Josh was a stunt puller and this was a doozey and Diego could hardly contain himself.

"Cut it out!! Stack the mats!!"

Diego tried, honestly. He ran in circles with a great deal of energy. He clutched at his stomach in the constant hilarity. *Josh dangling helplessly.*

It was at least a broken ankle. "Just give me half the mats!"

No, it was a broken hand.

Hold on, I can fix this. Let me find the scotch tape. I'll have you back in no time.

"Deee-ay-gooooo!" Josh sounded like the kid—the little girl with the siren.

Hold on a minute. I'm in the middle of something. I'm a little bit busy here. If you'll let me catch my breath, before I have to build the foothill…If you can, I'd encourage you to wait.

Diego was frantic—panicked and still laughing. Josh was suspended animation.

The mats were every which way—as all mats should have been—taking such a magnificent fall. Diego had to sort them and then he had to pile them. Josh looked on with intense interest. His arms began to throb in the unnatural strain, but he managed to hold on for virility's sake. When he dropped at last, he fell on a cushion of Diego's monumental making.

"C'mon, Josh. I'd never leave you hanging." *Not forever. You're all my best friends.*

Josh swiped at Diego, a kind of begrudging affection; the only manly admission of warmth.

They helped lock up the gym. It was nearly midnight, and it was the hour that made them seem giddy. Everything was funnier, everything was imbued with an extra measure of something. Kenneth couldn't get his arms around it, but it felt sort of brotherly—maybe that was the distinction. He had more in common with Diego than he knew, both of them from immigrant families. Kenneth's family was from Laos; Kenneth's father worked the night shift; Kenneth's mother took over in the daytime. They couldn't afford babysitters; they had struggled to get to

Conyers, just to stay in the middle class. The job had been a godsend—the job at the gym—and Kenneth had never confessed it. Diego and Kenneth had so many similarities but, mostly, they just weren't big whiners.

The three boys looked up once, before they dimmed the lights and they could see the markings in the rafter. It brought smiles to their faces, that unspoken tribute that overshadowed the smell of spent vitality.

We were here once and we did small things with great intensity of feeling. We were young and we were splendid boys and of this we testify, boldly here, suspended.

It would stay there forever; the dust was that thick—their own sort of makeshift memorial.

CHAPTER 4

"Come to breakfast!"

Diego was writing.

"Diego, come down here, *now!*"

Yesterday I got something that I have always wanted but should have asked my parents first. I got myself a puppy that is only 4 weeks old. I'm not sure what to name her yet.

"It's one-third lab, one-third Rottweiler, and one-third Australian shepherd."

Fabian had been both amused and intrigued. "Who told you that? You can't have genetics in thirds."

She is a small dog. At least she is a small dog right now, but it will grow up to be big…The only thing is that my parents are not very happy about me bringing a dog home. They said it is a lot of responsibility and said that I do not have enough time to care of it.

Which is true because I have a lot of things going on…I hope I can keep her, though.

"Diego!"

"Señora!"

He bounded to the kitchen and took his favorite seat. It was the sweet spot for the aromas, the idle chitchat, that feeling simply defined as home. It was on the kitchen counter that he confided nearly everything. *I got my first kiss after school.*

And how did you like it?

I liked it a lot, Mom.

That was the bond that they shared.

"He's special with Yolanda. I can't explain it. God did something incredible for her." Yolanda deserved such a blessing, to Jorge's way of thinking. Yolanda had earned the devotion.

"I asked Courtney out to the Homecoming dance."

"And she said 'yes,' I'm sure."

Diego ducked his head. He lost all brashness. "I was kind of nervous for a minute."

If someone were to come up to me and wanted to ask me right this second what is one thing that makes me happy…I would tell you this: the one thing that makes me happy would be when I'm with Courtney Hartford…Every time I see her it makes me happy and want to smile…I do not know what the future holds for Courtney and me, but I hope that it is something good.

He finished his breakfast, and he picked up Kenneth. Really, he didn't mind. Kenneth was apologetic, but he didn't explain himself. Kenneth couldn't afford a car.

The pair met later in the commons area of Salem High School and the buzz of the lunch crowd had escalated. Kenneth was a junior, a year younger than Diego, and news traveled fast in their circles.

"She thinks *I'm* cute?"

"That's what I heard." Diego grinned, ear to ear. "I'm telling you, my friend, you have to ask her out. She wants you to take her to the Homecoming dance."

"She's a senior, Diego. Are you absolutely sure? I mean, are you *absolutely* sure?"

"If you don't go over there, I'll do it myself. I swear to you, Kenneth. I will."

Kenneth licked his lips. He almost felt queasy. The seniors were camped on the tables. The underclassmen sat on the floor and few were privileged to approach their inner sanctum.

Diego read his mind. Diego was privileged. "I'll take you there if you'll do it."

Kenneth swallowed hard. Kenneth couldn't think, so Diego shoved him, hard.

He came face-to-face with the most mesmerizing set of eyes he'd ever seen before. She was a senior and she was beautiful and the sound of her laughter made him want to run for his life. The cacophony of noise from the commons dissipated; not everyone witnessed the drama. It just felt like they did—it just felt like complete silence as Kenneth stood in extreme awkwardness. The seniors at their tables, in their advantaged ranks, staring at him in bewilderment. It was sheer audacity and the young woman's face mirrored the discomfort that Kenneth felt.

It was a terrible mistake. So much so that Diego took one step backward, and then two.

I'm not with him. Don't ask me what he's doing. I barely know the guy. Diego edged away purposefully and there was nothing disloyal. It was all part of comic genius.

"Do you wanna go to the dance with me?" It came out rushed. It came out preposterous and childlike. The words ran together so that the sentence shrank and withered in front of the crowd. Kenneth was dying and the girl's face turned red and there was nowhere to stumble or hide. It was the longest pause, and then it was a movie—a really grotesque, nerdy movie.

"Yes," she said and Kenneth blinked twice.

Diego was nowhere to be found.

+≡⚊≡+

Diego sat forlornly on the kitchen counter, and there was no reasonable explanation, no excuse for his behavior. It would have been, could have been the best night of their lives and Diego had ruined everything.

It all went the opposite of what I expected...During dinner we did not talk at all. I had lost my voice a little because of the Homecoming game versus Heritage High School. We went to the dance and walked in one hour late...I saw a couple of friends across the commons area...I then walked back to the entrance and did not find my date. I looked for her for about 35 minutes and I could not find her. Having about an hour left in the dance I decided to go have some fun with my friends. Then something happened with a good friend of mine and my date found out and was very mad at me.

It was the edited version that he spared his school journal because Diego had kissed another girl. *Not in front of Courtney. That would have been mean.* "I really don't know why I did it, Mom.

"I'm not mad at Josh. He did the right thing. He told her because she deserved the truth."

Fabian had found Diego driving in circles, peeling out in his Mustang. It was disconcerting to see him so angry. *Kenneth, you have to do something.* It could be terribly annoying, but Diego was reliable. Diego was cheerful—happy. There had to be some things that always bounced back: the sun in the morning and Diego.

"Sometimes there are consequences for our actions. Dieguito, you hurt her feelings," Yolanda said. It wasn't a bad lesson for him to learn now, and yet it still pricked a mother's heart.

Diego was pining and penitent and raw. He jumped down from the counter and she held him. "Things might work out. She might forgive you. But trust is hard to redeem."

He found Jerry Smith when the ache was unbearable and then, too, the grades were still slipping. Diego had mood swings that no one else saw—except for the head of drama. There were certain expectations that he was compelled to fulfill. Diego was popular because he shimmered. Even when he was serious, few people took him seriously, and so he resorted to the theater—Mr. Smith was gifted that unusual glimpse because he allowed for the development of character.

Out of the hardship had come a plan and it was the last despondent talk Diego would ever have with his mentor. He didn't feel like sharing it, not just yet—but Diego had actually thought ahead. He did have a tendency to get caught up in the moment, but there was some secret brightness inside of him. He held it to him, this wish and this dream, and all he had to do was graduate from high school.

It was just a closing point, something positive to say. "I think I'll keep going to her church." Somewhere along the way, his family had become Seventh-day Adventists and then they'd stopped attending altogether. Jorge's business occupied so much time, but Diego had heard once that his father had gotten his feelings hurt. He didn't know the how and he didn't need the why—what he really wanted was the prayer.

Deep inside of him, alongside that new goal, Diego sought solace among Courtney's congregation.

Diego's first broken heart was mended by the rush—the culmination of his entire life's offering. To be a senior in high school with so much to wake up for was like a carousel ride. The outside world blurred and everything revolved around him in that gilded, fairytale swirl. There were ups and downs, but the platform was stationary. There was security amid all the bright colors.

He wasn't pleased with his first performance, but his cheerleading squad still took third. Diego's mother carried a video camera everywhere, and when George got the flu, she still filmed.

"Georgie, are you sure?"

"Yes, ma'am. I am."

George had thrown up all day.

"We can't miss his game, Mom." George took a wash rag, and he held it all through the game in case he hurled on the field.

Diego was compartmentalized. That's what it was. Kenneth understood it was more than competitiveness. Diego was a race horse with blinders on, running the track as he saw it. The intensity of his focus led him to do things that no one else would have even considered. They took fourth place at a competition, and it all happened at once because Diego so wanted to win.

They had tried to be gracious. Diego applauded. And then the first place team had gone crazy. They had dark blue uniforms, and they jumped up and down the way cheerleaders were prone to do. They were whipped into a frenzy. They were so elated, and Diego just had that urge. He joined their throng and he was clearly foreign, dancing in maroon and gold. He celebrated with them. *This is great. This is the honor I deserve.* And because he was reluctant for a good thing to end— because he liked second chances—Diego had entered the tumble off beforehand. Diego, the one-man show.

They were mini competitions, called jump offs or tumble offs, and they occurred during the tallying of scores. Each individual was allowed one pass— one attempt at a stunt. Josh and Diego paid the five-dollar entrance fee, and Kenneth groaned practicality. It was mortifying, really, to be so outclassed; some of the stunts were so far beyond them.

"I'm not going out there. I'm not looking like an idiot. Even you can't do an Arabian."

"I tried it a couple of times," Josh was undeterred. *Today just might be my day.*

Diego looked around and saw more skilled competitors bowing out of the contest.

"It's a *sign*, Diego."

"I don't think so. I think that makes more room for me."

"I can't watch this." Kenneth spotted Yolanda. His mother was going to immortalize it. His mother was filming it, for the record, and that was the added incentive.

Josh stutter-stepped. It was disastrous from the beginning. He over-rotated and landed out. Diego was next and it was destined to be worse. Diego had never even attempted it.

His first pass had been brilliant, overarching as he was able to with just one hand and then another. That had earned points. The crowd had loved that. He could have stopped while he was ahead.

He stutter-stepped twice and for a moment it appeared doable. For a moment, there was some finesse. An Arabian was a round off and then a back handspring, followed by a half turn and front tuck. *He was actually going to throw it. Diego was going to pull it off.* Diego misjudged his strength. He lost the easiness in his spring. He just tried too hard, and it propelled him too hard. Diego over-rotated, too.

"Oh," the crowd sympathized, all together, in unison. Diego clapped his hands, disappointed. He jumped up quickly with an "I can do better" swing in his dominant hand.

Diego positioned himself in the farthest corner. It was a serious breach of protocol. A competitor had only one chance to prove himself. The judges looked up in surprise.

"Wait, wait, wait!" He held up his hands. Perhaps the judges could have tackled him. Perhaps even that wouldn't have been an option—Diego had made up his mind.

He switched his lead hand and, for a moment, it was stunning and then he didn't stick the landing.

"Oh," the crowd moaned, together with Kenneth. The crowd was suddenly intrigued.

"Wait, wait, wait!" There was laughter in the stands. Someone yelled "stop" in mock agony.

"No, no, no," the same voice called out. The crowd joined in good-natured protest.

"Is he doing it *again?*"

"Oh, come *on*," Jorge laughed. "He can't be serious, Yoli."

No, no, no. But it was really too late. Diego could feel the crowd behind him.

He pulled all the stops, a catapulting round off that soared him into that magnificent back handspring. Diego was flying, which was only natural. Sometimes, he just swore he *could* fly. It was more momentum than the two previous stunts and he landed backward, on his hand.

"No!" the crowd was genuinely let down, and Diego halted in that most embarrassing position.

He looked at the mat and he looked at his hand and he looked at the crowd, so congenially deflated. He spun to face them; he stayed where he was, a mischievous smile on his face.

Diego improvised. Diego made do. Diego began to break dance, leading off with the offending hand.

The audience erupted into wild cheering. Kenneth and Josh doubled over. Diego rose and jogged off the mat with a carefree bounce. It was his rhythm in the chanting and the swell.

It was his conditioned response, his conditioned cordiality, his easy stride amid the adulation.

The Rincon family started plans for a house, a two-story house with dormer windows and five bedrooms. It had a formal dining room and a formal living room and a sprawling office on the second floor. There were three full bathrooms and a double-car garage—that was the part that mattered. Except that Diego and Fabian had huddled, and now they were one SUV short. They had each owned a vehicle, completely paid off, and they'd traded in the Ford Explorer. Their parents had been shy of the whole down payment, and they'd surprised them with the money for the house.

It was that kind of season, so much rebirth like springtime, as Diego took to the stage. He was going to be among the first cast to perform in Salem High School's new theater.

"You're all making history," Jerry Smith had extolled and Diego had absorbed the significance. *Let it be said, someday at this school, that I was the first, the original.*

Diego had been content to be part of an ensemble because he relished the fabric. Diego could take all the odds and ends and bind them up neatly in patchwork. Exquisite designs of all shapes and sizes—that was his inborn talent. But when Diego landed the part of Jimmy, it suddenly placed him at the coveted center.

The play is called "A Piece of My Heart." It is a very small cast in this play. There are only four males…It is about the lives of six normal girls that got pulled in the Vietnam war to be nurses. It talks about their lives in the war and everything they had to go through…Also how bad they were treated by the whole world. It is a very good play.

Diego took from the script what he believed—he only saw the bravery and the will. There were various shades of the era's climate, cast in gray on the pages. There was disillusionment, utter abandonment, hopelessness, and despair. Diego saw that which shined in his own heart, a sacred, smoldering ember. Diego did handsprings to entertain the cast in between the rehearsals. He resorted to the parking lot when the buses were full for a wider audience to appreciate him. He kept the intricacies of his character at bay for short bouts and fitful stretches. There just came a night when he sat on his bed and allowed the enormous impact.

Jimmy was the only main character in the play that died—and with such explicitness.

There was talk among the cast, among the female members, of taking the script to Washington, D.C.—of placing that portion of their souls at the foot of the Vietnam Veterans Memorial. It was a beautiful gesture, that somber reflection, etched into their beings. Some needed the tangibles, to try to touch the depth. Diego already felt the imprint. He identified with Jimmy—the embodiment of his destiny—and the heroic potential he owned. It wasn't the dying; it was the fighting that had taken the last drain of Jimmy's blood. Diego was nervous on opening night, but nerves were a sign of the preparation. It was because he had finally found a role that was worthy of all of his energy.

He gave it his heart and, more importantly, he gave Jimmy all of his dignity.

The play was never blocked to show the struggle, but to explore the internal strife. There was no blazing battle, just Jimmy wounded, the aftermath of the firefight. The nurse tried to comfort him, and there was the sound effect of his heartbeat, rapid and frightened and clinging. Diego was covered in blood and he was gasping and he had a mortal wound to his leg. The nurse tugged at his boot, and it was the most appalling moment: Jimmy's foot came off in the boot. The heartbeat flat lined and Diego rose to hover above his mortality.

Leslie Stewart had choreographed the light: it was dim and orange-red and then silhouetted. Diego became suspended between the earth and the sky. His figure was black and ramrod straight. There was an unprecedented discipline in his carriage—it was the fortitude, the erectness, the way he stood guard that took her breath away. There was the deafening roar of rotors in a jungle, bowing the grass to a benediction. And then the auditorium fell silent, deathly quiet. Diego against that burnished backdrop.

Diego, wounded. Diego, dead. Diego, laying down his life for his country.

With a clip so authentic Ms. Stewart found it haunting, Diego departed from the scene.

It touched him so deeply, wrenched him so profoundly, that Diego finally had to say it.

"I want to join the Army." They were outside Café Fonata. The cast was inside, celebrating their flawless performance.

That closely guarded secret, that brightness inside of him. He felt such enormous relief. All of the air expelled from Yolanda, and she gripped the steering wheel in shock and then in distress.

There was a voice inside of her. Someone was screaming. *No, no, no.* She was wailing. That was her head. Her voice came out panicked. "Why would you want such a thing?"

She waved at the parking lot, some abstract reference. The life they had finally built. "Diego you're loved here. You have friends. You have family. You have everything that you need."

I need to be heroic. I need something meaningful—when this part of my life is over.

Diego allowed her to process through it. Diego allowed the tears.

"Diego, you have absolutely no idea. The *Army.* You've been raised in a loving home. They'll yell at you. They'll swear at you. They'll grind you into the dust. Diego, that's not your heart."

"It *is* my heart, Mother." *It is my soul—my heroic potential here, beating.*

It was just the play and the uncertainty and, of course, the stage. Diego was passing through a stage.

"I'm asking you, then, to wait one year, Diego. That's all I'm saying right now."

Diego eyes fell on a massive hurt.

"Promise me that, Diego."

"I promise," he whispered. He lost his voice—the deepness, the resonance, the resilience. An excruciating strain passed between them, their first full wedge of disagreement.

It took several minutes for Yolanda to compose herself, crying softly in the parking lot, alone. Diego had always had that walk characterized by boundless energy, and it displayed some sudden stiffness.

The rhythm was crutched, the buoyancy was subdued. Diego's spirit was limping.

He never thumbed through the script again. He only clutched it to him once. *It was very sad and I hope I can put it all deep in my mind and remember it forever.* Major Michael Davis O'Donnell had been listed as Killed in Action in 1978. "If you are able," he'd written in Vietnam, "save for them a place inside of you and save one backward glance when you are leaving for the places they can no longer go.

"Be not ashamed to say you loved them, though you may or may not have always. Take what they have taught you with their dying and keep it with your own.

"And in that time when men decide and feel safe to call the war insane, take one moment to embrace those gentle heroes you left behind."

It was saved inside of him along with a sermon from the "Book of Revelations"—not fire and brimstone, but introspection. He sat in a pew in Courtney's church on Sunday, and it settled over him lightly. He wouldn't come like a thief in the night—to steal him away in the misconception of his youth. When Jesus came again it would be to redeem the world, to restore their final peace. It was the clergyman's concept of wars and rumors of wars that caught him slightly off balance. It sounded colossal and it wasn't colossal—not in his country, and not yet. Some shiver ran through him, some lucidity of thought, when the preacher presented one surety: whether the Savior came to earth in all of His glory, or they simply died first was less relevant.

Sooner or later, he said, Jesus came.

And one way or another, they'd meet Him.

CHAPTER 5

The devil arrived in America before Jesus did, on September 11, 2001. Jorge gaped and put trembling fingers to his lips, and then he buried his face in his hands. Up to that point his most devastating day had been the Oklahoma City bombing—it had looked so much like the DAS building in Colombia, an exact replica of the defacement. Diego paced the living room with the images of the assault causing an actual implosion in his brain. It seemed to him that something holy and sacred had been systematically divided and violated, a hideous parting of the raiment just before the crucifixion of the innocent. The decimation at Ground Zero was like Satan himself barging through heaven's gate—and though he knew that God would not, could not surrender, he felt the greatest despair of his life.

There was the vague sort of hurt that clouded children's eyes. It was in George's expression and it stung him. There was Tí Tí's untouched laughter—the full grip still on childhood—that put him over the edge. He shut the door on a room that had been soundproofed against the bang of the drum set. A phase he had gone through, like the time he had bought a puppy. *Like the Army*, his mother still thought. It was because he was older, because he was an adult that the children looked up to him for protection. He slid down the door, dissolved on the floor in racking, inconsolable sobs. He felt the powerlessness; he felt the betrayal; and more crushing than ever before, Diego felt the insignificance.

He was never going to be a doctor; his grades had brought him up short. He was never going to be a lawyer like Fabian; he didn't have the intellectual fire.

What Diego knew was that some men were born to be CEOs, and some were born to be small business owners like his father. Some men were born to climb the stairwells of highrises when all of the world around them was crumbling. He watched the three firemen hoist the American flag atop the rubble, in a stirring reminiscent of the thrust on Iwo Jima. Someday he might don the heroic uniform of a policeman, or a firefighter, or a rescue worker.

But, in 2001, Diego wanted more power than a reactionary rescue—Diego wanted the first strike at the borders that would never allow for another attack.

He was an immigrant and when he'd touched down on America, he'd offered it some sacred thing. That's what America was—even with all its imperfections— a melting pot of devotion. People still came to the United States after more than two centuries to dream and to build and to contribute. The devil couldn't do that and so he'd enlisted his legions to tear them all down in revolt. Well, the devil would care to step aside because in this one thing, Diego was right. To one end he'd been born and to one end his family had come, and God help the next terrorist who threatened it. He rose up in fury with such unusual clarity because it took such great hold: he was a warrior at heart and the time had come again when the world was in need of a warrior.

In some deep recess that he had never let slip, Diego needed the reciprocation of feeling in his adopted homeland. He sweat like an American, his heart and mind burned like an American, and he hoped she loved him as much. It had taken longer than his father had imagined to be accepted for citizenship. If Diego was willing to take up arms for his county, lay down his life for her—then perhaps he would win that final cleave of her affections; perhaps he'd be wholly hers.

On every United States military base, in every part of the world, the hair on the soldiers' necks was being raised like that of a snarling, cornered dog. There was a palpable readiness, that fearsome animal straining against a threadbare collar. They were chomping to be unleashed, and it was an awesome and a dreadful thing, seeing the men and women of the armed forces rise like an impenetrable wall around valor. Diego felt left out and he'd never felt left out and so he made a quickening resolve.

He'd promised his mother he'd wait one year, which meant he could leave in five months—less than half a year to put a life with meaning and all his natural instincts on hold.

He started to calmly descend the stairs, with an unusual measure of peace. He took them slowly, not with a pause but a deliberateness, and then he faced his parents abruptly. He took a deep breath, and he couldn't make eye contact with her, couldn't see the severe blow to his mother.

"I'm joining the Army."

Jorge's head snapped up, and his mother released an audible gasp.

"We'll talk about this later, Diego."

His son was undeterred. He steeled his jaw in one of the few defiant moments of his life.

"It's my country to defend, Papi."

That sweltering day at the Colombian airport and Diego's very first steps—the teetering baby ones into outstretched arms, and the joyful, uninhibited ones on American soil—it seemed that every hop, skip and jump hung thick and strangely poetic between father and son. They were wrenching words in the wake of the September 11 attacks, and momentous in the wake of the war.

He was still such a little boy, Jorge thought, studying him in earnest—a little boy with a sly, infectious grin and that newfound conviction in his voice. He had the bold, callused hands of a lifelong working man, and then the sensitivities of some kind of soulful preacher. A nineteen-year-old could only be so all-at-once innocent and idealistic if he'd had it both hard and good.

Diego was so grown up before his time because of the extremes.

"Vayase."

Go then, Jorge said quietly. America was his soul mate, and his son was right to protect her. His heart was right. "Join the Army," Diego's father gave his blessing again, and his mother turned her head.

There was a haunting, piercing pain in her breast, taking her breath away.

Jorge's business had been hit hard by terrorism, as if sanitation was suddenly a luxury. People had been too busy buying up duct tape and plastic to have their carpets cleaned. The woman who sold flags and the man who stocked gas masks had experienced a small windfall that year. It had felt like the rest of Atlanta horded its money and its little ones crawled on dirty floors. Jorge had been at a loss to understand it. It was like Sherman's Army had marched in again.

Fabian almost felt a prick of conscience as Diego left for the recruiting office in January. The show of loyalty had occurred to him, too, in the aftermath and Afghanistan. They'd watched the broadcast, the announcement of the first missile strikes of Operation Enduring Freedom. Children had begun dancing and musicians were singing in streets that had been void of music for so long.

It was the United States' freedom and humanity's freedom, and yet something held Fabian back.

"You check it out. Let me see how it goes." Diego had smiled in understanding. He would case the joint—case the Army the way he'd once scrutinized the elementary school.

With the exception of George and Stephanie, the Rincons were permanent residents, a distinction only surpassed by true citizenship. Only the citizens got to vote and Diego pressed the recruiter. Soldiers were, in fact, put on the fast track; in time, he could win that status, too. Diego was what was known as a green card soldier, and the green card had come just in time.

In some secret part of her, Yolanda had prayed that maybe the card would be denied. A backlog here, some bureaucracy there, and Diego's enlistment would be delayed. And then she saw the strain and the ache and the passion, and she lost heart on her wish for her son. She turned it over to God: *if he's meant to be a soldier, let the card be the sign.*

Diego bounded into the house with such elation that she felt that most unusual pain. The truth was he probably loved no one like her, not with the same protective ardor. That was the irony: it was *her* world, *her* home and *her* future that Diego sought to safeguard. She had taught him such faith and such will and devotion that it was she who had compelled him to service. She had instilled in him such conviction, such exactness in morality that Diego could never have wavered. He held up the green card, and she carried the camcorder to Fort Gillem as she'd carried it faithfully, all through those high school years.

Diego doing handsprings, Diego's win by takedown, Diego raising his arm, squared.

"I, Diego Fernando Rincon..."

I, Diego Fernando Rincon.

"Do solemnly swear..."

Do solemnly swear.

"That I will support and defend..."

That I will support and defend.

"The Constitution of the United States..."

The Constitution of the United States.

"Against all enemies..."

Against all enemies.

"Foreign and domestic..."

Foreign and domestic.

"That I will bear true faith..."

That I will bear true faith.

"And allegiance to the same..."

And allegiance to the same.

"And that I will obey the orders…"
And that I will obey the orders.
"Of the President of the United States…"
Of the President of the United States.
"And the orders of the officers…"
And the orders of the officers.
"Appointed over me…"
Appointed over me.
"According to the regulations…"
According to the regulations.
"And the Uniform Code…"
And the Uniform Code.
"Of Military Justice…"
Of Military Justice.
"So help me God…"
So…help…me…God.

Again it was Reagan who provided the parallel for Jorge—he saw shadows of his son in that first inaugural speech.

"Under one such marker at Arlington lies a young man—Martin Treptow—who left his job in a small town barber shop in 1917 to go to France with the famed Rainbow Division. There, on the western front, he was killed trying to carry a message between battalions under fire.

"We are told that on his body was found a diary. On the flyleaf under the heading, 'My Pledge,' he had written these words. 'America must win this war. Therefore, I will work, I will save, I will sacrifice, I will endure, I will fight cheerfully and do my utmost, as if the issue of the whole struggle depended on me alone.'"

Diego's eyes filled as he departed for boot camp—saying goodbye to the Mustang. He gave her a love tap, one last rev in the driveway and turned off the ignition for good. There were always casualties when times were tough: like the World War II rationing of sugar and silk stockings. Sports cars were like clean carpets, some bygone extravagance in a burn felt all the way to the coast.

We can't hear you, had come the restless call of one of those broken down workers in Manhattan—the firefighters, the emergency response teams, all the police officers gathered at the devastation of the Twin Towers.

"Well, I can hear you!" the President had cried back to him, to every American through a bull horn.

"And soon the whole world will hear you!" he had resolved.

Diego had experienced no small stir.

He jogged easily to his mother and gave her a final hug, as if the issue of the whole struggle depended on him. Some men felt it like that—like firefighters and police officers—that's what Yolanda thought as she waved goodbye.

A man heard the blare through something like a bull horn, and even felt it differently, too. It was all the difference between the protectors and the protected—all the difference between a stir and a shiver.

CHAPTER 6

If any of you have a history of respiratory problems—any respiratory problems at all, raise your hand. The drill sergeant's command was deliberate and delivered slowly so that there could be no misunderstanding.

This includes a history of bronchitis...asthma...pneumonia. Any respiratory problems at all...

The silence was awkward. Some of the men shifted. *Let's get on with this thing,* their feet seemed to intimate. Diego was the only one who seemed to be concerned. Diego stood very still.

The simulation of chemical exposure can be fatal if you have any of these respiratory conditions. You need to speak now...if you have had...any...respiratory...problems.

Three privates raised their hands at the word "fatal" and Diego inhaled sharply. He watched the young men with extreme interest as each of them was interrogated.

Did you indicate you had respiratory problems in your paperwork?

"No sir! I did not sir!"

It came in chorus, in triplicate. Diego winced slightly.

Well, that's just great. You're going home. You're going to be discharged from the Army.

Diego stopped breathing. Diego stopped shifting, a hollow feeling in his stomach.

It had occurred to him in the second week of basic training that friendliness and personal disclosure were not desired qualities for a new recruit. The darkness to which the men had first awakened at 0430 was so pervasive it had actually shrunk his thoughts. There was the shrill call to formation and the groggy coming to that had made Diego want to curl to the bottom of his bed—resort to unconsciousness—and then there was the prickling sensation of wonderment as he had tried to remember where he was. It had all been followed by a string of incomprehensible orders and screaming that had jerked him to an upright position and suddenly aroused all his sensitivities.

What in the name of all that is good and holy was I thinking when I joined the Army??

He had had such thoughts throughout the week, believing that if the men didn't die in combat someday, they were going to be bored to death. *The reception battalion at basic training is a nice little piece of Army love,* he had grimaced. They had endured any number of three-hour waits for paperwork and haircuts and extremely long needles—Fort Benning was meant to be elite, intense, and the only manly endurance it had seemed to produce initially was standing. The men had been like cattle, so lowly in the beginning week that the drill sergeants hadn't even summoned the energy to yell at them.

He had been anxious enough for action, and he had gotten it in the second week of all the manly inclines to which they would be subjected. The drill sergeants had suddenly grown hair on their chests and subwoofer tubes in their lungs. Their living quarters had been chaotic, men stumbling to brush their teeth, stumbling to relieve themselves, stumbling to get dressed and make their beds. Some of the men had slept on top of the sheets so as not to waste time—which was of the essence.

Time and volume had seemed to be life and death to a drill sergeant after the reception battalion.

Drop and do twenty!

Don't ignore me!

Drop and do twenty!

Don't eyeball me!!

Drop and do twenty!

You're out of the Army!!!

All of that dropping for nothing.

Diego's heart was in his throat, stuck in his throat, and he didn't budge. He had not run and awakened, dropped and awakened, and pushed so hard that puddles had formed at his feet from the sweat. He had not flexed arms that had the ache of immovable steel from shots that went clear to the bone. He had not come so far to get kicked out with the dishonor of something like sloppy paperwork.

Diego was not being discharged from the Army for a little thing like asthma, even if it killed him.

It struck him, halfway through the shock of the gas chamber—the "Devil's Playhouse" as it was and was not so affectionately referred to at Fort Benning—it struck him that the resolve and the obstinate thought and the devotion to his most cherished heart's desire might just kill him. It was like being a child again, arching his back and coughing blood and his eyes rolling back in his head all at once. He felt as if he hovered above his body. He was suffocating in a small apartment in Bogotá.

He had entered the chamber, secured the seal in the mask, then pulled the straps and resealed the mask in seven seconds. The privates had been lined up in the room for five minutes before they were commanded to break the seal. They had closed their eyes and held their breath for what seemed like a long ten seconds.

"Secure your masks! Reseal your masks!" the drill sergeant had barked. They'd obeyed.

It had been the same deliberate, slow talking drill sergeant and he had sounded far away, in a tunnel. The men had lined up in groups of three, waiting their turn to assemble in the center of the chamber. The first group of three had stepped forward and pulled their masks. They'd been asked a simple question. One man had gagged; another had answered quickly; it was an all-for-one, one-for-all kind of exercise.

The first man gagging had had more trouble, and then all three of them had struggled composure. No one had been able to leave until each of them had answered that simple question—Diego had felt his heart fall.

It had plummeted steadily, from his throat to his feet. And then his heart was in his big toe, dragging.

He removed his mask and immediately it seized him, thrashing him about like a rag doll. The burn was intense enough that men had been warned to remove their contact lenses: the vapor would melt them into their eyes and possibly even blind them. There was a peculiar pop in Diego's ears and maybe that's why he suddenly heard voices, distant. He had made friends easily enough at boot camp—what else could he have done but talk to his neighbor when he had been using a bathroom with no stalls?

I'm having an asthma attack. They had forgotten their duties and Diego had accompanied his wheezing friend to the hospital.

The Army physician had handed him a note: "Restricted from the Devil's Playhouse."

I'm having an attack!
You should have been restricted!

I'm having an attack!
Give me your social!
Let's get this thing over with!
Tell me your social, privates!!!

Diego couldn't focus. He was trying to focus with so many people screaming at him.

I sealed my mask in seven seconds. Did I take it off?? I'm not breathing!!

"What is your social??!!"

He tried sounding it out.

There is a six. It starts with a six.

Diego began crying—not the emotional discharge—but an uncontrollable weeping from his eyes. The release of the tear gas in the chamber made him suck and puff, and there was nothing but burning, the sting exploding in his lungs. *There's a six. There's a six.* His mouth was wide open, and no sound could be elicited from his throat. He started to gag. His nose felt like a hose, all the fluid bottled up, and then suddenly spurting downward. The more he tried to talk, the more he retched, and then, suddenly, there was another explosion. White smoke filled the chamber, and Diego could no longer see his hands or his feet or his mask. His comrades were invisible and he was drowning—a soupy, acid fog that pooled and devoured him whole.

He was dizzy and he stumbled, his mask dangling helplessly. There was no coherent thought, no reason. He had a tingly, sprinkling kind of feeling, as if not just his legs but his whole body had gone to sleep, numbed. Everything pixilated: the smoke, the mask, and his nose felt like someone had punched it.

He was losing his life; he was going to die. He thought first and last of his mother.

He tried to scream, but it was not possible. He was being strangled from within. He saw a light—a distant glow of light—and in his incomprehension came a sequence of numbers. He clawed at them, fingernails scraping on a chalkboard. *Had he clawed out loud, in the chamber?* The light grew brighter, broader with each second, and he staggered toward its escape.

There had been a video camera, near the entrance of the chamber; Diego had taken special note of it. The Army filmed, made highlight videos, and it was a personal challenge to him. A drama student, a brave young warrior—well, surely he would make the cuts. His arms and legs trembled. *Was he having convulsions?* He tried to stop drooling, stop shaking. Somehow he had passed and he stumbled forward and it was hard to see the camera through the waves of water. His nose was still running in the assault of sudden sunlight. He weaved forward, then side to side, willing his lungs to the outside air. There was no sound, except his gasping; his hearing was gone and then, too, his balance was failing him. He *felt* the camera. Without glancing sideways, he brought his head slowly up. It caught him in profile. He held up a thumb and wiped at the saliva, the vomit a mere hint at his pain. He was buying that video. He had said his number. *He had done it. He had done it. He had done it.*

It was the closest to death he had ever come, and he had stared it down with remarkable intensity. He had believed he could perform, but when all had nearly been lost, the muscles of his courage had flexed. He straightened a little and then again, each step coming easier outside the chamber.

He had done it for his mother, and he'd write her about it later—share with her that instinct, that contraction of valor.

Diego had not one, but two battle buddies, and each lay on either side of him. One slept on his back, his tonsils showing, the tension entirely drained from his face. Diego's body was coiled metallic, the rigidity of the Army still rousing him. He could sleep through anything, except motivation, which was based on very real need.

He had the zeal for it: even classes seemed easy when it was life or death in the equation. On top of that, he was good with his hands and the mechanical nature of his duties suited him. It wasn't mundane to disassemble his rifle under the pressure of time and battle. He closed his eyes and pictured his weapon with the reverence he would have paid to a muscle car.

Great men understood the attention to detail that was warranted by great machines.

Clear your rifle. Remove the sling. If dirt or corrosion are seen through the vent holes...

Remove the hand guards Push the takedown pin. Pivot the upper receiver from the lower receiver. Push the receiver pivot pin. Separate the upper and lower receivers. Pull back the charging handle. Remove the bolt and bolt carrier. Remove the charging handle. Remove the firing pin retaining pin. Put the bolt assembly in the locked position. Remove the firing pin. Remove the bolt cam pin. Turn the cam pin one-quarter turn and lift it out. Pull the bolt assembly from the bolt carrier.

If parts are dirty or damaged—remove the extractor pin. Careful, careful. Do not damage the tip of the firing pin.

Lift out the extractor and spring, but do not separate the spring from the extractor. Check the spring function by pressing on the extractor. Press in the buffer, depress the retainer, and release the buffer. Remove the buffer and action spring. Separate the buffer from the spring.

Cleaning the receiver was next and he used a bore brush, working through the flash suppressor. Lying on his back, it caused him to flinch slightly, running his fingers through the process. He envisioned the disassembly, the cleaning and inspection, the lubrication, and then the reassembly. There were so many intricate steps to M16 maintenance and he was increasingly consumed with his performance.

There was either *go* or *no-go* in the completion of each task, and the workings blurred in such time constraints. In the heat of combat and under pressure, a well-maintained M16 was a soldier's most vital appendage. It was Diego's right arm that would suppress the enemy and swallow ground with something like the horsepower of a Hemi.

Hey, Mom. Come here a second. Hold the extractor pin. Check out this rifle, people.

He wished they were there to give audience to the achievement and truly appreciate his experience. His mental exercises were contributing to his proficiency, making him better and faster each day. That was the impulse, the striving for excellence, that didn't allow him to fall asleep readily. There was a stream of consciousness telling and re-telling, a pattern he succumbed to each night no matter how exhausted he was. *Thirty seconds to completely disassemble it. One of the most elite rifles on earth.*

Did you see that, Dad? I'm improving a lot. It's all in the repetition.

Diego aimed to lead, to be the pacer—like stock car racing. It was all about setting the standard. He'd been placed in F Company 2-58 Infantry, and it seemed that was a pat on the back. *There are four different groups, Mom. Mine is the toughest. It's called the "House of Pain." I'm going to feel so proud when I finally graduate. It is going to feel like I have made an accomplishment.*

One of his battle buddies snored and interrupted his thought process. *What a sorry excuse of a gender. Women were pretty when they fell asleep.* For a moment, he just missed something as simple as the smell of perfume.

They're coming to film us—the "History Channel"—that's how prestigious we are. I repelled a fifty-foot wall today. I felt like I was in the FBI...

The four-mile run was so easy for me, Mom, but wow—what an experience—in that gas chamber...It went through my head, when they asked about the asthma, that this was the possibility of a lifetime...

I'll be able to apply for citizenship—once I get to my duty station. Maybe after that we can get citizenship for Mom, too...

Don't worry, Mom. I'm okay. At least we're all where we belong.

He had to mentally load and discharge his weapon, and then his brain could relax. For a few stolen seconds, he abandoned himself completely to the wave of homesickness in his heart. It made his eyes water like the Devil's Playhouse as he held a picture of George and Stephanie in his hand. He missed his mother's kitchen and it was more than the cooking, though the Army food left something to be desired. He arched his back suddenly with the groaning and rebellion of manhood taut in his tendons.

He was acting like a mama's boy—a Foxtrot warrior and that would not have gone over well.

It wasn't so shameful: he just wanted to sit lazily on the kitchen counter and allow for the appreciation of his day. He would take in the scent—the simmer on the stove and the smell of cookies baking in the oven. There would be the cleanness of sheets as they were washed in the laundry room; she would pour in some fabric softener. She would massage all the soreness from his shoulders and back, and she would ruffle his hair when she kissed him. She would listen to his stories, cluck sympathetically—those drill sergeants yelling at her baby…

She would smile gently and then laugh out loud, Tí Tí echoing her for no reason.

He reached for the image and then it was gone, leaving such stinging space.

That's what he missed at basic training: that contrast of softness that made him more masculine than ever. He had always told her everything, even the mischief, because her gaze was as persistent as truth serum. She would have scolded him a little for trying on the drill sergeant's hat while they waited for their commander in his office.

It had an acorn band. I looked like Smokey the Bear. I put my feet on his desk…

"What were you thinking, Diego??"

He smiled in the dark. *I was thinking it was pretty funny, actually…*

She would wear a stern look and then turn her head, before he caught the flicker of amusement.

It's hard for me, Mom—to constantly lay low. I'm having an identity crisis.

Over watch positions, tentative defensive positions, temporary fighting positions. He was nearly always prone with complete conformity. *The strain is killing me, Mom.*

I have to lay low and then I have to move quickly—because the Army is nothing like your kitchen. I have to pick a background with no silhouette, Mom. Nothing can expose my position.

He folded his arms behind his head and squeezed his eyes tight in his tangent. He was in a desert, was training his sights on an enemy about to make his rush.

In a case like that, he's a rapidly moving target, stealing from one concealed area to the next cover.

But there's a moment of decisiveness, that opportune time, when the enemy actually slows up. It's at the beginning of the rush, and at the end of the rush, when he pauses every so slightly in momentum. It's in that flash of a second when the enemy's most vulnerable to the rifle I have aimed at his chest...

Diego bolted upright, trying to censor himself. There were some things a mother shouldn't hear.

He was too keyed up. He rubbed at his temples. He felt real envy for his battle buddies. They were so contented in their apparent dream states, so surrendered to the fatigue. He was always overcome—this idea he had—that to graduate in Foxtrot was to reach a pinnacle. If, by his natural athleticism and God's good graces and practice and learning and more practice...

If he could just outperform, outdo and outshine—he was *going to be* the best of the best.

He was down to four hours, only four hours of sleep, before awakening to the next torturous day. He hugged it to him, like a soft down comforter, because he had the Army Code of Conduct memorized...

Article I: I am an American, fighting in the forces which guard my country and our way of life. I am prepared to give my life in their defense.

Article II: I will never surrender of my own free will. If in command, I will never surrender the members of my command while they still have the means to resist.

Article III: If I am captured, I will continue to resist by all means available. I will make every effort to escape and aid others to escape. I will accept neither parole nor special favors from the enemy.

Article IV: If I become a prisoner of war, I will keep faith with my fellow prisoners. I will give no information or take part in any action which might be harmful to my comrades. If I am senior, I will take command. If not, I will obey the lawful orders of those appointed over me and will back them up in every way.

Article V: When questioned, should I become a prisoner of war, I am required to give name, rank, service number, and date of birth. I will evade answering further questions to the utmost of my ability. I will make no oral or written statements disloyal to my country and its allies or harmful to their cause.

Article VI: I will never forget that I am an American, fighting for freedom, responsible for my actions, and dedicated to the principles which made my country free. I will trust in my God and in the United States of America.

"I will never forget that I am an American..."

That was the part that kept him going.

Mom, the Army wants me and needs me...it even expects me to act like a citizen. She loves me, Mom—my country loves me. The exhaustion came in overpowering waves.

His hand began to twitch slightly in the blackness. He finally succumbed to sleep. As hard as it was, there was some utter fulfillment that was only perforated once in a while by that longing. He began to dream and he was running in camouflage, from cover to cover, all the way home to his mother's kitchen.

Hamburger, pizza, pumpkin pie!
These are the foods that you live by!
Feel the fat running through your veins!
Your cholesterol's gone insane!

F
F
F is for Fatboy

A
A
A you'll eat anything

T
T
T is for Twinkie

B
B
B is for bring me more

O
O
O is for Oreo

Y
Y
Y are you a fatboy!!!

Diego felt the drumbeat, steady in his chest. He had legs and that fuel economy. Despite the cadence and the nonstop running, he had gained eighteen muscle-bound pounds.

He wanted seven more—he would *never* be a fatboy. His abdomen, for the Army record, was a washboard.

He had never shot a weapon before in his life, and he was still struggling to adjust to the kick. With scores like those he had earned in his practice runs, he was barely going to qualify at basic rifle marksmanship. His gait was controlled as he headed downrange, a five-mile run with all of his gear—*it was easy, so easy*—and that bothered him more. He needed that smoothness in the discharge of his weapon.

The qualifications had come on a Wednesday, and Diego had to aim extremely high. He had only shot 23/40 the previous day—one less at his next try, and he would have to re-start the program. He needed a 30/40 to be a *sharpshooter* and 36/40 to then achieve *expert*. The tension was palpable as he eyed a ground swell, casings littered throughout the rifle range. He slung his weapon and rolled his shoulders; he tried his hand at deep breathing.

His palms were sweaty and he licked his lips. He needed to relax, unwind. He needed a rhythm. He searched for a rhythm, and then he began to sing in his head. His shoulders dropped slightly; he succumbed to the beat. He had fired 150 rounds earlier. *It's going to be easy. It's going to be easy.* He put that slow, gentle rock in his head.

If he aimed for *expert*, he might achieve *expert*, but really it was all very relative. It was like telling himself he had a ten-mile run so that the first five miles were a breeze. He aimed for expert, so far beyond the mark—there was no room to do anything but qualify. *I'm the best of the best. I'm in Foxtrot Company.*

I'm an expert, he whistled low.

The M16 was noted for its accuracy. The weapons were slick and clean as whistles. Considering the maximum effective range, he sized up the targets and the terrain—it was razor sharp, everything visible, entreating and incredibly close. He zeroed his weapon, adjusting for elevation and windage. *The kick was going to feel so very natural.*

Diego suddenly shimmied and settled. He aimed to become worthy of his weapon...

Pop.

Reacquire the target.

Pop.

Get in the zone. Feel the fire.

Pop.

Pause.

Pop.

Pause.

The target threat came sporadically.
Pause.
Reacquire the target.
Pop.
Accurate, lethal, direct fire.
Pause.
Pop.
Pause.

It wasn't as if he could rock and roll. He just took it one trigger pull at a time.

The concentration flowed through his veins. It contracted like ice with every shot. He had only two rounds left. A pop and then a pop. His shoulder absorbed it, a very good pain. The cartridges yielded with near delicacy in their precision; they lay deflected and satisfied on the ground. For a moment, he relished the silence of his weapon—and then the relief gave way to euphoria.

He had shot 30 percent better than the day before: he had only missed the *expert* mark by one target.

He had done it. He had done it. Like a silver medal. He rose in the exultation. The next thing he knew the men were at attention as the commanders approached them, jerked on the right front pocket of their battle dress uniforms. They tugged hard and they pinned meticulously, an emblem of distinction that not every soldier earned. Diego's eyes averted once from the strict formation, and only then was the accomplishment visible. His lip still quivered slightly from leftover nervousness and no one but the cameraman saw the intensity in his eyes.

He had had a weakness and he'd overcome it—he had actually turned it into a strength.

"Hey Fabian," he wrote, *"F" stands for Fat Boy. Did my mom tell you that I shot 35/40?"*

I'm a sharpshooter now and I got a medal…I also got "first class" on grenades…

He threw his pen down with other results pending—he had been chosen to represent his platoon. Only three other men had been tapped for the honor. He trotted to the course, suddenly jubilant.

"You ready, Rincon?" There was a surge in the demand. He appeared too casual, too natural. *If he could succeed at the firing range…*

This is my thing, people. Just stand back and watch me haul.

"We're going to win. Don't worry about it." His voice had a lilt of renewal. He'd finally slept—what little the Army afforded. He was only just banking the coals.

He had shown improvement—significant improvement—from his first physical training test to his fourth. He had had thirteen weeks to drop his two-mile run by a minute, and he'd already dropped it by two. At the last PT, he had done fifty-eight push-ups, all of them legitimate. He had done sixty-two sit-ups, about one per second—it had been his warm-up for the event of the day.

He kicked at the dust with his dominant foot like a thoroughbred, high strung and raring. To an outsider it appeared like an "aw shucks" kind of motion, missing what reeled in his head. *Steady on the backstretch. Spare the overdrive or you'll never make it. Endurance, not speed, is the key.* He tuned out his buddies; the fire was rising. There was that unmistakable tingle of a good feeling.

The field had that spirit, like Sparta and Athens—the toil, the tradition, and the triumph. It was awash in great ghosts, the legends and contemporaries, who had cut their teeth on infantry soil. Omar Bradley, Dwight D. Eisenhower, George Marshall, Patton, and Colin Powell—they'd all come from Benning and they weren't crushing shadows anymore—they were like gloriously welcome shade. The World War I Armistice had yielded the acorn that had branched into that mighty, old oak. He felt the virility of Fort Benning's schooling, allowed its surge up his backbone in soothing expectation.

He took first to the sprawl of the monkey bars which complemented arms taut as iron. If fatigue ever set in, one was often prone to take a double-handed grip on the rungs. It was understandable, but entirely wrong—Diego knew how to work gravity. He swung, continuously, from his left hand to his right, his legs evading dead weight for momentum. He rocked his hips slightly which gave the illusion he could glide, even walk on air. One pole read "selfless," another "service". They mounted red, white, and blue, and then surpassed.

He reached the logs where crossing offered a reprieve, but he didn't yield to the temptation. It was easier to maintain the churn of his legs than it was to jumpstart his heart again. There was a low wall hurdle, an unnatural pause where his competitors' fingers strained for the top. "Honor" and "courage"—it was the most telling of obstacles—Diego had the bound of a deer.

He conquered its scale and a dozen others, some looming and some like pummel horses. He shimmied on his back under a maze of barbed wire and crab-crawled until his trapezius muscles screamed. His internal clock kept impeccable time. In his heartbeat, he *heard* himself beating the others. He cleared and bent and jogged and pushed, until he saw light at the end of the tunnel.

That's what it was, telltale sunlight, as he emerged in a slither through what resembled a culvert pipe.

The men could walk it—completion was enough—that last patch of dirt to the finish. Diego sighted the woods, the furthest objective, so that the end came as a pleasant surprise. He had the final plod of a marathon runner just before he bowed at the waist. He clutched his knees and exhaled hard: *rigorous training, strict discipline, efficient organization.*

He was all that Omar Bradley had envisioned a soldier to be and he straightened himself with great pride. *He had done it. He had done it.* For the second time, he had won the obstacle course.

He went on to place first at the next competition; the confidence course just more of the same. And then he came to the Eagle Tower—that great watchtower of enhanced performance, where athleticism and practicality met. He mounted the wooden ladder to the eagle's nest with his eyes fixed securely on the sky. It was a startling blue, the sun was intense, and his leg muscles worked without slack. There were horizontal hardships strung end to end, to be crossed and vanquished in suspension. They were all made of rope, like a high-wire act, dancing against the brilliant beyond. There were safety nets below that lay like checkerboards, crisscrossing the red Georgia clay. He would never fall to the net and be trapped in that spider web of failure and shame.

The point was balance—all those hours of trying to stand on his hands at the gym. The first rope suspension was easy, just an aerial walkway, and then he took on the middle suspension. He stayed horizontal, but that wasn't the hard part on a single rope that stretched from one platform to the other. He had to stay on top of it, slip like a snake across its upper edge.

Don't look down, Rincon. His left leg remained straight, using the rope like a guide wire. The other was curled, an eye hook closure, his right foot securing the hold. Hand over hand, just like the monkey bars. *Stretch and reach and pull.* It wasn't so bad, looking straight ahead, closing the gap like a zipper.

His concentration was extreme and hard, but he had that optimal kinesthetic awareness. He sensed the sweep, the sheer agility, moving across the third suspension. A member of his platoon was sliding, effortlessly, across a rope ladder, inverted sideways. Diego pulled harder, kicked his speed up a notch, to make it more quickly to the opposite platform. The men were swimming in opposite directions as he heaved himself onto the stability. He cranked his head to see the young man's technique—it was the economy of movement that intrigued him.

There were footholds and handholds and a myriad of methods, but his comrade's was the surest and swiftest. Some were using a crossover method, literally pulling themselves across the expanse. The legs were precariously placed in that instance, narrowing the body to the rope. It shifted the weight to a tenuous posture instead of lowering the center of gravity. One man was using his legs like a brace, putting his hands in a position of catch-up. It was effective and secure, but it overworked the arms—he was practically dragging himself horizontally.

No, the grace and the speed were in a mechanized flow of medium-sized steps and grasps. The young man's body was never overextended, nor did he shortchange his motion. When his feet were spread on the lower rope, his hands conjoined on the upper; when his feet were together, his hands were spread and he kept his knees slightly bent. He absorbed the spring inherent in the rope with a steady resistance that was parallel and equal. He looked the part of a water bug, skittering across some suspended pond.

"All right. Let's go!" It was Diego's turn, and he was inheriting the pattern of the gods.

He could hear the commander. *Keep it moving!*

"You're doing a good job right there!"

His heart took flight—to get a compliment when, in fact, he was showing off. He eyed the final descent. It was just an entanglement: a mesh of squared-off trappings. Diego observed another man and again it became very clear.

Put your hands like this. His battle buddy nodded and jumped ahead, a vertical grasp on the netting. *To do it any other way caused too much give in the wrist.* His buddy descended with ease.

Diego followed with the fluidity of air, a luxurious, unbroken line. He fell backward to the mat in utter triumph, just as he neared the bottom. It felt as soft as a featherbed and, for a heartbeat, he let himself revel in it.

It was happy disbelief, the quiet realization that he was in a physical class all by himself.

It was because Diego had been in a stage of development—in his mother's womb when Reagan had graced Colombia. It had given him that imprint, that special brand of optimism that had forever shaped his perspective. He had immigrated in the late 1980s, when everything seemed possible and promising and indomitable. Once idealism like that took root in a soul, it could never be fully extinguished.

There might be doubts, there might be more terror, and there might even be long, lasting wars. In a heart like Diego's, they were only measurements—the obstacles to be met and hurdled. They were coming to the rescue; Diego to the rescue. The United States military would never allow permanent defeat.

To be an integral part of such a fighting force—to be needed and even to excel—they were proving his commitment, and he was answering the call with resounding, victorious mettle. For time immemorial, there would be this one pause: his before and after "the service." All of his life had been a dress rehearsal, compelling him to this one opening night.

It wasn't the pre-dawn hour or the exertion: Diego was accustomed to both. It was nerves by the time he approached the culmination of all he had learned and perfected. A week's worth in the woods—the field training exercise—it was like the World Series going all seven games. Every drill and skill, every mold of his character, was about to come into play.

There was an audience of commanders, but that pressure was less than the critic of self-evaluation. The air was pitch black, and its only discernible edges were distinguished by the thick competition. Diego felt a rush and his body protested, pounding him with profound fatigue. He wanted to hurl through the first formation, preparing to set out for the field.

And then suddenly he awakened—it was that prickle of a good feeling—it was *this*, his moment to shine.

He had never been so in tune with his body; had never felt his mind sharper or keener. His sense of purpose was pinpointed and pierced, like the stars, ever constant and aligned. He took his seat, awaiting the transport, and his face wore that readiness. They arrived at the range at 0725 and were lined up with orders to run.

Each man had his gear and Diego was in back, his weight totaling 235 pounds. The added bulk came in a rifle and two pairs of boots, with multiple socks and various shirts. He wore his standard uniform—the BDU—his wet weather gear, a hygiene kit, a K-Pod. The list went on, some men fell behind, and Diego was slowed in his plod at the rear.

It was just a small incident, the kind of thing that could have happened any day at Fort Benning. It was just a story that had originated at Fort Bragg that helped to keep things in perspective. As competitive as Diego was, he needed some reminders to help him stay focused on teamwork. It was the mark of true leadership, the kind of solidarity that forged the anchor of their resolve.

A reserve officer in his mid-thirties had been recently activated for the global war on terror. Like many others, he had left children and an expectant wife at home. He had been a U.S. citizen, of Middle Eastern descent, who had been raised in both the U.S. and the Islamic world. His language skills had been critical, and he'd been called on to interrogate first in Afghanistan.

He had been needed overseas, for his cultural understanding, for his savvy and for covert operations. He had been given the option to stay and fight in Iraq, or to go to airborne school at Fort Benning. Fifteen months of missions had left him severely weakened, and he had had only five weeks to get in shape for the school. The training had been brutal for a man of his age, on top of the past fifteen months. He had had just one trial left—a five-mile run and one knee was shredded from service. The platoon had begun to run at a record pace, and the officer had fought not to scratch.

They'd passed the three-mile marker on an oval track, and he had felt good about his performance. He had trained for that distance, and it had not been until the fourth mile that he had begun to feel the buckle. He hadn't been sure he could make it all five miles, given the pace of the platoon. After the fourth mile, the platoon had veered onto a path away from the main course.

There had been no way to tell how much farther they had to run once they were off the track. He had felt the awful foreshadow of collapse in the deflation of his lungs. He had struggled for breath, and then he had slowed. He had felt his own failure imminent. All of that work and he would have had to re-start the training, or maybe simply give up. At that very moment, he had felt a push, a forceful hand propelling him to take the next step. It was a nineteen-year-old private who had slowed his own pace to make certain the officer finished.

No sir, he had willed him. *You will not quit, sir.* He had continually laid a hand at his back.

At every lapse and every cave, the private had pressed him to the finish line. It hadn't been orders—it had been that priceless brotherhood that won on the battlefront. Reminiscent of the young private who had pushed at Fort Bragg, Diego was leaving no man behind.

No sir. He was steady. Diego encouraged. Diego remained at the back.

It was 0945 when the Alpha team reassembled, and took the prone, unsupported position. Diego was breathless, sweating profusely, and dehydrated as he shouldered his rifle. He had eaten two crackers, a little bit of cheese that had dissolved in a mixing bowl kind of feeling. His hands were shaking, his vision was distorted; the exhaustion was pummeling his brain. He filled the rifle's chamber and, in the fog and the ache, he underestimated the flow of the oil. There was a kick and then a puff as white acid smoke began to persecute his nose and his eyes. He blinked and pushed through it, coughed bitterly, and pushed through it, another benchmark of forty rounds. *Not bad under pressure.* He was forged into a battle squad—and this time he got to lead.

By 1022, the men were heaving. Diego's stomach felt like an ironing board. It was wet from the steam and flattened by the heat, hard and contracted as metal. A teammate staggered; his face was pale green, perspiration running in torrents down his neck. His voiced sounded swollen, unnaturally thick like he was trying to talk through cotton balls. He looked like the Hunchback of Notre Dame, swaying grotesquely in his labored descent. They were headed downrange, their first mock battle, and Diego tried to uphold him.

"I'm gonna get killed." The color had drained; there was nothing highlighting expression. To be shot in mock battle was to be dragged like a corpse, let someone assume all the equipment. They were going head-to-head with formidable drill sergeants—like a high school team against pros. The sense of urgency was acutely real and then, too, it was a matter of pride.

"Give me your load." Diego stopped him, took on an additional seventy-five pounds. His quadriceps jolted, seared in the pain so that he uttered an audible groan. There was that fleeting thought—*it might be a luxury to get shot and let them take the load.* There were no Abrams tanks, no combat engineers to clear any ground swells of treachery. It all came down to a nimble assault, and Diego was handicapped in mass. His thighs quaked violently; his ankles writhed.

Let's go men! You can dig deeper!

He was excessively weakened as he lumbered forward, about 300 more meters to the conflict. They reached the battlefield, and his comrade lurched forward to reassume his load. The private's face was red from the overexertion, the random blotches of fair skin.

At least he had color...

Let's go! Let's go! From the wood line came a ghastly splinter.

There was a telltale burst, and the men ducked for cover, answering the retort from the ground. Their low crawl was slow, impeded by the burden, which was just the way the drill sergeants liked it. The men were as green as the underbrush, as encumbered and dense as the forest. *They were ripe for the picking.* A team member fell. He was dragged, sure enough, like a corpse.

I'm not going to die! Diego lunged forward, entered the danger zone. He took a hot rush from clearing to clearing, the concussions hammering at his feet. It was the surge of adrenaline—he rolled to his non-firing side as if he was taking home base. And then the twist of the gear clipped his great wings, and he lay at unnatural angles. He scissored his legs, back to prone, the looming threat at ten o'clock. *Fire! Fire!* The weapon erupted with a great deal of pleasure.

The battle ended swiftly, after only fifteen minutes. He wasn't exactly the last man standing. He was crouched offensively, but still alive, and apparently that counted for something. He made a sober review of the carnal damage: over half of the men were dead or wounded. The drill sergeants were calm—strangely calm—for a company in such dire need of improvement.

The pale-faced comrade, whose gear he had carried, had survived it and that brought Diego comfort. Otherwise, they'd been annihilated, completely overrun, and the air just felt sticky and dismal. In a real life scenario, outside evaluation, it would have mattered more and then less. To have remained alive—well, that would have been everything—until placed in the context of their defeat.

Half of his buddies would have been dead, and the bloodbath might have forced a retreat. When the men ate, it was silently—crackers and peanut butter that stuck dry and choked in Diego's throat.

At 1330 they secured the jungle, and Diego pulled security on the perimeter. It was back to the tedium, the mind-numbing boredom that played at the fringes of his discipline. He became engrossed with a fire ant, oblivious to the muzzle it crawled. He picked up two twigs and coaxed it to the straight one, flicking the tip with his finger.

"Hey, little buddy, go round and round." He twirled the stick in sheer idleness. The ant ran faster—and faster and faster—trying to keep pace with the treadmill. Diego kept a journal, and he wrote in his journal: *playing with a red ant.*

Not anymore, it died, he conceded. Must have been the hyperventilation.

He took the second twig and dug at the dirt, seeking another distraction. He was caught in the meltdown of sheer fatigue and the afternoon sun that weighted it. Anything would have done—anything at all—so long as it had propped up the eyelids. He ached for spontaneity, that eternal fix that had so often bridged his weakest moments.

To suddenly jump up and yell, "Snowball fight!" It was the extravagance of life as a civilian. There was no snow, not in Georgia, and certainly not in May, but he liked the overall sound of it.

Snowball fight! They were powdering each other and feeling the chill down their backs. It was a total free-for-all, where improvisation reigned, where the sport—*the sport*—was the thing. They stood out like sore thumbs, the dark green camouflage obvious and stark against the white. He was leaping unexpectedly, vaulted, suspended, and then landing pillow soft in its embrace.

A snow angel! They were laughing. Just like Tí Tí had in their first and last snowstorm in Conyers. It was that touch of the whimsical, the impulsive grace, in the middle of being pummeled in battle.

No more snowballs. Angels for everyone. My mom will make us snow ice cream…

He stared at the twigs, dead and brown, and that's when the whole thing occurred to him.

One stick was straight and the other was bent—not terribly bent—but imperfect. They had been set alongside the most formidable foe, the drill sergeants, the straightest of sticks. It was a kind of clairvoyance that filtered through the clusters, the sunlight speckled on the leaves. They had been annihilated, completely overrun, but there would never be a more imposing measurement. They had clashed with nothing like a ragtag army and Diego seized the idea whole. It was the degree of difficulty that swelled in his chest. *I just fought against the best.*

He rolled to his right, squirmed in the abruptness of all that illuminated his thoughts. It was that largeness of spirit that made his next movements uncharacteristically jerky and comical. It had aerial rootlets, a three-leaflet pattern, and a coarse-toothed clench on his uniform.

It had kept him company for forty-five minutes, and Diego could only laugh with his buddies. He spat in rebellion and saw his spittle like dew, contemptuous, on the poison ivy.

His drill sergeant was right: they'd done more by noon than most people did all day.

CHAPTER 7

"Hooah," Diego exhaled quietly, surveying the weapons cache. He had been told it was a quarter of a million dollars of firepower that had just been turned over to his watch. He took mental inventory of dozens of M16s, the grenade launchers and M240 machine guns. Four M249 Squad Automatic Weapons stood at attention, smug in their long-tailed stocks. It was the M249 SAW that elicited such reverence, such yearning as Diego ran his hand over the barrel. It was one of the mothers of all weapons in infantry squad support, that stream of suppressive fire. It was the scarcity of the M249 SAW that made it all the more coveted—Diego had to be the master of that machine gun.

The platoon had established its virtual patrol base and Diego had pulled security for an hour, every other hour. He'd been awakened at midnight, at 0200 and at 0400, and then the whole camp had arisen at 0430. He had made his bed by covering his foxhole; he'd shaved and dusted himself off. He was rounding off the minutes to the next piece of action: the platoon was gearing up for their first RECON.

Diego had learned that reconnaissance missions had one key ingredient: stealth. The mechanics were textbook at the outset of the mission, but decisions were soon made on the fly. The point was to fight only when necessary as combat might hinder the objectives. They were to gather information in one of three categories—enemy troops, a terrain feature, or a locality. The commanders were given the ultimate latitude, as much as the mission would allow. It was their duty to assess, to both gather intelligence and to evaluate the performance of their men.

The metallic rap of enemy fire assaulted them almost immediately. The terrain was a longsuffering plane of corrosion with severe patches of undergrowth and some long trench, like a gully. Diego cradled his rifle in his arms and took a high crawl through the concealment. His feet were swollen, the color of red plums and they balked at his slide past the undergrowth. The drill sergeants shot blanks from the M249 SAWs, and the impression was gut wrenchingly real. Diego rolled to the right, fired a three-round burst. There were flashes from the M16's discharge. He rolled to the right again to evade the exposure and began a new rush to that gully. The drill sergeants were baiting them—there was high visibility—and Diego saw the retort from ten o'clock.

Fire. There was the high-pitched puncture from his aim on the embankment of the gully. One man was down. Diego had killed him. He was 200 meters from the enemy's position. He felt a kind of jolt—the sudden sizzle of energy that taunted his trigger finger. A team member motioned to him. *They had revealed their location.* They had to get out of the gully.

The men backtracked slightly—that would be unexpected—not to take the unobstructed path in a sprint. There was a slight depression and the men ascended, so flat they were chewing at the dust. They sidled alongside a fallen tree, then rushed in spurts in a great arc. From the density of the forest, they saw their man, furtively creeping to protection.

Diego's heart exploded in the sudden swell.

They took their first prisoner of war.

The dead man was walking when the mission was over: Diego's casualty approached him, pleased. He didn't say much—just gave him forty rounds instead of the usual twenty. Diego had been entrusted and he turned to his battle buddy. "Here. Take an extra ten."

See, I'm a team player, he wrote in his journal. And then RECON began again.

Lunchtime followed, and a lot could be told about a man's character each time he was allowed to eat. At 1208 the hunger was shocking, every nerve, every tissue crying out for food. There was chicken and rice, pound cake and peaches, and Diego's salivary glands contracted at the smell. Some men had started eating, but they'd received no orders. Diego clasped his hands in near prayer.

Maybe it was a test, and maybe it wasn't, but Diego sat dutifully for five minutes. The desire was so strong that when the orders came, he could hardly take time to chew. It was the best MRE he'd had in his life—it was the fresh air that made him ravenous. No one spoke, except one team member, who suddenly talked to his Jell-O.

It was the sleep deprivation that spawned the mumbling. In two days, they'd slept less than three hours. The men were cooking in the excessive oven of dehydration and stress and exhaustion, too.

"Is it just me, or is it 100 degrees Celsius?" There was an immediate swell of agreement.

"Yeah man, it's hot." They all jumped in. No one liked the idea of cracking up.

Diego dug his foxhole at 2030; it was so much harder once the sun had set. The commanders dropped by with an eighty-pound rucksack to go with their Night Observation Detection System. He had slept for exactly twenty-two minutes when he was aroused to take up his load. They were going on an experimental walk through the woods, with the NODS and the added eighty pounds.

Diego trudged bleary-eyed. *This is important.* He considered slapping himself silly. He didn't have to. They entered a twilight zone that took his breath away.

The scopes made the view lucid. The world was greenish, except for the ghosted white grass and leaves. Diego stayed with his battle buddy through the forest—the first ten meters were crawling with life. He had never seen a kaleidoscope as rich or as eerie and in his awe was a renewal of resolve.

He could have the NODS and he could have the M249 SAW. *Imagine packing that vision and heat.*

A few men tripped in the unseen and the immeasurable—their depth perception stolen. One man apologized, his civilian manners sounding stilted amid the deep concentration. Diego proceeded cautiously, as smooth as a mountain lion, on the prowl for some long lasting enemy: it was only inexperience that made him mortal and, with time, he would hunt that down, too.

He slept fifteen minutes, was awakened for guard duty, and rose with the weariness of the dying. His lungs seemed minute, so shrunken and compacted his heart felt dislodged from his chest. He imagined it pounding, the size of a ping pong ball, outside the walled-off cavity of his ribs. His head rolled back, as if the stretch could somehow pull the rip cord of inflation to his brain. He was on duty for two hours—no one relieved him—the extreme agitation kept him alert.

At 0300 he stumbled back to his foxhole and saw that the source of the negligence was unstirred. It was the worn out team member who had mumbled to his Jell-O, and Diego felt his anger go slack.

To be a good soldier was to sometimes shoulder the weakness as valiantly as one led the charge.

He surrendered consciousness the moment he settled, to such fatigue the earth felt like goose down. His arms were so weary they draped at odd angles, and his expression loosened to a downturn. That was the sap of the energy in the field—

even his face lost vitality. There was a telltale twitch and then his arms flailed wildly. The ground heaved itself inside out.

It was 0319 as he grabbed at his rifle, taking his temporary fighting position. His eyes were filmed, but it seemed they were ambushed; the rounds were coming right at him. The drill sergeants cleared the high brush in a hot pursuit—Diego riddled the road. He sighted two sergeants in his direct line of fire and his M16 made a blood curdling scream. An M240 splintered the enemy in a stream of combustion at the same time it lapped at Diego. The shells discharged, stinging, and then it was over—the enemy in an all-out retreat.

The men were stunned silent, and then came a sole utterance in the dust. "I think they were trying to kill us."

He lay down in a stupor, his heart still racing. It was 0335 when he drifted off to sleep.

At 0400, he was rudely awakened—it was time to start a new day.

They were ambushed again, on their way to supposed church services, and ambushed as they attempted to eat. They were ambushed at noon, somewhere around nightfall, and then sunrise—the pattern was infuriatingly random.

"Camo up!" It was mid-morning and the men obliged, preparing for the dense forest coverage. Camouflage might have been an art to more dexterous fingers— all the shading and highlights that transformed human flesh into a chameleon. Diego shined his battle buddy, using the loam, working from the forehead to the chin. He polished the cheekbones and the prominence of his nose, then picked up a light green stick.

"Don't smile, man." His buddy did just that, his teeth suddenly gleaming from the mask.

"Looks to me like you'd be the one with the problem. You smile, Rincon—it's all gums."

The men were nervous, not terribly talkative, keeping their weapons nearby. The succession of ambushes had frayed their nerves, like a never ending concussion of depth charges. They were trapped and committed—it might have been training—but the hostility from the drill sergeants felt real. Diego was impatient as his face took on color, a jungle cat picking up scent.

Nothing happened, and that heightened the apprehension—not to have the release of the stress.

They had orders for a bunker at 1015. The M16s commanded their forces. There was the roll of their thunder, the screaming bleed of their entrails, as

Diego's team powered them out. Diego got to call for a right flank and then the bunker was theirs.

All right, men, good job! Let's go!

They were moving out to another set of woods, another set of foxholes to dig.

The sun was white hot and the sweat was glistening on their foreheads in a sickly, unnatural glow. They looked like scarecrows, their eyes bloodshot bulges in complexions battered by the elements. Diego leaned on his shovel, his arms leaden, and that was what triggered the fury. The drill sergeants were trying to train them in music appreciation—all the compositions and instruments of war. There were the symphonies of dissonance, the harmonies, the percussion of classical, orchestrated battle. The M16 had the tat of a snare drum and the M249 SAW was, comparatively speaking, a rich, deep baritone. Some rhythms were sporadic and indirect, and others resonated right to the core. They should eventually have the skill set to distinguish even the armor—to play by ear all the wheels and the tracks. The only lost meter was sometimes the distinction of the aggressor, the fire of friend or foe.

The men sailed for cover from the M16s, priming their own rifles in defense. They tuned their instruments to the pitch of the enemy, the frenzied *Flight of the Bumblebee*. There was a stiff crescendo, and then the awful awkwardness of some performer missing his cue. Diego's rifle was hopelessly jammed, and the others soon followed suit. They had spent their ammunition, and their weapons fell mournful, the hollowed-out chamber music of taps.

Diego's team seized the power machine gun, the M240, and they unleashed its bass on the drill sergeants. It roared like a cannon in patriotic overture, so gallant and fruitful and dominating. He expected a medal—that was the supremacy that had suddenly encouraged the swell. Their ingenuity, their dogged stand sang with the empowerment of an ovation.

The skirmish ended; the men lay dazed, but smug and victorious in their triumph. For a moment, they heard Spanish—it *had* to be Spanish—the fluidity of a passionate tongue.

There was a new vocabulary, so near to an art form; Diego had never heard anything like it. Profanity was the brushstroke of their military canvas, so all-encompassing, so broad in its color. In this new third language, swear words were qualifiers, adjectives, adverbs and pronouns. They could be subject and verb, preposition or dangling participle—that was the Renaissance of the militant.

All those rules he'd learned in English grammar, and there you had the irony of the Army—the drill sergeants spoke *something* like Spanish. It was a free flow, a string, just about any old word where they wanted it.

$#%#@&!...
What were you thinking...
$#%#@&!...
What in...
$#%#@&!...
Were you thinking...
$#%#@&!...
Were you thinking???!!!

Diego was speechless. The Catholics crossed themselves, more than one "Hail Mary" in double time.

Apparently they hadn't been thinking—not thinking at all—when they'd suddenly let loose with the M240. The ambushing forces now had intelligence—significant, life altering intel.

Because...
$#%#@&!...
...of...
$#%#@&!...
...that...
$#%#@&!...
...weapon...
$#%#@&*!...*$#%#@&!...
...the enemy knows...
$#%#@&!...
...you...have...
$#%#@&!...
...a...whole...
$#%#@&!...
...platoon!!!!!

And when the enemy knew there was an entire platoon, there was going to be **$#%#@&*!* to pay.

The men covered their foxholes, nearly two hours of work, and they were forced to retrench again in punishment. At 1815 they were secure in their berms when one man decided to stand. Maybe he experienced a spasm. Maybe he was just stupid. The men used one of their new words. It was a miserable punishment they had to complete in less than two minutes, and the misery increased when they failed.

They had carried the man's squad 100 meters, and they had exceeded the limit by nine seconds. *You'll do it again!!!!* The drill sergeant had seethed, adding five more men to their payload.

In the thinly veiled blanket that came with twilight, Diego looked over each of his team members. He was a trainee team leader, and it was a mixture of sympathy and frazzled consternation that he used to nudge them awake. "Hey, no sleeping on guard," he sounded terse, but his own eyelids objected to the weight.

He fell asleep, standing up, which earned him another good workout.

He crawled to his berm at 2200, truly wishing to die. The crickets hummed softly, like a bedtime story as he drooled; his mouth went slack and feeble. At 2217, the acoustics rocked. The maestro had raised his baton. They were ambushed again, and Diego's heart groaned, fumbling for more ammunition.

At 2230 a new threat appeared—two drill sergeants had jumped out from the wood line. That was what snapped them, every ounce of reserve—the men began to shoot for the sake of shooting.

It was midnight and obscure, the thick trails of moonlight cloaked in the cloud cover of pending summer. Diego's eyes scanned in quick, short bursts, the irregularity of contracted figure eights. It was a cat and mouse game and Diego felt the edge, all of his good humor shredded.

He was the hunted, the mouse, the *rodent*, the lowliest of creatures in the forest.

He was stationed by a log—a massive log—when he heard the snap of a twig. There was a rustle of leaves, incoming motion, and he steeled his jaw in sheer madness. *How many were there? What were their weapons? How could they have gotten that close?*

One team member motioned and Diego nodded, taking a low crawl through the cover.

He stifled his breathing as he stole toward the wood line, but he couldn't squelch his own heart. The drumbeat of his fear was pounding at his brain, splitting his ears in rebellion. The enemy could hear it, that frantic pulsation, could smell the sweat of his dread. He felt the small hairs rising to attention, as rigid as soldiers on his neck.

Tsssssssssssss.

What was that?

He motioned frantically. It had a wing as intrepid as Special Forces.

At any moment, something elite would swoop down on them. *Why couldn't they make out his form?*

They reached the protection of those giants of embedment, the oaks with their sway over peril. There was another light crack, and Diego winced as a twig cried under his presence. He leaned against a tree, his shoulders tense, bracing himself against the firmness. He was almost on top of him, this phantom assailant—he swung his barrel—three o'clock.

He seized the trigger, the annihilation of all that plagued him, wanting and awake in his wrath. The drill sergeants had hounded his daylight, had taunted his twilight, had stolen his midnight and then some.

The vengeance was his—this lone would-be sniper—he raised his rifle to the fray.

The enemy practically lifted to his sights.

Let it rip!

The sniper was a snake.

There was a long, clumsy pause that collapsed in relief in the same way a fever broke. The delirium abated and pooled at the neck in rags of perspiration, warm and sticky.

"That would clearly be of the garden variety. Nothing with venom there." His battle buddy's tone came so sardonic it pierced the blackness with impressive wit.

Diego coughed it up, the sudden oxygen that sharply inflated his lungs. His chest was shaking and then his stomach was shaking, and he just couldn't help himself. They were like six-year-old schoolboys buckled and snorting, trying not to laugh through a prayer. Diego sat hard, cradling his rifle with enormous dead weight on his thighs. The tears streamed down his face, his brain was exploding. He had to put a fist to his mouth.

The unrestraint, melodically funny—it was the first good music to his ears.

The drill sergeants were human, almost friendly, on day six of FTX. *This is the last hole you'll have to dig.* The euphoria had been palpable and earned. Diego could envision it—the finish line of the field training exercise—without his usual octane spare. He could make it that far, and only that far; Diego was on his very last leg.

At 0945 they had three objectives. First, they had to plow the road. Second, they had orders to destroy any enemy in their vision, and, third, they had to assault and obliterate the enemy's bunker. One team was chosen to lead the assault: it was Alpha team, supported by Bravo.

The wedge of their orders drove them to a sand pit, and that's where the v-shape distorted. Diego broke off, took up the left flank, deviating for twenty meters.

"*Cover!*"

There was a harsh cry in the heat. The rupture of lead was deadly. The enemy was down, and Diego led his team, sidling along enemy lines. There was a bounty for their effort, the men gobbled it up, ravenous for ammunition. They were exultant and methodical as they stole the magazines, and then stole the forest in pieces. There was a stilted scan as they waded through the brush, and then Diego spotted the abnormality. The green was too flat—not dead, but discolored— enemy camouflage at two o'clock.

They swarmed the two drill sergeants with a surprise attack, trying to swallow ground. They took a late report. They moved out again, the bunker was finally within reach. *Carpe diem.* They set their jaws, scrambling for the valor of their grenades.

The men who had been athletes in their former lives had a competitive advantage. Throwing a grenade was somewhat like throwing a baseball, as deceptive and precise as a strike. In training, the pitching mound stood at about forty-five meters, the maximum effective range for a kill. Timing was everything, depending on the defense, the grenade could splatter mid-air or blow from the ground. The men didn't hold onto them longer than necessary, nor did they release them too soon. There would come a day when the smoke screen of practice would clear to the concussion of real combat.

Diego was the one who got to release it, on the fly, and the men instinctively braced.

It was stunning in its report, the collateral damage instant, swelling, and then infected. It was an open sore, weeping and bleeding from the vital organs of the drill sergeants' resistance. The Bravo team rushed, the great vultures of clean-up, a high-speed chase to the bunker.

"I Am The Infantry, the Queen of Battle, Follow Me!!!" came their war cry.

There was another tossed grenade, another report, and then abruptly the battle was won. The woods were subdued, the defiance of the oaks suddenly bowed to the greater shade of their deliverance. The drill sergeants came forward, that worthy opponent, that slave master of toil and strife. Diego's throat locked on the unmixed emotion, the paradigm shift of his life.

It was so rewarding, so exalting, so clear—the brutality, the deprivation. It had all been for him, they had proven *him*—he had passed, and they had made him a man.

"It [was] said that Napoleon lost the battle of Waterloo because he forgot his infantry—he staked too much upon the more spectacular, but less substantial cavalry." It was hard to imagine Franklin D. Roosevelt's claim—for who could have forgotten the infantry? The battle was never more spectacularly heroic than among those who took it on the ground.

From the ignoble trenches Foxtrot 2-58 rose like a phoenix, charred and battle-worn and soiled. They were a beautiful sight, the rough cut of a diamond emerging from its strangle of coal.

They marched in three groups, in impeccable formations, before a crowd at graduation. Jorge strained to pick out his son's form—there was a mass of tight haircuts and taut bodies. His heart took flight as they made an about-face and he witnessed the transformation. Diego's eyes had a jarring new glint from advanced individual training—they were compelling and fighting and focused. They recited the creed, the company standard aloft in controlled, gut-forced voices. It was the flawless constraint that perched above the might—like the glorious float of Frances Scott Key.

Jorge was presented a blue cord, the braid of the infantry that entwined them at last with the legacy. Diego stared straight ahead, the core of his discipline making him as stout as a statue. It was the special recognition that George Washington had afforded. Jorge felt his jaw clamp on the emotion. He secured it fast on his son, beneath the epaulet, the scepter to the crown of Class A's.

The United States of America had always had some kind of might, not found in its superior defense systems. They had the precision weaponry now, the laser-guided missiles that could secure an area in a matter of milliseconds. But that same small space had taken the unfathomable mettle of hundreds of men, swaying forward on enemy soil. They had advanced and bled, moved back and bled, the eternal stain of liberation on Iwo Jima and Normandy.

They were amazing developments—borne of the Space Age technology—and, even so, it all paled in comparison. The might of the military, the muscle that carried them, was found in the heart of its soldiers.

The image of their gallantry and all those who had preceded him—from the American Revolution to the Gulf War—they were the inflections of his countenance, Diego's countenance shining, and willing, and able.

Willing and able. That was the trumpet that blared in the blaze of the hot June sun. Diego was headed to the famed Fort Stewart, the 3rd Infantry Division (Mechanized), the "Rock of the Marne." His statuesque halt came suddenly to life as he was turned blue and his father stepped back. The richness of his heritage, the fortune of his future—he owed it all to a singular vision. He leaned toward Jorge with absolute spontaneity, the pleasure and the sacrifice and the hardship—he kissed his father on the cheek with what seemed like the last remnants of boyhood still apparent in his smile.

It was his finest hour yet: he had become a man and a soldier all-at-once, and he reassumed his ramrod position.

THE
SOLDIER

Freedom is never more than one generation away from extinction. We didn't pass it to our children in the bloodstream. It must be fought for, protected, and handed on for them to do the same, or one day we will spend our sunset years telling our children and our children's children what it was once like in the United States where men were free.

—Ronald Wilson Reagan

FOREWORD
WITH JORGE RINCON

I never felt such powerlessness in my life: all those people running through the streets, crying for help, and all that black smoke billowing against such a beautiful, blue sky. I thought about the desperation of those people, trapped inside the Twin Towers—the kind of hideousness that could make a man jump to his death, propel him into nothingness like that.

A man will do anything to live when the faces of his wife and his children are indelibly etched in his mind—when he knows they are waiting for him, aching for him to come home.

It was so horrific inside those blazing buildings that they abandoned the image and *jumped* to their deaths. So many times I've wondered what they saw, what they heard—what they *thought* when their last sure footing gave way beneath them.

Every soul was a brother and sister. They were all *my* countrymen.

I felt so betrayed that something like that could happen here, in the United States—that something like that could happen with God watching over us. I looked into Diego's eyes as they showed the crash sites, and I knew he felt the same anger, the identical despair. I buried my face in my hands, and I wept as I had never wept before. He placed a compassionate hand on my shoulder, and I felt some electrical impulse pass between us. So much history passed between us in that anguished touch.

Do you know what it is to be born into that kind of recklessness, that kind of savagery? I escaped all of that with my little family a long time ago, another

169

lifetime ago. We came to this country to be at peace, and we never did anything to hurt anybody. Those people in New York, at the Pentagon, in Pennsylvania—they were just going to work, making this country work, providing for themselves and their families.

Many of them were just average people, like us, trying to make a go of things.

The terrorists tied my hands, all my hopes and my dreams, on September 11, and my son Diego—my valiant, sweet son Diego—loosed them again. He asked me what I thought. He asked for my permission and, of course, I told him to go.

What kind of father would I have been—what kind of American would I have been—if I hadn't been willing to assume the sacrifice as readily as the blessings?

With all my heart, I told him to join the Army and defend this country that had given us so much. I never wanted us to experience such a reprehensible day again, and somebody had to see to that.

No one wants war, least of all a parent—it's the most excruciating pain. To look at a son or daughter and think, but for war, but for the bombs and the bullets and the chemicals, that young, vital body could go on forever. You look at the epitome of health and strength when you take in the image of a soldier. You see that it can all change in the blink of an eye. Your children are going to lose innocence, that's for certain. And then they might lose an eye, or an arm, or a leg. They might lose their lives, and you can only ask yourself this: if our way of life, our freedom, and our families, and our God-given rights are not worth fighting for, what is?

If the Iraqi people don't deserve the same blessing of freedom I have known, then who does, and what makes us so selective?

If we cannot rise to the occasions when humanity hangs in the balance, what can we stand for, ever?

I have wished so many times when I have seen people taking to the streets, lying down in the middle of the streets to protest the war—I have wished I could just ship them off to Colombia for one month so that they, too, would know the hardship. I tell you, one month in Colombia, living the way Yolanda and I once lived, and they would quietly, gratefully go back to their homes. They would wish to bow at the feet of the people who lay down in makeshift cots, and sandstorms, and trenches, and holes—those soldiers who seek any place to lay down their weary heads, just so they can wake up to lay down their *lives* for us.

Seeing Diego raise his hand, take an oath for all those people who had suffered—seeing him take an oath that transformed him in an instant from boyhood to manhood—that was the most powerful moment in my life, and it will be forever cherished in my heart.

Diego grew to a giant of a man the day I witnessed him actually resolve to *do* something. Most of us felt the churning and the anger and the sadness, and Diego chose to respond.

My son was part of the greatest army in the world; and he fought, side by side, with the bravest defenders of liberty and truth and justice we will ever assemble. I cannot tell you the reverence and awe, the nobility that still stirs in me when I think of him marching with such precision. I still see him saluting with such exactness, such fidelity, and courage.

Believe me when I say that I have only one problem with the United States Army.

It is that they've told me I'm too old to join, too old to take my son's place.

I think of those people in Iraq who were just like me once. Held captive for so long, wondering how they were going to feed their families, living day to day, paying always for others' mistakes—for a dictator's mistakes. It's a terribly hard thing to be subject to rulers who don't have your best interests at heart. The Iraqi people have suffered more cruelty, more torture, more barbarity than I ever did, but I can understand a part of their misery.

The poverty of the soul is a multicultural emotion I can truly appreciate.

If I am the last person left standing in this country after the War on Terror— the last person to defend the legacy for which my son fought and died—so be it.

George Washington once said this: citizens by birth or choice, of a common country, that country has a right to concentrate your affections.

The United States of America is my home now by choice, and she has more than earned my devotion.

CHAPTER 1

I wouldn't give a bean
To be a fancy pants Marine
I'd rather be a
Dog-face soldier like I am

I wouldn't trade my old ODs
For all the Navy dungarees
For I'm the walking pride
Of Uncle Sam

On Army posters that I read
It says, "Be all that you can"
So they're tearing me down
To build me over again

I'm just a dog-face soldier
With a rifle on my shoulder
And I eat raw meat
For breakfast ev'ry day

So feed me ammunition
Keep me in Third Division
Your dog-face soldier's a-okay.

The term "dog-face soldier" dated back to the Indian Wars. It was not a derogatory expression. Over the years, different versions of the song had been sung, and some were more politically correct than others. Major General Albert O. Connor of the Third Infantry Division had once verbalized to Walt Disney Productions a particular caricature. He wanted a mascot to represent the ideal infantryman: "heroic but humble; fierce but gentle; quick-witted and wise, with a confidence and dignity that comes from having proved himself."

The 3rd ID song was epitomized in "Rocky, the Bulldog," which took its statuesque guard on post.

Fort Stewart had always been shrouded in cagey forests, every tree, every bush on guard. Its woods could be secretive, survivalistic, and then they could abruptly explode with raw mettle. The land was defended and acted as a defense—the soldiers and terrain, one and impenetrable. The 3rd ID staked its claim to fame on being the only rapid deployable, mechanized division in the Army.

Diego stepped foot on the sprawling garrison with the bright July sun on his face. In the summer of 2002, it was easy to be egocentric, easy to believe that it all existed for him. He had inspired that respect among his family and friends, that public deference that seemed to come with the uniform. In Conyers, he had passed veterans whose faces bore the emotion, an unmistakable regard. Perhaps it was a realization that their youth was expendable, that their most virulent days had come and gone; perhaps it was relief that the full weight of humankind lay on fresh, idealistic shoulders.

Or perhaps it was sadness, the weariness of battle, of man's inhumanity to man. Only ten months had passed since the September 11 attacks and the pain still reeled in many eyes.

Hinesville enlarged the imprint of importance, the post's largest neighbor, and the county seat of historic Liberty. To Diego, it had the aura that all places did which lived and died with their youth. The Army was industry; the Army was occupancy; the Army was omnipresent. The bedroom communities had a special intermingling of sleepy Southern towns, with the fleeting tenancy of the combative.

"Enter to Learn—Leave to Lead": there would always be the neighborly orders and the exits. It was like a good schooling, a great institution, a college town with resounding attitude. The troops might be individually transient, but there would always be ranks, great swelling rank and file. In 2002, the soldiers carried the pressure and the honor and the glory of a nation's held breath just for them.

Among all the impressions, from wide-eyed romanticism to deep-seated fears of living up to it all, came the illustrious history which sustained Diego most, the past avant-garde and its permanent mark. The Third Infantry Division had been heralded the "Rock of the Marne" for its flesh and blood stand in France. General

John J. Pershing had referred to their stranglehold in World War I as "one of the most brilliant pages of our military annals." Inexperienced Doughboys—in their first ever fight—had been ordered to the Chateau Thierry.

It had been on the Marne River, on the road to Paris, that the Germans had made their last great attack.

The 3rd Division had been ordered to hold the line exactly at the river. "With one foot in the water" had been the French directive on July 15, 1918. The Germans had launched their offensive, assailing the Allies in the dead of night with the pent-up retort of their stranded position. American forces had pounded their boats and the footbridges with the scathing intensity of their machine guns. The enemy advance had been forced to swim and that's when the real assault had begun.

The 38th Regiment had knitted its strength with the French 125th Division. The French had been overtaken and quickly retreated, exposing the 28th Infantry Division to the enemy fire. Most of the 28th had been captured or killed, leaving the 38th Regiment to close the ranks. At the time a Lieutenant Colonel, Ulysses Grant McAlexander ordered a horseshoe formation to withstand the German barrage from all sides. In a seven-mile barricade across the Marne, the 4th and 7th Regiments, too, had to shift their forces. There were pockets of defense only three platoons deep and still the 3rd Division held steady. In one shallow area, there was but a thread of survivors and the Germans failed to break them. When the battle was over, with four out of ten men lost, the Americans had upended the enemy. There was not one break in the line, not one German soldier who had taken a foot of the Allied side. In time, the 3rd Division pursued the Germans in a bloodbath, all the way to the Ourq River.

The division was assigned to the US III Corps and then to the 1st US Army to take on the first American offensive in the war. They occupied Saint-Mihiel while the remaining divisions drove the Germans to the Woerve Plains. It was there, near the border between France and Germany, that a bone weary 3rd Division received orders for another offensive: the Argonne forest along the Meuse River was their final battleground of the war.

On September 26, over half a million infantrymen advanced through the mud and the tortured terrain. The Germans were surprised, but heavily fortified, and they scrapped for every inch of the forest for days. One week passed and the 3rd Division received the nod to take over the agony of the advance. One by one, the infantry picked off the positions of the Germans entrenched in the woods. Six days later, the forest was cleared and the troops were allowed to rest—except for the 3rd Division, which was ordered to the hills to abolish the last of the resistance.

It had taken three weeks of constant combat to annihilate the German forces. When the brutality had ended, the occupation had begun, following the signing of the Armistice. From combat to peacekeeping, the celebrated division had an indelible etch on the granite heritage of the United States Army. The legacy had continued through World War II, and through the viciousness of Korea and Vietnam. Be it Operation Desert Storm or the War on Terror, the Third Infantry Division would always serve as a spearhead. It was that sense of power, the exhilarating twinge in Diego's spine, as he reported for duty on post.

There was a childhood echo of insecurity that generally plagued even soldiers. Like the first day of school, Diego was naturally curious but couldn't overtly display it. He shielded the pique with the fallback of duty, attentive, restrained, and stoic. The private next to him did the same—exceedingly terse and focused. It was a façade, of course, the aloof demeanors, the halting mannerisms, the detachment. It would be something casual, some unassuming moment, which would eventually cement them, brothers. The rigors of training and the strain and the sweat would peel back the layers of dissension. All their hopes and their dreams, all their vulnerabilities would be exposed in a prop field somewhere.

The private eyed him with a baby soft complexion, so smooth that any blemish would have shown. When he had to shave—if he had ever had cause to shave—the razor would have worn his skin raw. That was the paradox of Mike Creighton's face, thrust atop that mountainous body. He was stout and ruddy, and in his bald youth was something too cynical and surly. He had had a hard time of it once, a defiant kid whose last chance at civility had been the rigors of the Army. It had all worked together, the density of his upbringing, to safeguard the abiding compassion.

The funny thing about Creighton, not easily discernible, was the immensity and grace of his heart. If he was shown kindness once, he would never forget it— he would die for a touch of goodwill.

He really didn't glower directly at Diego. It was more of a warning to maintain some distance, to give him some time to adjust. He had been perpetually cornered and wounded enough that he would have to step forward on his own. A few generous scraps and he would tame to the friendliness; Diego sensed that inherently. One of the commanders had observed the gift back at boot camp— the talent for the ensembles, and the light. The exception shone brilliantly among such militant standards; it was the contrast that made it so evident. Diego was sunshine, his shafts paled somewhat by the conformity of drab Army colors. But he was light nonetheless, playing off the harshness, intensifying the prisms of his comrades. He softened the edges and he warmed to the chill and he brightened the depressed and downtrodden. He breathed life into the dark corners with a touch so gentle, one was never intruded upon. Standing beside Creighton, Diego was Will Rogers with a strange twist on the widely known axiom: he had never met a man he didn't like, and there was no one who wouldn't eventually like him.

Anthony Farina was instinctively drawn to Diego, the openness fused with a strange forbearance. Specialist Farina was an engaging sort of extrovert—his warmth rarely shrugged off in his discipline. Standing at attention, he displayed an easiness it took some time to understand: Farina was tough, but he was never rigid, all of his high-tuned energies stemming from loyalty.

Sergeant Chad Urquhart acknowledged none of the subtleties as he surveyed each of the men. That was the oddity, the enigma of his old school drill, eyeing each soldier with contempt. He had complexities, as varied as his childhood, resentment and gratitude constantly combating within. It seemed his father had been hard on him—had had punishing expectations so that it had melded him into sheer stone. He demonstrated little patience for flexibility, for the compassion that had once been denied; and still he was thankful for his father's iron hand, for the restraint it had formed in his character. He thought a lot of his father, and he really loved the men in his squad—it was going to be painfully hard for him to show it. The mismatch was going to be horrific for a young man like Diego whose sole purpose in life was to please.

Farina foresaw the impending crisis, Diego being a shade of himself. His was the guileless manner that had once been Farina's, before his four years in the Marines. They were both small town boys, some of Atlanta's suburbs almost as rural as Farina's hometown in the heartland. They had that hopefulness—that finely honed leadership that came from being big fishes in small ponds.

High school had granted them the repetitive exposure, the means to take risks and absorb the outcomes. It was the small town kid who, more often than most, got to succeed or fail so publicly. In Conyers, Georgia there had been the teachers who had noticed when a kid was having a bad day. And then in Dale, Indiana— for Farina at least—there had always been the open doors. The sage old men who spoke simple truths and the women who still liked to mother him. It was an entire community, so interwoven, a boy could practically trick-or-treat the whole town. Leaving a place like Dale, Indiana had brought a rude awakening—an anonymity so severe it had made courage plummet, absolved all the hard-earned accolades. Diego would certainly feel the pinch of obscurity and Urquhart would add to that feeling.

The decision was subconscious—he was Diego's team leader—Farina was compelled to protect him.

Diego startled Farina as they began the physical training regimen. Just watching him stirred something powerful. Specialist Patrick Sawicki was swayed by it, too—it was an athletic genius, untouchable. It wasn't the ease or even the strength, though both of those qualities struck them. It was that the first workout was brutal, a veritable torture, and something exuded from Diego like joy. It wasn't in his face, which was rock-hard competitive, nor was it in the intensity of his eyes. It was in his skin, that thin veil of joyfulness that existed to define such great potency. Every muscle was distinct, the workings of a makeup that seemed to cry out for the tests—it was flawless endurance that begged to be proven, that never faltered or tired.

They ran and they ran and it was in that new moment that their sweat gave off some kind of pheromone—the first human pheromone that would make up the chemistry, that would make up for all of the rest. They were that semblance of near schoolboys, some of them teenagers, all of them wanting of friends. But unlike mere schoolboys, the bullets might fly some day, and familiarity meant more than companionship.

Observing Diego, the dependability of his reflexes and the more than abundant will, it occurred to Farina that if he ever did battle, he wanted it to be with someone like him.

They spoke to each other briefly, the terribly discreet small talk that centered on the duties at hand. The soldiers who had come directly from AIT had grown accustomed to the strangulation—the physical output had been so difficult and then, too, the chitchat was punished. There were two deprivations that had caused Diego to suffer most: in-depth conversations and girls.

Diego's voice was deep and non-descript when Farina met up with them in the barracks. Creighton had been assigned as Diego's roommate, and Farina took stock of them both.

"So where's the Southern accent?"

Farina was met by Diego's shrug. "I moved to Georgia when I was five."

"And you?" Farina probed. Creighton stopped short of "drop dead." He answered because Farina was a superior.

"My Mom was a sergeant major. My dad served in Vietnam." He had spilled a near mountain of history. There was too little interest in either man to result in much of a stand-off.

It was Diego who saw the inroad, made the next link unassumingly, chipped right to Creighton's soft spots. He was a soldier who loved guns, who spent a lot of time with his old man.

"So your dad can really shoot."

It was said with such genuineness that Creighton was bound. "Yeah, he's pretty good. There's a range—not too far anyway. We shoot and we fish a lot."

"My dad was a bodyguard when we lived in Colombia. But I never really shot a rifle until now."

Creighton studied Diego, the politeness, the manners—*so that's what he had escaped for the Army.*

He wanted the citizenship. That had to be it. Otherwise, the kid didn't fit.

It was a slight error in judgment, but one that was pardonable because Creighton let down his guard. They were both lacking something to his way of thinking; and need was an immense kind of bond. The first glow of camaraderie settled in their walk as they reported to the company quarters. *Volens et potens*, the insignia read. *Willing and able.* The 2nd Battalion, 7th Infantry Regiment.

Diego had been assigned to Alpha Company, otherwise known as "Rage."

Private First Class Robbie Brooks was behind the front counter as the three soldiers entered the office. The hub of "Rage" Company was standard regulation: functional with as much charm as a warehouse. The tables were wood, the chairs were metal, the XO title was etched like a cattle brand. The paint was old, some leftover color that no one else but the Army would buy. There were men milling around with the pre-game kind of look reserved for a moderate opponent. It was all one big locker room—the boys club of the infantry—minus the playful flip of worn towels.

Brooks was a military brat and that brief introduction to Diego seemed to account for a lot. *How ya doin'…nice to meet you*—not one of those cordialities applied. A wide open stance and a slap on the back and a big grin were going to be slow coming. To meet Robbie Brooks was to be offhandedly observed, to be sized up in a most interesting way. There was something of detachment that was oddly reassuring because Brooks avoided the rush to rash judgments. He nodded his head in general acknowledgment, neither overextended nor rude.

Farina had reached out to him, had taken the passivity as a benchmark of composure and gravity. He was partly right, believing as he did that Brooks and Diego were a study in contrasts. Diego with his levity and his center stage kind of pull, and Brooks with his spear carrier qualities—time would reveal that they were both exceptionally good at getting attention and an audience. In reaching verdicts on human nature, Diego achieved the most honest assessments through a hands-on type of interaction. Brooks managed to accomplish the same read through surveillance, no more intrusive than camouflage. That hang-up of a kid whose father had been a major in the Air Force, who had bounced to so many different schools—it would all succumb gradually to disarming friendliness once he'd deemed a man worthy of his allegiance. Brooks had the identical sudden bursts, the quirky energy that Diego often displayed in his humor. And then he had that frankness, the penetration in his eyes that showed he listened intently.

The men were at ease, which allowed the faint shifts as the new guys began to pair off. It was nearly imperceptible, the willful migration, most cautious for the lowest of ranks. In the underlying strain, in the wait for the orders, which would rescue the more socially awkward, there came an assuming voice, a rich impulsiveness that overrode all of the tension. Specialist Michael Curtin made an entrance, sounding good-natured and uncharacteristically demanding.

"Where *is* Brooks? I *need* to see Brooks." He was pointed to the most abhorrent of bathrooms.

The office was energized as the new guys watched curiously—seven rhythmic raps at the door. The most diligent review in a Class A Inspection wouldn't reveal even a miniscule flaw. Curtin's presentation was consummately squared away, the model of a soldier's kind of soldier. He had recently earned his Black Beret, made it through the Ranger Indoctrination Program. Therein lay the inconsistency, the mystification: he had simply passed on that milestone of moments. He was the prototype of Special Forces in his discipline and his instincts and, incomprehensibly, he had abandoned the pursuit. He'd been told to drop—to do 100 push-ups—and he'd suddenly stood up and said "no."

"No, I don't think so. Not today, sir. It's a nice thing you're trying to do for me...

"I really appreciate it, but not anymore." *Not today and not ever again.*

There had come "the talk," the commander's encouragement that stemmed from an assessment of burnout. Curtin had come so far in such an elite undertaking—that had been the well-meaning rhetoric.

Despite his sociability, Curtin had said little; he wasn't one to bare his soul. He had responded in the impeccable, curt kind of language that had made him worthy of his beret.

"No sir," he had steeled. "I prefer the infantry, sir." *There's nothing you can say or do to change my mind, sir.*

That had been all; he'd been quietly dismissed with orders to go to the 2-7.

The company bathroom wasn't a lingering hideout given the potential for bacterial breeding. There were no friendly magazines, no comfortable odors, no oversight from women. Without the decency of their wives or their mothers, Diego wondered if the place had ever been cleaned. The hole that housed the toilet became the first sign of comedy—the insistent tapping that measured a wide spread of grins. From the other side of the door came a rat-a-tat-tat, the echo of Brook's firm response.

Curtin changed the rhythm and the rejoinder was the same, a sly smile stealing across his face. It was true that Brooks counted his friends on a single hand, and one had earned his opposable thumb. It was the one finger that separated mankind from the animals, made Brooks whole and useful and balanced. He remained in the bathroom for an intolerable amount of time, the two tapping some Morse kind of code.

Diego expected the door—when it opened—to do so coyly in the joke. It swung wide abruptly and in that erratic kind of humor, Brooks pushed Curtin to the side. His blatant disregard, the lack of eye contact did nothing to conceal the impression. It was a thinly veiled mask on a rare solidarity; Curtin was clearly his best friend.

The friction was palpable as Urquhart made his entrance, a charisma more properly attributed to intensity. Farina bristled, all of the lightheartedness gone— in a blink came the tight snap of reins. His home state of Indiana bordered Kentucky, the grassy farms known for select horse breeding. There were exceptional thoroughbreds, colts of the highest caliber, but one had to know how to ride them. Urquhart expected a hard run on the bridle through every stretch of the track. Even the great race horses needed the small slack if they were going to be paced for the win. There were some high-strung horses whose natural instincts to compete responded with greatness when challenged; and then there were stud horses that had to be gelded to control a train wreck of passions. Knowing the difference, understanding the responsive mouths of horses who rose steadily to the slightest nudge at the bit—to Farina's way of thinking, that was the instinct that seemed to be missing from Urquhart's leadership style.

"Keep your eye on the prize," Curtin whispered to Brooks as they gave way to the razor sharp orders. The goal of the training was to establish the checkpoints that would give priority to the allied movement. The METT-T—the mission, enemy, terrain, troops and time available—all pertained to one aspect of insurgency. It was guerilla warfare that could make checkpoint security as thorny and lethal as combat.

One of the first goals of insurgency was to overthrow the government and it was daunting to take on the establishment. The modern terrorist camps were thin on personnel and emaciated when it came to their resources. They had no means to materially damage armed forces and so they relied on psychology. Among their most common tactics were attacks on small elements, like the checkpoints that symbolized the safety nets. It was no hollow victory to create the perception that armed forces were inadequate to safeguard the populations or their properties. The guerillas were deceptive, often indigenous, which lent to the blend with civilians. They held few obligations to society at large and, in fact, they craved vulnerability for their people. If they could manage to draw fire, better yet incur casualties—anything to afflict the civilians—the small accumulations would add up to a victory that would serve to weaken the resolve.

It was resentment they wanted, the constant harassment that might lead to a breakdown of coalition support.

The afternoon stretched long as the squads worked their strongholds, Urquhart intolerant and meticulous. There was an uncoiling of nerve with the Concertina wire that Farina felt he had to assuage. Diego's tendencies for perfectionism were clear and so, too, was Urquhart's dissatisfaction. The harder the men worked, the more Urquhart hassled them so that the job of small encouragements fell to Farina. Despite Diego's athleticism and his generally sunny nature, Farina could see he was a soft-mouthed horse. It was the Army, of course, but Diego was naturally obliging and Urquhart was still yanking his chain.

Diego focused intently on one task at a time and it was rules of engagement that preoccupied him. His face took on darkness from Urquhart's whipping and then, too, from that sour briefing. There were stragglers and deserters, the general populous and terrorists and all of them might look like mere farmers. "They might come in trucks. They might come on foot. You have to make a split-second decision...

"Fire the warning shots and if they continue to advance—if they threaten you—smoke them immediately. That's your ROE. *Those are your rules of engagement.*"

It was one thing to kill a man in a mock battle with the drill sergeants—that was just fierce competition. In the war games with opposition forces there was no blood, no surviving family, no error that couldn't be rectified. Diego's jaw tightened in the whirlwind of thought. *What if he killed someone, innocent?* To fire that weapon was to somehow play God, to make an eternal kind of judgment.

Farina had had the same introspection once, and he had had to weigh it in the balance of his faith. As a young boy, he had always walked to the sacred Arch Abbey and visited with the Catholic priests there. Farina was a churchgoer, finding something healing and straightening each time he attended Mass. It was the richness of the ceremony and the sameness of worship that made him feel right with God.

Seeing the Savior as he hung on the cross, he had always sensed a renewal of power—God had made him and God could fix him. Together, they could work anything out.

He reminded himself of that abiding grace as Urquhart stalked their perimeter. As much as faceless terrorists and ambiguous regimes, Farina struggled to love that one enemy. Urquhart's berating came to him clipped and controlled and it was that singular quality that got under his skin. He was something like dynamite, Farina thought, with a short fuse that miraculously smoldered at the cap. Something kept Urquhart from completely exploding, the primal heat within millimeters. His carotid artery had a peculiar pulsation that never touched off the fire in his eyes. Perhaps it was purposeful—the old crazy like a fox adage—because his tirades were the means to a great end. The cohesion was visible, the body language of the new guys, banding so quickly against him.

To forge the alliances, there had to be the tangibles—the foe they could see, hear, and feel. Before there was deception, before there was war, before there were great rounds of mortar…

There stood before Farina that human embodiment, an intense level of aggression, aimed at them all from within.

The Rincon children scrambled from the van with a summer camp-like eagerness. It had been a four-hour drive from Conyers to Fort Stewart, and they were hungry and cramped and tired. They had stopped at a convenience store that would serve as their commissary for as long as Diego was on post. George and Stephanie bought themselves treats, and enough food to appease the return trip. It was the weekend ritual of retrieving Diego, a commitment they had made as a family—Monday through Friday, the Army could have him, but his place on the weekends was at home.

"You'll come back on Sunday?" Farina's question was rhetorical. Diego had retrieved his cell phone from an unremarkable stuffed animal, a tiger that chanted the song "Wild Thing." The animal had a zipper to a covert cavity that had once hid his contraband at boot camp. He had placed his call from his room in the barracks—his family was just outside Pembroke.

"Esfero roto," his father had quipped, a rough Colombian translation for "pen broke." There was something in Jorge that never wanted his second son to feel abandoned on the weekends—Diego wasn't sure of the history, but it hearkened back to a children's school and it was the source of a fierce resolution.

Farina watched Diego pack with a twinge of envy, reuniting with his family so easily. His wife had stayed back in Indiana, and the decision clutched at his chest. Jillian had just given birth to their second child, and he was missing that whole wonder of infancy—the clouded eyes, and the utter dependency, and the sweetness that bathed the miracle. The endless field orders, the transfers and the extended duties were a far cry from stability; he knew that. It was the best thing for the children; that's what he told himself, sleeping alone at nights. His girls would know the serenity of a small town and that was a blessing—Jillian was right to insist on a real home.

"I'll be back on Monday." Diego was nonchalant. "As late as I possibly can be."

Farina's whirl was quick. "You'd have to leave your house at one o'clock in the morning. Your parents won't go for that."

"Wait and see. You don't know my family. We're night people, anyway."

There was a perplexing inflexibility to Diego's smile, and Creighton regarded him, expressionless. "You should come back at seven. Miss PT. I think I'd enjoy seeing that."

The unspoken, of course, was consequence and punishment, and a whole squad of overworked carotid arteries. Creighton's impertinence had the desired effect as Diego turned on him, affronted. It was the idea—that was all—the very idea that sparked the impulsive lunge. The floor on which they stood was thin and industrial, and Diego used it like a springboard.

The element of surprise caught Creighton off balance. He crashed against the bed, reeling tilted. He was a good five inches taller, and so he tried to press his weight, the stoutness of his arms against Diego. Creighton had size but Diego had agility, anticipating movement by focusing on the waist. The waist was the last portion of the body to react so that Creighton's head fakes and his hand batting were useless. It made for a good match, and Farina stood apart from them, engrossed in the outlet of energy. Nearly everyone wrestled; it was the pastime of the Army—the protest of so much manly pressure on lingering adolescence.

For all of the strong wills and the thrashing and striving, there were certain rules that governed the contests. The first one was injury—the avoidance of severe injury—in an occupation where complete physical strength was imperative. The second rule was similar in its reverence to the body: *never tap a man out.* In a world with few subtleties, they somehow felt the brinks and stopped before the exhausting of their opponents. It was a gentlemanly kind of arrival when the pair was evenly matched and they sensed the impending collapse. Creighton and Diego breathed hard as they knelt, a draw in the friendly exchange.

Diego's cell phone rang with insistence and Farina grabbed at it, muffled the receiver to Diego's panting. He was responsibly serious as Diego motioned downward. "Yes, Mr. Rincon, he's coming."

People to see. Places to go. Diego became animated again. He blindly threw his clothes and his personal toiletries into the rucksack on his bed.

Creighton was a helper, flinging anything small into the mouth of the pack.

"Cut it out. I'm in a hurry!" Diego threw back his razor.

"No, that's true, you wouldn't shave. A little boy like you." Creighton slipped the razor into the rucksack as Diego turned his attention.

"Hooah." Diego finally shouldered his load, transformed in the sudden elation. He was going home and, all at once, he appeared taller, his skin taking on a sunlit kind of glow.

"Look, when you get back—we're headed to the field."

Farina wasn't trying to dampen the excitement.

Diego waved him off, and Farina caught his arm, lest he be misunderstood. "All I'm saying is it's been a rough week. After the field—I promise we'll do something fun."

"You're really going to miss me," Diego smiled ingenuously as his phone sounded, impatient and loud. Farina followed him downstairs with a renewed stab of yearning onto the grassy compound of Building 629.

He didn't stay long enough to be introduced, their trails forking at the pavement. The post was flat and less vegetated than its surroundings—for Georgia, he had an uncommon line of vision. He saw a child with dark, flowing hair running with all of her might. Diego swept her into his arms. It was a great outstretch of brotherly affection.

Farina's oldest daughter had that same silky abandonment—only there were blonde tousles of locks when she awoke. They brushed at puppy brown eyes that glittered in the morning as he cradled her and twirled her hair in his fingers. The sigh was subconscious, but the dull throbbing in his throat was palpable and poised to break. It was four months until Christmas—until the next block—and he would have to endure it that long.

The van pulled away quietly, without the acknowledgement of the exuberance or the chatter inside. Farina mulled the fate that brought the abundance that secured such abiding love. If anything, the Army was a study in fortunes with so many varied walks of life. *How was it all decided? Their homes and their families and every breath after that? How did God decide who got to be loved, who got to be free, or who suffered? How did He decide each man's destiny—how each man lived and how he died?*

They were the purpose-of-life questions and it was only the past year that had borne such poignant reflection. Since September 11, Farina had searched for meaning in the smallest of occurrences, even in the placement of men under his watch. God had decided, for whatever reason, that theirs was a generation to do battle. And God had decided, for whatever reason, to put Farina in charge. The bond was so natural, the compulsion was so strong, that Farina viewed it like a calling. He felt strangely enough like he'd known many soldiers before; as if they'd always been meant for this time. There were no drafts, no sharp delineations that either spared a man or obligated him to service.

There were just volunteers locked in two rhythmic cycles of Ecclesiastes—a time to kill and a time of war.

The SUV reached the intersection, made an abrupt right before Farina reached it on foot. Lost in their own thoughts, neither Yolanda nor her son's team leader saw all the crossroads, the small interventions. Diego always reserved something to tell his mom later, something that only she would appreciate. She clung to each inflection, each story, each reassurance that her son was adjusting to the Army. She still struggled with his decision, but she had wanted him to make friends, had wanted someone to reach out to him, had wanted someone to care for him, too. No one could love a boy quite like a mother, and so she'd prayed to God for some angel.

Farina walked on, a little disheartened—with the exception of his job, he felt somewhat insignificant. All those years at the Arch Abbey and the sermons and the parables, and he missed the divine connection in his loneliness. The weekend was welcome but relatively unremarkable except for his own humble part.

All the world was a stage and he'd come exactly on cue—the answer to a mother's fervent prayers.

CHAPTER 2

It had often been said that history turned on small hinges, and this was a hinge kind of night. A soldier, just returned from airborne school, approached the wood line in the damp and burden that Georgia forests exuded with rainfall. His boots made a sucking noise as he slopped through the field, pretending indifference the closer he came to the clusters of hooches. There was something brewing, the sky was bulging, and the air was tense and electrical.

The young soldier's skin had a familiar richness, even in the weighted gray of the overcast. His eyes were bright, intense brown pools as he surveyed the forest for friendliness. Never mind rank, there was a pecking order to the clusters—the men had already bonded in his absence. Whatever his outward calm, the leisure in his steps, he was as anxious as any newcomer could be for shelter and a tent mate to lighten the load.

"Hey Rincon…" someone called out to him, and he twisted his neck, searching. There was no one behind him as he sloshed through the prop field and the young man frowned, disconcerted. He approached the wood line, twenty meters out, and the faces appeared to be unconcerned still. And then, suddenly, a group of soldiers waffled, saw that he was a stranger—their eyes sized him up, cold and skeptical. There was a prickle on his neck and he steeled himself for what was about to be a long night.

Diego and Farina were the first to reach out to him and, though Diego was enormously proud of his physique, he was not so wrapped in vanity that he could have discerned what Farina perceived immediately. The man before them was twenty-something, Hispanic, with piercing eyes. He had that same telltale charm, the warmth and the flow, something striking in his demeanor. It was noted that every person in the world had a twin, and Farina stared as Diego extended a hand—as if he had been granted some magical power to reach through a mirror to himself.

The relief in the young man was obvious and enormous, someone drawing him in amid the blackness and the impending storm. "Adrian Cavazos," he offered a firm handshake in the renewal of confidence. *PV2.* "Thanks, man."

Cavazos wore a white-gold wedding band, one of those immediate distinctions that caught Creighton's eye as he unpacked. That he retained it in the field was a telling sign, a man who wore his heart on his sleeve. The ring was too shiny, too polished and unmarred to have been on his finger for long. Creighton never judged a man—not when he was married—until he had seen the wife.

In the glow of mere acceptance, Cavazos failed to notice his was the only group without a tent. He offered his poncho, which gave them a total of three tarps to string from the trees. That was his first interaction, besides the idle chitchat, that accompanied the task at hand—Cavazos was a builder, and the initial bond would come in sheltering each man from the storm. The sky pitched darker, twisted and ugly, and their little group had the mesmerizing draw of a fire. They huddled in the shiver of the beginning pelts of rain, the sound of the drops soft and sporadic.

Specialist Patrick Sawicki made his way to their lean-to and flicked at their ponchos with disdain. "I don't think it will hold," he said arbitrarily, and then he spat near Cavazos.

"Who are you?"

"Listen Patty Cake—you can't just barge in here…

Cavazos interrupted Farina. "Adrian Cavazos. I was at airborne school." It rolled off his tongue with a challenge.

There was a discernible pause, the deep consideration of the Army and its enigmatic rule. With increasing frequency, young men like Cavazos were finding their way back to the infantry. Bound for other forces, the marks of specialization for which the Army charmed and wheedled and begged—and then with sudden schizophrenia, the Army issued its returns, as if it had to beef up the basics.

There were rumors, of course. Always rumors in the military, and quite a few were uttered in the same breath with Afghanistan or Iraq. Diego was intrigued, but not too unsettled. More and more, he had begun to believe it would never come to that.

"This is why I'm you're only friend, Sawicki. You have to learn some manners. See Rincon here, he's *polite*. You could learn a lot from Rincon."

Sawicki attempted a glare at Farina, but the intensity was only half-hearted. The truth was he just liked the tension in friendship. He walked away with a snort.

"Nice to meet you man," Sawicki called over his shoulder, not seeming to take note of Diego. He smiled to himself as he saw Diego's grip on the stake that secured their shelter.

"Basic at Fort Benning?" Farina dismissed Sawicki and Cavazos nodded his head.

"Delta 2-58." he replied, "I finished in mid-June."

Diego's head snapped abruptly. "Hey, I was in Foxtrot, 2-58. You must have been right next to us."

Cavazos became animated; it was the small commonalities that always formed the attachments. "When did you graduate?"

"June 6th."

"Hey, that was a week before me."

They settled to the ground, each man radiating his own self-assurance that prevailed in one prominent trait. Diego was genuine, Farina was warm, and Cavazos was magnetic. He was Diego's soul mate in his expressions and mannerisms, but there was also more of an edge—it might have stemmed from tougher days on the streets, or perhaps it was just the second love of his life. Football was like war: he had never thought of being tackled, but of how far he could run down the field. When all eyes were on him—when he cradled the kickoff and eleven men promised to pummel him—all he saw was the goal line, shot like a cannon, scrappy and poised for a good fight.

It was Farina who spotted the tendency for hyperactivity; saw that Cavazos was the hub of all energy. Unlike Diego, whose amiability soothed, Cavazos' tended to stir things. It was his perpetual motion, some close relative to discontent that somehow completed their circle. "Here's the thing," Farina suddenly announced. "We'll tell everyone you're cousins."

Farina had that friendliness, but he could also pretend insolence. Cavazos stared at him, warily.

"And that name has to go." *Cuh…vah…zose. Who can say that in the middle of shooting?*

"Cvos." *See…vose.* That's your name now." The matter seemed to be closed. "This is *Recon*, Diego Rincon, your long lost cousin from Colombia. I don't care if your grandma's from Mexico, Cvos."

"My grandma *is* from Mexico."

"Well, there you have it. Get your story straight. We'd say you were brothers but we can't pull it off—not with the different last names."

The big brotherly affection, their past history preceding them—Diego abruptly leaped from the ground. From where Cavazos stood, it was entirely unwarranted, and it stunned Farina to awkwardness. His arms flailed briefly, trying to recapture balance, and then he fell headlong into a puddle. He flung a mud-caked hand at his aggressor's ankle, and Diego managed to hopscotch the comeback. His flight from the puddle lasted only a moment, and then he returned to the brink of fairness. He let Farina strong-arm him into the water and they clashed like pigs in the mire. The rain drizzled, constant, making tearstained rivulets down the exposure of their flesh. Farina shook himself, the frenzy of a wet dog, and Cavazos turned from the assault. "I hope you didn't eat before you decided to play in the water," he said.

Diego's teeth gleamed in the dark.

"Do that again, Recon. A little wider this time—I'm not sure I saw all your gums."

Diego took off his boots and wrung his socks on Farina. There was little comfort in the effort. His feet were purple, bruised still from running, and objecting to the damp and the chill. He snuggled to Farina, quaking in his misery, the rain now coming in torrents.

"Don't touch me, man. That was a bad idea." Farina shoved at him roughly.

"It was fun for a minute." It came with such wistfulness—Diego's sheer reason for living. Farina's laugh was begrudging, his head in his arms. He could never stay sore at Diego.

The men were soaked, pelted on the outer limits of their makeshift shelter by the sheets of driving rain. The ponchos collapsed with so little flourish that a wonder settled over the group. Cavazos scrambled to salvage the essentials, but his rucksack was caught in the downpour.

Someone cursed the rain.

Someone cursed the infantry.

Someone cursed Sawicki for good measure.

They sat cross-legged and from his outside peer Sawicki saw three bumps of heads in the tarps. It was one of those moments they'd laugh about later—but Sawicki was amused right away. To be so wretched, freezing, and isolated, under a drenching cloak of their own making…

He left them to their whining, a familiar voice crying out, questioning why they had all joined the Army.

The men picked up exactly where they'd left off, their chatter always reverting to women. It was their only solace, come rain or shine, the diversion that never failed them. As Cavazos curled up in the thin embrace of his sleeping bag, he longed for the touch of his wife. Cavazos was a newlywed, and there was something painfully absent—the soft, sweet breaths as she slept. It was worse in the rain, to think of their apartment, despite all the wear and tear. He even missed the bathtub—the stupid upstairs bathtub that dripped until it drove him mad. It was like the Chinese torture method that stole all his sleep and still he'd kill to be next to the bathroom.

"Do you really have a girlfriend—or are you just making that up? We'll like you, Rincon, either way." It was Cavazos' opinion that girlfriends were like seeds—no matter how dormant, they suddenly took root in the seclusion of the field. The single guys needed the fantasies, they needed the anticipation, and, at that moment, they needed the warm glow. "Guys who don't have girls, you know. All of a sudden they got 'em. Once they get out *here…*"

"Nah, she's real. I met her after basic. Look. She gave me a picture…

"There's only one thing you should know about me, Cvos. I *always* have me a girl."

He produced a photograph of Catherine Montemayor, with silken blonde hair and blue eyes. Her pose was sultry—that portrayal of attitude—but a sweetness abounding from her smile.

Cavazos snickered, "Get a load of that. She wants you to know what you're missing."

Farina laughed hard, enough of a disruption that Cavazos didn't pick on him, too.

"Hey, do you have any kids?" Farina turned to Cavazos.

"I hope not. We got married last month."

Each man laughed, except for Cavazos, whose face took on gentle reflection.

"I was never committed to any girlfriend. I swear it. Not even one. And then I met Naemi. You meet someone like that, and there's no comparison. There's no reason to look any further.

"Really, she was the reason I joined the Army. If I wanted this marriage to work, I'd have to have a good job that would help support my family. She's a very smart woman. She doesn't need any distractions, and I just wanted her to focus on school.

"The Army pays the bills. Naemi finishes college. We go on to the next chapter of our lives."

The tone of his voice took it for granted that somehow his new friends understood. They wouldn't be goading him, not about this one; in the relationship was something off limits and special. Every word that was uttered remotely about Naemi was going to be tinged in respect. He'd met her waiting tables at an Olive Garden in Harlingen, and he'd been swept away by her goodness.

Her smile was all-encompassing, as big as Texas, as genuine and promising as the Gulf Coast. She was pretty, she was kind, and she was on to him from the start—there was nothing that got past Naemi.

Cavazos was a smoker; he'd charmed and bartered to get cigarettes throughout basic training. That's when it occurred to him—he'd met Diego before—his battle buddy had been the supplier.

"Hey, I remember you. I *wrestled* you." Diego smiled unintentionally and nodded. "Why didn't you say something?"

Diego only shrugged and Cavazos mulled that quirkiness.

He'd beaten him in wrestling. That's why Diego said nothing. Still competitive to the bone months later. Cavazos smiled to himself. He had to get a cigarette; the lure was suddenly too strong.

Creighton and Private Allen Black had been battle buddies since basic training. They remained inseparable and exclusive in their campsite. It was an awkward introduction, as if he'd gotten off on the wrong foot, bumming a smoke right away. He had to explain himself, really work it—Sawicki pulling the stake, the rain, and the intense need. He held up the pack. "They got completely soaked," he said, trying to garner some sympathy.

Cavazos was shrewd; he knew he'd intruded and, at the same time, he was keenly observant. Creighton smoked his exact brand, and Black had his same back-up, the identical wood-tipped cigars.

Creighton towered over him, issued him a hard look, and flipped a cigarette his way. He was a tough one to crack. Black was more congenial. "So where you from, Cavazos?"

"Near South Padre Island. A little town called Harlingen."

"I've been to San Antonio before."

"I was there for a year. Just before I met my wife."

Let's wait and see the wife.

Creighton remained completely stone-faced. He took one last, long drag then snuffed the butt with his foot, grinding it excessively for Cavazos' benefit. Cavazos eyed the butt, tried to keep the conversation going, a sly smile playing at his mouth.

"Naemi's father was military. He's a Gulf War veteran. Retired First Sergeant Moses Mendoza, Jr."

"Did you join the Army to impress the guy?"

"No, I just wanted a good start for both of us."

There was another stilted pause.

"Hey, why'd you join, Creighton?" Cavazos lobbed it to him, easy.

"I wanted to make my parents proud." He lit another cigarette and turned his back on Cavazos.

Creighton was obnoxious, and Cavazos kind of liked that, the strange bedfellows of war.

"Hey, what are you guys doing this weekend?" Cavazos offered it casually. Nonchalance was the key.

Black was free—which meant so, too, was Creighton. Cavazos tried to close the ranks.

"I'm having a barbecue. Over at my house. Farina and Rincon are coming."

"Recon's my roommate." It was the first voluntary utterance.

Cavazos had not been aware of that.

"We don't have a car." It sounded like an excuse.

"Don't worry. You just call us. Naemi and I will pick you up."

Black nodded once, non-committal, and the three of them smoked and talked for two more hours.

Cavazos' small home sat on Gilbert Street, a corner apartment in a complex half empty. His wife's laughter bubbled from an open front door as the men parked their vehicles haphazardly. The lot was crowded so that the trucks and SUVs found a home on the grass, under the trees. Naemi extended a firm handshake—a guy's kind of girl—and offered them food and drinks right away. They circled four kitchen chairs around an antique Army trunk Naemi had salvaged from a yard sale.

There were certain small moments that defined lasting friendships: the collapse of the tent had been one of them. And then the first visit to the Cavazos' home would seem larger than life someday when they found life could be snuffed out so quickly. Creighton had reserved judgment until he had met the wife, and then he had completely succumbed to her charms. The apartment on Gilbert Street became the inner sanctum, the hangout, the place so many of them called home.

It was the constancy perhaps that attracted the men—there was always laughter and good food. The patio smelled of barbecue, there was a spare room upstairs, and the downstairs toilet was a haven.

"Come here for a second," Black motioned mysteriously, and every man followed him to the bathroom. Five grown men tried to squeeze themselves into it as Naemi stared at them, perplexed.

"What's going on? Is there something wrong?"

Every man had his eyes shut, deep breathing.

"Air freshener," Black said, as if that explained everything. "You can't imagine until you've been in the field…"

Diego flushed the toilet for everyone's benefit, the men watching the water rise with reverence. "I really missed toilets," he broke their reverie quite earnestly. They all seemed to be just as enthralled.

"Hey, don't try that upstairs," Naemi giggled. "That one doesn't work so well." They had been adding water manually to their second toilet tank for nearly a week to try to make it flush.

The men were too absorbed to hear her—it was better than a PlayStation. They got markers and began to autograph a magazine cut-out on the wall. They closed the door and the object of their ceremony read, "Laugh at inappropriate times."

The diversion was short-lived, as their down time often was—the men seemed relaxed, but distracted. In addition to the four chairs, the Cavazos had one sturdy table, a portable lawn chair, and a futon couch.

"Stop hogging the couch, Creighton." Diego forced a seat, plopping himself on Creighton's legs. They had begun to display the constant bickering of certain married couples, entirely comfortable and exasperated and compatible. Cavazos sized them up—thought they had become too like-minded—so naturally, he had to break them up.

"Come with me, Creighton. We need some more drinks."

He might as well have yelled "fire" to the group.

Three able bodies stampeded the hallway, like little boys on their way to a swimming hole. Inside a kitchen that was long and narrow there was a singular pop of oil in a skillet. It was marked by consternation—Farina's consternation as the dinner party headed for the door.

"You don't all need to go. Guys! Come *on*," Farina's voice turned stern as his plea went unheeded. "Hey! You know, I could use some help in here—like I'm the one doing all the work."

Black made a "blah, blah, blah" kind of motion. "Farina, you're entirely too sensitive sometimes."

"I am not too sensitive."

"Whatever."

Whatever. Farina was cut off by the impassive close of the door.

He muttered to himself in the quiet that pervaded—for a minute he thought they'd all left. Diego stood surprisingly shy in the kitchen doorway, struggling to vocalize a favor.

"I'll stay and help you."

Farina's face suddenly brightened. "Sure, little brother. C'mon."

They rummaged through the cupboards until Diego produced another skillet. Farina showed him how to cut up the chicken. "Now when you soak the bread, use a half bottle of extra virgin olive oil. You have to cut the bread diagonally.

"Just make sure you don't cut it all the way through. You coat the inside pieces with butter, and then you bake it for fifteen minutes at 325 degrees."

"What does this mean here—mince the garlic?"

"It means you chop it up really fine."

Diego nodded and watched Farina de-vein the shrimp before throwing them into a pot. "You'll know they're done when they lose that opaque color. They'll turn pink when they've boiled long enough."

"You're going all out."

He did like to cook. "You know, Diego, this is how you can really woo the women."

Diego ducked his head, a sly smile overtaking his face. "Yeah, I thought I might make it for my girl."

"Uh-huh." Farina smiled dryly. "That's what I thought. I know what's going on in that head."

Diego had met Catherine at an outdoor concert, when she'd been inadvertently separated from her friends. He was the first and only boy she'd brought home to her parents who had secured their approval—period. She displayed the patience to sit beside him hour after hour as he fiddled with that mistress of a car. Her laugh was infectious and she had given him butterflies the first time he'd said something funny.

Diego was passionate about women, but he tempered his feelings to be cool— he never mentioned her first name.

"I took my girl out to dinner the other night. The salad was eighteen dollars! I said, 'Hey, baby, you see that lettuce? Chew it really slow…it's like fifty cents a leaf.'"

"Eighteen dollars! For salad? Where'd you take her?"

"Some she-she joint in the city. My parents gave me the money. I just didn't want to spend it all—not *that* much money on food.

"I mean, look at it this way: it goes in; it comes out…that's why I like rice and beans."

Farina slapped Diego on the back. "Well, your family's going to love this. I guarantee it. You can call me if you need any help."

"Yeah, speaking of which…where *are* those guys anyway? Dinner's going to get cold."

"Listen up—white wine with chicken. Red wine with beef. And the guys are going to show up with cheap beer. You just wait and see."

"When I make this for my family, it won't matter anyway. No one in my family drinks."

Farina looked at him curiously.

"It's against our religion."

"That makes me thankful I'm Catholic."

Diego looked over the table. The shrimp was artistically arranged. The forks and knives had been set in their proper places. Farina had gone to the trouble of actually folding the napkins. The chicken was glazed brown, falling off the bone. Naemi had made dessert, a homemade coconut cream pie. It kind of felt like home, the smell of fresh bread overtaking the apartment.

"It's a very good spread and those guys are *late*."

They had no choice but to resort to Nintendo.

People to see and places to go. The irony completely escaped Diego. He drummed his fingers on Naemi's Army trunk, slouched in righteous indignation. "You know, you put a lot of work into this, Farina."

"I know. They're ingrates. Welcome to the infantry, brother."

Another hour passed. They had gone to River Street. Or they were probably clubbing as Diego spoke. It was the mention of Savannah that suddenly reminded him—it was exactly why a guy needed pals.

"I bought my girl clothes there. And I'm looking at these pants. And I'm thinking, 'no way.' They're too small. So I called her up and she told me the sizes again, and I think I really insulted her.

"I mean she's skinny, Farina, but these looked *tiny*. I'm telling you, I didn't think they'd fit."

"What size is she?"

"She said she was a size five."

He retrieved the clothing from the shopping bag and held them up.

A pair of jeans, a couple of sweaters, a blouse in her favorite color.

Farina snatched them immediately.

"I bought them at Abercrombie & Fitch."

Farina couldn't stop laughing. He didn't even bother to look at the tag. Abercrombie & Fitch *for kids*.

Diego took the ribbing exceptionally well. A mixture of humor and chagrin on his face that was cut short by a grand sort of entrance—the inner circle was triumphant as they stood in the doorway.

"Farina, you got me all wrong."

They had been to Savannah all right, but the thing about Cavazos—he would have never gone there just to buy *cheap* beer.

+⫘⫘+

Fabian had volunteered to pick up his brother. He waited for two hours near the 2-7 motor pool.

He allowed one more hour and then he called Diego's cell phone.

I promise I'll be done soon. Don't leave me.

Fabian drummed his fingers on the steering column. He released a drawn out sigh.

It wasn't that they'd merely co-existed in the same household; they just weren't as close as some brothers. They were comfortable in their patterns, they got along, the occasional overlap of opposites in their egocentric ages. Diego went to parties on Halloween, and Fabian stayed home with the little ones. Diego had girlfriends, and Fabian had good grades. There was nothing wrong with that.

When did Diego become so responsible? It struck him as funny in the shadows. There was sharpness to the night, a biting sort of humor, surrounded by the regiment in overtime.

Diego in his discipline. Diego in his punctuality. Diego conforming and serious. It descended on him slowly with the time to really think—Diego becoming a grown-up.

A group of soldiers eyed him as they approached the crosswalk. Someone called out and a familiar form appeared. Fabian felt relief, a genuine affection as Diego climbed into the car.

"Thanks for waiting, man."

"Did I have a choice?"

Diego half embraced him from his seat. He cursed the hour and the excessive demand and praised names that Fabian didn't recognize. The older brother sensed it—a slight shift in the wind, some rustling beneath the yellow glow from the street lamps.

He studied Diego's face which had never been lined and had seemingly never grown tired. It still bore the optimism, the natural upturn, but it was strangely void of true bliss. That's what evaded the expression that was different—there was something almost weary in his smile. Diego was so happy to see him, so happy to go home, and it was so subtle that on any other face it might have been undetectable.

It was a fleeting joy when Diego's life had once seemed to be just one long stretch of exuberance.

They listened to alternative rock from a station in Savannah until the static became an annoyance. Diego was at ease with Fabian's silence, that familiar thinking man's music.

"I need your advice." Fabian said it so cautiously that even he missed the concession. "There's a girl. At church. Her name is Shannon."

Diego's face slowly spread.

Fabian's eyes remained on the road, and yet he still felt the swagger, the sudden expansion of the chest. Diego stuck his tongue in the side of his mouth, cocky and assuming he'd be consulted.

"I'm trying to play it cool." It was a slip in semantics. Fabian meant "easy," "unhurried."

Diego heard "smooth." Diego heard his middle name, and he launched into all his favorite come-ons.

Fabian couldn't retract it, and he couldn't stop laughing. "You know I can't say that. Only you get away with that stuff."

"Try it. Just say it. Just practice a little."

"No-ho!" Fabian was all over the road.

You know how there's a class clown and everyone expects him to be the class clown so that whatever comes out of his mouth is funny? "Diego, if I say it, it'll come out all wrong. It'll sound like it's forced or something."

"Well, I think I like this girl."

Fabian blinked hard. Diego had never approved.

"What did you say? You actually approved? Why did you say that? You haven't even met her."

"I think she deserves you."

It was the tone *and* semantics. Diego meant "worthy," and Fabian heard the sincerity. Maybe they weren't so far apart on things. Maybe they had just been lazy.

The two reached Macon and they filled the car with fuel and Diego's admission was offhanded.

"If it really comes down to that—Diego, you'll be ready. You're like the consummate soldier."

"It might just be talk. It might just be threats. If I were the Iraqis, I know I'd back down."

"If you were reasonable. Does Saddam strike you as reasonable?"

"Yeah…I guess you have a point."

"But he ought to be scared at least. Look at the Gulf War. Look at Afghanistan. The military doesn't mess around."

"Hey, you know I was thinking about the Gulf War the other day. Do you remember when we used to play on the old Army stuff?"

Diego's face lit. "Hey, yeah, all the leftover equipment the military brought back. I'd almost forgotten about that."

"It was right after we moved to America, wasn't it?"

"I thought I was one G.I. Joe." Diego stared at the faint outline of timber, so much darkness in the uncharted woods.

"Yeah, and now look at you—BDUs." Fabian mulled another impending war. His younger brother was kicking tail around the world. It almost pleased him to think of him in battle because Diego needed the backdrop. Diego could spring even from the abject of combat and emerge as the conqueror, always. He pictured his brother in a blaze of glory, doing some heroic thing. Knowing Diego, he would have a hot date in Baghdad. He would fast-talk the enemy into switching sides.

"I'm ready, Fabian. I'm a soldier. Fighting is what we do."

It settled in peculiarly, not an ounce of bravado. Just a statement of fact.

They pulled into the driveway and they were greeted by their parents and they resorted to their rooms in exhaustion. Fabian slept downstairs and Diego slept upstairs, but they both had west-side rooms. Fabian's view overlooked the backyard and the woods sidling up to their property. Diego's window offered a bird's-eye view of the street—Diego always saw himself going places.

"Remember to take a shower!"

Diego groaned. His mother appeared in the door.

"Baby, just turn on the water for a minute. Your father will never know the difference."

Diego smiled in their conspiracy and went into the bathroom. Stephanie followed him with anxiety on her face.

"Hey wiggle worm. Did you miss me?" he asked playfully. His sister nodded vigorously.

She tugged at his hand. She led him down the hallway. They stopped at the balcony that overhung the front foyer.

"My animal's stuck," she pointed. It lay on the overhang, well past the chandelier. It was hopelessly lodged on the ledge on the opposite wall. The stuffed animal was suspended beneath the window.

Diego considered what would happen if he passed out. He was that tired as he ruffled her hair.

Don't worry, Ti Ti. This will be a cinch. You'll always remember this trick.

Diego scaled the railing, solid as a wall, and he crouched in contemplation on its shelf. Georgie's eyes blinked wide and then they turned frightened. "I told my Mom we needed a ladder."

"It's okay, Buddy Boy."

"Oh my gosh." George had profoundly adult expressions. There was the toy and at least a fifteen-foot drop. His face took on fearful shock.

Diego sailed above the open space of the foyer, floated beyond Georgie's prayers. He lit like a cat and tossed the stuffed animal, and Stephanie scrambled in joy. He surveyed the return and there was a comic expression of puzzlement as he was forced to consider gravity. He hadn't really thought of all the angles—at least not those outside his little sister's predicament.

He inhaled sharply and soared back toward the balcony, like Spider-Man with no stretch of thread. He hit the wall hard, the impact of his landing nailing him squarely in the chest.

"Oh my gosh," it came quieter the second time. George closed his eyes on the calamity. Diego had a finger-hold sway on the balcony, but he managed to pull himself over it.

There had been that loud "oomph" simultaneous with the crash, and Yolanda stood in the foyer with her hands on her hips. It wasn't quite anger and it wasn't quite admiration. It was a mother's universal sigh. She listened for the bound of footsteps on the stairs; it was impossible for Diego to walk them. He ran some and skipped some, and there was a telltale rustle of certain sweatpants at all hours of the day.

There were no more disturbances. She heard a quick jog to the bathroom, and then the seclusion in his loft. All the noise stopped. Diego had closed the door on his soundproofed room. Diego had fallen asleep.

It was that sense she had at three o'clock in the morning that caused her to sit upright. Even from a muted room, she distinguished the panic. She bolted from her bed and rushed down the hall.

"Diego, wake up, baby." *Dieguito, it's okay. It's just a dream. It's okay.*

She tried to rock him and soothe him in his cold sweat. Her second son had always been such a sound sleeper. He was incoherent and his body trembled and tears streaked down his face.

Diego, what is it? He began to cry softly.

Diego had dreamed Fabian had died.

CHAPTER 3

"Let's go to Baldinos." It was the home of the giant Jersey sub, just off the main entrance to post. It was a departure that week: Brooks had taken a liking to Taco Bell—two square meals there a day.

He hated the chow hall and by the looks of their barracks, a lot of the men shared his scorn.

"You guys are *pigs*," Cavazos pronounced when all he found was an empty pizza box, stashed inside the refrigerator.

There was a year's supply of Texas Pete hot sauce, though. Every infantryman had hot sauce. "What's up with that, anyway? I must have missed that class that says you have to eat it with everything."

"A Mexican? From Texas? What's wrong with you, Cvos?" Black hurled the pizza box in disgust. "People just come in here. Make messes in my room. I have a roommate with yellow sheets. There's somethin' wrong with that, you know what I'm sayin'? A guy with pale yellow sheets."

"What's wrong with Cvos is his wife has to call him to make sure he eats every day."

"I don't think I'd talk, Creight. You live over there. I think she baby-sits you, too."

"Hey! Just where do you think you two are off to?" It was the rhetorical question that often made Black sound slighted.

Brooks and Curtin liked to golf on the weekends.

"Jersey here got us a tee time."

That's what they called Curtin—Jersey—from Howell, a tight-knit bedroom community. His accent was strong, he was the oldest of five children, and he'd once been a security guard at a gig for Tommy Lee. He had been on security detail, too, for a punk group, The Donnas, and he hadn't allowed them backstage. He didn't think they looked exactly like The Donnas.

Nope, I'm sorry. I have orders.

His father had been Army, and his grandfather had been Army, and his family apparently had his tenacity. His parents had been the only ones on the road on September 11. They had taken off for Fort Benning just after the attacks. It wasn't every day that terrorists assailed your country, but it wasn't every day your son graduated from basic training either. There was going to be a war—their son would fight in that war—and sometimes a boy just needed his family.

It was funny the things the soldiers discovered about each other, swatting flies at gunnery.

The pair picked up Specialist Joseph Finley, and they hunkered down at Baldinos and inhaled a signature family size. It had been quite a week and their conversation turned predictable in a celebration among friends. Curtin hadn't taken one portion of the news terribly hard, because Curtin had a way of buffering the caustic. Rincon and Cavazos, on the other hand, had been visibly upset when Urquhart had been promoted to staff sergeant and subsequently appointed their squad leader. Curtin had been promoted to the rank of a corporal in the formation of the third squad, the super squad. The Willing and Able were reinforcing for what seemed to be inevitable—Curtin assumed they were headed to Afghanistan.

Brooks had procrastinated his enlistment for years, though he had always known he'd sign up. He'd carried that lineage, a grandfather who had served and earned a Silver Star in World War II. And then, of course, his father had brought home the office, the calling of the Air Force every day. It had always surrounded him, like the air that he breathed; he knew exactly what was expected. He could not really pinpoint it as September 11—he had just suddenly felt it was time. He had assumed all along he would go to war after that, and it was neither an attraction nor a deterrent. The decision didn't transform him into any big hero— it was nothing like snatching a baby from a burning building. Truthfully, he just liked to don the uniform, something buttoned up and square that made him *feel* like a better man. If the only occasion a person had to meet a serviceman came in a brief introduction to Brooks—well, then, he hoped he was inspiring, that his casual interaction was an exceptional reflection on the Army.

That had been his draw to Curtin from the beginning. Brooks was proud of the milestone. Curtin was going to take some flack for the sudden advancement because it was hard to take orders from peers. *You were just like us a couple of days ago, and now you're bossing us around?* Urquhart and others placed such enormous trust in Curtin that he'd been promoted from a private first class to corporal in a matter of months. Brooks anticipated the resentment, and it was at Baldinos that he made that conscious decision: in front of the squads, he would always refer to him, formally, as Corporal Curtin. If, as his best friend, he was willing to show that deference, then surely the others would follow.

Diego was not so confident as he passed Baldinos in his prized Mustang GT. He had finally done it—a canary yellow Cobra with custom fog lights and steel inserts. It was a souped-up engine, and he'd installed twelve-inch subs and a shot of 75 HP Nitrous. His face was clouded in something dark and brooding, the end of life as he knew it. He had had a visceral reaction, a heave in his stomach, and his head still swam in dismay.

He couldn't quit the Army, but the thought had crossed his mind, barely making eye contact with Urquhart.

"The guy needs to relax, have some fun once in a while. I work better when I'm happy." There was a little-boy tone to Cavazos' bellyache and a kind of wistfulness in his pain.

"I don't respond to yelling. I'm serious, man."

Diego wasn't responding either. The Mustang slowed, sputtered, and then expired on General Screven Way.

It was one of the main arteries in which all the traffic converged, the blood mix of soldiers and civilians. He eased to the right, but he was still a blockage, damming the five o'clock flow. The gas tank had breathed the last of its fumes, and they were stuck a half mile from a service station.

"What do you mean you ran out of gas?!" Cavazos panted as he pushed.

"I put in three dollars!" Diego shouted—something about money and car payments.

It was as if he'd joined the Army to pay off the Mustang. Every dime of that first monthly check. A four-year commitment to Uncle Sam and a four-year commitment to the bank. He had ten dollars left after the first payroll, and then he blew the second payoff on parts.

"Hey, do me a favor. Don't give me a ride again!"

"What are friends for?!" Diego grinned.

The turmoil of the day had suddenly evaporated. For some weird reason, Diego was happy again.

"Give me fifty cents."

"How much you putting in?"

Three dollars if you give me fifty cents.

Alpha Company left in a matter of weeks for the high Mojave Desert outside Fort Irwin. The size of Rhode Island, it was the most realistic environment for force-on-force and live-fire training. Entire brigades clashed on its surface in a simulation of real conflict. It was more than an exercise. The formidable OPFOR could make men into gods—that was what they were after. The U.S. military was only as strong as its opposition forces and, in the Mojave, the opposition was fierce.

"We have something to prove now." First Lieutenant Brian Johnson had taken command of the Outlaw Platoon. They were an overworked bunch, ramrod straight with an attitude that was worthy of that vigilante nickname. Diego's first impression of the tribal chief had been focused entirely on his cerebral nature— Johnson was a bookworm in the truest sense, one who devoured paper and fed on the paste in the bindings. It just hadn't taken long for Diego to discover that Johnson was anything but bookish.

He could be firm and uncompromising and then alternately funny. Cavazos saw that even Johnson made mistakes. He covered them comically, which was all the more winning; he allowed for the human nature. Johnson would turn down a Purple Heart someday, feeling the wound didn't merit the recognition. The injury didn't begin to touch the life-altering wounds of someone like Bob Dole, and Johnson still had all of his limbs. He didn't begrudge other men for their tokens of a little shrapnel—it just wasn't his cup of tea.

"We're the best platoon here. Let's make our presence known." Johnson also wasn't big on stirring speeches.

Diego wished for Johnson's easy swagger that could sell anyone on his virtues. The confidence seemed to make the platoon leader larger than life, at the same time his charisma was inclusive. Johnson always remained one of them, perhaps because they began to mirror him, a platoon taking on the persona of its leader. He was an icon of a soldier, and they had begun to affectionately refer to him as "The L.T."

He squinted and blinked hard, twice, as was his habit whenever he addressed larger groups. It came down to endurance and scrupulous work and their precision through all the hot, dirty jobs. A month in the field took a quiet confidence, something akin to the autonomic nervous system. The OPFOR was just a stimulus that provoked an automatic response—it was destined to cause a contraction of their merit.

They reacted to the conditions, to the adversity and all the tests with a steady, inspiring spirit. With each passing day, Johnson saw not only improvement, but the binding solidarity of champions. Their skills were razor sharp; their heads were in the game when the game simulated life and death. He saw something special—what a commander could never really dictate—he saw that his soldiers had chemistry.

In the infantry, the proximity drew men together and the hardships forced them to get along. Somehow Johnson's platoon didn't have an air of being compelled, though—their unity in the mock battles seemed to come naturally. It was the commander's job to assess the flaws, to play off the strengths of each squad. There were only a couple of weak links, and there came the exceptional character: the stronger ones carried them like rucksacks. There were no glaring breaks, no breakdowns in morale; they just quietly compensated where they had to. It was a beautiful sight, a well-oiled machine, and Johnson had never been more pleased.

Diego was typically the model of that proficiency and compliance, but he didn't necessarily like the authority. Not that he ever voiced that; it was just a crawling in his skin to the vice grip it had on his creativity. He was obedient because it was pleasing and because the inherent straightening of the Army would eventually make him stronger. Cavazos and he had come across a description that hadn't fit the usual term for a required component of their NBC kits. Diego had given it the old college try and had moved on to the rest of his packing for the National Training Center. Training for a nuclear, biological or chemical attack was always serious business—he plainly understood that, the horror of the gas chamber forever burned in his brain. He thought he had chosen a suitable alternative, and he realized his mistake at NTC. Farina made him drop, the standard number of push-ups for leaving behind the components in what the men called the "ice pack."

"I'm sorry, Sergeant Urquhart. I didn't understand the description. I thought I did, but…I didn't." Diego's hands began to sweat; he tried to remain professional, groveling as he was obligated to do. Urquhart had made the men lay out their equipment—on three separate occasions. The NBC mask was one of the most critical components of protection, and their disregard was insulting.

And then it wasn't the berating; it was the tone of Urquhart's discipline. Diego always found him excessively harsh and demeaning. A Jerry Smith would have said, "not good enough"—nothing personal—just do the thing over.

I'll do better next time. Just tell me what you're after. I won't let you down. I promise.

He was forced to low crawl, to drag himself with one elbow and that guide wire of a knee with his face down. It was his face in the Mojave Desert, the tear at his skin that shamed Diego for meters on end. Urquhart threw him a gas mask, a stick to a dog that he fetched and muzzled too long. The mask constricted 85 percent of his breathing in near triple-digit heat. The lens of the mask became fogged in the strain, and Diego's eyes were singed in the moisture. He struggled for relief, suffocating in his own sweat and saliva and lack of oxygen. At fifteen-minute intervals, he was allowed to drink water, then don the mask and low crawl again. The rest of the company stared in disbelief. "Farina, you have to stop this."

There was no mortal danger, nothing he could do. It was more painful to watch than to participate.

The vegetation was sparse, even less than the Joshua trees which the religious ascribed to the prophet of the Exodus. The Joshua tree with its limbs outstretched, beckoning them all to some promised land. There was no such mercy, no visionary motive behind the humiliation and baseness. When Diego arose, his face was streaked in grime and something resembling hot tears.

Diego liked to get dirty, up to his elbows in noble effort, but he didn't like to be made to feel dirty.

Diego's special loyalty, the fact that he would have crawled further, intentionally, to save a friend on the battlefield—it was that gallant nature that incensed Farina further when Diego had to wear the gas mask for a day. There were unspoken rules, the rough guidelines of their masculinity that kept complaints at a minimum. But there was also a code of conduct, of reasonable conduct, when it came to the dignity of the men.

Johnson was prone to extend the latitude, to place implicit trust in his leaders. Diego's omission had been a serious one, and morale was serious, too. There were going to be times when Johnson voiced his displeasure. "They know you're a sergeant already…

"You don't have to walk around flexing your rank." It was a stinging rebuke for the fatherly intonation.

Urquhart argued back vehemently. He had to build character; his men had it in them to be faultless. It was the mark of a good leader and Johnson allowed the exchange out of due respect: Urquhart was a new squad leader and he felt the strain and he was worthy of Johnson's correction. He perceived Urquhart's strengths in addition to his weaknesses and he considered the person, as a whole. He took everything into account, the degree of difficulty, and the intentions, and the well being of his troops.

"Ease up on your men." It came out tempered and calm, but it was an unmistakable order. Urquhart didn't like it, but Urquhart obeyed—he was an exactly obedient soldier.

Diego sat atop a vending machine in the corner, his perch precarious and isolated. It was the only place he could get a strong cell phone signal; the only place that afforded some privacy. His was not the anger, the churning bitterness which had kept Cavazos from sleep. His friend had been beside him, through every inch of sand and gravel, and his hands bore the marks of the hardship. There was more fire in Cavazos, a meltdown of temper, and he wished he had it in him to change things. It took more strength than he felt at the moment, so much self-control to keep from lashing out.

He hadn't joined the Army for an easy road, but he had expected a fair one. He had parted from Diego with scarcely a word; their shared animosity transparent.

Diego didn't cry as he put his head in his arms. His desperation was beyond that. He finally had that despondence, that look of a thoroughbred, its spirit chiseled away. The never-ending criticism and the oppressive hand and the degradation had broken him. It was a darkness that would have affected Jerry Smith deeply, and Diego was alone in his calamity. He placed his call to Conyers and the depression subdued him, and then it overwhelmed him.

Farina felt a stab of contrition as he tossed and turned in his tent, in his irate insomnia.

How was it that Urquhart couldn't see what Farina did, the effort and the goodness and the heart?

He's doing just fine. The kid's doing well. One image prevailed in the soured night.

It was Diego crawling through the rocks—not the recent punishment, but a drill that had shred their endurance.

Hey, Farina, take a picture!

"Recon, are you out of your mind?"

"No, I want my family to see this!"

Farina had had to laugh.

That was the will. That was the sunny disposition *That* was the strength when it was harnessed right. Farina almost pitied Urquhart for the lack of vision, for the blindness of ambition that robbed him.

Farina and Urquhart had something in common: they both thought they saw the potential. It was Urquhart's aim to ensure that his men were prepared—that the punishment was so severe they never forgot the basics. And then Farina pitied Urquhart for the ignorance and the rigidity that would keep the men under his charge from realizing greatness. Farina just felt it was easier to channel the energy than it was to try and revive it.

Diego had never been known to say an unkind thing, nothing intentionally mean or low. It was a reputation that had preceded him to the military, and it had stuck with him right up until that moment.

Yolanda bristled as he recounted the past days, as he uttered that first disparagement. His heart wasn't in the last words he uttered, and the emotion was too thick in his voice.

"I've made my decision, Mom. I don't know how I'll do it. But I'm going to stay in the Army."

━━━━

The last mission of NTC was the most scathing of the attacks, even with close air support. The OPFOR mounted the AT-5 Spandrel, a portable anti-armor weapon intended solely for the destruction of vehicles. The simulation of the assault had the devastating effect of the newer fire-and-forget anti-tank missile, the Javelin. The Outlaw Platoon had never witnessed such a blow, the M1 Abrams tanks torched and incapacitated in daylight.

They had convoyed for a time, impenetrable in their breach of a tank ditch at the forefront of a mine field. The warheads had come from an explosive nowhere, annihilating every track. Five men had dismounted on the run, escaping their lethal metal housing. They were the last men standing: Johnson, Curtin, and Brooks, flanked by Sergeant Eugene Williams and Specialist Richard Snavely.

The enemy was entrenched, heavily fortified, as the men paralleled the ridge line. They had made it to the first tank ditch and then the field had opened, a bear trap of anti-personnel measures. They were dressed in full battle gear, clothed against a chemical attack, bounding for 1,000 meters. In the absence of his suspenders, Curtin's NBC pants dropped repeatedly in the rush to the battle. A bridge appeared passable, but there was a never ending tinsel-string of Concertina wire through the terrain. Curtin's pants dropped again, and a low chuckle sounded from Brooks as he strained to catch him in the field.

"What do we do now?!"

"We made it this far!" Johnson ordered a death charge. They would join the 82nd Airborne and Brooks rolled out the M240 machine gun for cover as Williams did a manual breach of the Concertina wire.

In a training exercise, as intense as it was, Brooks had the luxury of awe. There was no demolition equipment, just the raw strength and agility as Williams infiltrated the labyrinth. He snipped and he manhandled and he stretched and crab-crawled. Brooks lit up the enemy before him. It was virtual triumph, a glorious blaze, a swell to be conquering and alive.

There was a fatal flaw in Curtin's combat gear and the commander tapped him out when it was nearly over.

"You're dead," he said.

"And you're dead, too."

Brooks succumbed with a grin.

"We put up a good fight, though."

"It was a good fight." Curtin had grown up studying the Bible with his father. *I have fought a good fight, I have finished my course, I have kept the faith.* It came naturally.

The pair began to laugh and then they dropped to the ground to share a water bottle, exhausted.

Sergeant Williams had remained alive; he had come to a splendid end. And Diego, in his own way, had survived it. The Outlaws had just earned that coveted honor—they were named the top platoon. Their name was immortalized on the rocks at NTC, just as Johnson had envisioned. It was the best he could have hoped for when the ultimate training for war was to actually go to war.

There was a telling order from Lieutenant Colonel Scott Rutter when the Outlaws returned to Fort Stewart.

The flack vests were in, one for each platoon member, the last puzzle piece to imminent combat.

Johnson's wedding had been within days of Cavazos'. There were no perfect words, but Johnson had to prepare his wife.

"Body armor like that is only issued when we're about to go to war."

It was useful against some attacks and futile against others; but, always, it was reserved for that duty. They had been the number-one platoon—the white-hot platoon to emerge from NTC.

Of course it was comforting that they were all good soldiers, that they were proven and ready for battle. There had always been that chance, that risk a woman took, when she fell in love with a soldier. Cheri tried to be stoic, and she masked her worry and the pain of possible separation. Johnson was the luckiest. He knew it as he held her, had known it for quite some time.

The December that followed had a number of clear days, the startling blue above the moderately cold snap of Georgia winters. And yet it seemed to be a colorless month, a low-hanging fog overcoming the base. It finally settled in the middle of the month to a chronic grayness and into moody flurries of rain. Diego's squad ran in the gusts for long stretches, a pounding of pavement and clapped thunder. The inspection that trailed them was equally burdensome, but Farina was satisfied with the effort. They were counting the hours to their four-day break, to Christmas, and to the comforts of their own homes.

"The squad passed inspection. They did *well* overall. You can't take this break from my men."

Farina was livid. *And you can't take it from me. I'll die if I don't see my girls.*

Urquhart was unmoved. "I'm not satisfied yet." Farina thought it would feel good just to punch him.

"I'll tell you what. If you clean all the equipment, if I can't find one speck of dirt…not one speck, I mean it, Farina…bring it here tomorrow, and then I'll consider letting you have your four-day."

Farina wore the strained succession of resentments that followed all of his previous discussions with Urquhart. There was a swell of mutiny as Farina almost apologized for the unfairness that was his own near undoing. The stockpile of equipment loomed insurmountable because soldiers saw each piece in parts. It was a mountain of work and Farina wondered if his expression could match the encouragement he pretended in his voice.

Diego imagined the sadness, his family's holiday without him. Diego had to try.

It was nearly midnight, the end of a grueling day, as the squad assembled to scrub down their CIF issue. There were thirty-five pieces, sleeping bags, ruck sacks, cartridge belts, and canteens.

Not one speck of dirt. It was mindless and pointless and Diego's head nodded as he cotton-swabbed the canteen lids. By three in the morning, they succumbed to the monotony. Diego fell asleep on the couch.

Cavazos and Creighton began to wrestle. *Get back to work. We're almost done.* There was a pleading to the entreaty—Farina's baby girl—the only resilience left in the room.

Creighton had an idea, the same one he'd had all night that was interspersed with long strings of insults. It began in coarseness and ended in vulgarity with a "let's bring it all covered in mud" in between. Creighton had bent over backward, had practically done cartwheels to win favor, to earn leave for his birthday—just once. Farina surrendered to Creighton's disillusionment: Urquhart would find something wrong.

Diego called his mother at the end of the next day. His voice was heavy and cheerless. "I really tried, Mom. I did my very best, but I can't come home this weekend."

The Rincons had been invited to spend the holidays with the Schmidts, one of Jorge's regular clients in Social Circle.

"Please call me Pamela," Mrs. Schmidt had once encouraged, and Jorge had politely refused.

"I call you by your first name—I'll have to charge you less." It was his usual comeback, good-natured. But there was something warm, unusually inviting about her manner and the Rincons had become quick, close friends. Their oldest son, Casey, was patient and kind to Stephanie—and Austin was a pistol, like Diego. They had an enormous house that overlooked a pond in the woods, a horse, eleven cats and seven dogs.

"I can't believe it, Yolanda. The place is so clean. Even with all of those pets."

If Jorge said it was clean, then it was truly immaculate.

"Phillip's done well in his job, baby."

It was a Currier & Ives postcard, a wrap-around porch with a view of the pristine fields. There were tall, sturdy oaks that had the nod of a plantation, sweeping and secluded and stately. *The perfect setting for such a significant occasion. Diego might not be home for a while.*

Yolanda felt a catch, the swift disappointment that flustered her. "Okay, Dieguito. It's okay."

She hung up the phone and surveyed the kitchen with all the sweet aromas, the abundance. Chicken and rice and empanadas and the refrigerator stocked full of guava juice. The tree was so plentiful with the skirt of its Christmas presents that it overflowed the dining room. She had turned on the lights and the ornaments sparkled, then flickered to a blur in her eyes.

She would go to him. They would get a hotel room. They would just spend the holidays in Hinesville.

There was a sharp rap at the door and she blinked back the discouragement, put on a brave face for their visitors.

Diego stood in the doorway, that unabashed grin, and Yolanda swept him to her.

"I'm here!" *I'm wight here. I'm wight here, Mommy.* "You know I was just teasing you, Mom."

It was a joyous antagonism that was swallowed in the embrace as she squeezed him tight in her arms.

Diego swung his legs from the kitchen counter, his arms and shoulders taut and exposed. He sat on his hands which further emphasized the perfect V-shape to which his body had conformed.

Fabian squeezed the bulk of his biceps. "Maybe I should join the Army now."

"They'll never take you. You're too lily-white."

"Oh yeah? Happy Kwanzaa, man."

Stephanie and George erupted in a fit of laughter.

"Whatever, Anthrax."

"I'll take you out."

"No wrestling in the house. You know the rules."

They did, in fact, know the rules.

Fabian and Diego shared knowing smiles, an exchange that was lost on their mother. They still had a curfew, no later than midnight, and they'd committed a sin comparable to leaving on shoes in the house.

Let me take the heat. We'll tell them it's my fault.
Why you?
Dude, I'm going to war.

Diego had been right—how long could they ground him? Diego had always been smart that way.

The breach had gone unpunished, but the point had been a mute one. Diego was becoming an introvert. He had broken up with Catherine, a decision that had lasted just over a couple of hours.

You know you're not going to wait for me. There had been tears and slammed doors and Yolanda's quiet intervention.

Dieguito, time will take care of it. If she's truly right for you, then she will wait. If not, it was never meant to be.

It was her second nature and so much hard experience—they were all implied as Yolanda lifted Diego's chin gently. "If you truly don't care about her, that's one thing. But don't take counsel from your fears."

I need your help, Mom.

"I think I should do something special for Catherine before I leave for Kuwait."

"You could take her to dinner at Frontera. Aunt Elsa has coupons for you."

Diego shook his head. "I don't want to leave the house." He jumped from the counter in disquiet.

He had grown protective of every moment since the Christmas break and then, finally, he had detached himself entirely. One by one, the outside haunts had slipped through his fingers until home was all he had clutched in earnest. He had gone to his last movie, had gone out with his buddies, and stopped at a drive-through for hamburgers. Fabian had hurled French fries, backward through his own sunroof to Diego's open convertible. They'd revved their engines and he'd caught a few fries in his mouth, the ones that Fabian had aimed well. They'd driven home separately and he'd hunkered down after that with the playfulness and enthusiasm fading. It was a long and mellow goodbye to more carefree days, as if he might never be young again. That's what it was, not a permanent farewell, but a painful relinquishing of the lightheartedness. Every last touch, every nuance had to be shrouded in home because the rest seemed to be prematurely aging him.

"The Army gave us blue t-shirts. *Light* blue t-shirts for PT in the desert. The enemy will see us working out a mile away.

"Now, does that make any sense to you?"

If there was some logic, Fabian would see it.

"Not unless you work out in the sky."

It brought an unusually wry smile to Diego's lips.

By Jorge's standards, the structure was a shed; by the neighbors' it appeared to be a cottage. There were two glass windows with shutters and flower boxes that were always adorned with silk garlands. The interior was carpeted, and cleaning the shed required no more effort than cleaning the formal dining room. It had been Yolanda's idea. She set out her best candelabras and china reserved for special occasions.

She had to go grocery shopping and Diego called her once, panicked in the near breach of etiquette.

"You have to get a card for her. Pick out something romantic."

"I don't know how you feel, baby."

"Okay, read me the words and I'll tell you what I like."

That one's too puppy love. That one's too old sounding. That one's just lame. I don't like it.

What does it look like?"

Okay, I like that one. When are you coming home?

It wasn't the card or the roses or even dinner—not even the ingenious privacy in the shed. It was the space heater next to Catherine's chair—it was that Diego had remembered a little thing like that. Catherine always got cold, and Yolanda felt a tug as the lights in the neighborhood began to snap on in their twilight. The candlelight glowed from the coziness of the sanctuary, two teenagers playing house. There were apparent shadow dances, a dip and a sway, and then they weren't really children anymore. They grew up—not before Yolanda's eyes, but in the echo of soft laughter drifting into the woods. It bubbled uninhibited and then it grew fainter, weighted by the hush of their seriousness. They were two teenagers playing house except that one of them was old enough to go to war.

"What are you thinking?"

Diego shrugged, playing with the key chain in the Mustang. "I don't know how you'll take this."

"Whatever it is, you can tell me, Diego. Please."

The sky had that severity, netted in stars, sharp and pointed and lucid. It was satin black, chilled and unyielding in the way that made a man feel small in comparison.

"I love you," he said. The stars softened and blurred. She whispered it back in his ear. He caressed her face and the honey blonde hair and he kissed her in the driveway of his house.

There was a man-to-man talk in the backyard swing the morning after the candlelight dinner. Across the country, there were those sacred moments, all those fathers and sons on back porches. Creighton's father was that sage first sergeant who would ship his son some witch hazel when he arrived in Kuwait.

"It will help with the heat rashes and the thing about witch hazel—the enemy won't smell you coming."

Dad, that's just jungle talk. Creighton stared at the ground with an unexpected tenderness. *Vietnam and the stuff of his old man.* "Maybe we won't even fire a shot, Dad. Maybe we'll just die of the boredom."

Russell shook his head, worked his hands, tried to find the right words. "Someday you'll be sitting in a foxhole somewhere, talking about hamburgers and milkshakes. The next thing you know, your buddy will slump over. That'll be it. He'll be gone," he said.

"When someone's that hurt, you can do a million things, but you can't go back in time, son. Death is death, and you can't change it, no matter how hard you try. I want you to understand that, Mike. Don't blame the medics. You might see death once. The medics—they see death every day."

He gave his son tracts—Christian tracts—to hand out to his fellow soldiers. "It'll matter a lot over there. You wait and see. Even the atheists will need Jesus."

Creighton's face was backlit in a newfound sobriety and he began to rub his fingers like his father. He hadn't seen combat so it wasn't what they called the thousand-mile stare—not yet. It just looked a lot like it, the same world-away gaze that Fabian saw in Diego.

It hurt like crazy, something fierce and protective sweeping a big brother's soul.

All those long talks in the Mustang from Conyers to Fort Stewart with that scratchy signal from the radio. It had forced them to actually interact and something had matured drastically—now that Diego was deploying. It was a terrible sting, a lasting remorse so that Fabian had signed on as his right-hand man. *I'll fix the car up for you. You go fight wars and I'll keep things going on the home front.* Diego, the epitome of the U.S. Army, so confident, so fearless, so indestructible. That was it, when it was boiled down—the expectations that Fabian finally grasped. It had to be hard, too, to have the pressure, to be the nice guy, to always play the hero.

Diego's face wore unmixed anguish in the time he had left to be brave.

Creighton's dad had tried to strengthen his son and, conversely, Diego tried to steel his father. In the backyard swing, the cold nipping at their hands, he allowed the bow momentarily. It was the frost of January and then it was something harsher that reddened his cheeks at midday. "Pops, they told us the terrorists might arm the children. If I saw a little boy with a rifle…"

He trailed off and turned haunted eyes to Jorge. "I couldn't live with myself."
It was said so low, barely above a whisper, that Jorge felt a sharp pain in his
chest.

"I signed all the insurance papers. I'll leave you a copy. You'll get $250,000."
The chest pain grew unbearable, and Jorge thrust his hands forward, an
instinctive flinch to halt him. "You see these two hands. I can always make
money. All I need are these two hands."

Jorge cradled his son's face, suddenly rough and despairing. He was pleading
and he didn't know why.

"Dieguito, I cannot make you again."

He pulled his son to him fiercely.

Please bring Diego home safely. Yolanda clutched the phone in the kitchen, in
the tearing trust to which no company commander was immune. Lieutenant
Colonel Scott Rutter was to lead Alpha Company and he would only make one
other similar phone call. He wished that he had a hundred soldiers like Diego, he
said. He was proud of him, for his loyalty and his dependability. He wanted
Yolanda to know how much he appreciated good parents—for raising that kind
of a son.

There was humility and tenderness and a kind of concession that leaders didn't
make everyday. "Ma'am. I will do my very best to bring them *all* back. I can and
will promise you that."

There was a poignant emotional checklist that Diego had to complete, just days
before he deployed. He drove his Mustang to Salem High School and scanned the
sprawl of his formative years. Jerry Smith met him near all the old hangouts with the
sadness and the agony trickling down his face. It was hard to bear up when he didn't
agree politically with any one premise for the war. That was the human drama,
shared between a mentor and a friend who was so young that Mr. Smith ached. The
inner turmoil nearly took his breath away as he held out his arms to Diego.

He looked into Diego's eyes, and he hated the war and nothing in his mind
could have ever made it right. And then he saw a fire, an inexplicable conviction
that had never burned in Diego before. He stepped away with that last jarring
hug, his little son so bold and so proud. What he saw was that the war was right
for Diego, and he surrendered with his most supportive smile.

Diego flashed his own grin, and there was shattering pain in Mr. Smith as the
engine of the Mustang roared. Diego squealed from the parking lot, left telltale
black tracks, that little piece of his heart.

Diego called Kenneth and it was just a phantom trace he left on the caller ID.
It faded in time and Kenneth consoled himself that the war would take little time
to win.

He understood why Diego had left no message—there were probably no words for such moments. Kenneth just wished for the richness and the resonance; he just wished for the formality of a goodbye.

┼╪═╪═╪┼

The men of 2-7 marched to waiting buses in the early morning hours of January 23, 2003. The sun hid its face in a final show of respect, in the mournful sympathy of rain. No thought was given to swirling debates on diplomacy or Congressional acts of war. It was inconsequential that Turkey had outlined tenuous conditions and that there was talk of a stalemate in the U.N. There was a gray zone of grief overshadowed by dignity and formations and the abrupt snap of loss. The men's uniforms were being pelted by the outpouring of the sky as each infantryman faded from view.

Naemi Cavazos walked the pathway along Cottrell Field afterward, the loneliness and the hurt sweeping at her in the wind. It had been a four-hour goodbye outside Alpha Company that had strained the serenity of her soul. There had been delays, more preparation, and more delays before the troops had marched away in that drizzle. She had focused on the bright spots—that was her nature—the small things that had sustained her resolve.

There had been the three-year-old daughter of Sergeant Williams who had run in circles, twirling her father's booney hat in her hand. Her mother had awakened her in the middle of the night for the last embraces that might ease some future regret. If something should happen—if Williams didn't come home—his little girl would always have that faint memory. It was Mya's innocence, still dressed in her Clifford nightgown, and the laughter that had graced their dawn.

"Baby, you know—I probably won't see any action. We don't even know there'll be a war."

But if there is, I'll be here. I'll be right here, Adrian. I'll be the one holding down the fort.

It's what her father used to say: "You hold down the fort." And she would hold still and hold on and hold back. Adrian needed that assurance, that light in her eyes, that beacon that anchored him to shore. If when he crossed the ocean again, if he came home changed, if he came home with less than two legs—Naemi would be there; she would always just be there; she was his constant, his hope, and his whole world.

He'd die from the boredom, like Creighton had said, from sitting on the border, and even if they went into battle—

Look at her father in the Gulf War. Look at Afghanistan. Were they all just being naïve?

In her heart was that experience—that dread and that calm—was it better to have been raised with the ghosts? To have taken that widow's walk so many times, that vigilant watch for a soldier? Did her background help her? *Her father had come home.* She had that pattern to cling to. She had that pattern, always nagged by the fear—the men in her life perhaps dying.

He was on a flight by now to Ireland, and there was a sudden, piercing pang of remorse. It was a destination—a honeymoon—not a real stopover for war. The hills cascaded verdant and pristine, the sheep were like soft puffs of clouds. The outland was graced by the elegance of castles and the villages were charming and cozy. It touched her like a dream, that softness, that splendor of ordinary life *somewhere else.* The rain was streaking against cottage windows, the glow of lamps lit for *someone else.* It was gray and damp and streaking down her face, that rain for somebody else.

She couldn't have known as she pressed past the field the bittersweet spring of her longing. She stood at the spot where eastern redbud trees would be planted later, the pathway of the Warriors' Walk. There were no limbs outstretched; no seedlings of warning for each fallen man who would be memorialized. The field stretched endless, flat with no break, like the Normandy landscape of 1940. She had called it out at the last minute—had yelled to Diego. *Good luck over there!* That big smile. Her looking glass was dazed on a grass that was dormant, brown, spent of the lifeblood of the men. No toil, no sweat, no call for PT sounding from the layers of their soil. She had never felt she belonged on that part of the post, a civilian, amid the rank and the file. It took her aback, the forlornness, the barrenness, the cavity they had left in their wake. It was hers, after all, every particle and blade, echoing the striving of her husband. Her eyes were glazed, she was sifting through consciousness—trying to breathe, to make her heart beat without his pulse. Nothing would ever be clear or bright or lucid until Adrian was back in her arms.

Time stood still at 11:11 and so she set forth a new pattern. She stood and she prayed as she would every day; it gave her a new sense of purpose. In the morning and at night, at 11:11 she summoned, entreated her courage.

It was a small thing she did; but she had to have meaning. Faith was the opposite of fear.

At 11:11, in an Atlanta suburb, Yolanda sat quietly on Diego's bed. She pushed the play button on his keyboard, and the strain drifted haunting, bereft, down the hall. He had worked it repeatedly, until it was perfect, a final remembrance to keep her company.

She hugged his pillow to her, the smell of him still overpowering, weeping to the melody of Beethoven's Für Elise.

CHAPTER 4

Somewhere in America, people slept, and drank ice cold milk, and went to shopping malls. Somewhere in America, where there were trees, and streams, and flowers they took long walks in parks. They windsurfed or snow skied, depending on their climate; there were moderately predictable weather patterns. When it was cold they went inside; when it was too hot, they turned on air conditioning. There were sensibilities, somewhere in America.

The troops landed on Mars, a red planet of swirling sand that riddled their skin like fire ants. It assaulted them first thing, a constant irritant in their eyes, their noses, and throats; the enemy they could not contain. They hadn't arrived in season—the storms were most prevalent from March until August—and still a fine mist shrouded their sleeping bags, even the underwear they wore. Kuwait just blinded a man; and, after the dust settled, what they saw they didn't believe.

There was no patchwork of shade: no trees or bushes or even long slivers of grass. The landscape was forlorn, desolate, but for the occupation that skirted its northernmost borders.

Diego set up his cot with the rest of the company, row after row of camouflage sleeping bags and personal effects spilling out of their rucksacks. The first night was bitterly cold, and the soldiers were plagued by mosquitoes, trying to draw small, shivering breaths. They suffocated themselves in the bags, trying to evade the malaria; by mid-day, the tent was oppressively hot. Their belongings were covered in flies and Diego felt like a pig, roasting on a spit. It was the beginning of a mindless routine of living like animals, bunkered in the same slop and sameness of oversized tents, the grit, and the tedium.

Only forty-eight hours had passed, and the 2-7 was ready, primed for war just to get out of Camp Pennsylvania.

The men tried to write from the prone position in their beds, filling out form letters for their families. It had come down to that—men big enough for battle and too juvenile to be trusted with their own correspondence. The postage was pre-paid and the cards were white, except for two rows of neat, black type:

HELLO <u>Mom and Dad</u>, I HAVE ARRIVED IN KUWAIT SAFELY. PLEASE SEND MAIL TO THE RETURN ADDRESS.

Perhaps the military thought it was preserving manliness, making such a polite, blanket request on behalf of the soldiers. Diego had no shame. He had written in the letdown: *Send me anything that you may think I need. Give this address to everybody…*

There was a strange glow in the tent at night, like a hospital room where the lights never truly faded. In it, Diego could see a few of the men toss and turn, trying to settle with their arms wrapped around some kind of softness. Their towels and their brown t-shirts—their socks stiff with sweat—everything hung like putrid, taunting ghosts on the lines overhead. The homesickness did not come in waves as Diego expected it would: it was ever-present in a general malaise and half-heartedness.

Somewhere in America kitchens smelled of waffles and eggs in the morning, and laundry had that fresh, clean scent. People showered with soap and shampoo and conditioner, and their water was extremely hot, even when the January rain pounded the pavement. Diego saw Tí Tí through the kitchen window in such overwhelming strikes and mirages: Tí Tí in her pajamas with her long, disheveled hair, spilling down her back.

He punched his bag trying to squelch the hurt, trying to pretend he was just trying to get situated on his cot.

"I think they'll make a movie."

It was like the first drop of rain, a mildness in a ripple on a pond.

"Who?" It was muffled by Sawicki's arm over his face. He had almost drifted to sleep.

"Us," Cavazos said. "They'll make a movie of *us*. Like *Blackhawk Down*, or *We Were Soldiers Once*. I think Tom Cruise should definitely play me. I mean I know he's not Hispanic, but he's got my charisma, you know?"

"What do you *mean* by charisma? Do you mean you've got some magnetism, or do you mean some intensity, some fire?"

"Well both. I'm sexy, Sawicki. And I am pretty brave. I would definitely have to say both."

There was a chorus of derision. The men were suddenly wide awake and a rolled up t-shirt hit Cavazos squarely.

"If there was a movie, *I'd* be the star. Tom Cruise would have to play *me*."

"Oh yeah, that'd work, Farina. 'Cause to draw the women we'd have to have a sensitive leading man."

"Well, one thing about it, Sawicki. We'd have to make you the loner. You would have to be the guy with no friends."

"I have a wife."

"Yeah, you're a real keeper. Not quite sure how that happened. But you're a real keeper, Patty Cake."

"Do you know how he met her—this is classic. They were both counselors at an Easter Seals camp. He taught special ed. This guy worked with children. Is that just scary or what?"

"You know, she saw my name on the list of counselors. She just saw my name and she knew."

"Knew what, Sawicki? *Quick, you better run*. Find yourself another camp, girl."

Diego laughed hard. It just felt good to laugh; maybe it wasn't even that funny.

"I'm thinking Ben Stiller could pull you off, Sawicki. Ben Stiller with crazy eyes."

"Who gets to play me?" It was Diego's lack of guile, to think out loud and set himself up like that.

"The ladies are fond of you. Maybe Benjamin Bratt." There seemed to be consensus on Diego's character.

Cavazos was pleased, to have pegged him so easily and won that unanimous vote.

"Hey, how about L.T.? Who could play 'The L.T.?' The platoon commander—that's an important one."

"Tom Hanks," Curtin said. *Of course. Tom Hanks.* He had precedence in *Saving Private Ryan.*

Williams was also key; he had to have a big role, one of the best NCOs the men had ever known. "Sergeant Williams. That's easy. Gotta be Will Smith. Definitely, played by Will Smith."

"And Sergeant Tolbert—that's Denzel Washington." Sergeant Ronald Tolbert was officially a tank gunner. Unofficially, he was like the camp psychologist, the soothing one who talked them through all of their problems.

"You know who could play you?" Cavazos turned to Farina. "Keanu Reeves, don't you think?"

Farina mulled it. "I think I could see that…

"Yeah…he's a high-speed guy."

"Why do we always say that—guys in the Army—who started that anyway? I'm a high-speed guy with a high-speed knife and a high-speed M16."

There was a pause in the debate and then Sawicki took the credit. "Okay, it was me. I admit it. I was the first guy in the entire Army to ever say 'high-speed'—and then Al Gore and I invented the Internet.

"I also came up with 'hooah' and it just caught on. Everyone wants to be like me."

"Go to sleep, Patty Cake. We're impressed enough that someone let you graduate from college."

"And work with children."

"And reproduce."

"Hey, you leave my baby girl out of this."

"I think if there a movie, I know who play me." PFC Erwin Rendon's frame suddenly overpowered his cot. Rendon was from Ecuador, and he was selective in acknowledging the letter "s" in either of the languages he spoke. It was a useless consonant; it tied up the tongue and, really, he swore quite well without it.

He was 6'3" and burly and he would have been formidable if it wasn't for an oversized heart.

"Leonardo DiCaprio. He can play me."

The tent erupted in hysterics.

"*Leonardo DiCaprio*—what is he, a blond? *Dude*, he's the size of your forearm."

"I like him, though. I see his movies. He alway get the girl in the end."

It was said with such innocence; there really was some logic, a thought process not of their planet. "Okay, okay," he recanted." Maybe not him. I think Kevin Costner then."

Diego rubbed his eyes. He couldn't catch his breath in a laughter that ached in his stomach.

"Please, man, I'm serious. He my favorite white guy."

Diego's cot was shaking.

There was a story about Rendon that became legendary, after the throes of combat. It was one of those windows, the anecdotal kind that gave a panoramic view on his nature. The scene was a shower stall, a coveted appointment because that's how they earned cleanliness during peacekeeping—by appointment. He had lathered himself up, in the toil of Baghdad, the exotic leisure of mere soap and water.

Rendon was friendly, and so he had called out when a British soldier happened by his stall.

"Hey guy," he had said.

"Hey," had come the reply, too much femininity in the pitch.

Rendon had stared, horrified. *A woman in their showers.* He had been flustered for only a second. He had just grabbed a towel, not bothering to rinse off, and he had run from her, all the way through the local hospital.

"There a girl. In the shower. She's British and she saw me."

Sawicki had mulled that in his political mind.

"Well, I don't think you should hold that against the British. At least they're here," he had muttered.

"I think 'The Rock' should play Rendon."

The suggestion had come from the cot beside him.

Every funny man had a sidekick, and Erwin Rendon's was Private First Class Paolo Ronquillo. He had come from the Philippines in 1997. *It's Rone-key-lee-oh,* he had enunciated it. The men had never quite gotten it. *Run-quill-oh. Ronny Q. Whatever.* They were loathe to be bothered with details.

Ronquillo was bright. Ronquillo was articulate. He marched to a different drum. His face was sincere, even when he wasn't, and so his expressions were always mixed. He had the markings of a bygone school president except for the sardonic humor—Ronquillo had a purity and a childlike trust to him and still somehow came off as jaded. It took exactly one beer to fuzz his world and so he rarely drank.

None for me, thanks. It's all in the moderation. You know how I get if I drink.

Really, they didn't. He never lost control, but there was no starting point, no convention to begin with. *I think "The Rock" should play Rendon.* It was such a sensible thing to say that the men waited for some kind of wisecrack.

Ronquillo shrugged and they began a checklist of the men in Diego's squad, with an offshoot of friends sprinkled in the mix. PFC James Lane was so incredibly young, had joined when he was seventeen years old. They had to think on that one, skipped him momentarily, and moved on to Creighton and Black. Brad Pitt for Creighton. In his most tough guy roles. They struggled again to pinpoint Black. Jet Li and Ronquillo—that was a natural. Curtin could be played by Orlando Bloom. Curtin warmed to that. It was one of his favorite characters—Legolas, famously arrow-whipping in *The Lord of the Rings.*

"Hey, what about Brooks over here?"

The men thought hard. Brooks was complex. Vivid and engaging, but reserved.

"Russell Crowe."

There was a swell of agreement, and then a handful of dissenting voices.

"What's wrong with Russell Crowe?" Sawicki was in favor. "He can be offhanded. He can be coy. He can be tough. Look at *Gladiator.*"

"He's too old for Brooks," someone said, and above the protests came the loudest rebuff.

"Did you just say 'coy?' Did you actually just use it in a sentence? Did you just use coy to describe one of *us*? Cvos, did you actually say 'fond of' earlier? What's wrong with you people? What's wrong with you coy boy? We're men!

"We're...going...to...war!" Farina arched in his sleeping bag, as if bound like a mummy, trying to flail lose of his shroud. He cursed at the constraint. "Stop talking like that!" We're the infantry! Okay?! We're *men!!!"*

"Easy there, buddy. Whoa, Indiana Jones. Somebody needs to take a nap."

"Viggo Mortensen." It came from a corner.

"What?"

"Viggo Mortensen."

"He has an established relationship with Orlando Bloom. He's a little bit edgier, though."

Brooks smiled to himself. He was neither convinced nor put off; he offered no opinion at all.

"There's that seven-minute lull in the conversation. Quick, somebody fill it. Hurry."

"Okay. What about women?"

"Ohhhhh. We *have* to have women. They can play our wives and stuff."

"They gotta be hot."

"Oh, they'll be hot."

"Not as hot as Mrs. Sawicki, of course."

It was a whole new tangent and Cavazos drifted off, taking first dibs on a cameo appearance.

"Hi love. Hey baby." Black smooched his hand; the phone line seemed to snake for miles. "I miss you so much. Look at him, Creight. He's slobbering all over himself."

Rendon turned his back. He was in a sour mood—so distracted he'd even lost a chess match. He was the defending champion, and he should have advanced to the semi-finals at Camp PA.

"It's because he didn't get any mail from her today. Now isn't that just precious. I tell ya."

Rendon tried to be discreet before he hung up the phone. "Bye baby," he kissed the receiver.

"I'm surprised I'm not taking *your* calls over here, Black." Cavazos' voice carried insolence. *"Can I speak to Allen? This is one of his girls."*

"Now, man you know I wasn't getting any cell phone service."

"He gave them *my* phone number. They were calling at all hours of the night. *Hello...I'm Black's answering machine. Sure. No problem. Let me drive to the barracks. See if I can find his sorry self.*"

Ronquillo snickered. "And when you walk in, you know what he's doing? He's *charging* his phone. No kidding."

"Why you charge the phone when you got no service?"

"You shouldn't let your batteries run down."

Rendon turned his back for the second time in disgust. "You're too much for me, man."

"I need my 'me' time. You know what I'm saying? It didn't hurt him to take a few calls.

"Hey Rincon!" Black interrupted himself. "What'd your mama say?"

Diego turned around with a self-satisfied smile. It had been a six-hour wait to make the call.

Mom, don't you worry. I'm not getting married. No matter what you hear. "I just wanted to be on the news. I told a reporter that I had gotten engaged. It was the only way I could get on TV."

More clearly than the lizard that had scurried at his feet, Diego had seen his mother's reaction. She had stood in his bedroom, that second floor loft that overlooked the driveway and the street. It was overcast in Georgia, and she had ducked her head in the soft smile that couldn't help disapproving. "What am I going to do with you?" she had asked.

"Send me another package."

Diego had hung up the phone with a strange twist in his stomach. It was the waiting and the boredom that made him dwell on things. "My mom couldn't pick me out!" Diego called back to Black. "She said, in uniform, we all look alike!"

"Oh, well now, that's true. Look here at Brooks and me. No one can tell *us* apart."

Brooks smiled wryly. Black was black and Brooks was not even close. "I do tan easily." That part was true. "And then sometimes *I* get confused. I think I'm Cvos and then I think I'm Black and then sometimes I think I'm Ronquillo. It's that 'Army of One' thing. I can't help myself. I just don't know who I am."

"You know, this here's an ad for cultural diversity. Somebody take a picture. Somebody show our quota. We got us some kind of quota going on right here."

Diego sauntered away, left Black to his politically correct musings. Cavazos headed to their tent.

It was a miserable day, the heat and the itchiness of monotony swelling in his brain. Cavazos needed action, something meaningful, and he thought in his idleness on the most grotesque insect: it was known as a camel spider and they'd been told more than once that it could eat an animal whole. The spider was as long as a soldier's forearm and it devoured its prey, even humans, from the inside out. It started in the intestines and worked its way to the gray matter and it was all very spooky stuff. It was a myth, of course, though there were camel spiders and they *looked* like they might do serious damage.

The real predator was the tedious cat and mouse game—someday Kuwait might just swallow Cavazos whole. More than the war, he hated the waiting for war, the constant nibbling at his psyche.

"Stop toying with me, Rincon." It was late in the game and Ronquillo moved a pawn from its opening position. It was a strategy meant to be equally exasperating because Diego had won long ago. "Just call checkmate. Get the thing over with." His white pawn could neither advance nor capture Diego's bishop. He couldn't interpose and Diego was dancing adeptly, hovering but not checking Ronquillo's king.

Diego was pleased with himself. *Dart in and out. Wait for the more glorious kill.* Diego wouldn't be satisfied until he'd captured all the pieces, until every pawn was a prisoner of war.

"He stinks at chess. I don't see how he wins all the time. He doesn't even understand the rules." It was true Diego had just taken up the game—to have something else in common with Fabian.

Johnson smiled dryly. "That's like saying the Lakers stink. But, hey, somehow they win."

"He just moves a lot. He's shifty. That's it. He's got no strategy at all."

"Checkmate." Diego leaned back in his chair. The smile on his face was smug. He had made it to the finals and Johnson kept reading, some amusement tugging at his mouth.

It took so much to ruffle Diego that Cavazos had to think hard. Creighton sat down on his cot in protest, his patience worn razor thin. His military Star card was new, the plastic issued by the Army, and the bureaucracy was a backhanded slap. He couldn't withdraw money—they'd sent him to war and he couldn't even access his paycheck. He rubbed his temples as if he might explode; it was a pressure cooker inside the tent. There were too many bodies, too many indignities, and the heat just agitated him more.

He was as stir crazy as Cavazos, and he sensed the alliance the minute Cavazos motioned him outside.

"I'd like to see him mad. Seriously mad. What do you think we should do?"

A mischievous smile crossed Creighton's face. He peered inside the tent.

Several men were stretched out, writing letters home. Rendon was meticulously scribbling. He had mammoth hands, but his characters were tiny as if he had a sacred duty to conserve paper. His choice of words was long and flowing, but the mechanics shrunk them so that they were nearly illegible. He poured out his feelings, and then he folded the papers and he never sent the letters to his mother.

She was having a hard time, a seamstress in New York, afraid to answer the door. Rendon's younger brother had been deployed on the USNS Comfort—all of her boys in the waves of combat. She didn't leave the house for fear there might be news, and she didn't answer the door for the same reason. Rendon wrote her about their sandbox, all the pains and the humilities, and he told her about each of the men. Diego was kind and Black was funny and Cavazos could never sit still. "Mike Creighton is a white guy but, Mom, you should meet him: he has a big, Hispanic heart."

He pictured her in Manhattan, in their shoebox apartment and always she was crippled in fear.

Curtin, too, was writing, making a plea for his family to send something overseas to Brooks. Brooks never received packages, rarely got letters, and Curtin felt the sting of reproach. Brooks had family and he'd been known to drive home to Florida nearly every weekend to see them. It didn't make sense, and Brooks never let on that he'd held to his own hard and fast rule: there would be no word until the fighting was over, until he'd made it out alive.

He couldn't fathom his last words reaching his sisters after his own funeral. *Hello everybody. I'm doing fine.*

Except that he'd been killed in combat a month earlier. The mail could be that slow.

Creighton waited until Diego left for the mess tent, until all of the letter writing ceased. He stole to Diego's cot and took a can of black spray paint and painstakingly left a message on Diego's pants.

"It's like encouragement," he smirked to Cavazos, allowing the paint to dry in the seat. He hoped Diego would spot it in the desert camouflage; if not, that might be even funnier.

It was perhaps the close quarters, day in and day out, but the men were keenly aware of the mood shifts. The tentacles of relationships spanned the ocean, and they embraced or throttled morale. Farina entered the tent and he still seemed pensive, but it was clear the load had been lessened. It was the magic of Sergeant Tolbert, some gift that he had for renewing the soul in private visits.

Tolbert was intuitive, approachable, and interested, which made him like God in a way. When the prayers seemed to bounce off the pitch of their quarters, there was Tolbert, that sounding board.

Farina was transported thousands of miles, his mind so nestled in Indiana that the Arch Abbey sang. *Father, thank you. I really needed to talk to someone. I needed it explained to me that way.*

Creighton and Cavazos edged away from Diego's cot, and there was no such sanctity in their expressions. They wore the nonchalance that had come with much practice at pranks and the hot air that they always blew afterward. They covered their sneers and they covered their tracks and they covered for each other at all costs. Diego returned and the pair locked eyes once and then they almost forgot the joke.

Diego took a seat on Farina's cot, and it was covered with letters from Indiana. The children from the school where his mother-in-law taught had written to express their support. Every once in a while the soldiers got shipments like that: drawings and misspellings and beginning grammar. And then some of the hometown kids who had written were in junior high, and they had soul-searching praise for the troops. *Anthony Farina. You are my hero. I wouldn't have the courage to fight like you do.*

He had held that notebook sheet for a very long time, his chest tightening on the effect of the words. He ached to live to see his baby's first steps and that sparkle in the eyes of his four-year-old. Sometimes he didn't feel like such a hero; sometimes he didn't feel he could take one more step.

"All you have out here are the men beside you," Tolbert had comforted him quietly. "They're your brothers, Farina, and you have to put your trust in them the way those school kids put their trust in you."

That was the thing that had settled him finally, and Farina smiled softly as Diego shared the adulation of southern Indiana.

"This is awesome."

"Yeah, it really is. It means a whole lot over here, you know?"

"So what did you think, when you heard we were attached to the 3-69?" Diego's digression caught him off guard.

Farina paused thoughtfully. "Well, it's an armor battalion. Soldiers can do what the tanks just can't sometimes.

"I'll miss some of the guys in Alpha Company, but we're Outlaws, you know? We might as well live up to the name."

Diego picked at the sleeping bag. "We're the ugly stepchild. Nobody loves us, Farina."

"They may not love us, but they'll always need the infantry. The ground's where it's at, little brother."

Farina paused. "I think I'm going to re-enlist."

Diego's face was unreadable.

"I can make a career of it. I have the stuff, I think. I'm looking at Special Forces." He blew out a hard breath. "I just have a lot on my mind. My kids and my wife to take care of. You know I stood in line for two and a half hours today just to get on the phone at Camp New York. I started talking to my wife and then I got called to leave. This whole thing is *not* family friendly. All the moving and deployments—this is my third, Recon—the third time away from everyone I know. But if I can get this promotion, if I can make E-5 Sergeant, I'll have options and a pretty good pay raise.

"I'll tell you one thing I'm not going to work two jobs to support my family back home."

There seemed to be something on Diego's mind, too, but he was hesitant to utter the words. Farina had always envied him, that carefree nature, that live-in-the-moment kind of slack. There was something disheartened, a subtle worry that played in the gentleness of Diego's eyes. Farina had sought Tolbert, and Diego had sought Johnson, and the platoon leader had tried to talk him through the crisis. Johnson knew the Bible backward and forward, and Diego had such burning questions.

Farina was religious and so Diego hinted. "I'm glad I was re-baptized at boot camp."

It didn't hang as heavy in the air as he'd thought it would, and Farina seemed to understand. "Now's the time to get it all straightened out, Recon. Before you go home to Jesus. If He decides to take you, then you'll know you served your purpose. Just get things straight while you're here."

Diego looked away, and Farina had to add it: "I don't know how this all turns out.

"I know somehow that God is in complete control, and I know things get messy in a war. People die and war isn't fair and this life isn't fair—but God *is*. All of us are free to make choices and you and I—it's our moment—the ones to fight to defend those choices. It's a God-given right, Rincon—that freedom of choice—and *we* were born to defend it.

"God doesn't always intervene right way. He just rectifies all the mistakes in the end."

There was a fine line between unloading the burden and dwelling on the more morbid thoughts. Something Naemi had once said struck Diego deeply in the context of Farina's eloquence. They had passed a sign for a consult with a psychic who had settled in Hinesville—an Army town. It would have been nice to have all the answers, to know if he'd live or he'd die. Or maybe he just wanted to know that he'd live; maybe he didn't really want the truth. Not one of the men had ventured to the psychic. Most of them had chosen church instead.

"I don't really believe that everything is pre-destined," Naemi had waxed thoughtful in the car.

"If everything is decided, then why bother fighting?"

God expected them to strive.

+>===<+

The edge to Camp PA grew palpable in the afternoon as the day stretched long and blew harsh. Daytime flew and the hours crept and no one could get a handle on that idiosyncrasy. The nerves had frayed and then finally unraveled. Farina's voice took on hardness.

"It's time to go to Baghdad. This war was started twelve years ago, and now it's time for us to finish it."

"I think I have sun poisoning," Diego sat down hard.

"It's the fluctuation in temperature." The air had been cool at the range they'd established, but the sun had remained unforgiving. In all of his travels, so many climates, Farina had never experienced anything like it. "It's hot and then it's cold and then it's both all at once. This is the best vacation spot ever."

"Welcome, my friends, to the beautiful beaches of Kuwait." Sawicki flung his gear on his cot.

Diego rolled to his side and it was then that he discovered it—that little piece of advice from his friends. He clutched the pants in a reaction that was immediate and full and surpassed all previous expectations. It was better than irritated. Better than mad. Cavazos stood motionless in his wonder. Diego leaped from the bed with a remarkable threat. Diego actually threw a fit.

He found the spray paint and he found Creighton outside and he hurled himself at his chest. There was a hard flail and motioning and stray men gathered around, one of the few spectator sports in their sandbox. Diego pinned his body and Creighton threw sand in protest at his eyes and mouth.

"I hate when he does that. He fight dirty, man." Rendon had to pull for Diego.

Creighton rolled on his back and Diego sprayed, every square inch of his inseam and then some.

"Now that's not subtle. Creighton was subtle. A little tiny message, you know."

Diego unleashed his fury until the can was spent, until both men gasped and tapped out.

Cavazos paced the perimeter. "He completely overreacted," but truly Cavazos was pleased.

If it was an overreaction, it was also a chain reaction that sent the men over the edge. Wrestling broke out in wayward patches throughout the camp, a cauldron of frustration boiling over. Rendon wanted the action and he tried to get the outlet, "C'mon, Sergeant Wills. *Please.*"

Williams was clever. The higher ranks would never touch him. "I'm sorry but I don't wrestle privates."

"Don't wrestle privates? Why you say that? You know I can take you. *You're scared.*"

Williams smiled wryly. "I would but I can't. I just cannot wrestle *privates* today."

There was another brief sandstorm, and it abated with the sluggish fall of the sun, a fairly distant cousin to dusk. As Farina had claimed, there were two types of environments, the blaze and the bone chill that curtailed it. The men played with a lizard and they built a cardboard sled from a leftover care package they'd confiscated. They slid on the sand dunes until they exhausted the cardboard, until all they could manage was tumbling. It was the end-over-end antics that brought up the subject, the opportune lull to tell a well-guarded secret.

Lieutenant Johnson was lazed in his portable chair, absorbed in a copy of *Band of Brothers*. He sat outside with his bare head exposed to the wrath of the sun in its decline. He used a Bic razor, a manual stroke, to achieve the smooth baldness that branded him. He wore dark glasses, small, round lenses that reflected the brashness of the heat. He assumed the pose of Socrates that was his habit, his index finger thoughtful on his cheek. Brooks leaned over him with his chin on his fist, Auguste Rodin's renowned statue, "The Thinker."

"Hey, Lord of the Flies," Cavazos called to Johnson, "we found out Rincon here was a cheerleader."

"You'll get his attention if you yell 'bookmobile' real loud. He'll run after it— like a kid and an ice cream truck."

"*I* was a cheerleader."

"Sawicki, don't lie to me."

"It's *true*. In *college*. At *Radford*."

Sawicki's voice increased an octave with each point of emphasis. It was a thick northeastern accent that always played the defense.

"What do you *mean* by 'I was a cheerleader?' What do you meeeaaaann by that statement?" Cavazos used one of Sawicki's trademarks. The answer with a question, the elongation of *mean*, and the eyes slightly squinted.

"What do you meeeaaaann by what do I meeeaaaann? Do you mean am I cheerleader now? Clearly not now, Cvos. Not when I'm a soldier. Do you mean that you think I could be both, because I can't. Do you *mean* was I a cheerleader in *Kuwait?*"

"Prove it, Patty Cake. Do a little trick."

Sawicki, who knew just a little bit about everything.

"Let's see what Rincon has in him first."

Cavazos' laugh was predictable.

Johnson creased the page and leaned in his chair with his hands folded, abruptly and fully attentive. "Okay, let's see some tricks. Do a little cartwheel. Something to boost morale."

It was the reason Cavazos regarded Johnson as a friend, that likable, offhanded manner. They were both sarcastic, but loyal enough that laughing at the men felt like laughing at themselves.

"Come on now," he urged. "Don't be bashful. We have *cheerleaders* among us. Give a yell. Inspire us."

"Hi." Clap, clap. *"My name's Diego."* Clap, clap, clap. Cavazos' attempt doubled Farina over.

Diego took on that "aw shucks" kind of look he'd carried at basic training—the same kind of glint that had flickered in his eyes just before he'd annihilated the competition in the obstacle course. He worked his shoulders and his triceps and quads and he stretched for a moment in earnest. There wasn't a lot of spring in his combat boots and little give in his DCUs. He surveyed the distance of the undeviating quadrant and the men thought he was putting them on. The sand was a tough mat; he swung his arms back and forth to get the blood pumping again. He breathed in, then breathed out, one short quick exhale, and then he coiled in all of his gear.

It was rough on his hands, like the lick of a cat's tongue, as he propelled himself through the series. It was amazingly cathartic, to shrug off the constraint—that regiment that had so overshadowed him. The soldiers didn't know him like the folks back home, not the showboating or the spontaneity or the joy. Diego had squelched that untroubled part of him the moment he'd taken an oath. There were some traits, unheralded, because he'd kept them from the men—even from Farina, his brother. They thought he was quiet and somewhat unassuming and Diego felt his heart soar.

He stuck his landing, back handsprings in triplicate and a couple one-handed for good measure. He leaned on his legs, panting in the effort and the flushing temperature of an oven. There was a stunned sort of hush, a few blown breaths, and it was Johnson who broke their stillness.

"Was it just me or did he just go like—I don't know—the length of a football field?"

"Wow," Brooks stared.

Cavazos' laugh was short. "I had no idea. I swear."

He's such an athlete. Farina felt a strange swell in an articulation that wouldn't do Diego justice. There were so few luxuries and so much degradation in the primitive captivity of Kuwait. Diego had risen above them all for a second, had exalted and transcended the baseness and the stagnation and the depravity. Farina felt a salute in him, the grace and the elegance and the dignity his friend had restored.

Diego's smile dazzled and he should have taken a bow, right there in the theater of their war.

"Okay, Sawicki, show us what you got. We don't have all day."

It wasn't true, but Cavazos liked the pressure. Sawicki hesitated.

"I'm really not that limber."

"Just do a cartwheel or something."

"Really, it's been quite a while, guys."

Cavazos pushed him and Sawicki had to take a run at it. He gave it what he could, and then there was a chorus of "boos."

"What was *that,* girly-girl?"

"I threw women in the air. What did you expect from me, Cvos?"

"I expected more than that sorry sight."

"Oh, give him a break," Johnson placated. "He was probably on a pep squad or something."

"A pep squad?" Brooks mouthed. He shook his head to one side. *No, I really don't think so.*

"I'm sorry, sir. But Sawicki's not all that peppy," Cavazos echoed Brooks.

Diego just seemed discreet. Brooks sidled up to him. "Can you teach me to do that? Spot me?"

More of the soldiers gathered around. Diego was the hottest ticket in town.

"Absolutely not." Johnson was stern. "I don't want you guys getting hurt." He resumed his reading, and the men shared knowing looks. They were forced to peel off in small groups.

They feigned the groans, the rumblings of small children who never got to have any fun. And then they met Diego behind the tent, with two of their men pulling security.

Johnson at six o'clock. Johnson reading. Johnson going to relieve himself.

"How do you do that?"

Diego refrained from his old habit. *I don't know. Just go do it.*

Diego stood patiently with a column of soldiers. Diego actually coached.

+┝═══╡+

Creighton and Cavazos split from the group, away from the grunts and the stretching.

"Listen up, Creighton," Cavazos played the Irish lilt he'd recently acquired in Kuwait. There were Irish near the camps; they sold the men swords and it was the way they'd addressed him—*Creighton*. The accent had stuck with all the flourish and warmth. "I'm going to do you a favor."

Cavazos had a way of positioning his own favors so that it appeared he was on the giving end. *I'm going to do you a favor. I'm not going to leave. Because I'm so interested in what you're saying. I'm going to stay here and smoke, in the same room. I know it's polite to go outside. But it's all about you. You're the important one here. I'm your very best friend.*

Creighton shifted, "What do you want?"

"I want you to use my credit card."

Creighton looked down, stared at his feet on the cot, at the soiled sweat that would never wash out.

"It's hard enough over here. You need to have money."

"I'll pay you back. I swear it."

"Oh, you'll pay me back." He had to say it. Because he was frugal and he needed to ease things.

There was clearly emotion, a touched kind of gratitude that just wasn't Creighton's style. Cavazos was popular for all of his charm, and for the kind of teasing that made the men face themselves squarely. But he never allowed a good man to lose face—there were some things he never exploited.

"I really appreciate it. I mean, I really…"

"I know. Maybe you should send her flowers."

Creighton brightened. Cavazos was one of the few who knew: Creighton was going to get married.

Cavazos rummaged through his rucksack and produced the wallet. His boots were a whole different matter. It wasn't a coincidence—Creighton's were gone, too, and they began to ransack Diego's space. They remained empty-handed and Cavazos stood exactly in the middle of the tent, overcome. That many beds, that many cubby holes; there was just too much ground to cover.

"I'm gonna kill Rincon."

"Look through Farina's stuff."

A logical guess. Not bad.

They found each pair of boots underneath his cot, their happiness truncated instantly. Cavazos owned the look, that peculiar flash when he'd been had and wouldn't concede. It was a begrudging smile that stole across his lips. His plan for revenge was immediate. He carried the boots to the edge of the cot, put them on, and wobbled outside.

Creighton followed him, the unnatural slip of the tongue in shoes that were missing their laces.

CHAPTER 5

The pranks weren't funny if done repeatedly. Each side stopped for a while, for the suspense. It was almost as enjoyable to see the cold sweat, the wonder before their formations. Every morning there was that moment of truth—did a man really have all his gear? Sometimes yes. Sometimes no. Sometimes things just went missing. Diego found his Under Armor shirt in a sleeping bag, rolled at the bottom of another man's cot.

It was only a matter of time until their space would shrink: the 101st Airborne was incoming. The infantry was going to be kicked out of Camp Pennsylvania to wander like nomads in the desert. There were barely enough hooches—it was the life of the grunts, the life of the guys on the ground.

In London, in Hyde Park, there were hundreds of thousands of protesters who had taken to the streets in their furor. There were anti-war demonstrations in Glasgow and Belfast, and some protesters lay down in rebuke. They thought the United States was acting like an island, great hordes of mavericks and isolationists. It was funny to Diego—not his usual funny—just something misunderstood. He thought he was right, he hoped he was right because, truthfully, being there to liberate a country—it was the most *un*island-like thing he had ever done, the most selfless act of his life.

There were smaller rallies around the world, and Diego took his own position. He sat in the field in a foxhole of sand, in a bed of extreme discomfort and deprivation. Farina had packed his gear, prematurely, and he had been waiting for an interminably long time. General Charles Krulak of the United States Marine Corps called it the "three-block war."

"In one moment in time, our service members will be feeding and clothing displaced refugees—providing humanitarian assistance. In the next moment, they will be holding two warring tribes apart—conducting peacekeeping operations. Finally, they will be fighting a highly lethal mid-intensity battle. All on the same day, all within three city blocks. It will be what we call the 'three-block war.'"

The infantry was set to undergo vigorous training for Military Operations in Urban Terrain. MOUT training was the last crucial piece before they entered the more lethal combat zones. Every man thought of Somalia—it was natural to be haunted and motivated by the horror of that mission. They'd learned a few things, and it had all accumulated into the Army's best simulation ever. Diego whistled softly as they overviewed the city, their makeshift urban environment. The construction was crude, but it was in the middle of the desert. *Your tax dollars at work, boys.*

Sawicki was dumbfounded and then he was elated. "Thank you, George W. Bush."

The truth was it was dilapidated, and poverty-stricken, and exposed—that was really the point. The presence of Special Forces made the place so realistic that Cavazos was transported to Baghdad. It was that knowledge base of the experts, not the rough intimation of buildings that capped the set-up exceptional.

They had been given precious resources to do their jobs better, to live to fight another day.

They trained to immense precision, all the scissor strokes of clearing one-room huts and occupied buildings. The larger the space, the more intricate the floor plan, the more intensity the search required. They lined up back-to-front and kicked down the doors and shouted and shot when they had to. There was a sniper on the rooftop, but they couldn't take him out. Rooftops were often sacred places. The innocent civilians, the source of their protection, often resorted there to pray. The Fedayeen Saddam—*Saddam's Men of Sacrifice*—were trying to lure them into a trap. The counterinsurgency would aim at coalition forces, and snap decisions would have to be made. There might be rocket-propelled grenades and deadly mortar rounds and humanitarian aid in the mix.

There might be Red Cross workers and women and children—or a little boy holding a box. He handed it to the troops and he ran away and Farina shuddered at the thought. It was the brief on a real life scenario that had plagued two soldiers; the child had handed them explosives. *God rest their souls.* It made Farina sick, but he needed to know these things.

The volleys could ricochet on urban terrain, and Diego learned how to evade. He shot over any number of varied walls, and Curtin covered his men as they darted between buildings. Brooks advanced and fired and knelt and advanced and pummeled the enemy. A feeling of awe, of serious accomplishment, swept them in their final days. It was a new level of readiness, so many gaps filled they hadn't even known existed.

The next time they entered a zone of such enormity, the bullets and the blood would be real.

All the leftover boxes and the remnants of MOUT training were gathered and piled high. It was Army protocol that turned into a moment as the men set fire to their debris. Diego stamped his feet against the shiver of their gaunt landscape and then the air assumed a sudden vibrancy. The bonfire took courage in its elevated status, one of the few high points in Kuwait. It was galvanized by a stir of a small, chilled breeze and it climbed to a welcome inferno. Farina opened his overcoat in the face of the heat, allowing for the freedom of motion. Diego's head fell back in the uninhibited laughter that so often accompanied Farina's storytelling. The men began to segregate in the same intimate groupings that typified their squads. There was a soft and continual drone, punctuated by the outbursts, all interspersed by good company. They mingled and jostled with the dancing flames illuminating each man's skin.

There were contractors at the site, the retired military, who had guided the men through their training. *Been there. Done that. You boys will do just fine.* It gave the soldiers a boost to see the back-up. The bonfire roared and crackled its approval, and Johnson took a long, thoughtful look around him. *Let freedom ring.* There was the embrace of sentiment like that, glowing in the flicker of their fire.

It was the supreme kind of feeling that existed between warriors, between men with a noble cause.

It was February 22 and orders came down from Johnson to write a final letter home. Diego sat down quietly with heavy thoughts, a renewal of the seesaw of deployment. There had been no articulation for that last glimpse on civilization in Ireland—pretty girls and quaint shops and a language that made perfect sense. All the beauty had faded to the specter of the sky's ambivalence when they had finally taken off for Kuwait. There had been a funny sensation in Diego's stomach, a churning he couldn't attribute to air sickness. It had made him recite his favorite passage before he had closed his eyes. He had felt like he was living a scene in a movie, a poorly written one at that. His mouth had twitched and he'd begun to mumble in his sleep, suddenly a very long way from home. He was captured in a jumbo jet, and then he was in the desert with no intention of turning back. He squirmed again fitfully with a pen in his hand and it was always the same kind of restless foreboding.

Even in his dreams, the resonance of the 23rd Psalm of David filtered its way into deserts and dragons and the airlift of clouds overhead.

"Hola Mother," his mind was in Conyers. He wasn't sure he should say it.

The Lord is my shepherd; I shall not want.

He maketh me to lie down in green pastures: he leadeth me beside the still waters.

He restoreth my soul: he leadeth me in the paths of righteousness for his name's sake.

Yea, though I walk through the valley of the shadow of death, I will fear no evil: for thou art with me; they rod and thy staff they comfort me.

Thou preparest a table before me in the presence of mine enemies: thou annointest my head with oil; my cup runneth over.

Surely goodness and mercy shall follow me all the days of my life: and I will dwell in the house of the Lord forever.

"So I guess the time has finally come for us to see what we are made of. Who will crack when the stress level rises and who will be calm all the way thru it. Only time will tell. We are at the peak of our training and it's time to put it to the test…Mother, I love you so much…I'm living my life one day at a time. Sitting here picturing home with a small tear in my eyes…"

Diego had no idea—the emotional impact of the letter. The international rounds it would make.

He turned his back and Farina couldn't be sure, but he thought Diego was crying.

You're surrounded by too much estrogen, Farina. Well, Sawicki had brought on himself the same fortune. Cavazos' face was marked in severity; each man isolated and straining for words. Brooks seemed subdued, but he became animated quickly when pressed to write anything down. "It's a jinx. I'm telling you. I'm not writing that letter. You might as well say you're going to die."

Curtin and Creighton gave him circumspect looks and continued with the task at hand.

It was like having a baby, Farina thought, when the ache of pregnancy outweighed the fear of the delivery. When a person was so anxious to get out of the current state, that labor pains suddenly seemed welcome. Until the contractions came, of course, and his wife squeezed his hand and there was very real torture in her eyes.

"Let's get this show on the road." His letter finished on an icy tone. "I want to see bombs over Baghdad."

They gathered for another briefing on a critical mission, what the commanders referred to as the Karbala Gap. There was a natural depression, a previous sort of impasse, which made the desert concave. The primary mission of the Outlaw Platoon could be summed up in two words—it was the buzz phrase, the soon-to-be-overused phrase—*regime change.*

"The Outlaw Platoon will pass through the Gap between the town of Karbala and the reservoir on the way to Baghdad. What makes the Gap critical is its deadly entrapment. There is a high probability of getting gassed at the Gap."

Johnson was many things—above all he was a teacher—and he tried to spell things out clearly. If they were hit with blood agents, their blood would be unable to clot—they would bleed out through their mucous membranes. Nerve agents might cause them to twitch and convulse and involuntarily urinate like lab rats. Blister agents were intended to ravage the skin—to eat the tissue right down to the organs.

If fears were confessions, Johnson had two: he didn't want to be permanently disabled or gassed.

The chemicals were able to float above the basin, and then seep into the depression on the men. It was the Devil's Playhouse with no escape hatches, no safety valves, and no cameras. No mere tests of endurance or cogent thought— and no thumbs up at the end. Saddam Hussein was a madman, and he was going to get desperate as each day passed in the conflict.

It was imperative they cross the border in their chemical suits; the clock was winding down.

If ye are prepared, ye shall not fear. That Biblical verse came to Diego. The Karbala Gap loomed with its head-on suicide attacks that might leave them all seizing and foaming. He had a job to do and knowing each detail, knowing all the minute possibilities—for some reason that empowered him and gave him direction, something practical, finally, to grasp. It was like the MOUT training. *Just let me run through it; just let me see what's ahead.* Diego felt liberated in the somberness, a grave sort of confidence restored to his steps.

They moved out to their tactical Assembly Area, and there was more of the mischief that had plagued them at Camp PA. All the men were gathered in squalor and hooches, resentful of their exiled status. Diego stole Cavazos' socks and, in his haste, he dropped one of his own.

Urquhart spied it and picked it up in disdain. "You can sleep outside tonight, private."

"For a sock?" Diego looked at him, disbelieving. Counting to ten didn't work. *They were about to enter a combat zone. What was the point of the punishment?*

He saw the lapse for what it was, and what it was absolutely not. It was not stellar discipline to leave a sock outside, and it wasn't a cardinal sin either. He dragged his sleeping bag into the descending chill, the arid, unyielding of their wasteland. There was something inside of Urquhart that was like the sand, that couldn't absorb the warmth while he had it. And like the sand, he couldn't radiate it for that reason once the sunlight had faded. Urquhart and the desert were trained in absolutes, and Diego might never see the variance. Urquhart couldn't tolerate the shadows or the temperate; Urquhart was unnerved by the gray.

"I want these men to be at their best. I want these men to get promoted. Are they or aren't they the best squad here?" Their reliability was always Urquhart's best defense.

Diego used a flashlight to address the envelopes. He had bought cards just before he had deployed. He might have forgotten a sock, but he hadn't forgotten that. Diego planned better with his heart.

Mom, you know you were my first valentine. That one had been sent long ago. *Hello Mom and Dad.* His father would have liked to buy the upgrades for the Mustang himself.

Hey buddy boy. What's up? Just doing my job, waiting to go home…Be good and listen to your mom and dad…Take of your little sister because she is special.

Thanks for the drawings…I love you so much. Give Tí Tí a kiss for me.

One card for Fabian, and one for Stephanie—where would he be on April 13, on their birthdays? It was just some optimism there'd be another mail call. *Hey wiggle worm. You being a good girl?*

I hope so, because if you are I'm going to take you to Toys 'R' Us when I get back…Take care of George for me. I miss you so much. My little angel. Love you.

He had begun to sign his correspondence, "Your no limit soldier." And then, of course, he always signed his full name.

He awoke in a veil of mist that was nearly the humid imprint of Georgia. His sleeping bag was drenched from the fog that had rolled in overnight from another solar system. The weather wasn't strange—it was a vast conspiracy to which even God seemed to be contributing. By the following evening, they were in a downpour reminiscent of Savannah in the middle of hurricane season. The platoon was short on tents, and Curtin volunteered to take the outside post. If there were trenches to be dug, then he picked up a shovel; that was Curtin at his best. Brooks couldn't leave him to such solitary misery so he laid his sleeping bag beside him. They were pelted by the wind, and the sand blew over them in a scathing blizzard of dispute. They became buried in small dunes, and Curtin tried to poke his head out—it was a carbon dioxide trap in the nylon. The raindrops that came next fell with such weight; they were like lead and Brooks began to laugh.

"It only rains here like four times a year, doesn't it?"

"Let's just stick it out. See how much worse it can get."

Curtin had always loved the rain and he sensed the alliance: Brooks was entrenched for the duration. The sky parted fully and it was as if legions of destroying angels spit their wrath on the men.

It came in sheets. "Aaaaaggghhh!" Brooks yelled once, and it had that distinct edge: *it's a good pain.* They rode out the storm not just for defiance sake, but for the story they would make of it later. They would sit around someday, the veterans of the War on Terror, start with faint smiles, and end with "good stuff."

They scooped their way to the morning sun when it broke over the huddles and the Bradleys. In the fighting vehicle was a heater with a small reservoir. Lieutenant Johnson used it to boil water. He stood over the steam, warmed his hands on a cup, cut from a plastic water bottle. The men wore beanies and fingerless gloves, and they naturally migrated toward their leader. The pull was inevitable, borne of the privation of being homeless and discontent.

"I can't find my shirt." Both men began to snicker. Brooks and Curtin were unshaven and bleary-eyed. Curtin eyed the odds and ends of their overnight beating, a shrewdness lighting his smile. His gear was scattered to the four winds perhaps—it was hard to tell in the massive burial. He thrust his arm into the sand, to his shoulder, and wiggled his fingers.

"Ha!" he cried, hoisting his prize from the wreckage. In his hand, incredibly, was his shirt.

Cavazos had slept on the bench of the Bradley at their tactical Assembly Area. He was the man assigned to monitor the radio, and he picked up news the others didn't. "I'm telling you guys, we gotta have Turkey. We get Turkey, we join up with 4th ID. I want that extra pounding, coming from the north. The more the merrier, you know."

"They might not give us the launch pad, Cvos. We can't count on that support, just in case."

"When the shooting starts, I'm only counting on one thing: the guy fighting next to me."

Diego said it so quietly that the softer resonance actually overrode all the louder voices. It compelled the rest of them to vocalize it quickly—they were the Outlaw Platoon—they didn't need backing from anyone.

Johnson was more than a witness to the deflation when the news from *BBC Radio* eventually broke their camp. It was a slap in the face and one of the worst morale killers he'd seen in his military career. "They're not backing *us*? They're protesting *us*? In the streets of *New York*?" There was a visible sink in Brooks' shoulders.

"Jersey?" Diego stared at Curtin for some explanation. He had been the closest one to 9/11.

Sometimes Diego wasn't sure he deserved all the ardor, the way some people put the soldiers on pedestals. But he sure didn't think he deserved the shades of Vietnam—all those people chanting "baby killer" to the troops. If the activists had only known the longing for home, the will and the hardship and the backbone. For any man or woman to be the object of their disdain was the ultimate disgrace and betrayal. The role of Jimmy still stung him at times: his boot in a nurse's hand. He searched the faces of his friends in the self-denial and filth, and he took the thing personally for them. They were giving their all for something larger than themselves, and so many of the protesters weren't even minimally affected.

"You have to do something." The injury was worse than a bullet wound to the gut. *You don't know my mom, but she will fix this.* "Get everyone in the family to help."

Jorge and Yolanda went to work straightaway to write letters for all of the soldiers. They called Anna Maria and enlisted the children until they had three letters for nearly every man. *God bless America. We love our troops.* Cans of mixed fruit and potato chips and peanuts. They sent the non-perishables, and they sent wet wipes and lip balm and eye drops and lotion. *We're praying for you to come home to us soon. You have our undying support and our gratitude.* It would take up to a month for a package like that to arrive, and it would eventually be returned to the sender.

It wasn't that all the February writing had finally paid off—most of the correspondence originating in the U.S. had been sent in January. The mail call that week just brought an unprecedented outpouring. The men sat gratefully in the sand. There were drawings of stick figures under blue sky and sunlight with green grass and trees and flowers. "Hey now, that's a *share* package. Give me some pogey bate." A few of the men smiled again.

Rendon closed his eyes on the soft scent of perfume, and Farina almost felt like a saint. His mother-in-law's hometown had adopted Brooks through Operation Home Fires. Curtin smiled as he recognized the writing on the outside of one of the envelopes addressed to his best friend. His sister had come through—Brooks had as many letters as Diego had clean socks from his family.

Johnson's smile was one of relief. It almost made up for the rest.

CHAPTER 6

The sunlight on the desert glared with such intensity because there was little if any visual letup. No shadows of variance, no shade to spare the eyes from that everlasting heat and strain. And yet there was a moment, at the close of the day when the desert exhausted to a brilliant smolder. It was found in the sunsets, like the luminous glow of a lamp from God's outstretched dwelling above the earth. Particles of sand, so thick they were visible, scurried the pallid blue light. The result was a shaft of fiery warmth, the brushstrokes of stunning copper and scarlet.

Just before the scattering, the sun revealed something more—so peculiar Private Charles Hall had to get a picture. They had moved from the first tactical Assembly Area to a position three kilometers from the border. Hall rushed back for his camera and there was a chilling sensation that prickled Diego's arms.

The outline was so distinct, the phenomenon the sun had yielded—there was a ghosted horse, winged, in the sky.

In a peaceful land, the shimmer would have been Pegasus: some starlight of dreamier days. But it wasn't Pegasus, and it wasn't nighttime; it was some gargantuan, celestial sign. A smaller group of soldiers, perched outside the Bradleys, saw the pale horse of the Apocalypse before them. It was not as disturbing as it was awakening, to see the symbol of death and the sword. They were nearly prostrate in the cradle of civilization, some line both promising and ominous in their horizon. The haze that settled over them was like a sacred anointing—they were liberators on great metal steeds. They understood collectively the foretold prophecy, and they stared in stunned disbelief.

"It's an optical illusion."

"No, it's not. It's the 'Book of Revelations.' God knows we're going to war."

They needed a diversion, to forget for a moment just where they were and why. Diego looked back once to see that the image had faded, the goose bumps still clinging to his spine. Rendon offered the bag from his ProMask kit that normally held his gas mask. Three other soldiers did the same, laying them in a diamond-shape on a flat. They found a discarded 2x4, and Diego made a baseball out of MRE packaging and strapping tape.

"Hey batta, batta," Cavazos heckled Sawicki just before he took a swing with the wood.

The baseball lobbed crazily, its poor aerodynamics landing it short of the base. "Sttttttrrrriiiiiikkkkkeeee...one!"

"That's not a strike! I didn't swing! It didn't even get to the plate!"

"I had to call something," Ronquillo was also the catcher. "Keep your eye on the ball."

Diego stretched a single into a double and wrapped his arms around second base. There were ruptures occasionally of the overriding jeers from the men in their makeshift dugouts. It was all overridden by the perpetual buzz, the drone of so much chitchat between each man in the infield.

"Did you just seriously slide, man? Those aren't baseball cleats."

Diego shrugged in his DCUs.

"I'm very competitive, Farina."

"You're a nut. That's what you are."

Diego threatened to steal to third base.

"You're clearly going to be MVP."

"Well, clearly." Diego was gone in a flash, running as though he'd never get another chance. By the top of the fourth inning, he had added two runs and two singles to his earlier double. He should have had more stats—he demanded more stats—they forgot to keep track of RBI.

"He's head and shoulders above everyone else—athletically speaking, of course."

"Of course," Farina nodded in agreement with Sawicki as Diego brushed past home base a third time.

Farina stuck out his foot and tripped up Sawicki. Sawicki kicked back a mouthful of sand.

"Hey now, no fighting, not in the infield," Cavazos wagged a finger. "Do I have to pull you two out?"

"Patty Cake started it."

"No I didn't."

"Did too."

"Did not."

"Did *too*."

Cavazos' sigh was exaggerated and lost beneath the flair, a rocket of thunder overhead. The Tomahawk cruise missiles had been hammering Baghdad since around 0600 that morning. Still, there had not been one round fired to the south, and the men were a World Series away from the fighting.

"What the…" Farina started.

"It's an incoming scud!!!" the radio operator squawked, his eyes saucer-sized in his broadcast.

"Headed south. Unknown on chemicals." The men scrambled for their ProMask kits.

"Where's my Pro-Mask??!! Where's my mask?????!!!!!"

It's somewhere near center field!!!!!

They went to MOPP4, the highest level of defense against an NBC attack, the men completely encapsulated. They closed all their over-garments, rolled down and adjusted the mask hood, and put on rubber gloves with cotton liners. In the desert heat, a soldier could just as easily lose consciousness, frying inside his protective gear. For that reason, commanders were not so hasty—the inherent outcome a close second to the exposure.

"Look guys, don't panic," Johnson tried to restore order among them. "There are going to be plenty of scuds."

He adjusted the headset and awaited confirmation. The radio resumed its chatter.

"Downgrade to MOPP0, Outlaws," Johnson talked and listened to the radio net simultaneously.

"The wind is blowing the opposite direction. I repeat, downgrade to MOPP0."

The men picked up where they'd left off in the game, Corporal Richard Snavely with two balls and a strike. Snavely was half German and half Puerto Rican, which accounted for a lot in their interactions. The men called him Snuggles—he was the fabric softener bear and no one recalled who had ordained him that. Snavely was just crazy enough to keep them all sane, the Hawkeye Pierce of their tent banter. He didn't wax as poetic as his alter ego of M*A*S*H, but he was spontaneous and comically warped. They figured someday Snavely would rise up and declare the war dead on account of his own lack of interest.

"Not even close, Dogs. Not even close," Snavely pooh-poohed Saddam with disdain.

An hour later, Diego picked up the least unappetizing portion of his dinner and stood to place it reverently on the hood.

"Do you know what this looks like?"

Cavazos scrutinized it and flipped it counterclockwise for effect.

"What do you think? They make this stuff in New Jersey, don't they?"

Curtin wasn't even mildly amused. "Except it says right here, Cvos— 'Made…in…Texas.'"

"Oh that's funny. You're real swift with the comebacks."

Diego poked it again, propped it up like a hood ornament. "I had a dog once and Missy never left any little treats like this."

"Stop talking like that."

"You're a little cranky, Big Mike."

"No, you're just getting on my nerves."

Johnson smiled to himself. *Sometimes the children bickered.* And sometimes he egged them on.

"You're just mad, Creight, because you lost to Rincon."

"I could have beaten him at Spades."

"That's funny because I seem to have heard *he* beat you today. He's not that far behind Williams now."

"That was beginner's luck—just like chess…" His voice trailed off and he frowned. A missile blasted what was left of their hearth-and-home kind of bliss. Each head jerked skyward, the screech of the Patriot plunging them to an unprecedented hush.

The first scud missile had landed in Kuwait, forty-five miles south of their springboard.

"At least this time it's one of ours…" Lane spoke faintly.

Taking out one of theirs.

A second Patriot streaked their dusk, leaving a long tail of vapor. In a matter of thirty seconds, Diego had instinctively ducked twice. The threat was undeniably real.

Urquhart's mouth was set in something unreadable as he approached the body of his squad. "Those were Patriots…intercepting two scuds…

"The Iraqi missiles were headed for us."

<hr />

They received the Operations Order to move out at night, exactly at 2300. At 2000, Baghdad had been attacked with artillery and A-10 bombings. There had been the tracers followed by a series of booms that concussed the ground where the men staged their deployment. Diego let out a low, soft whistle, "It feels just like a movie..."

The rockets red glare, the bombs bursting in air.

"...or maybe the Fourth of July."

Creighton was unusually soft spoken. "It doesn't feel like Independence Day to me."

The same sobriety fell over the others, each stationed at intervals near their Bradleys.

"That's weird," Farina said. He was attaching his rucksack to the fighting vehicle, frowning something mixed.

"What's weird?" Brooks asked. It was the tone of Farina's voice. There had to be something wrong.

"I just had déjà vu—like I've been here before. Don't you think that's kind of strange?"

Maybe they had all been terribly engrossed, but a few of the men peered at him blankly.

"I'm sorry. I didn't mean to interrupt or anything. I was just talking out loud. Just, you know...I had déjà vu."

"Oh, no, by all means. You did the right thing," Brooks said. "Seriously. When something like that happens, you should just stop everything you're doing.

"Stop all conversation. Tell everyone you know...

"Hey, I just had déjà vu."

Farina smiled self-deprecatingly.

"Tough crowd," Snavely muttered in passing.

Their Operations Order had come twenty-four hours earlier than expected. There had been a preemptive air strike in Baghdad. The Commander-in-Chief had ordered an assault on a bunker, at what intelligence assessed to be a command-and-control center. Earlier intel had placed Saddam Hussein at the scene and, for all the infantry knew, he was dead. It was business as usual—business and ignorance that never interrupted the bliss.

Johnson had the platoon sergeant gather the men and ask them to circle and take a knee. The finality of the moment was overwhelming and a relief; the men appeared to succumb gratefully. Black took Creighton's hand and Creighton took Diego's and so the chain of unity continued. With all of the earnestness his soul was known to afford, Sergeant Tolbert pleaded for them and pleaded for their great undertaking.

Diego felt himself repeating each phrase, a hallowed echo of feeling.

"Lord, help us to be honorable."

Please, help me to be honorable.

"Guide us in every movement in battle."

Guide my every movement. Help me to perform well. Help me to be brave for my mom.

A few yards away Rendon, too, was immersed in an unprecedented wrenching of his spirit. He wouldn't have claimed to be terribly religious, if formal church-going mattered. He did have a keenly developed relationship with God—one image, etched in his mind. His Father was kind and merciful and everything was negotiable so long as God had the final say. He was white and, compared to Rendon, physically speaking, God was thin and all powerful, but delicate. Like all best friends, He had a nickname: it was "Flaco," which, in Spanish, meant "skinny."

Flaco, watch over us. Watch over all my friends. Please don't let anything bad happen. Help my mom so she's not so afraid. Help me get home to my family.

The mood was sober, the adrenaline running high as fate and duty enveloped them. Some rose with hesitancy, a final lingering, colored in shades of valor. Others dissolved from the circle quickly, filling the emotional space with last-minute activities. Every man's coping skills were not only evident, but magnified by the extremity of their trial.

For Sergeant Williams, the outlet was clear. They'd been debating the choice of music all day. Some thought they should play something patriotic when they crossed the border—and then others vehemently disagreed.

"We need the blood pumping. Like 'Bombs Over Baghdad.' But something just for the infantry. What's that song you like Curtin?" Urquhart held up his CDs.

"'Faraway Coast,'" Curtin said vaguely.

It was a song of resignation, of a daydream in despair that began with a man in the trenches. It was surprisingly dark for Curtin's upbeat nature. His outward longsuffering could be deceiving. He was relatively selfless so that his extreme protectiveness had shone through when he had become an uncle, and a godfather. He had held Kayla in his arms and he been hard pressed to share her, his most self-indulgent moments before deployment.

He had propped her on the couch, not two months old, trying to help her sit up at Christmas time. She had slumped over and he'd smiled softly. He had propped her up again. She had fallen sideways, trusting and pokerfaced. He had never felt like he might squeeze her too hard, or break her in the fragility. He had cradled her tenderly for as long as he was able, bent to kiss her in their brief, mortal cross of paths. Maybe there was a part of him that had known the moment was fleeting, and so he had been reluctant to give her up.

Maybe there had been a part of him that had needed to see her sit up, on her own, just once.

No matter the intensity of the sun in Iraq—the way it bore through layers of clothing to the skin—it couldn't lighten that overwhelming ache. "Faraway Coast" by DropKick Murphys wasn't much of a morale booster.

"Hey, maybe Rincon here would like Avril Levigne."

"Hey! We're making war here, not babies."

Diego tapped the outside armor of the Bradley. "Why don't they make subwoofers for these things?" Only half of the men had the Combat Vehicle Crewman helmets to pump out the power chords. Sergeant Todd Walker had spliced into the intercom to feed the music to the CVC helmets. In the back of the Bradley, that amounted to Urquhart and Curtin, debating the shared CD.

"I want something classic—none of this new-fangled crap. Something like AC/DC." Urquhart somehow managed to trump Johnson. "Hell's Bells is *good*," he added.

I'm a rolling thunder, a pouring rain. I'm comin' on like a hurricane. Johnson smiled and caved, not just out of consideration.

One could never go wrong with a classic.

Their fighting vehicle was loaded, top to bottom, like a scene out of *National Lampoon's Vacation*. "All we need on this gypsy wagon is grandma in a rocking chair, and we're ready to roll all the way to Baghdad."

"I don't think so," Cavazos jumped in quickly. "Let's just get in, get the job done, get outta there."

The radio broke his haste with a report on the scuds. One had landed at their former tactical Assembly Area.

For as outdated as the Iraqi arsenal had become in the last decade, it still threw a formidable sucker punch.

"It's time?"

There was a heavy pause. "It's time."

The music was all but forgotten.

Urquhart's squad drew together quietly, circling with arms around each other. They bowed their heads with exclusive solemnity, their mortality never more exposed. Each man took his turn, asking for divine protection and offering a sacred oath of allegiance. Some prayers were flowing and some were halting, but the feeling and the power were abundant to Diego. The ring was unbroken as they kept arms over shoulders, set their jaws in their firm band of brotherhood. *I'll be there for you*, was the unspoken covenant, tearful and penetrating in their eyes. When they rose they did so with a grand amen and a hooah that sounded strangely subdued. No one acknowledged the hard swallow of their air. For a moment, they all appeared scared.

They had trained, of course, to die for their country if needed, but each of them wanted desperately to live. They were all of a sound mind, and any man in his right mind didn't want the close quarter combat. Overhead came the flurry, the swoops and the stealth and the desert prowl of the Blackhawks. The constant drone and the rise of the rotor wash were really just preparatory for them. The air campaign carved huge chunks off the insurgence, but ultimately someone mopped up. Diego looked upon the tanks, those hulking steel shields, some swell of relief in their defense.

He was a former first sergeant from Diego's old company—First Sergeant Benjamin Moore. He had driven to the platoon's stranglehold on the border, now the launch pad to the Tigris and Euphrates. It was a final look on the Garden of Eden, the rebirth of civilization, their last sanctuary on peace and safety.

"This is what we've trained for," he talked with his hands—the longest, slender fingers the men had ever seen.

"We're going to make it. It'll be okay. Men...*now* is the time to be brave."

It was hard to believe for a soldier with Diego's upbringing that there wasn't some kind of foreordination. On the brink of Iraq is where history had begun and on the brink is where it would end. A patriot missile split their skyline again and First Sergeant Moore disappeared.

The men remained rooted, appeared somewhat startled. "*Where did he go?*" came one murmur.

Moore peeked tentatively from behind a Humvee, and he was met by some wide, knowing smiles.

"They've been shooting them for a while," an NCO's chorus was chiding. First Sergeant Moore ducked his head.

"...as I was saying, now is the time to be brave." He coughed ever so slightly as his carriage elongated.

The effect was magical; the men began to crack up. His eyes creased in warmth in the funny, unpredictable moment transitioning to the inevitability of war. If the men could have bottled sentiment, it would have been that feeling, keyed up in resounding laughter on the border. First Sergeant Moore had gifted it unwittingly and Johnson's smile was dry.

+≡≡≡+

Without the undulation, the desert appeared one-dimensional—except on the eve of the invasion. It was dense and layered with all of mankind's aspirations, the most recent ghosts arising from the Gulf War. Every grain, every flat field alluded to another man's fight that had culminated into a great calling: their one last chance to set the stage for some semblance of peace in the region, to root out the obvious evils.

So long as there was oppression, so long as there were torture and poverty and hopeless existence—there would always be the desperation, the struggle for escape, and the breeding ground for the fanaticism of the terrorists. The fire in Diego's belly that had prompted him to service had faded with the passage of time. What hadn't dulled was his will to make a difference, to stand up and be counted with the old warriors.

It was a strange intermingling, the fear and the fight in him, his smallness and then his significance. His hour had come—it had finally come—and in the terror he still wanted to be proven.

Diego was one of nine men assigned to Bradley A31. Only six passengers could fit in the back. There was a concave inlet that encircled the turret, and it offered the best seat in the house. It was nicknamed the hellhole for the contortionist kind of maneuvers required to get in and out. But Diego was a gymnast, his lean frame accommodating and, once there, he held a coveted position. He had the luxury of stretching his legs, of curling horizontally around the base. It was Diego's fate to be riding in the Bradley that was the command post of First Lieutenant Johnson.

His squad would be the first pierce to draw the blood when the entire detachment was deemed tip of the spear.

It had only taken the platoon a few hours in the Bradleys to initially approach the Kuwaiti border. The marathon lay ahead of them, the unfathomable cocoon in which the men would seal their metamorphosis. The oppressive darkness and the lack of privacy would both comfort them and drive them mad. The Bradley was a safe haven from the weaponry of the enemy, and yet its indignities would permanently alter them. The six men in the shallow cavern carried so much gear on their backs that their seats on the benches pitched them forward. They were forced to sit knee-to-knee, staring into a blackness pooling like ink, confronting all of their neuroses together. When the cramping became intolerable and their knees began to swell, they would have to lock legs to try to stretch. Sleep would be the reprieve from the insufferable boredom, the only numbness to their impending crisis. There were a few rare times when they might gain a visual reprieve, get to look through the scope of the turret. Even then, their view on Kuwait would offer no orientation, no familiar landmarks or nature-based splendor.

There was a sense of fierceness, marked by grave impatience, as each man took his place in the Bradleys. "This is it, men. The Combat Infantry Badge is the most important badge you'll ever wear."

Johnson's tone had become unmistakably decisive, and yet it still carried an air of compassion. They were staged and ready at 0400 with their company in the lead.

The first swipe at the border was tasked to the Third Infantry Division—they were to be the first full division inside. The engines revved, and then they revved some more, an idling that wouldn't stop.

Creighton squirmed in his seat, antagonized and intolerant. "What...is... going...*on?*"

They turned on the fan, an assault on their hearing that did nothing to circulate the air. It was like the Super Bowl, their game faces on, enduring some endless stall in the locker room. Cavazos rolled his head from side to side, just praying for some sign of motion.

Diego laid a frustrated arm over his face, agitated in his isolation. His blood was churning. *I'm ready. Let's go.* Hour after excruciating hour.

It was well after dawn when the lurch finally came, and no one ever really understood the delay.

Sergeant Tolbert manned the main gun and Sergeant Walker was the driver. Diego begged for a turn at the wheel.

"Are we there yet?' he pestered from the minute they rolled out, offering his services to navigate. Johnson was amused by Diego's eagerness, but at the same time it brought him up short. They were such little boys, still teenagers in some cases, and they carried the weight of humanity on their shoulders. For all of his ranting—or because of his ranting—Urquhart had trained them to be supreme and dependable. Johnson leaned to that notion, took solace in that notion, because even a commander experienced nerves.

When the shooting started, when they faced their own demise, would they buckle or rise to the occasion? Would his men follow orders or was there cowardice inside of them, lurking and ignorant and undetected?

Would he suck his thumb or wet his pants or do something ignoble in battle? He thought he knew the answer, but he could never know for certain until actual experience confirmed him.

"Maybe in a while...I'll let you drive," Sergeant Walker was fatherly and the oldest. Once an Army Ranger, he had broken his back in an airborne training jump. They called him Uncle Fester, of the *Addams Family* variety, and in that intimacy Diego tried to needle him.

"You're not sumping this Bradley," Walker rebuffed him. "Now, get back into your hole."

"It was an accident," Diego feigned far too much innocence.

"Whatever. I'll call you when I'm ready."

"It sure would be nice if I could get me some respect around here. If *someone* would stop hogging the wheel."

He released a dramatic sigh and then crawled back into the hellhole. Like a turtle in his shell, he settled into the dimness, his face taking on pinched severity. *If you're going to be in the Army, you might as well be a soldier.*

Those were Cavazos' words.

Cavazos had met an Army cook once upon a time and they'd hotly debated the merits of their prospective roles in the field.

"You're messed up."

"No, *you're* messed up," Cavazos had shot back, indignant.

"You're gonna take a bullet—get killed out there. I got me a safe job right here."

"Don't go cutting yourself, peeling potatoes, homeboy."

"Whatever. At least I'll be alive."

"Do they give out medals—for serving up this crap?"

"No. They don't give out no body bags neither."

"You're messed up."

"No, *you're* messed up."

"You are."

"You are."

"*You...are...*"

"Whatever, kitchen boy."

"Whatever, bullet magnet."

"I'll beat you down. Right here."

Cavazos had chosen the infantry just to spite the cook, and maybe he'd been right to do so; they certainly couldn't have been cooks, but maybe they should have considered joining the Air Force at some point. The thought came to Diego, somewhat randomly. It was because it suddenly seemed very appealing to soar undaunted above the fray.

No, he would have had to go to college first.

It was better to be in the infantry.

The atmosphere quickened, even in their blind stations, an electricity that bristled their necks. They approached the border and Diego clenched his jaw on that first-time anticipation. They had entered the war zone and there was no turning away as they spit back the last dust on Kuwait. Two long tank berms were on a parallel with five kilometers between them, a free-flowing tributary of sand.

The Abrams and Bradleys lumbered in a string, the grind of the convoy trumpeting their arrival. For miles there was nothing but that stream of churning, a serpentine crawl through the desert. The combat engineers had bulldozed through the first rise of sand, and then their wire cuts on the electrical fence had been meticulous. That was their skill set—their utter self-discipline and finesse in a gross motor kind of moment. Every heart pounded in the feverish pitch of performance in a monumental task. They had broken the second berm calmly, ushering in history below the stars' last blink of omniscience.

The first tank crashed the barrier and then another and another in an ascension not unlike their winged counterparts. Standing at the pierced barricade was like standing on a flight deck, the rush of the take off overpowering. One combat engineer cheered and another bowed his head, his eyes squinted on the extreme emotion. It was like an embanking sensation—something massaged the sand as the Bradley that carried Diego folded into an erect line.

The ground assault vehicles had come at that last stand in a wedge that funneled to a column between the two berms. Once past the second rise, the thrust of the Iraqi border, the vehicles had fanned out again. From an aerial view, their equipment seemed to form the anatomy of an arrow. The tanks at the forefront had that hopeful penetration, charting the course of the arrowhead. And then the tanks at the rear pushed destiny forward in clusters of metal feathers. Diego had taken his position behind Sergeant Walker. Their seats were back-to-back. Diego rode backward, but there was nothing backward about that small glimpse as he turned and peered over Walker's shoulder. It was in the shaft of their arrow, that uprightness between the two berms, that a handful of them nearly wept.

One combat engineer stood his ground, a lone silhouette against all of the fear and desolation. With the last strength he could afford, he swung the standard of liberty, waving them on with an American flag.

Something so enlarging overcame Diego in that moment that it rendered him breathless, almost pained in his pride. Through so much obscured glass, through the shell of his confinement, his soul was suddenly set free. The flag would never appear more vibrant, more rich and three-dimensional, than it did in its rise on the border. He crowded Walker, straining for a final glimpse, so heartened and stirred he was speechless. His heart burned with the fire, with the renewal of courage that imbued and sapped strength all at once. The transcendence lingered and then took on different shapes as the Bradley continued to move forward. The air had turned softly valiant, shrouding all of his misgivings and clinging to the callousness of the armor. It was as if he'd been given some choice after all—to shrink or live up to the moment. He inhaled its finality, unfurled in the flag, the banner wave of all previous decisions. It was a harsh, uncaring daybreak that had forced such hard thinking, but Diego had chosen liberty now.

The morning passed, the sun reached a climax, and then it appeared to bow to the might of it: the Army was so brazen in the first nightfall press that the

Abrams and Bradleys maintained a floodlight of candor. The columns moved forward with their headlights on—barefaced, full bore ahead. For miles, all a platoon commander saw was a brilliant white light—just one long, luminous thread. From Johnson's perspective, it was not so unlike the pierced track lighting that characterized that well-traveled interstate—between Los Angeles and Las Vegas, there was an uninhabited stretch where the civilian headlights star-studded the sparseness. It was one of Johnson's old stomping grounds, outside Ft. Irwin, and he was suddenly overcome by the boldness of the invasion. He was a long way from home in that striking pose—their audacity emblazoned on enemy terrain.

Their brashness was absorbed at the break of dawn. The columns rolled on, impervious to the blaze and depletion. Edging ever closer to civilization—the increased possibility of conflict—the men instinctively coiled for the discharge of their weapons. Their reflexes seemed to be overly taut and disposed. They stared at nothing in the faintness of the Bradley. It was the shadows that heightened the imagination—stark raving imagery in their minds. They were tortured for hours that way. The sun always seeming to be dipping somehow, all tides and time lost on the men.

In the fitful stops and starts, Diego had daydreams of home, his family, and Southern comforts. He kissed Catherine in the backyard swing, the crickets in a soft serenade. The moon was full there, as it had been in Kuwait, and the leaves shuddered with elegant decorum. In Georgia, the newer suburbs had long spindled pines and the whole trees swayed in the breeze like dancing umbrellas. The swing creaked gently in the rhythm of the forest as Diego traced her hand.

"I miss you," he whispered, and the tank ground on, the hum of it rocking him back to sleep.

He awakened briefly at the sound of voices. Cavazos' was tinged in aggravation. "Hold this for me, will you?" Black turned his head, and Curtin steeled his comrade's back.

It was the ultimate humiliation in the confines of the Bradley, but he'd waited as long as he could. Cavazos urinated into the only thing he had, a water bottle left over from not much of a lunch

It wasn't like Christmas, some cozy embrace awaiting them at their final destination. There would be no sweet reward for the monotony and the suffering of a trip that would stretch into weeks. That was the dissonance, the urgency to move on with nothing pleasurable awaiting them. They were generally good men, and good men had a hard time thriving in such darkness and gloom. The day passed uneventfully with a pendulum of emotions steadily ticking out their lives. Sometimes they felt restless, tense and ready, poised to just get the thing over with—sometimes they felt depressed, reconciled and listless, suspended in a labyrinth of disquiet.

They finally approached the village of Al-Khidr with an iron guard, the scan of the turret like a seeing-eye dog. It rotated warily, a low snarl in its protection, the main gun ready to lunge and lacerate. The 25mm main gun was flanked by coaxially mounted machine guns and a TOW anti-tank missile launcher with twin tubes. With the denial of eyesight came heavy reliance on that escape from the turret to sound off the alarm of an attack. Diego sat motionless taking short, shallow breaths, amid the perpetual whine of the scrutiny. Johnson lent his senses to Sergeant Urquhart, trying to paint a picture of the long road ahead.

Johnson was the literary one; Johnson was the narrator; he tried to be a book on tape. When Urquhart communicated back to him it was through the CVC helmet. Urquhart yelled his responses. It was the only way he had to keep the dismounts informed—to provide situational awareness to the men in the back. They had to get their bearings. They were entering a battle zone in something like a sensory deprivation tank.

The expectancy was so raw that Johnson's voice sounded foreign when he called off the pit bull of their fighting vehicle. Walker's clenched jaw went slack, so utterly slack, that it distressed Diego momentarily. He radiated the shock of a man witnessing catastrophe when, actually, what he was seeing was the reverse.

It was like a parade, the outstretched welcome from the villagers, caving to all sides of the road.

A friendly chaos ensued. The Iraqis were so enthusiastic—so curious—that Walker was afraid he might squash them. The villagers barely kept enough distance, and among their throngs were men and women, young and old. They called out something indecipherable, running alongside the road, waving to the troops in joy. Diego was riveted not by the shower of gratitude, but by the humility wedded to the affection.

The change in expectations was so profound and consuming because what Diego saw was himself.

An Iraqi boy, five years old perhaps, appeared like an apparition, his face full of strange introspection. He hung back from the crowd a bit, mesmerized by the flurry and outpouring of those who surrounded him. He held out his hands, tiny and empty, as if to demonstrate need. He took short, halting steps, something shy and remote, and in them was an epic kind of progress. He wore the cropped haircut that had once been Diego's when he'd stepped onto American soil. His smile was engaging if not so broad as the Colombian child he mirrored. They were baby strides and the resilience to advance to the brink of something extraordinary for the first time.

It was simply promise: an ideal he could neither fully grasp, nor ever shrug off again.

He might have had an incredibly difficult start, and he might yet have his battles to fight. But he was on to something suddenly, an opportunity that nothing but the very real struggle of coalition forces could secure. Diego felt a floodgate of emotion overtake him as the child drifted away like a dream. All of his instincts had been right, all of his aspirations worthy as he turned back to the deepest black shade of his hollow.

They'd been ordered to cross the border in their chemical suits, a measure that would encumber them for weeks. The squad was dressed down to MOPP2 in the imposing heat that cooked them in the cauldron of the Bradleys. Diego's jacket was allowed to drape open, a haphazardness the men assumed in their minds.

"All that worrying, and we were just met by friendly," Cavazos' voice echoed each man's incredulity.

A white SUV careened past their column, and Johnson barely took note of it. Their tanks were moving at thirty-five miles per hour—apparently a group of journalists wanted to jumpstart the war.

His complacency was shattered by a more distant development—what Johnson suddenly perceived in the landscape. There was a scurry on the horizon; there were men in uniform, manning fighting positions.

He felt the first crawl of apprehension that made all his hairs stand on end. He spoke tersely to Urquhart. "They have RPGs, mortars, and AK47s."

"Roger that." The enemy militia was still 300 meters from the Bradley in its forward moving position.

This is it. This is what we've trained for. The tension was riveted to the armor.

Johnson never ordered his men to dismount unless it was absolutely necessary. A soldier's exposure was the last resort—the Bradley's spitfire could take on so much of the fighting. *Let the steel take the heat.* Unless there were enemy prisoners. Unless there were buildings to clear. Tolbert manned the turret, ready to release the scathing equivalent of a human death charge, built into the Bradley's main gun.

The column of armored vehicles had a convulsive rumble that shook the ground in its advance. It felt like an earthquake, radiating seismic tremors for which Johnson assigned a number—on the Richter scale, it would be about a four: felt, but without damage to buildings. They were an entire task force, thundering in something Johnson thought of as a "shock and awe parade."

The shudder was so deafening, the vibrations were so appalling, that the insurgents stopped all their scampering. Johnson didn't have to see the reaction up close and personal: the Iraqis were wetting their pants. Their pupils were constricted by the glare of the desert, lost in the explosive whites of their eyes. Diego was right: Johnson knew the Bible backward and forward, and the book of Joshua—the city of Jericho—came to mind.

And it came to pass at the seventh time, when the priests blew with the trumpets, Joshua said unto the people, Shout: for the LORD hath given you the city…

So the people shouted when the priests blew with the trumpets: and it came to pass, when the people heard the sound of trumpet, and the people shouted with a great shout, that the wall fell down flat, so that the people went up into the city, every man straight before him, and they took the city.

It was the shout of their mechanized forces and the wall of insurgents flattened before his eyes. Every enemy fighting position was abandoned. The surrender was abrupt, and that was the eeriness as Johnson maintained his tone.

His voice was even and exaggerated in its deliberateness as he described the approaching men to Urquhart. "We got *seven* guys ahead of us. They've surrendered to the Bradley. There's an adobe wall, six feet high. If you dismount *right*, you will see the wall. You'll have three feet to get to the wall.

"Use it for cover." The Bradley was stopped. "Get your men ready to dismount."

Roger that.

Diego swallowed hard.

Lock and load.

The rear hatch of the Bradley was suddenly descending, and Urquhart exposed himself first. He jumped on the ramp, midway through its fall, with a few precious seconds to get situational awareness. He rode the ramp down and his eyes adjusted quickly to the first harsh assault of daylight. The sun was setting in his eyes. He called the right dismount—a soldier's left as he traveled backward—and the men were spewed from the belly of the Bradley.

It was a dizzying instinct Diego had on the fly. There were six Iraqi soldiers, hands in the air, in a mortar position.

Diego screamed at them, "Get down! Get down!" If the prisoners could have dug graves, they might have sunk lower.

The squad members searched them, their hands shaking and rough. There were five AK47 assault rifles with over 1,000 rounds. They had four RPG missile launchers and a mortar tube. They zip-stripped the prisoners, pulling the plastic cuffs tight.

"Clear that building!" The platoon split off in teams and took their next offense to a small warehouse. They stacked their formations, each soldier compressed, chest-to-back-to-chest. Their M16s protruded at angular intervals, one insolent against Diego's spine. The men smelled raw, the heavy breath of their starvation with little to eat in the past thirty-six hours. It mingled with the stench of their caked antagonism, laced with a newer anxiety. An intensity Diego had never known before stuck in his throat as he waited to spring on command.

Leslie Summer had taught him one thing—when it was time to perform, he had to focus on the mechanics, not the nerves.

If he focused on the mechanics, the perfunctory details…

Urquhart kicked open the door.

Diego had been poised on the hinge side of their entrance and he was the first man to rush to the left. Two more soldiers scissored right, one after another in a blur of shouts and primed weapons. They saw everything at once, and then nothing at all as Urquhart button-hooked from behind. Their tight wire on a discharge of automatic fire was as fine as the crosshairs on their scopes. They raked every cavity, every nook and cranny and still found no signs of life. Their edge out of the building was cagey and evasive, each man hugging the exterior wall. Diego stole a furtive glance, once at the rooftop, and then focused on the outlying rim.

Sometime between his first dismount and the approaching dusk, there had been the slam of a rocket-propelled grenade. Through the periscope of nearby Bradleys, a flash had been seen on a mound 150 meters ahead. It had come from the white SUV that had skirted the company convoy, intolerant of its mind-numbing crawl. The journalists inside had spearheaded the procession without the reactive armor of the Bradleys. There had been no shields of protection, not even embedded status, as the SUV had hurled through the air. It had landed overturned on the side of the road to Al-Samawah, its wheels spinning panicked and clockwise.

The village through which they had passed was home to Shiite Muslims, generally opposed to Saddam Hussein. First Sergeant Moore had stared in horror—what seemed like gallons of blood had splattered the SUV dash and the windshield. The slaughter had saturated the floor and drenched the front seats where a telephoto lens had lay intact. There had been no bodies inside the SUV, and he had scavenged the area, searching for any kind of clues.

"There was no one there," he later informed Johnson as the squads continued to clear the warehouse. "I can't believe no one was there. There was blood all over the place."

"Well, wherever they are now, they're badly wounded." Johnson blew a breath as his squads rolled in.

Small arms fire ruptured their approach. It seemed to come from a nearby building. The pending blackness had emboldened the insurgents and Urquhart's squad took cover.

"Where's it coming from?!" Diego yelled.

Every man went for his NODS. The Bradley's thermal was far superior to the men's Night Observation Detection Systems.

Tolbert braced in the turret, and let their bass drum rip, and the skirmish was incredibly short-lived. Lieutenant Colonel Rutter retracted the further escalation. The Outlaws were not to get decisively engaged.

Pulling out of the first firefight only meant to Johnson that they were going to find a night job somewhere else. He pulled back his platoon and monitored multiple radio frequencies. There were only three sound bites he needed to know.

"Roger that" followed by "hooah" were two of the critical utterances.

The intelligence reports played back to him in real time. *Iraqi armored personnel are guarding an overpass.*

Johnson received orders to advance the Bradleys to secure the strategic bridge. It was a critical link between their current state and the punishing run to Baghdad. There was no way around it. There was nothing to do but go through it. Some things, like the overpass, were that way. He uttered a "hooah" and ended in "amen" and that accounted for all of his catch-phrases in battle.

"We're getting fast movers in to drop ordnance." Johnson relayed the preemptive air power to Urquhart. Within minutes, two A-10 Thunderbolt IIs swooped the fighting vehicles. There was a jolt and a shiver as the first A-10 dropped its bomb on a structure 300 meters downwind.

The second bomb was released and the concussion opened a massive inferno in the night sky. The earth heaved again, at least two more times, and the enemy was smoked from his hole.

Johnson ordered the artillery barrage and the capability was unspeakable—so suppressive it cratered the entire site. There were last-ditch shots that came tinny and distant as the dismounts waited out the bombardment.

The A-10s were elusive and toxic, and then they were phantoms. Diego felt a small swell in their faithfulness. He'd heard once that the airmen referred to them as "the customers," that they held a special reverence just for them.

We exist for close air support, to keep the ground forces happy. We do everything we can for "the customers."

The onslaught would be truly measured by the decimation they found when the dismounts took the fight to the ground.

"Head to the overpass!" Urquhart's teeth didn't part in the restrictive clip that propelled them over the rise. His squad crept to the railroad tracks with the wariness of fugitives, their vulnerability flat lined and scary. Diego's movements were sure and intrepid, but his jugular vein felt completely exposed. It was over so quickly, so handily controlled that Diego gaped at the obliteration.

It was not a fraction, not even an inkling, of the pronounced "shock and awe" that was going to rock Baghdad. That was the point—to have simply stood their ground on the fringes, proven themselves in a fistfight from the trenches. He wasn't battered or maimed or even bruised, just hungry and tired to the bone. Diego seemed to drag his legs suddenly behind him, some weakness in the blood in his thighs.

The adrenaline overcame that. Five Iraqi soldiers lay dead, upended, as Diego's squad took to the streets.

Diego would always struggle mightily to distance himself from the crouching civilians, pleading and praying to Allah. They secured a block and took twenty-one prisoners, detaining one Iraqi man at a time. Each was fighting age, but two men shook violently and another had shed his military uniform for civilian clothes. Many of them wore the traditional Arabic male robes; the long, flowing dresses known in English as thobes. Diego explored their faces and there was nothing distinguishable to identify the friend from the foe. The shadows taunted the men in their first harsh schooling—light and dark conjoined. It took a strip-search to find that one carried a sidearm and one carried the Quran—both concealed.

There was a code of etiquette to which coalition soldiers adhered in which Iraqi officers were not searched in front of fellow soldiers. Such humiliation before the rank and file was a breach of cultural correctness. Diego and his squad worked through the four "S's": subdue, secure, segregate and safeguard. Every article was inspected and personal property and protective clothing were retained by the enemy prisoners. Under U.S. Army regulations, Enemy Prisoners of War were allowed protection from a nuclear, biological or chemical attack—even if the attack had actually originated with the very EPWs they captured.

They were halfway through the procedure when the road lights darkened, thick blackness overcoming the holding area. The Bradleys' main guns, poised at attention, braced for the certain uprising. Diego put a hard knee to his detainee's back, caught between personal safety and the Geneva Convention. His instinct was decency, in a low crouch from the enemy with his body protecting his prisoner. From an adjacent street came a sputter of fire and the turrets swung, deadly and earnest. The churn of the 25mm rounds blanketed the city in hot metal, and the enemy dismounts were blown like chaff in the wind. The insurgence was silenced, and then an eeriness fell over the collecting point, the vulnerability palpable and unnerving. Diego rolled his prisoner onto his back and stared at the shared trepidation. Beads of sweat glistened on both of their brows and, even in the obscurity, their pupils were unnaturally dilated.

"He's clean," Diego judged with more authority than he felt, his eyes never wavering from the prisoner's gaze. Under the umbrella of humanity, every man being his brother, Diego prayed that what he saw was redeeming. *What was he thinking? What were his intentions? Was he right to just let him go like that? Had he only been like one of the men standing to the side of their convoy, cheering and clapping and waving?*

If so, there was no jubilation, no joy in his expression at the moment—by now there would be some awful resentment. Diego moved on, the chill of his indecision torturing some very already tightly strung thoughts.

"We've zip-stripped them all, sir," Curtin held up a paper, a get-out-of-jail-free kind of issuance.

Johnson nodded. "Release them with their papers. Good job, men." It was anticlimactic.

It had been more than two days since they'd left Kuwait, and every soldier was exhausted—the nerves had heightened the pain and malaise that came with traveling in such cramped quarters.

"Load up." It was said so matter-of-factly, Johnson could have just as well said, "have a nice day." They crawled into the Bradleys and were plunged into an abyss again of the unknown and the unseeing of their confines. The simple pattern they relied on, their only sure habit, resembled a kitchen table where every family member knew his place.

Cavazos and Curtin took their seats toward the front, sidling up to the turret. Lane and Black were assigned to the middle seats, where their heads often rolled comatose in sleep. Urquhart and Creighton took the vulnerable rear flank, a certain psychology dictating at least Urquhart's location—he was the first man out, and the last man in—one thing about Urquhart, his bravery was never in question.

"Close your legs," Cavazos demanded of Black, who spread his legs wider to spite him. "I'm serious, man, you're in my space." Black became nearly spread-eagled.

"Ouch!"

"I told you, man. My space. Your space. There's an imaginary line...right... here."

"If there's some kinda direction there...I...can't...see...you," Black's taunt was short-lived in his weariness.

Diego pulled off his Kevlar helmet inside the Bradley and he wilted with his buddies in sleep. They had made it through their first skirmish without any sort of casualties. The release was overwhelming. In their profound fatigue came a short-lived oblivion to what the rest of the world already knew and mourned.

Two Marines had been killed in separate ground assaults, the first U.S. combat casualties of the war.

+>===<+

Long after the dismounts succumbed to sleep, the Bradley fighting vehicles came to a standstill. They formed the framework of a tenuous perimeter that evening that disguised the extreme defenselessness. Besides the overall casualty count, it was the second piece of information to which the lower ranks were not privy. Johnson had omitted the vulnerability purposefully—some things were better left unsaid.

There was a task force behind them: multiple companies and batteries that had that stretch of a rubber band just before its snapping. Once the Outlaws had secured the overpass, the platoon had been ordered by Lieutenant Colonel Rutter to remain in Al-Samawah. The mission was two-fold: first, set up a blocking position to prevent Baath party militia from coming out of Al-Samawah and attacking the task force; second, the Outlaws needed to direct the task force movement forward.

Just try to catch up with the task force tomorrow. Johnson and Tolbert had exchanged serious glances. The Bradley crews consisted of the commander, the gunner, and the driver—the mission was overwhelming.

None of the crew members had slept a wink in more than forty-eight hours. There had already been attempts at infiltration by the enemy dismounts, in the broad and bald-faced daylight. The platoon was going to be leapfrogged by the entire task force movement. In essence, the Outlaws had been ordered to a complete segregation to guide the ongoing convoys. At some point, they were going to be completely alone—outside of communication range with no reinforcements. They were going to be isolated, in the middle of enemy territory, with only the Bradley crews of each vehicle watching over them. It was like being an anthill—that was the size of it—in the vastness of all that hostile sand.

Eisenhower had once said that "farming looks mighty easy when your plow is a pencil, and you're a thousand miles from the corn field." All of the plans and even the training at times bowed to practicality and humanness. Johnson's head nodded repeatedly on duty, and he tried to ram through the fatigue with every possible diversion. Their lives depended on his watchfulness—the dismounts were unconsciously, obliviously depending on him. The most paralyzing thought occurred to him once, and he still struggled mightily to ward off the sleep. If *he* knew the importance of staying awake—and if *he* still couldn't manage the vigilance—how would the other unsuspecting Bradley crews pull it off in the mind-numbing black of their nightfall?

As if to prove the peril, the Bradleys were pelted by enemy fire throughout the night in a number of sporadic rushes at the perimeter. Tolbert retorted with a rap of fire that sounded leaden—even the main gun grew weary. They were firing on technicals—ordinary pick-up trucks with machine guns mounted inside the truck beds. The technicals were manned by one insurgent in back, trying to bait the Bradley crews.

One minute the sap of energy was so profound that Johnson's vision was distorted in waves—the next minute he was holding his breath in the duress, his focus almost laser sharp. Johnson and Tolbert tried to spell each other, and in one of those handoffs came a significant paradigm shift. It was the disruption of the tedium—another attempted assault that pumped the heart enough to maintain extreme awareness. They realized with some wryness that the Iraqis were providing sufficient adrenaline rushes to push them through the exhaustion in short bursts. The Bradley fire punched at an embedded machine gun and the insurgent flipped graphically in the technical.

Thank you so much. I really needed that assault. I now have thirty more minutes of alertness pounding in my chest.

They might have been the spookiest hours—their required diligence in that endless creep of a night. Except that there was comfort in the companionship of the convoys, rolling imperviously beyond them. Alpha Company passed them. Bravo passed them. Charlie passed. Headquarters passed. Hours passed as an engineering company sought to overtake them with all the other specializations. Artillery passed. Signal passed and so did Air Defense. Johnson watched the last of the columns drift away, allowing for all the safe passages. That's when the atmosphere truly quickened to something disturbing—a tingling chill in his spine.

"Get some sleep, sir."

"We're almost through it." Johnson refused even a momentary let-up. When the artificial lighting of the firefights bowed to the greater sunrise, the shafts would reveal their desertion.

Johnson's sole directives were a handful of maps, and that sense of their next tactical Assembly Area. *Don't get lost and don't get ambushed.* Lieutenant Colonel Rutter's orders had been firm and curt and something else. Maybe it was solely Johnson's interpretation, but Rutter had never sounded more grave. He folded the maps and he declined the rest because the spookiest hours were still to come.

He was completely spent by the time daylight broke. They were going to have to make a beeline north. He was on the brink of collapse and it would never stop—the worry would never stop.

It was Johnson's chatter through the CVC helmet. The drivers were advancing on auto pilot.

"Take a break, sir."

"Why don't *you* take a break, Sergeant Tolbert?"

"Because you got less sleep than I did."

It was a strenuous discussion that went back and forth, and Urquhart overheard the stubbornness on the CVC. He had slept with the other dismounts and his legs were fresh. "Traverse the turret," Urquhart said to Tolbert. "I'm coming up."

Tolbert moved the main gun to the twelve o'clock position.

"Sir, you have to get some sleep."

Johnson look startled.

"I'm giving you a break. And I'm not taking 'no' for an answer."

Johnson's protests had always been mixed before. He could display some tremendous modesty. That was the blend that Diego had picked up on—a dance in traits in which his confidence always took the lead. There was nothing in his voice just then to offset the expression of the enormous burdens he carried.

Urquhart gave him a look that bore common sense—the crucial decisions that Johnson would make in the progression of the war. Critical leadership required clear thinking and, from inside the turret, Tolbert almost sensed that important transition. It was the wisdom and understanding that Tolbert owned that came quietly through the CVC helmet.

"Urquhart's right, sir. Get some sleep. It's going to be impossible to stay awake the whole war."

They stopped to refuel and resupply at three checkpoints, their weekend passing in a continued stupor. Few but the embedded journalists kept track of time, perhaps because they were privileged to know daylight. These were the most perilous days yet, the intrigue mounting both in and out of the Outlaw Platoon's sights. At Camp PA, at what had once been Alpha Company's home, the 101st Airborne Division had come under assault.

It was an inside job, a fellow soldier whose hand grenade attack immediately killed an officer and wounded over a dozen others. The blow left troops sickened, dazed, and demoralized in the ever-increasing hostilities.

The 507th Maintenance Company was catastrophically ambushed, with not all of the dead and wounded accounted for. American POWs were being interrogated, paraded on international television in a stoic sort of terror. At Al-Najaf, a village north of the town of Al-Nasariyah, the Outlaws' old company, too, became entrapped. They survived the calamity only to reach Al-Samawah and face a more deadly upheaval.

The shoulder-launched grenades smashed the tanks from all sides in a scene that resembled the Somalian overrun of Mogadishu.

In the slow snarl of traffic, re-routed through the desert, Lieutenant Colonel Rutter told the last unit to penetrate Route 8 to use deadly force. "If you see they have weapons, you light them up. Your first obligation is to protect your life and protect the lives of your fellow soldiers. Those are my orders. That's your ROE. *If they have weapons, you kill them.*"

Johnson felt a renewed prick of nerves outside Al-Samawah, where a plateau stood with a single two-lane road cresting it. Approximately twenty kilometers from the escarpment was a vast complex, a suspected chemical weapons facility. The mechanized brigade climbed the crest with all of its reactive armor to clear the threat from the area. The Bradley ramps dropped to the sound of no fury, a disturbing silence engulfing them.

The company pulled security on the far side of the complex to ward off the enemy dismounts. It was unsettling for the possible motivations behind the abandonment—the Iraqis had fled, scaling back the offensive.

The company commander, Captain Jimmy Lee, led the advance to clear a new tactical Assembly Area. Johnson's platoon assumed the more rear guard duties as dusk overshadowed their procession.

It was a welcome flank, to be part of the group again, to be sheathed in the safeguard of numbers. The pleasure of reinforcement gave way to foreboding as the Bradleys pushed toward the edge of the horizon.

Perhaps it was the cleanness of the shifting sands that made the litter to appear so alarming. There was scattered debris, boots and uniforms, dropped in the haste of the Iraqis' flight. The men had been warned amply of the last-minute shedding that gave off the appearance of civility. They had witnessed the pretense before— the white flag surrenders, followed by the stammering fire of that falsehood. Each of the briefings and any previous atrocities paled to the stark visual that stretched before them. The platoon's misgivings were strewn across the desert in deceptive and ill-omened patchworks of all that militant clothing.

In time and the forward movement, the darkness revealed what the fading daylight had not. Through the thermal, the gunners saw people—enemy dismounts on the run. All the rats were jumping ship, and the Bradleys snaked forward, a methodical hunt that would end when the main guns bore down on them. They had the bite to deliver quick death and the commanders stopped short of releasing the venom.

Walker had to try to overtake the insurgents. The pursuit was stretching endlessly. The Iraqis ran for their lives, and he finally coiled around them in a death grip, in an impassable arc. When the Bradley halted, the insurgents were trapped, sprinting toward nearly thirty tons of armor in so many directions.

The squad members were enraged as they dismounted to the open desert, and Cavazos wore his kamikaze upbringing. He couldn't barrel upright, take the enemy on the run, but he had those kick-off return instincts. It rarely occurred to him that he might be shot; every thought was purely offensive. In Cavazos' world, he was never the hunted—he almost raised his assault weapon to the fray.

Diego felt a mental explosion that rollicked his head, an internal splaying of his stomach. He clenched his jaw, trying to suffocate the gorge that throbbed to the trigger of the SAW. The six Iraqis in front of them had thrown down their weapons and raised a white flag in their defeat. They had intended to trick them, even kill them, and suddenly they signaled mercy. Diego's finger twitched—there was only his honor that kept him from executing all six of them. His head pounded loathing as he took the first prisoner and threw him, hard, to the ground.

Diego began to pull security as the EPWs were searched by two soldiers, their AK47s and ammunition confiscated. Creighton and Black piled their belongings on a faint perimeter; all the Iraqis appeared to be Baath party loyalists. Shots began to clutter their darkness from what Cavazos figured was a quarter of a kilometer away.

"Check this out." Creighton flipped a bundle toward him. It was the bounty money for their heads.

They found more wads of cash and cassette tapes in Arabic, Saddam's repeated urgings to fight. The EPWs were spooked to complete complacency, a tentative watch on Creighton's pacing. He muttered something indecipherable, nothing masking an antagonism underscored by his size. In the two-kilometer spread of their assault, other members of the platoon faced much harsher conditions.

The situation was moderately controlled from the vantage point Rendon had—until two shots rung out on their perimeter. Chaos quickly ensued. He whirled to the scene where some of the first squad members had been patting down their prisoners. The dark and the distance shaded the scuffle, but something was clearly wrong.

Specialist Kyle Hartley lay on the ground. Specialist Hartley didn't seem to be moving.

His prisoner had been fighting him tooth and nail from the moment he'd seized him. Sergeant Chevallier Brown had laid the prisoner face down to strip-search him—he just appeared to be another insurgent. The prisoner had writhed, cursing them in Arabic, unruly and unintelligible. Brown had handled him roughly, had tried to contain him while Hartley patted him down.

As they had rolled the prisoner over, he had cocked an elbow, and Hartley had sprawled precariously, tripping over a rock. The EPW had instantly reached into his coat, a dominant hand groping near his waist. The prisoner had seethed, swung violently back as Brown unloaded, two solid shots to the chest. Two men had groaned on the floor as Rendon had spun in the blackness, trying to make sense of the bedlam.

Hartley was down. It shattered all of Rendon's thoughts. He had an uncontrollable urge to take out his own prisoner, to strike him into nothing but a bloody pulp.

Someone called for a CLS bag, the Combat Lifesaver Bag like those Cavazos and Diego carried.

Please save Hartley. Do something for Hartley. But they were all attending to the prisoner.

"He's okay, Rendon. Settle down…settle down!" A specialist grabbed Rendon by the shoulders.

Hartley rose, shaken but unscathed, and Brown stood rooted where he'd lowered his rifle. The EPW's eyes blinked incredulous for a moment, then glazed unnaturally cold. When they searched his belongings they found a photo, his wife's gaze soft and demure.

"I didn't want to kill him."

"There was nothing you could do."

"He might have killed Hartley, you know?"

"He would have killed you."

Brown relinquished a sigh. It didn't get any more intimate than killing one of the prisoners.

Some of the squads fell behind and they were compelled to roll north again, trying to close the gap between the EPW point and the remainder of their unit. At sunrise they field stripped their M16s near the tic-tac-toe of fertile onion fields. The soldiers gathered as a whole outside the Bradleys, every harrowing detail re-hashed. The prisoner had fought strenuously because he'd been an officer—they had gleaned that much from the eyewitnesses. They'd searched him in front of his men, that utter humiliation, but he'd borne no uniform or rank.

"He was a two-star general."

"More like a captain—their ranking system's different from ours."

"They'll do an investigation," Johnson was unruffled. "Given all the facts, the squad will be cleared. He endangered Brown's life—what he killed was the enemy. He did *exactly* as he was taught."

"He was dressed like a civilian," Diego said. "There's no more politeness. Not in war." His eyes shone suddenly hard in the daylight, a newfound practicality sparked in them.

Brooks said little, cleaning only one of two M240 B machine guns found in the platoon—"the hog" as he liked to call it. The weapon could be belt fed, fully automatic, and, even empty, weighed over twenty-two pounds. It was a flattering burden, that beast of firepower that Brooks had to constantly shoulder. He raised it to his chest, as if curling a twig, and Cavazos admired the strength. They were strange things that came to him, in the middle of the desert, in the middle of their war-tortured soil.

It was that Brooks was older, but still in his prime—they were all just hitting their stride. Every magnanimous trait, the outstanding potency had never been more finely honed. In the past, at PT, one could lay hold on certain personality traits by the way each man ran the six-mile. Cavazos was prone to take the lead, in quick bursts and sprints and then trot and then sprint again. Brooks always stayed behind, comfortable in the pack, but he was as steady and as disciplined as a stopwatch. He usually caught Cavazos, near the end, in a tortoise and hare kind of outlast. He never stopped or winced or seemed to be winded in that perpetual drumbeat of motion—neither did Diego, which was what made him supreme; he had Brooks' deliberateness with Cavazos' lengthened pace.

All three of the men pulled excessive security because of the nature of their weapons. They were used and abused on every perimeter, which resulted in the discoloration on Brooks' legs. There were nasty purple welts and small, broken blood vessels that suddenly caught Cavazos' attention.

"What, are you shooting up out here?"

Brooks met Cavazos tease in sheepishness.

"I have to pinch myself really hard to stay awake."

Brooks laid down his weapon, fully reassembled in the mind buzz that plagued them like hangovers. Even through his DCUs, his arms were stout, rippling the strength that manhandled his weapon. Cavazos assumed he could have carried the M240 machine gun, but he couldn't have done it with such ease. Every man complemented him and that notion was followed by another fleeting thought.

Their only weakness, their only apparent mortality, lay in that appalling fatigue.

Diego returned from the fringe of their consolidated perimeter where each man went to relieve himself. Cavazos, too, resorted to a berm that edged the civilian expanse. Mud houses were strewn past the outskirts of the farm, and the odor of the crops wafted just beyond his nostrils. The ground was like clay, absorbing none of the daybreak, so that the chill nipped his fingers as he removed his gloves. If they remained dismounted until mid-day, the sweltering would layer Cavazos' head in a fine mist of perspiration.

About 1,400 meters away, a white car was parked and idling—something in its standstill unsettling. Cavazos squatted precariously, trying to rush his routine, a prickling sensation at his neck. He ducked his head, then raised his eyes again to an eastern horizon, blinding. In the glare he saw figures, distorted in the haze, their long, flowing thobes moving in slow-motion patterns.

He had no toilet paper, another bygone luxury. He ripped at the bottom of his brown tee. The men had begun to use strips, the bottom of their shirts, and then they had started to tear up their sleeves. The trick was to keep enough of the shirt showing at the neck of the DCU to appear to meet standard regulations. The men had experienced extreme dysentery, salmonella poisoning, back on the border of Kuwait. So far as they knew, it was the worst biological weapon yet— they had lost all bodily control.

I feel like a baby. Bring me some powder. Black had uttered it under great duress.

And then he'd lamented the scarcity in childlike wonder. "Half a brown tee...just gone."

Cavazos threw down the strip and was hurried by his heightened sense, some urgency clipping at his combat boots. "Do you see that white car over there?" he motioned to Diego as he skirted the back of the Bradley.

They were near the end of their morning routine; Johnson stirred his coffee slowly. They'd salvaged enough hot cocoa from their MREs to make his most exotic blend. He shaded his eyes and Tolbert took his position, the turret widening its arc. The car inched forward in a slink from the gunner, and two civilians eased back to the farm.

There were just the locals, the goats and the chickens, and Cavazos began to relax.

Someday, when they were old men, they would sit around a table and drink coffee and tell stories and laugh. A real table with real chairs and real cups and real food, and they would joke about using brown tees as toilet paper. For the moment, all they had was that morning routine, but there was a great deal of comfort in that shallow berm. Perhaps it was the predictability; perhaps it was the companionship; perhaps it was just the normalcy.

Williams lounged easily in a stolen moment, humming in deep concentration. He appeared to be writing another letter home, but Cavazos knew better as he watched him. There was a flurry of scratches and then his eyes closed as he nodded, the intensity of a gifted composer. There was something heartening in that, too—to see a man so creatively alive in the wasteland, the bleakness that had snuffed out all inspiration.

"Sing for us, Sergeant Wills," Diego nudged him. Williams laid down his headphones. The thing about Williams was that he wasn't just smooth; he was soothing, appeasing, and constant. His own Bradley was often a scathing seventy-five meters from Diego's squad and he would trudge the soft sand all that way just to check on them. Williams was the rover, something inspired and self-appointed, an internal honing device that told him exactly when and where he was needed.

His voice drifted off and the last note, when it came, was melancholy, rich, and vibrant. It resembled the tones of the popular artist Usher, and in its sophistication came a simple swan song—it was the summary of Williams' essence, nothing emanating from him that wasn't ultimately pleasurable and pure.

There had been times when he'd ridden the men, when he'd had to reprimand them, when he'd been tough and exacting and unyielding. But admirable in Williams, Farina had always observed, was that he tried to do right by his men. If ever he came down on them, he sought each man out afterward, and made his peace with them right away. His high expectations were to be taken as a compliment, just like his music, the outreach of his soul.

"That's one cool cat," Cavazos said as Williams headed back to his own Bradley. Williams was a silhouette of absolute serenity pushing his way through the sand.

The sun had paced itself for most of the day, sapping the men in its steady and sure incline. By the time the infantry was ordered back into the Bradleys, it met earth's edge at a 45-degree angle. The ramp rose reluctantly on the squad's fighting vehicle and, just as it reached the same slant, Johnson spotted a tank gunner emerged from the top of a Bradley, like a chimney sweep against the sky. The gunner readied the main gun as they prepared to roll out in the fluid motions that repetition had created. He was exposed from the chest up, positioned in the turret with the intense mechanics of duty.

He was nineteen years old with no hesitancy in his form, his youth and his training fusing the decisiveness. Johnson thought he slunk into the hole with more work awaiting him inside the turret of the Bradley.

It was obscene to the ears and it shocked the radio waves.

"My loader's been shot! I need a CLS guy!!"

Urquhart's CVC responded in a thunder. "Man down! Man down! We need a CLS bag!"

Diego sprinted toward the Bradley with his Combat Lifesaver bag. Specialist Greg Sanders was crumpled motionless, inside the turret, a shot to the back of his head. It was a sniper who had sunk him into the Bradley, and Diego inhaled sharply. He stared at the wound. There was nothing he could do. Sanders had been dead the minute he'd taken the hit.

They were raked by new fire. "Load back up!" Johnson called out to Diego. Urquhart sidled the Bradley with him.

The men took refuge inside the steel, breathing hard in wonder.

Just like that. Walker pulled away to clear the tank and get a clear field of fire to engage the enemy.

"Get ready to dismount!" There was the unmistakable discharge of the main gun that followed Johnson's orders.

The Bradley gunners tried to eliminate as much of the threat as possible. The platoon was tasked to clear all buildings within small arms range of the tactical Assembly Area. It was a circular sweep, a 360 degree search. Dozens and dozens of farmhouses. The ramp dropped again and the hole was gaping as each team slithered out in defense.

"Alpha dismount left! Bravo right!" Diego and Cavazos took the lead of their respective teams with their SAWs. Diego's senses were assaulted again in a wash of tears as he struggled to blink back the harshness. They had dismounted in the middle of one of the onion fields, its harvest reeking and stinging.

"Go, go, go!" The men peeled off, ordered to raid one farmhouse at a time.

Their MOUT training came instinctively, but it was arduous work, a bootlace of intricacies and buttonhooks and adrenaline rushes. They sized up each structure, readied their weapons, and with a thrust of force opened a Pandora's box. The mounting uncertainty, the possible death at their doors, and the physical output amounted to extreme exhaustion. They returned to the Bradleys after five abandoned houses and tried to regroup in their safe house. Diego was winded. Sweat pounded from each pore and collected in puddles in his DCUs. He swiped at his forehead, trying to stave off the burn of the salt in his eyes, the pungency of onions at his parched lips. A collar of water soaked his neck and more collected in his armpits and the inside of his thighs. He felt himself shrinking, diminished in the task and the excessive loss of all his fluids.

"I'm smoked," Cavazos rasped as Creighton doused his mouth. "Hurry up. Gimme the bottle."

They were exceptionally rude and remarkably generous with only sixteen ounces of water between them.

"We got it," Urquhart said evenly as the CVC squawked again, calling for another round of searches. There were two other squads, but Urquhart had the mobile radio. "Get ready." Diego's legs screamed, but he willed them to move.

Rutter had had an uncanny omnipresence, though he split his time between the various forces of the 2-7. He had driven to the action, irate as a batted wasp when his men were cornered, or in danger. He had seen the Outlaw Platoon, often in real time, and he had taken proper note of their discipline. About the time the platoon had taken that lonely stand near Al-Samawah, the equivalent of taking a bullet for the company—about the time he had seen Johnson pull in with their force at the tactical Assembly Area, and seen they were all unscathed—about that time, he had been swayed by the idea that the Outlaws were enormously impressive. His confidence in them filtered down to Johnson, who observed his squads with the same swell in that long, methodical face-off. They rolled off the conveyor belt of their tracks with such intensity that it elicited incomparable pride.

In the wake of the fatality, there was some reassurance. *These are the go-to guys.*

From a second Bradley had come supplemental wingmen, Williams and Specialist Dustin Wheeland on the warpath. There were others in the mix, of course, but Brooks felt helpless each time the pair disappeared, stranded with his M240. With the monstrosity of the weapon came a schizophrenic duty—he could be the first man out, or the last stand. On this occasion it was his fate to stay behind, to man the stronghold at their base. He set his stance like his pace in the six-mile run, rock-solid and reliable and loyal. His legs were still fresh as Williams and Wheeland returned, panting and drained, to the Bradleys.

The tracks rolled a few yards as the two rehydrated and resolved, and then they were gone again.

When are we getting out? These guys are burnt out. Somebody...let...us...out...

Brooks sighed in the frustration of his fixed position, closed his eyes tight as was his habit in annoyance.

It took five hours to clear the outskirts of the village; the Alpha and Bravo teams were washed-out. Inside his own Bradley, Williams' head sunk. They had not found a single insurgent. There had been the occasional sputter from the 25mm of their fighting vehicle—the Bradleys had sawed a few loyalists in half. He just couldn't help thinking the same tortured stream-of-consciousness as Cavazos: the sniper had had him in his sights.

On the way to the berm where Cavazos had relieved himself. That prickling sensation at his neck. He had been in the sniper's crosshairs, the weapon had to have been pointed at his head the entire time.

Diego's wonder was voiced aloud as they patrolled ahead in the Bradley. "That sniper could have killed us. I could have died. Anyone of us could have died today."

Reality hadn't suddenly hit the men—it had knocked them into another atmosphere where they floated in the most isolating space.

Had Specialist Sanders had any inkling, any foreboding, any prescience at all? If he had died instantly—and it was apparent that he had—had his world just suddenly grown dark? Had his life passed before him, or had he suddenly found himself in heaven? What had been his last thoughts?

Did God give a person something grand—some lasting sort of vision. Or had he just been absorbed in that most mundane of tasks? Working feverishly on the main gun.

It wasn't like cancer or something with warning. *I'm sorry, but you only have six months to live.* No blood tests, no x-rays, and no doctors in white coats, trying to break the news gently. Up until that moment, Sanders had been completely strong and healthy and vital. I'm sorry, Specialist Sanders—I know you're married. I know you have a small daughter. But you'll never see them again. Not here anyway. That last hug on post…I'm really, truly sorry.

Specialist Sanders, I hate to tell you this—you have less than a split second to live.

Maybe it was better to die in a blaze of glory, to die on a battlefield in one's prime. The men certainly didn't want to linger; they didn't want to suffer; they didn't want to slack or waste away. How did God decide—why Specialist Sanders? God, after all, was in complete control. Diego personally felt a wave of guilt that came to him nauseous, the kind of feeling he had just before he might vomit.

He had an important piece of information that those closest to Sanders didn't even own. Sanders had died, and his family wouldn't even know that yet, living on the other side of the world.

They were loathe to pull security outside, on the ground, with the never-ending strikes on their huddles. Black refused to remove his Kevlar helmet, not for one second; not to sleep or to eat or to relieve himself. Johnson ordered security, one man up at a time to work the main gun on the Bradleys. Few of the men had experience in the turret. Tolbert gave Urquhart's squad a crash course.

The night was so lucid, the thermal energy so vivid, that Curtin spotted a mouse through the periscope. It scurried on the sand, all its life heat pulsating; he imagined he saw its nose twitch. The mouse was alive while all around them humans were dead, and there was a terrible unfairness in that. He tried to block that kind of whirling in his brain, tried to focus on something simpler.

Cavazos relieved him as their camp took on the stillness that always brought such immense longing. Back home, in Hinesville, he had risen at four to get onto post a bit early. By five in the morning, the traffic was at a standstill at the main entrance, and he barely made it to PT. He had learned if he rose prematurely, he could sail through the checkpoint and bed down for a forty-five minute nap on Brooks' floor in the barracks. There was always a lonely feeling, in that isolating drive, the moment before the houselights started peeping out from select windows.

It was a basic yearning—to be comfortable in his own bed, to succumb to a deep sleep with his wife.

He popped his jaw and he shifted his legs and he tried to take deep, invigorating breaths. The desert was mindless and the day's preceding searches had been endless; the sleepiness overtook him like a drug. Naemi had heard that a single cigarette could be seen a mile away in the thermal. Wracked in her phobia, she had sent large packages of smokeless tobacco in all the care packages to her husband.

Don't even worry, baby. The Iraqis don't have that kind of technology. He took a long drag on a Marlboro Light. When it did nothing to wake him, he put the cherry to his chin, inhaling the second hand smoke. He burned himself until the searing pain revived him, the sensation only lasting a minute. Brooks had insisted that a man never ran out of flesh to pinch—and bruising never caused lung cancer. Skin was regenerative—unlike cigarettes. In his mind, Cavazos brushed him off. He'd worry about cancer if he made it home alive. Right now, the artillery barrages were more pressing.

Diego relieved Cavazos and the drowsiness was overpowering, despite the cagey perimeter. He remembered seeing the sun sulk to an all-time low—the days and the nights had finally blurred. In the backdrop of a sunset had been a slow migration of the local population, their final attempts to evacuate a war zone. He had seen two forms, one in a head scarf, as if through the eyes of his mother.

It had risen to his throat in the good manners and grace that she alone had instilled. *Can I help you with that? Let me carry your little girl. Is there anything else I can do?*

And then suddenly there was a sniper, slipped into the commonness. A company coming under attack. A spray of bullets and the civilians scattering with their loads and then everyone ducking for cover.

He saw it in his mind as he'd heard that day. They'd killed an assassin, hiding among the sheep.

Take him out!! There's someone in the lambs!!! The sheep had bleated furiously in the uproar.

One lamb had crumpled amid the fire, and then a lone figure had dashed from the holding pen. There had been a quick volley and the sniper had suddenly contorted, his legs still willing him to flee. His head had rolled back and that was it. The would-be assassin had died. Maybe someone in the infantry had avenged Sanders' death that day.

Maybe not. There were so many, lying in wait.

Diego saw Rendon fifty meters away, tucking some notebook paper far beneath his chemical suit. The motion was noted as a trace of white in the thermal that watched over him throughout the night. The men's feet were prominent, the hottest part of their bodies because they were overworked and marched to near radiance. They were just a few lines that Rendon had penned in Spanish, the kind he could truly never send.

The Iraqis raise the white flag, Mom. They shoot at us. They kill our men. And then they raise a white flag...

If I make it through this war with this rule, Mom...I tell you, I'm not going to be the same man.

CHAPTER 7

The Outlaw Platoon was an internal reference, the kind of nickname assigned every day. That was the significance of an external bidding when Johnson received the categorical orders by radio.

"Outlaw 1, Able 3. Set up a checkpoint to only allow northbound traffic on Highway 9. Nothing headed south gets past you to influence the fight for the bridge over the Euphrates.

"I want the Outlaw Platoon. I want *the Outlaws* to stop all the Baath party loyalists."

"Roger that," Johnson was composed. He kept the exultation to himself.

We have our own identity. That was completely unheard of. The initial prick was one of pride. "The battalion operations officer dropped down to our platoon net to specifically ask for *us*."

It was relayed to Urquhart who experienced a similar rush, followed by terse and steadfast instruction. They had ridden seventy kilometers in another blinding sandstorm. The day had been ugly and slow. Curtin braced himself against the wind as he made his way back to the Bradley. "Let's get ready," he said. "It's outside Karbala. It's a checkpoint of some kind to screen for another unit."

Our guys are trying to take the bridge. We've been ordered to protect them from the Baath party loyalists. The orders reached the rank of a private first class, and Diego still felt the swell.

It *was* a compliment. It *was* terribly flattering. And then Johnson had one moment of regret—they were a known commodity now, and they were going to be tasked all of the tougher missions.

Captain Lee only needed two tanks and two Bradleys to outline the blocking position. "Give me Bravo," he told Johnson, and Urquhart's squad stayed back. Diego and his team members continued to clear the small farmhouses. Bravo moved forward to Highway 9. They established their fighting positions on a divided highway, south of Karbala, near a place called Al-Najaf.

It was midnight and lightly shadowed by the glow of the moon, the brightest the men had ever seen. It was just an illusion, the stark illumination, with no mountainous landscape to put its size in perspective. Urquhart's squad continued the raids in the dark as Tolbert settled in to monitor the radio.

The news came swiftly.

"Sir, there's trouble." Tolbert's expression was dark.

Johnson tuned his attention to the net, and what he immediately heard was some kind of horrible screeching. It came in contractions—individual words, more coherent than phrases.

Ambush! We're hit!!! We're taking fire!!!!!

From what Johnson gathered, Bravo had rolled right into it. Half of the platoon was mortally endangered. Johnson's own voice came to him foreign because something inside his gut screamed.

Urquhart's squad abandoned the small farmhouses and loaded rapidly in the Bradley. It was the first time they had had to mentally prepare themselves. They knew they were going straight into a firefight.

"What direction are they shooting?? Can we flank from behind?!" It was the longest ten minutes of Johnson's life. His foot subconsciously pressed the Bradley floor as if he could accelerate the flight. There was so much extreme drama playing out on the net. *This is taking too long. My men are dying out there.* In the hollow right behind him, there was palpable trepidation—hearts beating out of skulls among the dismounts.

Their Bradley had taken any number of pot shots from the insurgents on their grueling road to Karbala. They had often been awakened by the scan of the turret, followed by angry protests of fire. This was different. This was an anticipation that left a queasy feeling in the stomach. Alone in the hellhole and isolated in his thoughts, Diego's emotions came cursory. He was about to be immersed decidedly in battle, and there was only one comforting idea.

He had been re-baptized, that outward token of the devotion he'd offered to God at Ft. Benning.

Whatever happened, he had bound his heart in the way that he'd understood it in Romans. *For I am persuaded, that neither death, nor life, nor angels, nor principalities, nor powers, nor things present, nor things to come—Nor height, nor depth, nor any other creature, shall be able to separate us from the love of God, which is in Christ Jesus our Lord.* If, in fact, his mission was truly to deliver, to set free, no matter the type of bondage, then he was not so unlike those wondering warriors who had struggled on the road to Emmaus. He might be blind to the divinity that walked right beside them, but he only asked Him to abide. He felt as right with God as a young man could feel, not wanting to see Him just yet. He'd been baptized by water on the sacred soil of his home and now came his baptism by fire. It was going to pummel their fighting vehicle the moment they halted on Highway 9 in furrowed tracks and dismounted. Diego prayed in his hollowed shell. *Oh please, Jesus, abide here with me.* He repeated it in whispers that glossed over the actual words and settled on the fervency in his voice.

Two RPGs slammed into Bravo's tanks at the roadblock, nullified by their reactive armor. The men were burrowed in thin trenches and fighting positions, the gopher holes that always pocked infantry landscape. Brooks wasn't exactly prone and he wasn't exactly seated—some lopsided takeover of his cover. There was the telltale splatter, the streak of the tracers, and he knew they were seriously under fire.

It was comical at times, the outdated weaponry that U.S. forces had to swat back like fleas. It helped to look at it that way—to view the danger as a three-ring circus of fleas. Snavely was derisive and Brooks remained askew, some chatter in him overwhelming. He started to laugh, "Are they shooting at us, man?

"I mean, are they seriously...*shooting...at...us??*" That he emphasized his words, slowed the rhetoric, was an unusual break of demeanor. Brooks was a fast talker, always had been, the men sometimes telling him to breathe.

"They're shooting at us." There was still some incredulity that lapsed into more surreal humor. He couldn't help himself, he couldn't stop laughing, a low-pitched, nervous kind of hilarity.

"Are you crazy??!! Get down!!" Rendon called to Ronquillo as his squad low crawled to the Bradleys. They were desperate for cover, anything at all, even if their cover happened to be the target.

Rendon felt the heat of the RPG; it seemed to graze his face. There was a flash in his eyes, like the supposed flash of the muzzle when that sniper had suddenly peeked from the lambs. The crackle of the radios came distant but infuriating—some distressing call for backup. Rendon still crawled, but it didn't feel like a crawl—he felt his 180-pound frame move like lightning.

He was among the first to reach the safety net, and then he heard a familiar voice yelling.

"Friendly! Friendly! I'm making a move! Friendly at five o'clock!"

He shouldered his weapon, watching each back. There were more low crawls and approaches.

"Friendly!" They were moving in so fast and furious, it seemed he was surrounded on all sides.

They were gathered in like chicks under a mother hen's wing, except for one noticeable absence. He was poignantly missing, the last of their brood to be slow coming in and panic enveloped Rendon.

"Ronquillo!" he called. "Ronny Q, where are you??" A body lay motionless in the field. "Ronny Q! Is that you?" *C'mon, man please talk to me. Please get up off the ground!!!*

Ronquillo was unmoved and Rendon bit his lip. *Please. Not Ronny Q. No!*

He felt a sag, an audible gasp as all the air expelled from his lungs. He was going to cry and then he was going to explode and then Ronquillo suddenly stood up. He walked upright. He sauntered in. *Whatever, I'm here*, his gait spoke. "Incoming," he said it, nonchalant. *"Could you pass me the salt?"* was his tone.

"Listen, Turbo, could you be any slower??!!" Their team leader glared something mixed. It was the sarcasm of relief and the edge of annoyance. Rendon nearly came unglued.

"Don't you *ever* do that again, Ronquillo!" his anger came childlike and harmless. A man didn't go killing one of his better friends when death was at their threshold.

The tanks had been lodged in opposing directions to search all southbound traffic. It had the feel of one of the great Eagles songs: *you can check out any time you like, but you can never leave.* A white Toyota truck, a dime a dozen in Iraq, came barreling toward the tanks. The act was so brazen that bafflement reigned for a moment, a suspension of disbelief in their nightfall. There was an obvious median that split the highway, separating the north- and southbound lanes. When the pick-up truck broke all barricades, it breached them there, on that polarizing divide of right and wrong. The truck hurled inward, jumped the median and landed in a bunker in its frenzy.

It was clear the truck had been avoiding the tank, but its speed and its explicitness signaled the intent. It was a crazy world where civilians got confused and terrorists tried to act like civilians. The object of the insurgents was to get as close as possible just as the explosives were detonated. Every squad weapon opened fire on the vehicle, more than 100 rounds piercing the metal. A propane tank in the back of the truck caught some of the shrapnel and exploded in a ball of orange.

Urquhart's squad arrived on the scene exactly at that moment. When Johnson ordered the dismount, the opening of the Bradley ramp drew back a curtain. It was a hideously grotesque stage, the flames that devoured the truck and all of its shot-up occupants. Diego saw the dark outline of the heat on bent steel, which was the reverse of the thermal on the Bradleys.

Heat was black and black was white and then everything turned gray in the war. The inferno leaped higher, screaming and lashing at them. Cavazos' stomach churned. The men leaped forward and, in that propelling, there came a stunning and absolute understanding. They manhandled their weapons and the image before them was emblazoned.

War was quite literally hell.

The back of the pick-up had been full of chickens, penned in portable, wire coops. The feathers were molted to non-distinction, to lumps where the birds had been roasted. The fire burnt itself out and the men tentatively worked their way through the entanglement of Concertina wire. The truck was ensnared in all that wire and, in his labored approach, Diego felt the reflexive gag.

It was the most horrifying, appalling, most disastrous scene he had ever viewed in his life.

Some bones jutted sideways, the sockets in their heads gave the illusion of wide-eyed shock and accusation. The occupants looked young amid all their deformities, with dozens of bullet holes penetrating their skulls. The concave markings punctured every limb, the result of the squads' frantic pummeling. *What in the name of all that was good and holy were you possibly thinking—a kamikaze stunt like that?* Diego felt no anger, just that sickening gag in the stench of their ruin as he turned away. The bitterness lasted even as he choked back the bile—it was a never before tasted remorse. Brooks stared at the carnage and, when he had time to think, he would decide he could have gone a lifetime without seeing that kind of horror. And then he would think that it was better that he be the one—not his younger brother or his sisters. It was a distressful thing, to be exposed to the atrocities, but he was the one appointed to spare the others from the terror.

The Alpha and Bravo teams took their fighting positions and Diego cradled the SAW. The acrid smoke burned at his throat. It taunted his cracked, swollen lips. He'd heard that emotion was something of a rarity in places like Vietnam—that there had never been time to feel, to mourn, or to even think in the constant barrage of the enemy. The superiority of their weapons, their skill, and their sheer numbers negated that kind of numbness now—the insurgents danced in, left their mark, and danced out. At the end of each round came some reflection.

Diego's squad held fast in their berms, scanning their strip of the highway. They'd been instructed to shoot warning rounds at anything that moved, any traffic that threatened the roadway. A second pick-up truck approached the roadblock and the air was razed with fire. Five men jumped from the truck bed, scurrying like mice—mice who jabbered frantically in Arabic. Cavazos and Diego leaned against the bi-pods, their habit on directing clean shots. On the run, the weapon had a retractable butt stock that gave the men higher mobility. The snap was inborn, each time they hit the ground, they pulled the bi-pod like they blinked. The thermal picked up a signature: the fleeing men held something cold, something long like large tubes.

"Hey, Creight, do you see that?"

"Yeah, what are they *doing*?"

Cavazos called back to Urquhart. "They look like pipes! They gotta be RPGs! What do you think, Sergeant Urquhart?!"

"Hold your fire! Let's wait and see!" Urquhart called Johnson on the radio. All Diego had to do was get some heat in his sight and aim in the general direction.

It was strange how they saw all the traps laid out, the futility of gnats against a tiger. Except, once in a while, Diego felt more like a deer, some deer in the woods that actually watched as the hunter loaded his rifle. *That bullet's for me. It's intended for me and I have to outlast him, outwit him.*

"Hey, people, Iraqis. Don't worry about us. We'll just sit here and eat popcorn until you decide what you're doing."

It was because Johnson read a lot that he had the historical perspective—that he'd seen the vignette countless times. The first time the phrase had struck him he had been reading a historical novel about the Civil War.

"It's not the bullet addressed to your name that you have to worry about. It's the one that's addressed: 'To Whom It May Concern.'" It had sent small shivers up and down his spine and he'd thought on it, hard, for some time. As he'd worked his way, upward through the ranks, he had become increasingly comfortable with that notion. If he had a bullet with *his* name on it, that was fate and there was nothing he could do about it.

"To Whom It May Concern" implied some control. Those bullets were reserved for the mistaken. Those bullets could be avoided if a soldier utilized all of his training—if he worked to do everything right.

You will low crawl with your face plastered to the ground. You will do it because you play how you practice. Johnson was also an avid sports fan, and his men were not going to die because a drill was a tad bit uncomfortable.

Johnson remained with his mobile command post. Johnson remained in the Bradley. He could do more damage in directing the fire power from inside the fighting vehicle. He had better optics, he could monitor three nets on the radio, and form the framework for a bigger picture. He would do everything possible to protect his men first, and then balance that in the weight of protecting innocent civilians.

The thought of taking out some Iraqi, just the wrong man in the wrong place at the wrong time—it was all the reason Diego and Cavazos awaited orders. It was the reason they squirmed with their SAWs.

One Iraqi took a knee and the cold pipe swung wide in its arc. Urquhart yielded to the chain of command.

"Fire! Fire! Fire!" Johnson's order came screaming. The RPG was dangerously close to being launched as Diego witnessed the pierce of his own rounds.

He gauged the heat, picked up the flashes to the insurgents, and the Iraqis were mowed down before his eyes. The enemies' weapons were cold—merely litter—as it was seen through every thermal. But there was a glow of white heat that still radiated from bodies whose warm blood had been shocked in mid-pump. The coaxial on the Bradley had cut them in half as a protective measure, and still their strewn body parts glowed.

Diego leaned back in the stark realization: five men were dead at his hands.

The berm fell silent. There was no gloating, no bravado; Diego felt the tremble of near death. *Kill or be killed.* The sun had set blood red in the sandstorm earlier that day.

The violence wasn't enough, the human drama and the pelting they had taken from the wind and the grit—the sky opened its own tirade, a steady drizzle of rain that capped off the men's total misery. Each was incredulous as they hunkered in their foxholes: a chicken pecked its way to their berms. It had come from the white Toyota; it had survived the explosion and the spatter of bullets and then the weather.

Cavazos' lip curled in strange admiration, "That thing doesn't have sense to come in out of the rain, you know?"

It looked on them curiously, strutted to the rise, and weaved in and out of the SAWs.

"What are *you* lookin' at?" Cavazos rolled sideways. "You got to get out of the rain, chicken."

Diego smiled wide, a sign of genuine pleasure he hadn't shown since Kuwait. The chicken hopped on his barrel, perched in front of the thermal, and jutted its head in the inspection. "You see anything out there? I think we smoked 'em all." The chicken cocked its head as if contemplating.

"Hey, I'm a little hungry. Maybe we should have ourselves a fry." The chicken stretched its wings, indignant. Its feathers were as black as the midnight that had descended on them, downtrodden and streaked in the rain.

"I'm taking a picture and, if this turns out, I'm sending it out to your mama."

Diego posed for Cavazos with the chicken on his barrel. There were shots, the constant ping of enemy fire in their distance.

"Let's eat that chicken."

Diego shook his head, rarely one to dissent, a softness overcoming his face.

"Leave it alone, man. That chicken's doing nothing. That chicken isn't hurting anybody."

+≒≕+

"You almost died out there," Creighton turned to Rendon.

"Thanks be to God I didn't." *Thanks be to Flaco, watching my back.* He kept the term of endearment to himself.

"It's some crazy stuff out here," Diego sounded preoccupied as he wrote in a ten-page letter to Fabian. *How could he give words to killing a man, to seeing the unspeakable that had opened before them when the ramp had dropped?* Johnson was sipping his coffee, absorbed in conversation, and the rest of the men were detoxifying after the dawn. Curtin wrote a letter; Curtin in his stalwart kind of language: "There's a lot I can tell, but I cannot. We have seen a few small firefights and we are all okay. There's not much else to say but I love you all and you're always in my thoughts. Don't worry about me. I will write again the next time we can. Love, Michael."

When I saw the bodies it was the most horrifying sight you could ever imagine, Fabian. I could live my whole life without seeing that picture...

We walked where the other bodies were. They were missing arms, legs, and were lying all over the place. It was just like a movie. We buried them all. I felt sick to my stomach.

We got to a new [tactical] Alpha Alpha today and refueled and re-supplied. It is March 28, Friday morning. We got told about one hour ago that we will move out to fight the biggest battle yet. We are going into the barracks, the home of the 14th Medina Division. God protect us.

I don't want Mom to find this stuff out because I don't know how she will take it. I love you all so much. I'll do my best to make it home safely. Your bro, Diego Rincon.

His parents were still up, of course, given the time difference, given that it was only midnight in Conyers. Jorge had bought a walkman so that he could listen to the radio as he tried to keep his business competitive. He didn't feel like working, didn't feel like cleaning carpets when his son was fighting a war. His clients were kindhearted, allowing the glimpses of the newscasts that brought the battles right into their living rooms.

Sometimes he thought he could see him in the footage on Fox News; in uniform, they all looked alike. *There's Diego, clearing that building; there he is, rolling forward in that convoy.* An embedded reporter, Michael Corkery, filed stories on the Outlaws' old company frequently, but it was never enough to appease him. He wanted news of his son, specifically his son and his platoon, and that constant agony sucked the very life from him.

The worry shone tearfully as he methodically vacuumed, and a client placed a hand on his shoulder. "Jorge, he's fine. He's going to be just fine. He's going to come home very soon."

His children had cleaned carpets with him for so very long that Diego was like their boy, too. "He's going to come home and get married and have children. You have that whole beautiful life with him ahead of you."

Jorge nodded gratefully, trying to be a man, trying not to break down so publicly.

He drove to the house in a mist of memories, so thick it was hard to see the road. "Call us when you get there. Call us, Diego." They were the last words he'd said to his son at Fort Stewart. "Don't leave any part of yourself over there." He didn't know why he had uttered that. Pulling Diego to him in that final sweep, he'd felt him so alive, so intact. And then there'd been some explosion, some alarm in his brain that had made him blurt out the words.

Don't leave any little piece of your heart, Diego. I want you back in one piece.

"Be good to Tí Tí. Take care of your little sister." Diego had ruffled Georgie's head. It had been his last concern as George's unabashed adoration had backlit the sorrow on his face. He'd been passing a torch of care and concern to the most tenderhearted child of them all. It was that quirkiness in Stephanie that had caused the unexpected movement; that mirror on Diego's spontaneity. She had broken from her mother and leaped to Diego, wrapping her legs around his chest. She had squeezed harder and harder with her arms around his neck until Diego had buried his face in her long hair. He had smoothed the tresses and kissed her cheek and ever so quietly had come her small tremble.

"I miss you so much. Come back soon." And then she had composed herself.

Yolanda hadn't spoken; she'd just rubbed his cheek softly against hers as she'd pressed her hand to him. She had touched his face lightly and kissed his cheek and he'd smiled in a strange kind of grief. He had pulled back from her bravely, held two thumbs up. "Watch me. I'll be on the news."

Even from a distance, there had been the distinguishable breath that had come hard as Diego had walked away. He had faded beyond the street lamp and still his parents had sensed it—he had struggled not to look back as he cried.

Jorge was rocked violently in a mental storm between his idealism and soul-searching sacrifice. It was this notion he had—that he'd held to all his life—the same one carved on the Korean War Memorial.

"Freedom," it read, "is not free" and that conviction had been so surely etched in his heart. It was rock hard in the will that had brought him to America and granite-like in his support of the war. With the wall of resolve having been so carefully constructed, so meticulously shaped over time—it came as a great shock and a whirling to feel the frailty, the wrecking ball of his doubts. No matter the cost, no matter the climb, no matter the crosses to bear…they were all the stones that had framed his character. He had built them line upon line. If when the worst of assailants threatened to topple them, would he have the courage to stand? *No matter the cost…*

It was just so unbearable when the cost of freedom was a child.

He couldn't explain the terrible foreboding, the unleash of fury on his spirit. He was angry and brooding and so dysfunctional in his wrath that he separated himself from his family. He didn't enter the house but sat in Diego's Mustang for hours, gripping the steering wheel. Something bad was happening; he didn't understand it; there was nothing but blackness and despair.

"Diego, Diego," he cried out loud, dropping his head in his hands. Just the sound of his son's name suddenly caved all his strength in great and eternal racking sobs.

+≈=+

Diego had never been so hurt in his life, hearing the news as his platoon did. It came over the radio: there had been a catastrophic accident among Outlaw's old company, and among the casualties were friends. Johnson had been monitoring a number of nets on the radio—constantly interweaving the conversation threads. He had looked for the patterns, and he had tried to piece together the reports with so many of them coming in sporadic stitches. There were three words that had registered. *Dead. Paralyzed. Unconscious.* It was hard to distinguish the casualty count. *Did the words all apply to one man?* He closed his eyes, trying to listen more intently.

Being a Bradley commander meant being the navigator of a rather cumbersome, grotesque kind of animal. A great hulk like their fighting vehicles absorbed the enemy fire well, but was not easily maneuvered. It was nothing like graceful—which meant if it was on the attack, it was very much like an elephant, stampeding full bore ahead with blinders. Johnson and similar commanders had the marginal vision of the periscope, at twelve o'clock because the scope itself was stationary. The lack of depth perception on the flat and barren landscape made it all the more difficult to chart a course at night.

There was a revolting tone of panic and horror that came over the Alpha Company net. A Bradley from their old unit had been chasing Baath party militia—in the black of that desert canvas, the vehicle had been accidentally plunged into a hole. There was a swell of dismay and then a string of profanities that carried more awe than crudity as Johnson relayed it to the men. To be riding in a Bradley one minute, and then sunk thirty feet in the trappings of unforgiving steel—it was like dropping out of the sky at altitude in a metal morgue. The injury reports trickled in slowly to Johnson, and all of them were ghoulish and grim.

Sergeant Roderic Solomon was dead. Three infantrymen were seriously wounded—one of them was in a coma. Sergeant Kenneth Dixon had suffered a broken back, and it appeared he might be paralyzed. They were not so invincible, no matter their reactive armor and their training and their discipline and their youth. Hearts could stop beating, spinal cords could be severed, so that one minute one was riding along in a Bradley and the next minute life was over.

Or maybe it wasn't over—maybe it was just morbidly altered. Diego felt a lurch in his chest that made him dizzy. *Close your legs. Give me some room.* It brought shame just to remember someone saying that.

It meant they could move; it meant his physical form was still perfect, unaltered and whole.

Diego thought of Dixon, perhaps never walking again, and he curled his own legs tighter in sickness. No matter how hard he tried to sleep, it played repeatedly in his mind. Solomon had had dreams and warmth and a big smile, and all of that had been abruptly snuffed out. He'd been a Gulf War veteran who had begged to re-enlist, a father of three who had taken the younger men under his wing. For a man to never step foot again on American soil, for a man to never see his children again…

Diego wrote poetry, seeking some outlet. So much was churning inside.

Fabian:

One of our friends, Sergeant Solomon is dead and Dixon, another buddy, has a broken back.

I hate these people.

Plus we thought we got hit with gas one hour ago. They found two gas trucks driving and intel said that they were filled with chemical weapons. So they bombed the trucks. We saw the explosion and then we heard "gas" on the net. We saw smoke a mile up and a ring around the smoke. It freaked us out. It is so hot with the mask and we're all at MOPP4. It took them an hour to clear it for us.

Well, that's all so far. Pray for me and my pals. He had added it all in a postscript.

There was no elation, to be so wanted, the second time the Outlaw Platoon was tasked out. There was a brusqueness to the orders, a change in plans, as the call came over the radio. Alpha Company was being overrun at Highway 9 and, to the soldiers, it was a terrible distraction.

They were bound for the Karbala Gap—the roadblock was a detour, a pain-in-the-neck, untimely detour.

A man's gotta do what a man's gotta do. It was said with tight-lipped irreverence. There were no outward murmurs, but Diego and Cavazos shared a look that conveyed their frustration.

The SAWs had been giving them fits all morning; perhaps it was the sand or bad luck. They traded them in for M16 rifles from Alpha Company in a bittersweet reunion. They hadn't seen "Rage," not the entire spectrum of their forces for days, not since leaving Kuwait. It was a relief and it was sorrowful, news of Solomon and Dixon pervading so much thought.

Urquhart was intent and focused and hurried as they prepared for the handoff of duties. He didn't like what he saw, and neither did Johnson: the roadblock had turned into a checkpoint. There was a busload of civilians stalled on the roadway, all those bodies at a standstill on their perimeter. There was an unoccupied car in the middle of the median and stragglers all along the road.

"We have to search the cars now." It was a change in ROE. No warning shots and no absolutes.

"Fine," Johnson said. "Let's clean up this mess." They'd have a textbook throttle in no time.

"Want some juice?" Brooks sprayed Curtin playfully with a mist from the water bottle. They rode in separate Bradleys and there was that stolen happiness of talking while they could. Curtin gulped the water. He shook his head in good humor, drenched to the neck, and Brooks grinned, lighthearted.

"All right, Corporal Curtin. You're good to go."

Time to get back to work.

"We'll see ya." Brooks headed to his position, the most southern berm, away from the crowds and the chaos.

Urquhart's squad was conversely in the thick of things. He would have had it no other way. That left Rendon's team to guard the second berm where the EPWs were held captive by Concertina wire. Their fun was over, that brief interaction, caving to the maturity of duty. Rendon stood tall and formidable at the edge of their holding area, demonstrating far more patience than he felt. It was just after ten, and already the morning sun scorched him; it was going to be a bear of a long day.

"Alpha, get that man out of here!" Urquhart directed Williams' team to the far side of the median. "Bravo, we need to search that taxi cab. Let's restore some order. *Now.*"

The trickle of Brooks' clowning was already evaporating as Curtin made his move toward the car. Even when he wasn't marching, he looked like he was marching—Curtin in his undeviating stride. Farina picked out Diego, just by the graced assuredness of his walk, as the Bravo team edged out behind Curtin. He had flashed a large smile, too big for his face. *Okay, little bro.* Farina nodded. Somewhere in the universe there were onlookers, a crowd. Someone yelling to Diego, "No, no, no." He gripped his weapon in his Midas touch, the way he had of turning tumbles into victories.

"You can't stay here," Cavazos enunciated it at the median, hoping for some sudden breakthrough. If he said it slowly enough, if he said it strenuously enough, maybe his straggler would get the big picture.

The man lifted a leg and pointed to a foot. He had cleats on the soles of his shoes. "I understand. I know it hurts, man, but you cannot...sit...down...right...here." Cavazos shook his head, the universal "no" and the man began to plead with him. He pointed more vigorously at his swollen feet and made his fingers to move as if walking.

It was pointless to argue, but Cavazos had to argue. He couldn't point a weapon at his face. "You have to move," he said in clenched teeth. *Why are you jerking my chain like this?*

In some secret part of him, Cavazos felt pity. Otherwise, he would have used bodily force. Black stood to the right of him, his M16 pointed downward. "Go on," he motioned forcefully with it. "You have to move on."

"You have to turn around." Creighton ordered it to a man on a bicycle, twenty meters away from Cavazos. "Turn around and go back." He didn't understand. Creighton pointed north. The man was undeterred.

Rendon saw it all from his guard on the perimeter. It was a three-ring circus and he had a bad feeling. *Just get this place cleared.* Urquhart's squad was meticulous; they'd have things under control soon. He comforted himself in the steadiness of his friends. There had been a logical exodus to remove the taxi cab. Rendon squinted hard, something itching inside of him. He wasn't quite sure what was wrong.

The Bravo team surrounded the taxi cab driver and ordered him out of his car. The man on the bicycle was rooted to the spot where Creighton had last admonished him to leave. Urquhart attempted a callback on the radio and the frequency was lost near Al-Najaf. The man pack was down; it had to be reprogrammed with another set of frequencies to function.

"Lane, come with me," he pulled him aside in a hasty withdrawal to Ronquillo's berm. "We're switching out the battery. We'll be right back." Curtin assumed the lead role.

The driver of the taxi cab was non-descript to the Bravo team. He had a beard, olive skin, and a classic thobe. He appeared to be like every other civilian they had ever encountered on the road to Al-Samawah and in their heated march to Baghdad. He had shed no military uniform in his final moments and his rank as a colonel would only be awarded posthumously. The bounty he was to earn would be delivered to his family, more than any dinars he could have earned in a lifetime. In a CENTCOM briefing the previous night, Brigadier General Vincent Brooks had referred to the deceit as paramilitary death squads: *I don't know how you describe a group of people that would go in and out of uniform, that will move in civilian vehicles on a known battlefield, that will carry weapons, hide weapons, that will march children in front of them, that will take children away from their homes and tell their families that everyone will be killed if the males don't fight for the regime. I don't know what you call that. And I don't think anyone knows exactly what you call that.*

They still grappled with the words, just a few hours later. Some preferred the term *homicide* over *suicide bomber*. Whatever the semantics, whatever the motivation, it was the first such atrocity of the war.

Creighton and Diego positioned themselves on the passenger side of the taxi. Diego held the forward guard, his M16 locked and loaded, his sights trained on the front seat. The weapon felt light, a small liberation from the SAW, and yet it made him feel weaker. He shifted to a wide stance, shouldering the weapon he had started with, the weapon he would carry for the rest of his life.

"What do we do with this guy?" Black turned to Cavazos.

"I don't know. Maybe you should carry him."

"Hey man, he's *your* war bride." It struck them as funny. Maybe they were just so hard up for entertainment, but it struck them as immensely funny. Williams was serious, his eye on the taxi cab. He had seen Urquhart retreat for the radio. He was the senior NCO, a direct report, and he felt the nudge of responsibility. "Just get him out of here. I don't care what you do. I'm going to check on Bravo."

He strode purposefully toward the car in that last-minute decision, always something propelling him to help.

Williams had nearly joined Diego on the front line; he was ten meters away from the vehicle. The car was secured and Curtin led the driver to the rear portion of the vehicle.

The non-descript man in the white thobe walked calmly. He never made eye contact with Curtin. He seemed quite submissive despite the detachment, despite the vacancy of his expression. He was cold, but obliging. He sweated profusely and there was an involuntary flinch. It happened at the minute he placed his hand on the vehicle, and abruptly opened the trunk.

CHAPTER 8

The explosion was sudden, but not simultaneous as it ripped through the carriage of the taxi cab. The fireball came in a wave that Cavazos felt, then saw, then heard in three distinct bursts. He didn't perceive the five bodies that were silhouetted against the blaze, stick figures highlighted inside the combustion. Black was big and brute enough to take it on a knee, his rifle aimed in the general direction of the blast. He lunged forward with his weapon as if he could take the monster of depravity out, as if he knew exactly what to do. Cavazos saw all the particles come to him at once, like a tidal wave following the heat of purgatory that seared his skin. It stole his breath and then it roared—a shriek like an obscene banshee in his ears. It lifted him whole and hurled him airborne over the top of Black's ducked head.

The entire rock on their world happened in a matter of seconds. They were engulfed in the wide jaws of a monster.

The debris rained on Cavazos and Black like flame throwers, and the men struggled to get upright. A piece of the car, the size of a television, a wide screen came at them spinning wildly. It landed one foot from Cavazos' leg, and he hardly gave thought to its hurtle.

"Black, let's goooo!!! We gotta *go*!!!! Black was stunned stationary and Cavazos had to drag him.

"*Innnnn*—commmiiinnnngggggg!!!!!

"*Cover me while I move!!!*" Cavazos screamed, his voice lost and hollow in the pandemonium. He sat down hard, rolling forward in the berm and Ronquillo was prepared to draw fire. The men were panting, hunkered down with wild eyes, frozen, bewildered, and unthinking. Something snapped in Cavazos, even before he came to a standstill—the same instinct that had compelled him to the berm.

He ricocheted from the rise, clambered back up to the inferno, a horrifying realization. *"Those are our men*!!!! He swore in distress. "Our men are out there!!! Get…up!!!!!

"Get…*up*!!!!!" he cried again. The smoke was impenetrable so that he had to follow the trail of the burn.

Johnson ran, stumbling, twisting, hurdling the debris, and he was the first to reach Diego. He dived to him, scrambling on his hands and knees. Diego's face was turned upward and he jerked his load. He pulled at Diego's CLS bag and fifty pounds of Kevlar plates with all the ammunition. His load was so excessive, his rucksack protruded so far that it bowed Diego's back in an unnatural arc.

It was the first time, the only time, Diego had ever been stricken into any sort of ungraceful pose.

"Medics! Get over here!" Johnson screamed. Johnson felt for a pulse. There was none. The cloud was so thick—he strained to get a handle on how many were hurt in the triage.

Cavazos found Creighton just ten meters away from Diego, and his uniform was singed and bloodied. He lay face down in the indignity of the sand, and Cavazos rolled him over. He felt a pulse, faint and rapid, and he pulled a field dressing from his own CLS bag. His hands were trembling; he pulled it taut, struggling to keep the bandage sterile. Cavazos tried to stabilize him, and tried to keep his head steady, waiting in a panic for the medics. The Kevlar helmet lay lopsided and Cavazos set it aside. He tried to apply the dressing, tried to stem the flow. Out of the corner of his eye, Cavazos saw someone kneeling over another body.

The medic looked staggered and knelt at Creighton's side. "He's gone, man. He's gone." He put his hand on Cavazos' shoulder and Cavazos recoiled from the touch. "He's gone," the medic repeated, more forcefully, and Cavazos refused the words.

Cavazos had the overwhelming urge to hit him. "Do something!!!!! He has a *pulse*!!!!!"

Cavazos grabbed wildly at the medic's arm. *Do they train you guys to do something in combat?!*

He turned his back on the lack of sympathy, tried to squeeze more pressure on Creighton's wounds. His pulse was fading, fainter and more erratic, and Cavazos put a hand to his chest.

When someone's that hurt, you can do a million things, but you can't go back in time, Mike. You can't take it back. Death is permanent. I want you to understand that, son.

He could try to breathe for him. He could give the compressions. They could put in an IV, something. If the medic would try, if Cavazos really tried, they could save him. All they had to do was try.

"No, no, no, no, no, no, no."

Don't blame the medics, Mike. You might see death once. The medics—they see death every day.

Cavazos buried his head on Creighton's chest, wringing the bandage like a wet rag. "Please don't die, man. Please don't die." Cavazos whimpered like a child.

"He's gone," the medic repeated.

"Lord, no," Cavazos began to pray softly, pleading. He relinquished his grip on Creighton's wrist. All he could do was hold his friend's hand.

"Please, God, nooooo…*nooooo…nooooo…*" He couldn't let go of Creighton's hand.

There was too much smoke. Cavazos couldn't breathe. It was too wrenching and stinging in his eyes.

"This can't be happening…this can't be happening." Black began to pace in a frenzy beside Creighton. Cavazos backed away slowly. Someone was still kneeling over a body.

Cavazos turned. It was Diego.

"Recon. *Recon,*" Cavazos mumbled, his voice tinny and pounding in his skull.

Diego lay motionless, his eyes wide open, staring at something in the sky. He gasped and then settled, then gasped again. Cavazos felt for a pulse. Diego saw something peculiar above him, some light that flickered, registering enormous shock and wonder before his eyes rolled back in his head.

Why would Recon do that if he had no pulse? Cavazos cradled his face in his hands. He tried to sit him up. He wasn't that hurt. *He didn't look that hurt.* Except for the inner portion of his right leg. It was obliterated at the thigh. He was going to lose his leg and that thought brought its own peculiar sadness. Diego's boot was at an awkward angle. *He was going to lose his leg.*

Cavazos stared helplessly, the spark of life receding from Diego's eyes. He still seemed to gasp for air, something compelling him to give his life just one more chance.

There were small marks on his face, one that looked like a cat scratch above his right eye. That was it. *He wasn't gone.* He just couldn't be gone. Cavazos swayed back, desperate. His vision had become incredibly blurred. He looked up, past the crater and some enormous chunk of metal through a dust cloud. There had been a car there once, and now Urquhart knelt there—Urquhart was choking a man.

Rendon saw it, too, from a different angle. Williams' fingers were squeezing weakly. *I'm going to the car. I'm going to check on the men. I'm going to make sure everything's okay.* Always the last man standing, cool as ice—with Brooks and Curtin and Snavely.

Only Sergeant Williams wasn't standing. He was struggling for his last breath. Rendon stood in a hole, twenty meters from the EPWs and the shock was overwhelming.

Why was Urquhart choking Sergeant Wills? Why would anyone *hurt* Sergeant Wills? Cavazos lurched forward, suddenly overcoming the despondency and all of the powerlessness in his anger.

He had to defend Sergeant Wills—he was their champion. And then he saw Johnson working beside Urquhart. He had the same grip at Sergeant Wills' neck. He had taken over, his hands struggling to control the bleeding.

"You gotta pull through, Sergeant Wills," Rendon willed to him. *Please, Sergeant, you have to pull through.*

Johnson and Urquhart tried so hard. They battled so heroically. Williams quieted. He lay very still, all of the reflexes gone. He gave the last measure of vitality and resonance to the sand. His face went the color of ash. Cavazos closed his eyes on that most unkind of cuts: Sergeant Wills had been wounded most where he sang.

"Curtin?!"

"Curtin??!!"

The men began to yell, first terse and then unrestrained. Their last grip on hope began to fade in their tone with every successive call. Rendon thought hard: he had last seen Rincon pulling security, and Creighton had been talking to the man on the bicycle.

He shut his eyes and he could envision that march: Curtin had been searching a car.

Rendon had been running toward the scene when it had detonated—had split the sky like fire-laced lightning. There had been some nauseating swell in his gut just before that. He couldn't think what it was.

Something cold snapped—that uneasy feeling. Suddenly, he remembered. A handful of Iraqis had begun to flee: just seconds *before* the explosion.

"Get down, Rendon!!! *Get down!!!!*" someone had cried and, mindlessly, he had obeyed. The lightning bolts had splintered and then fallen in great, jagged pieces. One by one, they had dropped over his head, shattering his brain.

Creighton was gone and little Recon was gone. Sergeant Wills had died and he couldn't get a hold of himself.

Except for that hope—there was maybe some hope.

Maybe Curtin had survived.

"Curtin??!!!!"

"Curtin???!!!!!"

It came to him like a dream. *He was probably slow calling in.*

Hey, Turbo! Hey, Ronny Q! Could you be any slower? Don't you ever scare me like that again...

Curtin was slow to call in. That was it—that was all, and Rendon held onto that notion fiercely. His head was swimming. It was too much to take. Not Jersey, too, with the others.

Jersey so buttoned up, so squared away—so absolutely dependable. And that's when it hit him, what made him want to vomit.

Curtin would have never been slow to call in.

"Who are you missing?"

I'm missing Curtin. Urquhart had turned to Johnson.

The voices had been muffled and then they came to Rendon's ears, and they couldn't penetrate Cavazos' hearing. He worked his jaw, trying to get the sound back, trying to comprehend. The explosion had ruptured his left eardrum, and something was sticky and wet and blocked. The din was gone; half of his friends were gone; Cavazos was deaf and so alone in the desert.

It was someone else' tremble, someone else's sound—someone else on the verge of a breakdown. Curtin had been the one closest to the trunk, and Johnson had circled that perimeter.

"Urquhart," it came out so disheartened. Johnson needed help.

It was only the stark horror in Johnson's eyes that sucked the last hope from their breath.

Guys, I found Curtin.

"I found Curtin," Johnson said. It came out so soft that it sounded hollow and untrue.

More than 100 meters away, Brooks was bound to duty in a berm where the burnt flesh escaped his sense of smell. He was blind to the casualties and the calamity, but he had felt it the minute he had heard the blast. A best friend knew—a catastrophe like that—and the kick to his stomach paralyzed him. Curtin was dead and he stood shattered in his appointed place, a numb hand on his M240 machine gun.

The enemy prisoners cheered at the sight, applauded the blood and the watery eyes. It was too much for Rendon. He seized his rifle and was in a dead heat, sprinting toward them, appalled. He aimed his M16 at the first prisoner's chest; ready to go down the line. He was dizzy with rage; he couldn't wait to reach them; he would splatter them all on the run.

The team leader caught him, Rendon's massiveness heaving, and the team leader violently swung down his weapon. Rendon's chest roiled and his mouth worked as if he might spit on him. He locked his jaw in his wrath.

"Don't do it, Rendon. *Don't...do...it.*" His team leader held him and Rendon stared ahead in his hatred.

The EPWs held their hands high in the air, their near fatal laughter vanished. Their pupils had enlarged, but they still weren't penitent. Rendon's head began to throb. His arms and legs shook as he turned his back on them, the awfulness re-awakened in his vision.

There were no sanctuaries for his sight, and so he looked upward, his mouth in a helpless murmur to his Flaco. His lip began to quiver as something bitter melted in his lungs, and then he dropped his head and he cried.

CHAPTER 9

The small arms fire had erupted so quickly after the car bomb that Johnson thought it was a coordinated attack. Later, he might consider the possibility that the chaos just resulted in an opportunity for the enemy. He would probably never know the truth of that moment, except as it defined his gunner. Amid the burning and the clouds of dust and the shock and the enemy barrage, Tolbert had circled the wagons in a Bradley. He had taken the initiative, taken the defecto Bradley commander position, and roared the fighting vehicle to the scene. It had provided cover to those who were still alive and given dignity to those who had died. It restored the mobile command post to Johnson, and after that had come the extraordinary valor.

"What do you need me to do??!!" he had yelled above the chaos.

Suppress the enemy fire!!!

Tolbert assumed the command for the Bradley himself. Tolbert manned the turret alone.

Normally, there were three-round bursts from the main gun. Normally, there was a pause. A gunner assessed the effectiveness of each round and then adjusted the sight.

Tolbert in his insight, in his loyalty and reliability, let the main gun rip. It tore through the insurgents with a ceaseless batter in something Johnson had never heard before. It was as if Tolbert had turned the 25mm into a machine gun as he razed the enemy's uprising. He fired for so long, in such ferocious continuation—it seemed he melted the barrel of the main gun. It personified the anger, the horrific grief and gave voice to the anguish of the men. It wasn't just that he saved some lives that day. It was that Tolbert was hurting, too.

Johnson felt a painful catch as he listened to the stammer. He closed his eyes once to the perpetual drone. There were thunderous claps in that massive torrent—the bleeding out of Tolbert's heart.

He suppressed the fire so decidedly that the silence that enveloped them afterward was unnerving. "I want those men covered." The order pierced the stillness, and the platoon sergeant still felt compelled to repeat it.

"I want our men covered. Show some respect. Do it now," his jaw tightened.

Lane stared at the cavity, at the hole where he had stood and would have been if not for faltering frequencies. He was moved by a soft nudge and began to secure the perimeter with the remaining available men.

A mob descended on the scene from a nearby village.

"Get back! Stay back!"

"*Get...back!!!!!*"

There was nothing to salvage; the bus occupants had fled and the Iraqi on the bicycle lay charred and intact and very dead.

There had been a tree once, skirting the divided highway, and the Iraqis were gesturing, seeming to take note of that. Cavazos knelt before Diego, the villagers on the sideline, blurring before his eyes in waves. He squeezed them back, kept blinking rapidly, trying to find his voice. He was hoarse; he was quaking; the fluid was crusting in his ears—he felt alone in the noiseless desolation. His face had been peeled bone dry in the explosion, and then it was wet, incomprehensibly wet.

It was mercy that had deafened him so that the stillness was complete—the heavens, hushed, for his benefit. They were watching over him, God in His anguish, and the angels silently weeping with him, stunned. He started and stopped and started again, disjointedly mumbling to himself. His tears mingled in the blood, fell softly down Diego's face so that it appeared Diego was crying, too. The christening sting of smoke and sorrow filled his eyes. There was an appalling tightness in Cavazos' chest.

Our Father who art in heaven, hallowed be Thy name. Thy kingdom come. Thy will be done on earth, as it is in heaven. Give us this day our daily bread, and forgive us our trespasses, as we forgive those who trespass against us. And lead us not into temptation, but deliver us from evil. For Thine is the kingdom, and the power, and the glory, forever and ever. Amen.

He prayed it four times, until the devastation was complete, bent over the remains of his friends. He helped carry their bodies to the personnel carrier—a medic's unit that ran on tracks. It was an awful cavity, cold and dark. It wasn't even sterile or hollowed. It was worse than placing them in body bags, the obscenity of wrapping them in ponchos.

They'd been wrapped in ponchos when they were still alive, soaking in them on the night he had met them. Cavazos couldn't look at it—not that kind of closing of a casket that was so inhumane.

"Let's take a break. Drink some water." Johnson's voice had too much softness. "It's going to be okay." His hands were bloodstained. He had to turn away from his men.

The haunting, the hurt, the crushing tears in their eyes. Nothing could really touch the depth. Cavazos was reeling, still shocky, still trembling—Johnson had to get a handle on his men.

It was the most shameful thing he had ever said and it clutched at his throat in the cruelty. "I want you to divide up. Dig fighting positions. Right here, and then over there."

It was just something to do—they knew it and they surrendered. For as long as Johnson lived, he'd recall that. Not a murmur was sounded; not one voice of complaint. They did exactly as he had ordered.

He wanted to draw apart from them and cry. He had to scan the perimeter. He turned back once to see them, the silhouette of his soldiers, hollowed men in the blank stare of the desert. The handles of their shovels jutted up, then down, a foot on the blade in fury. They were bent in their grief, doubled over like old men, and still they continued to dig.

The personal carrier started, then drifted off. Not one soldier's sights turned to follow. They held their salutes in active hands on their shovels—a last stand in their fighting positions. Their rhythm was constant; their vision was blurred; they felt the grip sink into the sand. The carrier became a speck on the tortured horizon as the soldiers caved to the shallow tombs.

Cavazos had begun to scrub the inside of a Kevlar helmet, using the bottled water. The interceptor armor of the flack vest was red, the last traces of all the men's lifeblood. Cavazos' face was wet with tears again and he threw up, repeatedly, in the sand. He felt a hand, gentle at his back. He heard a voice soft and low.

"I got it."

Cavazos looked up and, in Urquhart's eyes, he saw the most tremendous sorrow and pain.

The area was secured in the sickly, gray drizzle that gave way to more blood red at midnight. The desert unfolded like a blanket of stinging nettle, the sandstorms relentless in their batter. Johnson woke up in the fog and the acid—

the scorched human flesh of his young men. He covered his mouth and his nose from the assault. He was having nightmares of his nightmares. He bolted upright to the shrill, piercing sound.

There was screaming from one of the berms.

Cavazos' hearing was impaired, but he was not so deafened that he didn't lift to the blood curdling sound of it. Black was racked in a tormented sleep. His battle buddy was gone. Cavazos tried to wake him from the thrashing. It was the wind that added to the frenzy. All around them the destruction still smoldered—the burn and the pungent taste of death in their mouths. He lifted his canteen and his throat closed instinctively; it had all taken on the flavor of the apocalypse.

The moon glowed red-orange—there was not even blackness to seep into their consciousness, deaden them. Farina curled up, trying to weather the sandstorm, and fighting a greater yield to the whirlwind. The worst pelting of the season had come that day; even the locals were in awe at the inhumanity. Farina clutched at his overcoat, his sackcloth in camouflage. *Where was God's mighty pavilion?*

They were on holy ground. God was rending the earth in a protest of the slaying of their most innocent. Farina was distraught, something swirling; how long had they been at war?

Rincon. Recon. Just ten days into the thing and already they had disintegrated like ash. He wrestled in such pleading to find solace from the anger and the churning and the full weight of the horror in his heart.

Hail Mary, full of grace. The Lord is with thee. Blessed art thou amongst women, and blessed is the fruit of thy womb, Jesus. Holy Mary, Mother of God, pray for us sinners, now and at the hour of our death. Amen.

He ached and he toiled in more heartrending prayers that made him sorrow at the great drops of blood. They'd been spilled in Gethsemane and just one child crying in the desert could have crushed Him, defeated Him soundly. He had fallen on His face; Farina seemed to fall on his face.

Tarry ye here. Watch with me.

The men's subconscious seemed to be conversely stimulated, then depressed, then unnerved in their shock. It was perhaps all pointless—by the very next day, they might all be gassed at the Karbala Gap. The shriek of the sandstorm would subside eventually, but only to the mind-numbing riddle of artillery.

They were back under enemy fire. It was dark and the Iraqis had no bearings; they were spraying mists of bullets in a fog.

Brooks sat up in his berm, fumbling for his Kevlar equipment—all the protection he'd abandoned in the storm. Each man did likewise, except for Snavely, who hunkered further into his hole.

Brooks struggled in dismay. He had taken out his contacts. The grit was ground into his fingernails. The solution was dirty, like gray-colored dishwater, stinging welts into his eyes. He draped his arms over his knees in futility; his coping skills were inherently gone. He'd re-dressed himself to MOPP2 and he was backward; his jacket was suffocating at his throat.

"Are you okay, man?" Specialist Joseph Finley put a hand on Brooks' shoulder. Even a touch like that was too much. An ounce of concern—just one show of kindness—and the dam was ready to break. It was intense human sympathy: he might have sobbed if the RPGs weren't so dangerously close.

Either aim or let us sleep! Brooks wanted to scream at them.

"No. I'm really not okay."

It came out like a whisper. *Keep your eye on the prize.* Brooks was never going to make it without Curtin.

"Not even close, Dogs. Not even close." Snavely uttered it softly.

It was just some act of grace; some offhanded affection; it was enough and Brooks didn't know why. His jaw went tight in the steel against emotion—he couldn't cry in the face of that. Snavely rolled over and then the berm was silent and then Brooks swiped at the distress in his eyes. He began to methodically re-dress himself, tried to shoulder some shroud of courage. He worked his fingers at the bridge of his nose and then he forced the spill back into his tear ducts. He pushed at his eyelids, pinching harder and harder, until he knew he could get through the night. He could not stand down and in the tortured sand dunes he tried to offer Curtin the wrenched bend of his character.

He squeezed his eyes shut to the barrage of the Iraqis, fighting the bitterest of enemies within.

The break of dawn was merely a shell, a spent-up casing from Satan's invective. Cavazos' eyes had the placid look of the sea after a violent and wind-tossed night. The men had been tormented to complete passivity; they were as vulnerable and fragile as glass. It seemed the tiniest of ripples would have broken them, and so they moved incredibly slowly.

They loaded the equipment into the Bradleys, a whale of Jonah about to swallow them whole. *You owe me $240, Creighton.* His absence was jarring—some awful hurt.

Farina moved wordlessly past the men, altered and sobered, exhausted to the depths of his soul. Dying didn't sound as bad as it once had—at least his friends would be waiting for him there. He tucked Diego's beret into his DCUs, ready to go to MOPP4. The Karbala Gap awaited him and he needed Diego's presence, his spirit to stay with him somehow. He crossed himself and looked up at the sky. He had two little girls and a wife.

There are a few rounds coming my way, Recon. Please, little brother, watch my back.

The men took their places in the Bradleys and welcomed that cavernous dark. They anticipated the lurch in the column, so many little particles left smashed in their paths. They had repelled each other like magnets—had avoided all their usual routines. They hadn't gathered for breakfast, for the hot chocolate or the coffee, the memories too painful and polarizing. And now they were back in their element, the magnetism flipped, making them one again and inseparable. Cavazos stared straight ahead at the vacancy and his knees felt naked, uncovered.

It was Curtin, sitting in front of him like a phantom pain, locking legs with him out of habit.

It was worse somehow than the actual explosion—the sudden and overwhelming emptiness. They had been severed, amputated from the group, and Cavazos could still see them, feel them. Diego was nestled in the hellhole; Creighton was on the other side, squirming and stubborn and smug. It didn't occur to Black or him—all that room now, and they didn't think to scoot over.

The camel spider had hollowed Cavazos finally, had eaten his insides out.

There was a subconscious decision on Cavazos' part, made right at the moment the Bradley ramp closed. It was the most survivalist instinct he had ever known and his greatest, most noble thought. The Bradley yawned and then it closed—an echo of sheer pain and, in the silence, was pure group dynamic. The men had magnified him, played off of him, so that the whole had never even appeared to have parts. They were going to be a catastrophe rolling forward: their limbs had all been detached. Their hearts had stopped beating at Al-Najaf, had died with Williams' last pulse. Cavazos' arms were wrapped around his stomach, an iron grip on that defensive position. He made no noise, and then the stir was distinct.

He forced himself to sit straight.

He had to battle for the men still beside him, and he had to battle for the ghosts that remained. His line of vision came into sharp focus—maybe there was some pinpoint of light from the turret. It was all that the men had, that faint illumination; it had to carry them throughout the war.

Moving out!!! It came like a clarion call. They had to keep moving out.

Johnson assumed his position, and there was one more physical lurch. The desert quaked and rumbled. The light was odd and flat. There were no sheens on the sand, or wavering mirages. There was nothing but cold, stark reality. It would never get harder; it would never be more trying than what they had just endured.

These are the times that try men's souls. The summer soldier and the sunshine patriot will, in this crisis, shrink from the service of his country; but he that stands it now, deserves the love and thanks of man and woman. Tyranny, like hell, is not easily conquered; yet we have this consolation with us, that the harder the conflict, the more glorious the triumph. What we obtain too cheap, we esteem too lightly:—'Tis dearness only that gives every thing its value. Heaven knows how to set a proper price upon its goods; and it would be strange indeed, if so celestial an article as freedom should not be highly rated.

It had rung out to those dispirited men—General Washington's men. They had come to The Crisis of the Revolution in retreat, in an icy withdrawal across the Delaware. They had been starved and bloodied and in tatters—nothing but a small band of brothers. They'd been severely outflanked, outnumbered, demoralized—Thomas Paine had forged the mettle of their redress. It was his rallying cry to them in a letter that had renewed their faith in a divine destiny, that marrow of the bones' assuredness:

Humanity's greatest potential could only be reached if humanity was truly able to exercise its own will.

These are the times that try men's souls. Perhaps they were on the verge of greatness in Iraq. If when the going got tough—trembling in the gut tough—they had neither to shirk, nor slack, nor wander…

If only when duty met the honor of their cause, there was the promise of a brighter day.

His wounds were open and gaping and raw, and he felt so wholly responsible. He wondered that he couldn't have seen the catastrophe coming. He wondered that he couldn't have prevented it all. If he could have said one last thing to his men, Johnson would have said, "I'm so sorry." He wondered—and would for the rest of his life—that he hadn't been able to stay awake the whole war. In that unbridled pain and the collective will to carry on, there came some odd sort of confidence. His men were now proven—he had just been proven—and the hurt was so binding and so enormous.

Johnson sustained himself because he had to: each man had chosen his path. Each man had stood at a crossroads: *two roads diverged in a wood.* It was the "Road Not Taken," by Robert Frost, that had drawn their heartstrings to near breaking. And then it was those woods that beckoned each man from courage—

all the longing and the sorrows of war. "Walking by Woods on a Snowy Evening" came to him soft and dream-like. The prose was haunting and reverential, what the rest of the world might never know.

A man had stopped in the woods and gazed on the forest, filling with a blanket of snow. In the polarizing standstill had come a yearning darkness, the utter aloneness of that one man. His horse had pressed him, disconcerted—the delay in such a black night. The woods had been mesmerizing—beckoning and beautiful—luring the man to the relief of escape.

To just give up to the delicate fall of snow, the gentle brush of the wind and the humanness—Johnson felt the enormous throbbing of a man who had shrugged off his desire to surrender to the shadows. The man had resumed his journey in his sleigh. The man had been called to duty. Johnson himself could not succumb, so far from home, on the fringes of utter civility. The Karbala Gap loomed in all of its depravity; that symbol of their most sinister, earthly depression. If they could get the enemy on the run, they'd roll all the way to Baghdad. If they could fight through their grief and wade through their grief, Saddam's statue would fall, in Firdous Square. They would stop and get shot at, stop and get shot at, but if they could just win every clay house, every raid...

Their training would kick in, it would pull the trigger, and their platoon would never lose another man. They were going to seek and destroy hundreds of munitions, overrun Saddam's torture chambers. They were going to be the platoon to find critical intelligence that proved Lieutenant Commander Scott Speicher had survived—a U.S. navy pilot had survived an F-18 crash in Operation Desert Storm, and they owed that search to a long, lost brother.

That was it, what they were after—the greater liberation—to shine the light on all the dark places. They would patrol every neighborhood, secure every school. The Iraqis would get back their country.

It was all but some daydream, and then it wasn't: that perspective would only be won in years. What Johnson knew in his heart, approaching the Karbala Gap, was that bravery had been won for a day.

They had voted with their feet. Johnson's men were marching on: faster, more furiously than ever.

In the back of the Bradley it became palpable, the monotony of character in their tracks. It lulled them to rest like a lullaby, then repeated itself in a grind. It pressed at the sand in the gore of its weight, then liberated every particle. Time and distance, time and distance, their grief was swept over again. They were rocked in an empty cradle and, in the hollow of its hand, they wept like children.

Cavazos' clothes were stained and soiled, desert camouflaged and bloodied in some places. Diego's blood was on his boot and he tugged ferociously at the laces.

No one would ever hide them again. That would be the lasting blow to his step.

He settled into the churning, into the numbness, and into the whirring of the track. It was perhaps that repetitiveness that had brought the poem to Johnson's remembrance—Frost's alliteration to the sound of the sleigh on snow.

They laid their weary heads in the deep.

They surrendered and let the blackness seep.

There were battles to fight before they could sleep.

So many battles to win before they could sleep.

THE
CITIZEN

*The ultimate determinate in the struggle
now going on for the world will not be
bombs and rockets but a test of wills and
ideas—a trial of spiritual resolve; the
values we hold, the beliefs we cherish and
the ideas to which we are dedicated.*

—Ronald Wilson Reagan

FOREWORD
WITH YOLANDA RINCON

I know what Diego would say to me right now:

"Don't cry, Mom. I'm okay."

I'm okay.

I tried so hard not to cry in front of him at Fort Stewart. He had always been so transparent. I knew he was hurting, too, and that my tears would only make it harder for him to go.

There was just something about seeing my baby in uniform as he prepared to leave for Iraq. The somber, stiff lapel and the rigid curve of his Army beret over those soft, brown eyes.

He was all-at-once so stoic and vulnerable I thought I might break in two.

Our boys never seem more valiant than they do in uniform, going off to war. That last heroic glance, the moment when they've never looked better, or even been better, is the searing image that burns in the brain alongside some haunting you're forced to acknowledge they might never come home again. It's the cruelest of ironies to see them rise to such heights, that fleeting glimpse of their perfection after all those restless nights—rocking them to sleep when they're sick, and helping them pick out corsages for prom dates, watching them shrug off piece by piece the childishness for manhood—knowing, all the while, that someone, somewhere wants to still that beauty and that progression. In the hollowness Diego left behind, I stamped and stamped at those horrifying thoughts—the idea that my child might ever be hurt or lonely or scared over there.

I stamped at them like a brushfire, trying to keep the worst thought of all from consuming me. I actually thought that if I *didn't* think, if I didn't give audience to the fears and the ache that threatened to tear me apart, it would somehow make a difference.

I stood there with so much longsuffering, so much dignity, as he took his very last steps on American soil. I was allowed to moan and tremble, cry out, when I pushed him into this world. Not a murmur of pain passed my lips as he quietly turned away, was wrenched from my side, never to return.

He slipped away so softly; he hugged me goodbye with so much affection. Something should have snapped inside of me. Something should have told me to fling myself at his feet, and never let him out of my sight.

My husband told Diego he could not leave a single piece of himself behind in Iraq, and my son's solemn nod—the intensity of that moment, reverberated through every fiber of my being to the heavens. I begged God not to take Diego. I told Him I could not live without my son. I knew He heard my prayer, and I knew that Diego was too strong, too alive, too invincible—and so was God.

Sometimes I think of all those painstaking, caretaking details of being a mother. How I used to bathe him and snuggle him, the softness of his skin against mine. How I used to be fearful when I trimmed his tiny fingernails and toenails when he was a baby, afraid that I might cut him.

And then I think how Diego still hated to clip his own toenails—some quirky foot fetish he had. I actually conceded to cut them for him, just before he deployed. I was his champion and all those little things I did for him—that sweet, appreciative smile he used to flash at me...

And when my son needed me the most, I was not there, and I could do nothing to protect or help him.

I wonder how long he lay there, bleeding. I wonder if he had time to see my face, or call out for me.

And I was not there.

They brought my son back in a coffin, draped in the American flag. I asked if I could see him, hold him, a mother's touch one last time.

I was told as kindly as possible that his body was not viewable.

I still wonder what that meant. Which part a mother could not love, could not caress when I'd stroked the soft curve of his face, and held the gentleness of his hands all those years.

I made him, and I still need to know which hole in him left such a gaping emptiness in me.

I still believe that Diego is going to walk through the front door. *I'm right here, Mom. I'm wight here, Mommy.* I'm convinced in such madness at times that he was only called to some top secret mission. He has to find Osama bin Laden, and his mission is so covert and so special—we just can't be told where he is right now, and the Army will notify us soon.

It is men's dreams, I think, that haunt me.

My husband had that conviction, and it brought us to America. They took such strong hold in my children's hearts that they carried Diego halfway around the world. Diego's resolve carried him to the end of it—so far beyond my reach that I cannot touch him, hug him, kiss him now. I will not hold my Dieguito again for a very long time, because I could not hold him back from his dreams.

In my own, someone takes me to his casket and there is a man inside. He is white. He is heavy and his nose is too small.

"That's not my Diego," I cry in such relief. "I knew the Army got it wrong!"

When I wake in the morning sobbing, I wonder, still, if someone didn't make a terrible mistake when they identified the body. I cannot reconcile a wound in my son that could not be healed, and I cannot comprehend that anything—anything—could have stopped that valiant, beautiful, heart.

Diego died in my sleep, and I cannot escape all of our dreams.

Please understand that I do not hate the people who did this to my son; I feel sorry for them. They did not realize the gift he was trying to give them, or know what a good boy he was. They did not realize that he went there to help them have the kind of life he once enjoyed.

It says in the Bible that on the fifth day of the Creation, God made the rivers and commanded the waters to fill the sea.

I believe He created them sufficiently deep and wide to account for all the tears that would ever be shed by the mothers of soldiers.

CHAPTER 1

Creighton's father was mostly right.

Soldiers alone couldn't turn back time.

Atlanta was eight hours behind Al-Najaf and Jorge awakened early in the morning with profound peace and hope. He didn't understand it, but the feeling was so overpowering he woke everyone in the house and announced they were going to church. For Seventh-day Adventists, the Sabbath was celebrated on Saturday. Services in Conyers began at half past nine.

The family had not been to church in ten years. Stephanie and George looked rather blankly at their father, but obeyed. Truthfully, George was glad to go; he was a young boy who thought quite seriously, quite often, about spiritual matters. He was anxious for some formal recognition during such a trying time as war.

The family was dressed impeccably as they took a pew at the back and Jorge passed a card with Diego's photo and name to the front for special prayers. Little George felt at home, so much devout sweetness and reverence in his face as he bowed his head. Stephanie looked quite behaved but inattentive, swinging her legs nonchalantly because they didn't reach the floor.

In fact, she was capable of absorbing every last detail and safeguarding it well in her heart.

Pastor Mike Leno was preparing a program that celebrated mission work around the world. A member of the congregation approached him—wanted to share something urgent with him—and it was not an opportune time. Truthfully,

Pastor Leno thought anything could wait until a more pronounced break before the worship service.

The congregation member insisted and passed him an index card. It had a picture on it and a pleading, handwritten note. The photograph was of a young soldier in Iraq named Diego—he was standing in front of an American flag and he didn't even look old enough to shave.

The pastor was humbled. Of course his congregation would honor the family with their prayers.

Pastor Leno's wife, Sondra, sought the Rincon family in the parking lot after the worship service. She saw that they were eager to reconnect with church members and saw that, as much as anything, they sought some desperate assurance about their son. It was a beautiful day, the sky a startling blue, and Jorge felt free of the terrible burden he had carried the night before.

God was God, in His heaven looking out for Diego, and the family returned home, renewed in the welcome space of oblivion—that time just before the time when no passage of minutes would ever be the same.

+⊱══⊰+

What Jorge saw immediately, at half past three that afternoon, were the tiny gold crosses on the chaplains' lapels. The men had no faces, no ranks, no medals or buttons, no names or voices—just crosses that grew to the size of Golgotha. They turned blood red and seized Jorge by the throat so that every part of him began to deflate and collapse.

A million years passed before him in that instant—Bolívar's men and Washington's men and Patton's men and the Savior, stumbling down the Via Dolorosa. Did he go to Yolanda because she had fallen? Did he try to find Fabian, call him? Did he go to George or Stephanie, or did he just cease to be nothing, feeling everything colossal, all at once? In the weight of the crucifix before him, in the sure knowledge that Jesus could take it all upon Himself—he thought for one second that the burden of his family alone at half past three on March 29, 2003, should have done the Son of God in.

Jorge's family, alone in the universe, shrieking, falling, moaning, wailing. *My God, my God, why hast Thou forsaken me?*

The family had been preparing a package for overseas delivery to Diego and Yolanda did not see the crosses, hiding as she suddenly did on the stair landing—thinking if she did not acknowledge the Army, they might not be real. They might just go away.

Her knees had buckled and she had sat down hard.

Otherwise she would have run.

She would have run and run and run until her legs gave out, and then she would have lain very still for the rest of her life. She would have lain in the blackness until God had come to pick her up and take her home again. Stephanie saw her mother crumple, heard her mumbling something quite clear and unclear all at once.

"No, no, no," her mother was sobbing uncontrollably. *No, Dieguito, no.*

Stephanie began to cry and George did, in fact, take off running—endless, blinding figure eights, around the backyard until everyone was certain the child had gone mad. It was utter chaos when Catherine arrived, hoping there had been some kind of mistake—hoping that because Jorge had been hysterical when he had called her, maybe she hadn't understood.

The casualty officers at the door were tangible enough, but Catherine was convinced they were lying. They had to be, she begged them as she fell to the floor, clutching desperately at Yolanda. From that near prone position, Catherine saw that everything was amiss. It was true—something terrible had overcome them.

The carpets were white, the front entrance gleamed, and no one had taken their shoes off in the house.

━━━◆━━━

Jorge was so distraught he was unable to give intelligible directions. Pastor Leno and his wife spoke with a neighbor. Just one coherent person who knew the area—they made their way to a newer subdivision after an hour.

The house was brick with cheerful yellow siding and forest green shutters and every portion of the yard spoke of painstaking care. As the pastor and his wife walked down the driveway they heard the sound of wailing voices, spilling from the open doors, sweeping uncontrollably into the street.

The pair moved from one family member to the next, tried to console the inconsolable. The grief was so heavy, the pall so pervasive, it seemed as if a dark suffocating mist blocked out all light and prevented clear thought. Any semblance of a normal conversation was impossible—Pastor Leno thought back to the book of Job. He decided that Job's friends had been at their best when they'd had the forethought to just stay quiet. He put his arm around the stricken parents until a uniformed woman, the casualty officer, appeared at the door. Jorge instinctively extended his arms and wept on her shoulder like a child.

The casualty officer's professionalism and demeanor remained unchanged, but Pastor Leno saw that she had to turn away to quickly wipe tears from her eyes.

Her role as a liaison was a brand new assignment, and she had never made such a call to a home before.

There was a letter, lying on the kitchen table, and it was dated February 22, 2003. Farina had sensed it: Diego had probably been crying—that final letter home that Johnson had encouraged.

Hola Mother,

How are you doing? Good I hope. I'm doing OK I guess. I won't be able to write anymore starting the 28th of this month. We are moving out. We are already packed and ready to move to a tactical Alpha Alpha (in Iraq). Once that happens there will not be any mail sent out. We will only receive mail that is less than 12 ounces. At least that's what they said. I'm not sure where exactly we're going to be at yet but it is said to be a 20-hour drive in the Bradley's.

So I guess the time has finally come for us to see what we are made of. Who will crack when the stress level rises and who will be calm all the way thru it. Only time will tell. We are at the peak of our training and it's time to put it to the test. I just want to tell everybody how much you all mean to me and how much I love you all.

Mother, I love you so much! I'm not going to give up! I'm living my life one day at a time. Sitting here picturing home with a small tear in my eyes. Spending time with my brothers who will hold my life in their hands.

I try not to think of what may happen in the future but I can't stand seeing it in my eyes. There's going to be murders, funerals, and tears rolling down everybody's eyes. But the only thing I can say is keep my head up and try to keep the faith and pray for better days. All this will pass. I believe God has a path for me. Whether I make it or not. It's all part of the plan. It can't be changed only completed.

Mother will be the last word I'll say. Your face will be the last picture that goes thru my eyes. I'm not trying to scare you, but it's reality. The time is here to see the plan laid out. And hopefully I'll be at home in it.

I don't know what I'm talking about or why I'm writing it down. Maybe I just want someone to know what goes thru my head. It's probably good not keeping it all inside. I just hope that you're proud of what I'm doing and have faith in my decisions. I will try hard and not give up. I just want to say sorry for anything I have ever done wrong. And I'm doing it all for you mom. I love you.

Your son,

Diego Rincon

P.S. Very important document.

Pastor Leno hoped that some well-meaning Christian wouldn't someday say something insensitive—something like "maybe this happened to the family so that they would get closer to God." To the depth of his being, Pastor Leno believed Jorge Rincon had made up his mind a long time ago to live a Christian life. He had come with a prayer in hand and the prayer hadn't been answered the way he had wanted, and still he was going to remain a believer.

Pastor Leno had discerned that, and he resented the implication that God somehow went around arranging killings and suicide attacks just to get someone to go to church.

He wasn't a political activist, but he thought the misperception of God was very much like the public relations problem the American forces had—being resented for the best of intentions and efforts, and blamed for someone else's violence.

In the twelve days between the Army's appearance at the house and the retrieval of the body, Pastor Leno grappled and he prayed as much as he ever had. He would have liked to have had just the right words to say, but he had only just met with war's greatest fury. He thought as he gathered the family together to kneel in prayer on so many occasions that he would never see soldiers or their families without feeling. Nor, for that matter, would he ever see the coverage that droned on and on with updates from Iraq in quite the same way that he had before. Homicide bombings and collateral damage would never be just abstract numbers again.

He felt as patriotic as anyone. He supported the troops wholeheartedly. But he was never going to be able to cheer them on again as one did for a favorite football team. The most terrible news took the forefront of the coverage, all too often packaged like entertainment. Pastor Leno was immersed in real life—and real death—and he could feel his actual metamorphosis in such powerful, wrenching strokes.

He tried to remember that God was still God after all, and he tried to resolve the notion that He was in complete control. There was something gnawing at him that a tragedy of such proportions was not His will at all. He had deep and lingering thoughts about war and what originated, ultimately, from the wounds of war. He attended a candlelight vigil for the Rincon family that overtook the neighborhood—a block of friends crying, hovering, and singing with brightly lit candles.

Diego's yellow Mustang had become a shrine, covered in flowers and balloons and messages of love and support.

The Rincon family carried the added burden of fame. Every moment was immortalized on film. The cameramen stayed a respectful distance from the family, only speaking when spoken to. It was a curious dynamic because the pastor saw that many reporters had a hard job to do as well. They were trying to report tragedy and avoid being overly intrusive—it was a-rock-and-a-hard-place kind of work.

Jorge and Yolanda struggled from time to time with evidences of prejudices, some of the media's opinions on the war aside: a notable reporter asked Jorge if he was in the United States legally and there was something inspiring in Jorge's reserve under such duress.

He took her by the arm, escorted her away from the crowd so as not to embarrass her. He requested quite kindly that she never, ever ask him something like that again, and then he continued the interview. The frustration really only mounted when reporters cut and discarded the sound bites from Yolanda—they asked her repeatedly how she managed to endure such a torturous time and she always said it was her faith in God. That seemed to be such an unpopular statement that her soft-spoken expressions eventually waxed futile. Yolanda withdrew in bits and pieces—a shame, the pastor thought, because it was she who best represented Diego's soul.

Jorge seemed to know instinctively that a live press conference was better, that people needed to understand him in context. It was the local Atlanta media he came to respect most because they could have easily edited his words. They represented his feelings the most accurately, and did not try to shape an agenda. It meant extra long sound bites sometimes, but then the family's sincerity seemed to demand that kind of regard.

Jorge discovered the hard way that face-to-face interviews were ideal: an article ran in *The New York Times* in which it was noted that Diego had been a "poor 18-year-old immigrant from Colombia, the son of a carpet cleaner." It wasn't the gross mischaracterization, the inaccuracy, of Jorge's economic standing—it was just plain ignorance that led people to see what they only wanted to see.

The reporter had conducted the interview by phone and, in the narrowness of that setting, she had assumed they were poverty-stricken. It was the beginning of April and copies of Jorge's tax return lay on the credenza, already completed and filed.

"Death and taxes," it had often been said, and it was clear that Jorge had paid his fair share of both.

Pastor Leno had not personally experienced anything that left soldiers shell-shocked or made men victims of flashbacks and endless rehabilitation. He only experienced the ripple effects from the battlefield—the shock waves that rolled the length of an ocean. They wreaked such enormous havoc on the family, the friends, the neighborhoods, and the entire community. The pain of death had been relatively short for Diego, but the circle of loss continued to engulf.

He didn't want to admit it, but Pastor Leno sympathized with those who just wanted revenge in Iraq. That meant there was another casualty of war, the compassion a clergyman should have felt. He underwent a period of numbness toward those who had surely suffered greater in other parts of the world. There were people who had lived their entire lives in conflict—to them this kind of violence was nothing new. It had been years since he had reflected upon an experience he'd had as a young pastor, but he thought on it often in the wake of Diego's death.

He had met an old mechanic once at an auto repair garage in the early 1980s and he had asked the man to fix his Honda. It had been a tough trip there: the pastor and a friend had managed to push the car into a little town near Eugene, Oregon. The owner had been defiant in his gesture to get the foreign car off his property and the pastor had been too innocently curious.

I lost my son in World War II! I'm not working on a Jap car!!

For the first time, Pastor Leno had had to come to grips with the bitterness that could rancor a man's soul and every generation's soul after that. Hatred had been taught by evil regimes and it had been cherished and handed down. It had somehow become tradition; then fact; then, finally, doctrine with each succeeding age group. He suspected that was the reason nineteen hijackers had flown planes into buildings, and Saddam Hussein had gassed his own people.

He suspected that was the reason there might always be a threat of violence, spilling onto American shores.

The second hand had ticked out a terrible time in mortality, swung a pendulum of grief that would always cause a family in America to speak of life in such definite terms. They had yet to be able to bring themselves to say the words—it was just "before that happened to Diego."

Pastor Leno could only pray for the kind of guidance that would help a devastated family find a better solace through the graces of God.

The war had already been won—long ago—at the cross. The rest was just mopping up.

CHAPTER 2

The end of March at Salem High School always went out like a lion, despite the old adage about weather. Seniors woke up one day, realized the end of adolescence was near, and tried to crowd every last flirtation and juvenile leisure into their final months—as if they were suddenly going to disintegrate by spontaneous human combustion, wherein nothing would ever be as funny or as playful, as dramatic or as hopeful again. The commons area had the perpetual drone of a beehive, and every locker and tile and notebook dripped in the melancholy.

Except on Monday, March 31, 2003, when Salem High School felt like a tomb.

The administrative office was friendly and glass, a hub of concerns and small exultations and parent-teacher conferences—and then it was a window on a pain so invasive it seemed the transparent plates would shatter.

"How could they take my boy?" Jorge nearly fell into Jerry Smith's arms, sobbing as the principal fought to distract the hordes of media from the intimacy.

It was clear that Jorge needed something, but he was unable to talk after that, to bring himself to say the word "funeral."

Fabian had to take over, ask Mr. Smith in a near whisper if he might do the family the honor of delivering a eulogy.

Mr. Smith had never really felt lacking before—it was a foreign sensation that made his knees wobble and his eyes suddenly flood in weakness. He didn't hesitate in his response to the family, but he felt very much like he'd been given the role of a lifetime for which there was no script.

It was Hamlet in tragedy and Romeo and Juliet in irony, and then it was like no other scene he had ever blocked. He had already lost his appetite and his ability to sleep, but the greater trial lay ahead in the forthcoming week.

Mr. Smith found himself standing before a life-sized portrait of Diego the day before the funeral. He was a lover of words, and he was an actor who had suddenly, inexplicably lost his voice.

He had had ten days to prepare, to try to sort through his feelings; there was not one single coherent thought or expression of thought except this one: the world was a lesser place without Diego, and that would not have comforted the family.

It wasn't just that Diego had been the ultimate performer, a young man so elegant with that unprecedented stage presence. Diego's gift and his grace and his beauty was in the fact that he had been so humanly plausible. He was gone and trivial condolences that he had been too good for this rotten world seemed so abhorrent—the truth was, the world could be a rotten place, and Diego's was a spirit so uplifting and so needed, he should have never died.

Mr. Smith was haunted by the stage and the audiences and the attention in which Diego would have reveled. He placed a tender hand on the reflection of Diego's face and he bowed his head in despondence. They should have given him that "A," just once, for squeezing it all in so exponentially. *Please, Diego*, he pleaded. *Tell me, little friend. Tell me what you want me to say.*

He knew he had to comfort the grieving, and still the casket mocked him: a confinement the very antithesis of the young warrior he had loved so much. He had been so alive—so boundless, so joyous—that tears began to stream down Mr. Smith's face.

Death makes no conquest of this conqueror. For now he lives in fame though not in life.

Shakespeare's eloquence could not touch the depth—for the real Diego had been so much more than the sudden personification of the war he'd become. He would cheat his young friend somehow if he relied upon another man's distant characterization. *Help me, Diego. Please help me*, he cried, in solitude, every thread disjointed and snapping. *I have to speak from the heart, Diego. Tell me what to say from the heart.*

It rose so softly, so imperceptibly, that Mr. Smith's face didn't recognize him, only gradually came up to meet the presence. And then Diego felt so close, his spirit so near, the room became muted, impressionistic, and blurred.

For a director, there was that hushed moment of impact when an audience had been stirred and mere applause felt sacrilegious. The house lights came up slowly in those instances, pale and non-intrusive to the illumination of the soul. It was a feeling rare, reserved for the most hallowed, the most poignant of all performances. Diego was vaulted, immortal against the backdrop of the burnished sun, the orchestra pit so stunned into silence that the auditorium took on that most eloquent melody of stillness.

Mr. Smith felt a warmth he'd never known seep into his veins and his heart, a salute so profound and reverent he held his breath lest the power leave him.

It was all so abundantly simple; his voice with such strength and fervor swelling from the dust.

Mr. Smith, Diego whispered with that gentle conviction. *Just give me the curtain call.*

Diego had given his short role everything, and Mr. Smith began to weep in the fragility of his senses. It was a final brush with greatness, and he'd been privileged enough to see it and touch it firsthand. The thoughts flowed so easily, pure inspiration filled him, begged his excruciating soliloquy. For the first time he understood what it was that had encompassed Diego—it was so easy, so true, and so gifted.

There was a story he'd heard so often of a young woman, another child he had mentored from the Caribbean. It was a sacred experience her mother had shared with him that suddenly formed the framework of his anguish. Just after the child had been born the elders of the village had taken special note of her, surrounded her in a circle, beaming.

"There is a hand of blessing upon this child that will follow her all through eternity."

They had said in it awe, with such deference and surety, that the infant's mother had wept. There was a light around the child's head, unlike the others, that would radiate to all who knew her. Mr. Smith had always cherished that story because he'd known the child so intimately—had believed it so ardently to be true.

Diego was a blessed one, and that's what Mr. Smith finally understood was the greater good they were supposed to learn from him. It became so obvious, the unfailing of it that could never be dimmed, not by death or by absence or time. If only others could have sensed what he did in that moment, the peace and the joy and the splendor—there would never be heartache, there would never be contention, there would never be war again.

He envisioned Diego in the sentry-like shadows, bidding the audience farewell—such immense sadness and grace and then accomplishment in that lasting, final impression.

Go blessed one, he murmured to the silhouette, the hurt so wrenching he thought he might break.

Go and I promise you, Diego: your light will be here. We will always carry it with us.

Go now my little son, with our blessing and yours, and take the most gallant of bows as you leave.

With the haunting clip of the about-face that had been inborn in him, Diego departed from the scene.

✛═══✚

The first session of the 108th Congress opened with formality and a prayer on the Senate floor. There were the usual tensions inherent to a two-party system, razor thin in the diversity of the aisles. Senator Zell Miller of Georgia stood to address his peers in one of those rare moments following the invocation: he not only had a case to plead, he was about to get bi-partisan support for the bill.

There was something special in his call to action, a sentiment of such power and praise and nobility. It was a reminder of why the Founding Fathers had chosen a clear voice for the people, allowed for the representation in such a colossal forum. Senator Miller was being given the chance to say what some could not say for themselves.

"Mr. President, I rise today to share with my colleagues the story of one of my Georgia constituents. It begins with a brave young Third Infantry soldier named Diego Rincon.

"Diego was a native of Colombia and he came to the United States in 1989 with his family when he was 5 years old. He enjoyed a life of freedom and safety that might not have been possible in Colombia.

"Diego was extremely loyal to the country that welcomed him. After the September 11th attacks, he decided it was time to repay his adopted nation.

"Upon graduation from Salem High School in Conyers, Georgia, Diego enlisted in the Army. He became a member of the 'Rock of the Marne,' Fort Stewart's Third Infantry Division.

"Sadly, Private First Class Rincon was killed March 29th in Iraq by a suicide bomber at a military checkpoint. Diego was 19 years old. Three other members of his 1st Brigade were also killed.

"In late February, Diego wrote his final letter home to his mother just as his Brigade was getting ready to move out. Let me read just a little of that letter:

"So I guess the time has finally come to see what we are made of, who will crack when the stress level rises and who will be calm all the way through it. Only time will tell.

"I try not to think what may happen, but I can't stand seeing it in my eyes. There's going to be murders, funerals, and tears rolling down everybody's eyes.

"But the only thing I can say is, keep my head up and try to keep the faith and pray for better days. All this will pass. I believe God has a path for me.

"Whether I make it or not, it's all part of the plan. It can't be changed, only completed.

"This 19-year-old was wise beyond his years.

"Diego joined the Army for the noblest of reasons. He fought and died in Iraq while defending our nation's freedom.

"And after his death, his family asked one last request of the government in return for their son's life—to be able to bury him this Thursday as a U.S. citizen.

"I am very pleased and proud to announce today that—with the help of the INS—Private First Class Diego Rincon has been awarded U.S. citizenship. This brave soldier will be buried Thursday as a citizen of our great country.

"But there are thousands of non-citizens fighting in our military right now.

"So, I, along with my fellow senator from Georgia, Senator Chambliss, have introduced legislation calling for citizenship to be granted immediately to any soldier who fights in our armed services and dies in combat.

"For those among our troops who are not citizens and die on the battlefield, I believe the least we can do is to honor them with posthumous citizenship.

"And I believe it should be done automatically by the government, with no delay and no burden on the families.

"Under our bill, the families of these brave soldiers would not have to fill out any forms or make any phone calls.

"This citizenship would apply only to the deceased soldier and it would not make the soldier's family eligible for any extra benefits or special treatment.

"It is simply a final gesture of thanks and gratitude for the ultimate sacrifice these immigrant soldiers have made for their adopted country.

"Thank you, Mr. President. I yield the floor."

<hr />

Diego's life had altered history; his light would forever shine as Mr. Smith had promised him. The bill inspired by Jorge and Yolanda's son would surely be passed into law. Meanwhile, the tragedy of the events surrounding his death had forever changed the rules of engagement in the war theater in Iraq. Countless lives were going to be saved in combat; a few immigrants, who had shed their blood as Diego, were honored. It was a fitting tribute to such a young man and it was the kind of thing that only happened in America, which made it a fitting tribute to the countrymen for whom Diego had died.

When Jorge thought of the goodness, dwelled on the heroism, he almost felt he could endure the next hour. It was a cold and rainy Saturday—exactly the kind of day to which Diego had been born. The hearse moved solemnly along the Stockbridge Highway and, in that downpour, there were large numbers of people lining the streets—tiny children on the curbs, the rain battering their faces, waving American flags to the procession. A few protesters had tried to make an appearance, but they were on private ground and were quickly enough dismissed by the sheriff's department.

Jorge saw that his son had honor in his homeland, and Jorge wept.

There were 650 people in attendance at the funeral. General James T. Hill, the Commander-in-Chief of the U.S. Southern Command was among them. Deputy Commanding General Keith M. Huber of the First Army stood to address the family and he seemed rather formidable at first. The brigadier general had been a lifer—garnered the kind of respect and decorations that would have made a young soldier like Diego feel as if he should kneel and fly at the same time. The general was as solid as stone as he faced his audience, the epitome of strength and valor and dignity when he began.

"There is no generation gap, no cultural distinction, as to why the young men and women join our Army today. They join for the same reasons that I joined thirty-two years ago.

"To make their parents proud, to be challenged, to be trained, to be educated, and to travel.

"To be part of something larger than their own egos…to join a family and be guided and inspired by the concepts of duty, honor and country.

"They learn that duty is a moral obligation, a responsibility—that we are all personally responsible for our actions and the actions of those with whom we serve. They learn that they have a responsibility each day to challenge themselves, to improve themselves, mentally and physically; to prepare for the next assigned mission.

"And, when given that mission, they have the responsibility in the duty to perform that mission to the best of their ability—regardless of the location, the adversary, or the danger.

"It is this concept of duty that willingly leads them away from all that they hold near and dear to their hearts—away from their family and friends and homes to places they may not be able to find on a map. They go to the defense of the ideals of democracy, in countries with different cultures and different languages. They learn about honor—it being their reputation—an especial esteem.

"They become persons of principle.

"They learn to treat everyone with dignity and respect. They discover selfless service and sacrifice. And they put aside their desire for personal comfort and personal safety.

"Private First Class Rincon came from the Americas, and as an American soldier, he solemnly swore to protect and defend the Constitution of the United States against all enemies, foreign and domestic.

"Diego did that." The general paused and took a labored breath and turned his attention to Jorge and Yolanda.

He was so proud of Diego. He called him one of his own. The Rincon's were surprised to hear the words come in Spanish. The general knew the pain and he knew the sacrifice, and he knew that Diego was on the right hand of God. He had but a handful of condolences to offer after that, but the general's mouth had become strangely twisted. It appeared that his English was clipped somehow—as if someone had a chokehold at his collar.

Jorge was confused, thought the general appeared mad in the split-second illogic of surreal moments.

"Soldiering is an affair of the heart. It is a special bond that soldiers earn through trust, mutual respect, and love.

"It is that bond that allows them to give their lives for others.

"There is no greater love."

It was extreme emotion. The general's eyes filled as he left the pulpit abruptly. He had struggled and it moved Jorge so that he had to put his fist to his mouth. He could not repress the audible moan. General Huber composed himself, presented Yolanda with three bullets from the twenty-one gun salute prelude to taps, wrapped in the American flag. Jorge began to rub Diego's dog tags like Aladdin's lamp, as if he could wish Diego back.

Kenneth had been asked to say a few words and he sat in numbness in his pew. He stared at the program and he stared at the words, *Diego Fernando Rincon*.

He hadn't known that—Diego's middle name—and it left him with an awful kind of hole. They just weren't old enough, and there had been so many things left to do and to learn. His address had been eloquent, his remembrances lucid and touching and entirely too poised. It came in a snap—the sudden realization, the most powerless feeling in his life.

It occurred to him jarringly as he dropped his face in his hand that he was never going to be able to stop crying.

Don Crocetti from the Bureau of Citizenship and Immigration rose to present Jorge with Diego's official certificate of United States citizenship. It was just then that an idea passed through Jorge's mind, too, a stream-of-consciousness thought that racked him all the more.

He extended his hand in the most gracious acceptance, and it trembled slightly in the acknowledgment.

Jorge was on the brink of a nervous breakdown.

It was the wallet that haunted him.

Jorge could visualize the most trusting of little boys, clinging to him as they had taken their last walk on Colombian soil together. And then he could see the young man—the boy who had breathed the American dream with such devotion that he had still gasped violently for it in the throes of death. Even as he had reached to touch the face of God, Diego had had one foot in heaven and the other on earth for as long as he had dared.

The Lord alone had preserved that wallet of money at the airport; had kept it intact, untouched, and unmarred. He had delivered it just after a Chevrolet Monza and before a green card in the knick of time. He had saved Jorge from death on so many occasions only to withdraw His divine protection at the last. For so long Jorge had believed, with all his heart, that it was God's will being played out for his great fortune.

Thy kingdom come, Thy will be done, on earth as it is in heaven.

He had uttered it at the airport, and he had been so deliberate, and then he had cried it and stifled it in his pillow. He had had some great mission and, until the Army had appeared at his door, he had never considered the great offering to be his son.

He didn't have the heart to blame God Himself. He had tried that as a child and it had never really worked out for him. To blame God for taking Diego was also to curse Him for blessing their lives with a child who had brought them nothing but joy for nearly twenty years. Jorge had broken Yolanda's heart after all of it—blaming the Army and war in Iraq was futile. The generals in the audience hadn't asked more than they'd given, would have wept openly with the family had it been the dignified thing to do. Diego had been a willing volunteer, and Jorge was not so arrogant as to believe that freedom was something he alone deserved. To say that the cost and the long haul of battle was not worthwhile was to take a coward's approach—to forget the atrocities of September 11 and to look upon the Iraqi people with no compassion at all.

But had they all been more important than his son and his wife's tender feelings—the anguish of a woman who had never expected anything, but that her child would come home? It was the hammer and anvil-like crush against terrorism that was also the punishing crucible to which Jorge succumbed.

If only he hadn't retrieved the wallet, he would have never had the money to come to the United States. If only he hadn't boarded that plane, perhaps Diego might still be alive.

His mind worked in circles—there was no beginning or end. He had to shrink from all the contention. He would have found a way to make it to America all over again for the very son who had perished. He would have found a way so that Diego might live the very patriot's dream that had stilled his heart in the end. The harsh ache of acceptance was made more agonizing by what he couldn't shrug off:

Freedom always found a way, and he bowed his head in that overwhelming hurt.

He looked upon the flag-draped casket and he couldn't grasp that Diego's remains were inside. He wanted his son back in such overwhelming wrenches and still he wanted salvation for humanity. He did not want people to remember his son the way he was in that box, betrayed by the ignorance of evil and bruised and broken. He wanted people to remember the precious blood that had been spilled for them—the selflessness.

He wanted people to think upon that gloriously empty tomb.

It was the closest thing to understanding God's character that Jorge would know in his lifetime. He clutched the certificate, Diego's citizenship to him, and he carried it to the coffin. He laid it atop Diego's resting place as Israel of old had once placed the most cherished of their burnt offerings at the sacred altars of the temples.

Whatsoever Diego loved, had loved him back with all of its heart.

Jorge knew that and he kissed the American flag in an effort to kiss the casket beneath and Diego beneath that.

He buried his face in his hands on the flag, and Jorge silently wept.

CHAPTER 3

Fabian had never asked to be in the spotlight—he had never even wanted to appear on the stage.

What was your brother like? He tried to fill the public's insatiable appetite for an impossible explanation.

He still felt he had to be the steady one, the one who didn't break down when everyone else fell apart. It was just that in dying, Diego had done something for his brother he had never quite accomplished in life: he had finally forced Fabian out of his shell. Fabian, the family spokesman, the ambassador.

He wasn't sure at times how he was supposed to feel except that he found himself wanting to cry badly. He sadistically played one of Diego's favorite songs as he sped east along I-16. It was the Dave Matthews Band, "Where Are You Going," and all the politics and the rhetoric didn't matter. All Diego had ever really asked was for the artists to give him the music that would give him the heart to keep fighting.

As articulate as Fabian was, he had never found the right words to describe the essence of Diego to those who hadn't known him. And then there it was, as thick as the Georgia oaks that blurred his vision in such a tumultuous ride. His father had stayed in his bedroom the entire day before, wracked in despair at the mere thought of revisiting the Army. Jorge drove in front of Fabian, in Diego's Mustang convertible, and Fabian could gauge his father's mood just by all the stops and starts in the four-hour journey. When his father cried, the powerful turbo of the car seemed to be overwhelmed, crawling along the back roads; when his father was belligerent and stirred, the Mustang flew at breathtaking speeds along the deserted highway. Fabian knew the acceleration and velocity were all bits of immortality—the momentous reminders of Diego that helped them move forward on roads less traveled. They had not been back to Fort Stewart since Diego's deployment, and it was only a tremendous suffering that had to be confronted, compelled them to face the old haunts one year later.

They had spoken to Adrian Cavazos by phone, but they had never met him in person. It was strange not to have a complete picture of the young man who, by all accounts, was Diego's twin. That was the thing that got to Fabian most—knowing the only chance he would ever get to see his brother grow old would come in stray glimpses through Cavazos. The last photo they had seen of Diego was young, and he would stay forever young no matter how long the rest of them lived.

On the seat next to Fabian, there was a memorial photograph Cavazos had sent to the family the past spring. It showed five M16 rifles, thrust bayonet-side down in the ever-shifting dust of Iraq. The weapons were set in combat boots, situated properly at attention. There were Kevlar helmets atop the weapons and dog tags which hung and clinked like wind chimes in the breeze. Cavazos stood to one side of remembrance in the picture, his figure and the remnants of his friends stark against the sand and a bullet-ridden wall. It was adorned by the lonely figure of an American flag. From the sideways angle of the photo, Cavazos looked so much like Diego—stood so much like him—that it seemed Diego was looking upon his own memorial.

It wasn't so bad for the family to think of it that way, believing as they did that it was probably an accurate portrayal of brotherhood: soldiers most likely looked upon themselves at times like that, felt a little piece of themselves die, whenever they lost a fellow soldier.

"Have a good day, sir. Welcome to the 'Rock of the Marne.'" It was the last checkpoint and they were back on post.

Cavazos stretched forth a somber hand to Jorge, and the pain in his eyes was unmistakable. He was a young man who desperately needed to face his demons and would rather have crawled into a thousand shell-shocked berms than face them in the grief of parents. Jorge pulled the young man to him, and it wasn't so much awkward at first as it was just plainly cruel. The resemblance to Diego was so remarkable, so uncanny, it took Yolanda's breath away. She felt her son in the surety of her embrace of him and the genuineness of his warmth. She clung to Cavazos at the same time she clenched her jaw in an iron will on her emotions. She couldn't squeeze the tears back hard enough and they fell on Cavazos' Class A uniform. The weeping of a mother who had just wanted one last touch, her son, her Diego.

Naemi watched the scene with the soulful ache of the one who'd been spared the suffering. Adrian had come home changed and unchanged in so many ways, but the real point was that he'd come home. When she'd learned of the death of Michael Creighton, Naemi had been told there were three other casualties. She had waited outside the apartment, on that dead end at Gilbert Street, expecting the Army at the door. There had been two neighbors who had sat beside her and held her hand for all of those hours—she had never really even seen them before, but they had refused to abandon her in her grief.

And now, there they all stood, her husband alive, and she'd never felt such a tearing. It was the story of Abraham and Isaac ascending with that chilling mountain to climb. Abraham ascending with that awful heaviness, that inevitability in his heart that pierced like no manmade sword ever could. God had provided a ram in the thicket that day, for Abraham and for Naemi. It was one of the mysteries she'd carry forever, that mixed hurt she'd take to her grave.

A battle to fight, an adventure to live, and a beauty to rescue it had been said. They were the words which came to Jorge's mind and all the things men needed according to John Eldredge in his noted book, *Wild at Heart.*

Everyone had known the battles and adventures of Diego, but his cousin Anna Maria had spelled out the rest. She had known something about rescuing, something about small heroics, because Diego had saved her once. When the world had been a frightening concussion of changes, Diego had done some great thing. He hadn't allowed the self-pity but he'd brought candy to history class, little familiar pieces she could actually taste. He'd brought her hugs and that endearing smile in a language that she understood. Anna Maria was indebted to him, and she'd spelled out the saving grace at the funeral, lest they ever be mistaken.

Diego's beauty to rescue had been his mother; and Adrian's looked on in sorrow.

Carlos had had a dream after Diego died in which he had wanted to tell him how much he loved him. He had never said it and he wished that he had and he had called after Diego, repeatedly. His cousin walked too far ahead of him to hear his cries. For a small moment, it appeared Diego recognized Carlos' voice and he had turned ever so slightly to acknowledge him.

Just as Carlos was going to run to him, tell him everything in his heart, Diego had turned into an eagle and flown away.

Yolanda wanted some kind of reassurance, her own sign, that maybe God hadn't really taken Diego unto Himself yet. She pressed at First Sergeant Moore at breakfast, wanting to know how they could be sure it was her son who had died. She did it while helping Stephanie with a bowl of cereal—that was Yolanda's instinct. She forced herself to get up every morning, just to do laundry and cook for them; just to keep the rest of her children alive. Stephanie had not really cried since the day the Army had come to the door; since the moment Anna Maria had taken her outside to feel the wind on her face. Wind was like wings, Anna Maria had said, and Stephanie would always know Diego was near when she felt its life on her skin.

First Sergeant Moore had eaten and slept and walked and worked beside Diego. He wasn't aware that Yolanda still left notes for her son in the kitchen every time the family went out. Nor did he know the feeling Yolanda had that she was being irresponsible and neglectful just to leave the home—a plague that made it seem she had left a baby unattended in the house.

She wrote short notes for Diego with every cell phone number imaginable because her son might come back someday and be startled to see that no one had waited for him after all. First Sergeant Moore only saw a devoted mother and an elegant and dignified woman who might never experience closure, but who deserved to hear the truth.

"I knew Diego, Ma'am," he said slowly. "It was definitely him."

Yolanda didn't touch her food. She stared at Stephanie's bowl of Fruit Loops, her lips tightening as she stroked her daughter's arm. The arm that had that unusual bow at the elbow and the small-scattered patch of hairs. Something had clearly just drained from her face, and for that First Sergeant Moore was so sorry. She was obviously seeking something to seal in her heart and that Diego had died instantly was not much of a consolation.

"Did you touch him?" Yolanda asked Cavazos softly, turned to him, aching, when they were alone.

Cavazos nodded, steeled his jaw.

"What did he feel like?" she murmured.

It was going to be as hard for Yolanda to hear it as it would be for Cavazos to say it.

His eyes dropped. "He felt hot, and his skin was too soft. Like it might come off in my hands."

Yolanda's gaze was steady, though Adrian thought he had seen her flinch ever so slightly.

"Is there anything else you can tell me? Anything at all?"

Cavazos felt protective and loyal and very drawn to Diego's mother; he didn't think anything he said would really help, but he tried to remember.

Something flickered in his eyes, the smallest grain of a detail in a mountainous holocaust he had shoved aside for too long.

"There were feathers around him," he uttered in a near whisper. "I brushed them from his face before I prayed."

The Rincon family allowed the soldiers to do most of the talking as the day wore on. It didn't seem conceivable in the weight of their initial meeting that a sliver of healing might come out of the conversations, but it did. Once Cavazos relinquished all of the awful minutiae once, it became somewhat easier to revisit his ghosts. Cavazos felt better, lighter, than he had in a year. He sensed the family's agony in hearing the occupation stories that went on without their son— but he also sensed some relief that what they had continued to do after Diego's death had been noble and worthy.

Really, they were all of them just looking for an audience to appreciate what they had battled, and what they had survived.

In the sacredness of the moment, Jorge shared with them his most impossible dream, some pressing he could never contain. President Bush had written the Rincon family a note, and Jorge had written a response just before he had left for Fort Stewart.

He had been helped with the translation; it was ready to be mailed, and his impromptu words reflected his outpouring:

As much as I loved and esteemed Diego, I never really knew the extent of his courage or the depth of his devotion until he was mortally tested.

My greatest consolations are that my son lived and died for something meaningful, and that I will see him again.

When I do—along with all of the years of anguish that will have passed in so many lifetimes without him, along with all of the insurmountable joy of that reunion—I will know his magnificent heart.

God knew it all along and now Diego knows it, too. He not only felt at home in God's plan as he hoped he would in an expression of a final letter to his mother—he went home in it.

Diego, as you know, was a finisher…My beautiful son gave his all.

I cherish my son's sacrifice and share his dream inasmuch as I want to join the United States Army. I have inquired about this possibility on several occasions and have been told repeatedly that I am too old.

Mr. President, it is true that I am forty-one years of age, but my heart still has something to give. After all the blessings my family has received from this country, I feel it my duty to protect and defend it.

I feel it my duty to complete the sacred work my son began.

Not one of the soldiers laughed at Jorge's letter, or his passionate declarations. Brooks was on duty, as Diego had first found him, behind the counter on C.Q. He didn't look up, and it appeared that several heads were bowed as the infantrymen led the family to Class A inspections. It was a company mandate being held that day with the Rincons as honored guests.

+‡===‡+

George was not the anxious, forlorn figure of a boy he had been ten months earlier as the family strode past Alpha Company. There had been a time when he had refused to eat, had grown more pale with each passing day, and his parents had been at a loss to know how to help.

Yolanda had finally gotten it out of him, the trembling of the purest, most soulful of little boys who not only thought on Diego—he thought just as much on the notion he was hopelessly lost; believed he had committed the unpardonable sin because he had been mad at God for allowing his brother to die. Yolanda had seen renewed torment flicker in George when Saddam Hussein had been caught by U.S. forces. George didn't rejoice because, truly, he had just wished that Saddam Hussein would die.

There were always going to be those kinds of holes and reminders, and ever so many deep wounds. It was the end of innocence and while Diego's death and the war had impacted so many, George was among those who would truly be shaped by such an immense history. Some children were at just the right age for a molding of such gigantic proportions. It had been Austin, Pamela's son and George's small friend, who had called him one day and done some remarkable thing in an hour.

George had begun to eat again, smile again, play again; and his natural skin tone had returned.

Pamela had asked Austin what he had said to George that could have possibly wrought such a change.

"Mother," Austin had chided her, propping resolute legs on the coffee table. "That was the beginning of what we call brotherhood."

It stood before them—the embodiment of that bloodline—so many of Diego's brothers.

Fabian turned to his mother in a remnant of normalcy, a hint of the kind of humor that had once pervaded their lives. The 2-7 had made Jorge part of their routine, allowed him to inspect the troops with First Sergeant Moore. He performed his duties quite gravely and reverently, pausing to speak with each of the men who had served with Diego. The soldiers were impeccable, their Combat Infantry Badges sparkling in the brightness of the sun.

Only the barrel-chested Rendon had a slight flaw, seeming to have outgrown his uniform in a sudden burst on manhood while he had been overseas.

"Pops is in the height of his glory now, isn't he?" Fabian whispered dryly.

Yolanda never averted her eyes, but a slight curl in her lips gave her away. She was a realist again. "Yes, I suppose that's as close as he'll ever get to the Army."

The platoon sergeants surveyed each block of the company. It was chilly, even beyond the shade. The American flag lifted enough in a stiff breeze that Stephanie huddled close to her mother in her best Sunday dress. There was a growing fire in Jorge's breast that made him unmindful of the cold. It had been requested that he speak to the troops, and it was one of the most bittersweet moments of his life.

"The United States of America is my country," he began. "It is the greatest county in the world because of our soldiers.

"Diego died for this country. You fought for this great country, defended it bravely. You are what keeps us strong."

He needed his English to be better, smoother; he didn't have the elegant command of his words that he knew in his native tongue. If he could have just spoken in Spanish, his emotions would have been bridled into long, flowing declarations that tamed the wildest impulses and compelled even the most complacent.

The infantrymen had been told beforehand that Jorge was an immigrant from Colombia, and he hoped that knowledge was enough for them to appreciate the contrast. He hoped he didn't have to explain that he knew what love and loyalty and liberty were all about because of what he had once lacked. He hoped he didn't have to describe his gratitude for light only because he had experienced the absence of light.

He rose to the full height of his stature, and he tried to give voice again to the swelling words that kept getting blocked in his throat. Perhaps it was that base humility; perhaps it was what the men sensed, not only what they heard, but soldiers who had served with Diego and soldiers who had only known him by name began to cry with Jorge. They stood in the glaring, morning sun that couldn't touch the chill in their spines and their tears glistened in the brilliance. It was the encouragement he needed and Jorge found his way in his own strange mixture of meekness and ardor.

"Bad people killed my son, but they cannot kill my American dream. You are the reason I still have my American dream...

"You are my heroes," his voice broke again. "And you will always be my sons."

They were ragged breaths that escaped from Yolanda and the children, but they stood ever as resolutely as the troops they faced. Maybe it had been that chicken Cavazos had talked about—the one that had pecked in their berms all night—maybe the feathers had come from the war horse in the sky, or maybe it was a sign that Diego was as truly free as the eagle in Carlos' dream. Yolanda looked again upon somber, stiff lapels and soft, tearful eyes, and so many shiny, spit polished shoes.

Wherever those feathers had come from that had brushed her son's face in his final exhale—she was going to believe for the rest of her life that the young men before her had indeed marched where the angels tread. Jorge stepped back from the platform and he let the moment stir in his heart, a sustainable character that would have to carry him the remainder of his days. It was not what they had collectively fought against after all—not poverty, not oppression, or even evil regimes. To battle those injustices was only human, and the sacrifice made it more than human.

It was what they had surrendered for the divine destiny of humanity, the reconciliation between their ambitions for duty and honor, and the anguishing crosses that had been borne and carried in that conviction. If he had had the vocabulary to utter it at all, Jorge would have echoed a quote of a quote—what Ronald Reagan had attributed in his first Presidential inauguration to Dr. Joseph Warren, a founding father:

"Our country is in danger, but not to be despaired of…On you depend the fortunes of America. You are to decide the important questions upon which rests the happiness and the liberty of millions yet unborn. Act worthy of yourselves."

Cavazos stood stoic with his eyes exquisitely grave and brimming and unyielding.

They had been worthy of the fight. The flag was still there, and everyone could see that.

EPILOGUE
FROM THE AUTHOR

The problem with sand is its infidelity.

It blows with every whim of the wind, saps the will in a scorching, daily punishment that slinks away at night. Sand has no ability to draw the warmth from the sun once the light is set and so it leaves a man spent and shivering when the darkness falls. The desert carries no imprint of loyalty, no deeply imbedded footprints of the armies that have crossed it, and so it retains no memories of its liberation. When blood is shed on sand, it often does not penetrate the thirsty soil, but stains like a mirage that bleaches in time and eventually fades to the shadows.

That is why, even as I write, coalition forces do not fight for sand in Iraq.

Diego and three of his fellow soldiers died on a windswept desert outside Al-Najaf. It took nearly two weeks for their remains to arrive stateside, to find their final resting places. Corporal Michael Curtin was buried in his hometown in New Jersey and there lay reminders both stark and serene. His family had a Bible verse and lyrics to his favorite Beatles' song engraved on the headstone, the one that echoes "we're going home." The *Two of Us* reads:

You and I have memories
Longer than the road that stretches out ahead

Just one row of markers away are the graves of two men who died in the World Trade Center on September 11, 2001. That's the oddity of New Jersey, where the War on Terror is flanked by such bookends as headstones. I think of the Curtins driving the length of the east coast just after the attacks to see the significance of their son's graduation. They had no idea, the repercussions—they were just trying to see the thing through. I think of the long stream of police officers who attended Michael Curtin's funeral, who knelt in pairs before his casket, prayed, and then rose to salute him. And I think of the mourners who gathered around and sang "God Bless America" at that tribute. I think of the Rincons and thousands of infantry soldier families helping their sons turn blue in the solemn infantry ceremony. If what I have to say now on a very personal note is not always agreed upon in the divisiveness of our times, just understand that I speak for the honor of those who can no longer speak for themselves. They volunteered for their duties and many families still cherish that and somebody just needs to say this.

I pray that I never painted a picture that war was a picnic, or that dying young and violently was desirable. It was a brutal, senseless act on the part of Saddam's regime at Highway 9, and it was a tragedy that will be felt for so many lifetimes to come. It was a heartrending outcome of war and, importantly, it was the fallout of a gargantuan struggle: there is a great good and there is a great evil, and make no mistake that the first strike was delivered by evil. In the United States of America, we still have the right to say that war is hell and yet there are worthwhile causes. You don't have to be a warmonger or conversely naïve to believe that there are some things worth fighting for. As I met with the survivors, cried with the survivors, was ultimately strengthened by the survivors—there were threads of faith and hope in nearly every conversation, a conviction that was two-fold. They believed their sons had fought a good fight, and they believed they would see them again in heaven. That didn't eliminate the sorrow; it didn't eliminate the horror; it just made the emotions bearable and the effort noble. One soldier articulated the loss in a simple eloquence when he said he knew his best friend was in a better place; he just really missed the future. He missed seeing his friend go to college and get married and have children and grow old. "He was just becoming the man he would have carried with him for the rest of his life," he said. The sorrow and the certainty can really co-exist, and that's the tug-of-war in the midst of war. It was a great and terrible irony that the Rincon family sought freedom and that their son died for someone else's freedom. That may account for the vast interest in their story in particular, but I do believe there's so much more.

People seem to remember hearing about that first homicide bombing of all the conflicts with some of the same emotions of the September 11 attacks. It seems to have registered, in both distressing instances, a sense that we'd entered a twilight zone. Some acts, even in war and no matter the scale, seem to resonate a more abiding shock in us than others. We've seen some of the worst of mankind in the past three years; and, out of that darkness and torture, we've also seen the brightest points of light. Perhaps one of the reasons for the fascination with the Rincon family is a very real longing felt by so many people: an ache for a return to some time-honored values, and an ache for a renewed kind of mettle. We were a generation largely unproven until the War on Terror and then something extraordinary happened. From the Pentagon to Pennsylvania, and to the brilliant skies of Manhattan, we were brought to our knees and a paradox: when we rose it was to something more ennobling and exalting than we'd ever imaged before. It would be hard to shrug off the nobility and courage of our fellow Americans in our major cities that day. Some were policemen and some were firefighters and some boarded planes for any number of reasons.

Along with that heroism has come a remarkable charge to not only answer the call, but to *finish* it.

We have it in us to triumph in the end if we can do like so many of the soldiers' families: if we can yet stand before our enemies and kneel before our Maker until the brighter day. That has always been the formula for overcoming adversity, no matter how great the challenges. George Washington did it, and Abraham Lincoln did it, and what's been coined as the "greatest generation" did it. Theirs was the first to see the sun rise again following a strike on America, and they were the pioneers who chose solidarity instead of selfishness, courage instead of cowardice, faith instead of fear. We talk about exit strategies and we draw the natural parallels between World War II and the War on Terror. We seem to forget, at times, the weight of men and women who have to draw themselves apart and make the momentous decisions. In Franklin D. Roosevelt's time, there was D-Day and the atomic bomb at Hiroshima, and those were the daunting plans near the end. The last century was bloody and the struggle continues and I'm grateful for the past avant-garde. We're fortunate now to have the overwhelming means to launch missiles with precision, at the same time we hand out humanitarian aid. What we can seize most from history, from the response to the events that unfolded at Pearl Harbor, is a priceless, remarkable heritage. If we will allow it, the legacy can still guide us through the dark, uncharted waters in which we must surely pass. A thing might be hard and the War on Terror might be excruciating, but that doesn't mean it's not right. In fact, the very things that stretch our heartstrings to near breaking for a season may bear the most lasting rewards. I met a businessman once in Manhattan just two months after the September 11 attacks and he had spent hours overlooking the devastation of the World Trade Center. He told me he did it because he wanted it to sink in; he wanted it to penetrate long enough and deeply enough that he could see his country through the strife ahead. I hope wherever that man is now, the same kind of fire and commitment still kindle. I have heard one theologian say that the most important word of our generation may simply be this: remember.

We can remember that all of us are, in some way, indebted to the vision of immigrants. We can remember that freedom carries a price no matter how long we've been here, and that we are not the only nation entitled to it. That we have the wherewithal to change landscape for the better at times is a gift as well as a burden. We can remember that we are all so inextricably entwined now that what is cultivated in faraway lands has a way of spilling onto our own shores. I was privileged last year to become acquainted with a former prisoner of war, a man who had dared as a teenager to defy Hitler. The leader of his group was executed, and his second friend was also imprisoned for the resistance. The labor and the beatings were so brutal for seven years that they envied the friend who had been killed. Karl-Heinz Schnibbe was German and, after one of his speaking engagements, he was approached by a Jewish man.

He was no mere audience member: he had lost countless family and friends to the Nazi holocaust. "Why?" he asked Karl. "Why did the Germans follow a monster like that? You are German. Explain it to me."

The simplicity in the answer from this man I so admired took me somewhat aback. It wasn't just the evil. He felt the more common people were so desperate for relief from the oppressive depression and the aftermath of World War I—they would have done anything, followed anyone who promised an alternative life. It was one man's perception, but he was once an important player in that arena. I can't speak for him on any other matter except that exchange. I just believe his response was one of the reasons for the Marshall Plan, one of the reasons for the immense resources invested in reconstruction after World War II. It is one of the reasons why we root out the entities that breed the same desperation and the terrorism in a few parts of our world now. It may seem like a long haul; it may be a terribly hard haul; but humanity is worthy of the haul.

Just a few months ago, on July 4, 2004 there was a discreet and small gathering in a hotel in Provo, Utah. It was an impromptu meeting that followed a religious patriotic service that capped off an event called America's Freedom Festival. Families had slept on streets overnight along the patriotic parade route to pay homage to liberty and those who had fought for it. There had been more than 60,000 people in the stadium when Jorge Rincon's family had been honored on stage for their sacrifice. The program, which included a tribute to former President Ronald Reagan, incidentally, was broadcast throughout the world to the troops. Everywhere we went the family was embraced, consoled, and paid appropriate respect for Diego's service. If there had been times when we had questioned the stomach of our citizens to see a cause through—to actually see the

War on Terror through—there was an enduring reassurance that we still had the stuff, that our hallmark nationalism was alive and well that week. Jorge and Yolanda Rincon came face-to-face with two pioneers from Iraq at their hotel later that evening. Emad Dhia and his wife, Basma Fakri, had been honored, too, for their efforts to rebuild a dream in their homeland. I wondered amid the tears and the feeling of that meeting and the unsurpassed gratitude of this couple—I wondered if in their soul wrenching of the past, they'd ever considered the possibility they might not see the fall of Saddam's regime in their lifetimes. Emad promised Jorge that one day they would return together to the site of the homicide bombing and to the site of Diego's spilled blood. It was a bittersweet irony that Emad was a native from the city of Al-Najaf, and that it was he who promised that visionary day. "It will take time," he said. "But you will see. Your son will not have died in vain."

I was struck as profoundly by one of Basma's comments made earlier during the Freedom Awards Gala. She was an advocate for women's rights in Iraq and she had faced a new ideal: approximately one-half of the population of her homeland consisted of women—it was the women who should finally gain a voice. When the hand that rocked the cradle was given an extraordinary new measure of liberty, an entire generation could be so profoundly influenced. I looked at Basma and I looked at Yolanda, that mother among all selfless mothers. I saw the promise amid the heartache because—if you want to know what made Diego so special—you had only to look at the one who shaped him.

All of the virtues and the atrocities of the world are sown in the human heart in such small beginnings. Weapons are just tools that can be used to completely destroy or protect or liberate. Nineteen hijackers stormed the United States, and they turned airliners into missiles. They merely came armed with a handful of box cutters; it was the human heart that compelled them. It will take not a few human hearts to turn the thing around now—to empower not only the hands that rock the cradles, but change the cradles themselves. But I believe, in our most unthinkable hours, we will be able to acquaint ourselves with valor and honor, having seen their faces lit so remarkably before. I do believe, in our most unthinkable hours, that we will raise the unfailing light that shines forth on future generations. I do believe that we can and will enable them to yet stand undaunted in the land of the free and the home of the brave.

I may not persuade the harshest critics of the war that what we are about is right, but I hope some can discern the historic and moral depth that has ultimately shaped the conviction. I hope, above all, what is plainly seen and appreciated are the soldiers who have fallen for our dreams. And I hope, in that same tenor, what is plainly seen and appreciated are the soldiers who still battle at home and abroad. I wished so often that everyone could have had the privilege I did on such a personal and human glimpse. When you speak to an infantry soldier and you hear of the deprivation, what it is to lay awake at night with the purest longing of home—the taste of his mother's cooking and the sweet smell of his girl and the feel of a long walk through the tall grass all brushing at him— you come to understand, in some small way, one of the ultimate definitions of sacrifice. It's the softness in such cold, hardened combat that makes his jaw ache so that it's too hard to dam what wants to spill onto his face. I wish that every American could hear of a fatigue so profound that rocket-propelled grenades and the constant barrage of enemy artillery didn't stir that same soldier when he finally earned his turn to succumb to some trench in the desert for an hour or two. All I humbly ask is that we remember that many of our forces continue to suffer a great deal—and then I ask that we remember that the Outlaw Platoon of the Rock of the Marne had it as hard as anyone, and remember them in the next deployment they face.

They lost half their squad in the first ten days of Operation Iraqi Freedom; the first to suffer casualties at the hands of that evil at that military checkpoint. They lost their brothers and they lost their innocence on a divided stretch of highway. No one will ever be able to really touch the wrench of that moment or the haunting as they mounted in the Bradleys the following morning without their friends. They had made that sacred pact before leaving Kuwait, an all-for-one and one-for-all kind of pledge—they were mortally wounded by a promise to which terrorists and explosives seldom give their honor. They battled and dreamed and laughed and hurt so hard alongside their fellow soldiers, there are ghosts that will likely walk beside them the rest of their days. But they overcame the sorrow and bridled the fury and never stopped their controlled and disciplined march to Baghdad until their job was done. We may never fully comprehend how difficult it was for them to mentally transform themselves from combat infantrymen to peacekeepers in a matter of hours. They had to beat their swords into plowshares so to speak to protect neighborhoods, to guard schools and mosques along the way. They have *all* had to learn to build literal and figurative bridges with the people of Iraq now that major combat operations have been deemed over. Just try to understand when things overseas get messy: it's hard to reach out sometimes to people whose friendly or deadly intentions you cannot always discern.

They carry the pictures of their families back home and the comrades they lost and the little Iraqi children they'll always wonder about. It's really all jumbled in their hearts at times, and those are the scars that will linger. Captain Johnson and Specialist Cavazos told me about a bucket brigade kind of night when the supply lines had been overrun. It was their most perilous firefight ever in the ground combat phase, in the swelter of the Baghdad International Airport. The task fell to the Outlaw Platoon—and that platoon only—to clear and occupy the Special Republican Guard barracks before nightfall. The men were being toasted in the deadly sizzle of a desert airfield without even the minimal luxury of water. The local supply was tainted, and there was precious little time for sanitation in an offensive like that. They secured the area before dark and then positioned snipers on the rooftops in observation points. The soldiers were drowning in saturated DCUs, the salt stains of their sweat indescribable. I imagine they must have felt something like reverence when a fresh supply of water came on a truck.

They dumped the bottles like madmen into five gallon coolers and they hoisted their salvation on a pulley made of rope. Picture those coolers and their heave past five floors that must have seemed like a mirage to the snipers.

Our soldiers lived like that and they relieved themselves in coffee cans and burned their waste with diesel fuel. And so many of the Iraqi people lived in the same conditions, as they had for years, sleeping in houses with no roofs. One family in particular affected the platoon members profoundly—a family with tiny daughters who shaved their heads in the heat. They, with so little, offered food to the coalition soldiers as often as they could out of gratitude. It was the father who had suffered most, who had lived with so many wounds—one of them two inches in width. It stretched from his neck all the way to his groin, courtesy of Saddam Hussein's elite Republican Guard.

No matter the domestic issues of the day, these soldiers did not fight for sand or try to take any part of it for themselves. They followed orders not only because they were dutiful, but because they aimed for something lasting. The stock market might never be anything bullish or bearish or glittering to a group of men who barely make enough money to cover their car payments. Social security remains a fairly elusive concept to someone just trying to survive the next deployment. Groups like theirs and the Rincons of the world seem to understand better than most that without basic human necessities—without ultimate priorities like hope and freedom and dignity and safety—everything else becomes inconsequential. They've waged war for a good many things, and in that supreme fight, they've seen that it is far preferable to take on the enemy overseas. It's better to come face-to-face with him in a surprise attack than it is to see it in their homeland: these are the kinds of catastrophes that destroy morale and any kind of loftier pursuits of happiness. Imagine the detonation of that car bomb, not at a military checkpoint outside Al-Najaf, but near Union Station at lunchtime or in a parking lot at Disneyland where Diego and Fabian once played.

They are trying to spare us that—some of them have shed their blood, trying to spare us that.

It is my greatest hope for Diego that the country he loved, lived, and died for will always be as true to his memory as he was to her. It is my greatest hope that her citizens will always remember what Diego taught us an ocean, a sunrise and that endless sea of sand apart.

That a patriot is not made, nor is a nation's providence shaped, by birthright alone. We are only as collectively good as the steadfast individual who resolves, at whatever peril, to bear not only the blessings but the burdens of that freedom we hold so dear. God willing, the lives of the remaining soldiers will be long, beautiful ones filled with as much forward splendor as past sorrow; a hundred times the peace and prosperity to at least try to account for the poverty and brutality of war. Heaven only knows—and heaven *does* know—these men and women have earned it.

Whatever the length of their lives and mine, I can only say that their story will always be engraved on my heart—that the soldiers and families with whom I've worked have done their best to set it into a stone: there were warriors once alongside Diego and there are corners of the world that are going to be better places for that.

No amount of time or shifting political winds should ever rob humanity's memory of that kind of vision and courage.

THE IMMIGRANT

Jorge, Fabian, Diego, & Yolanda outside Funza, Colombia

The couple's second son was unquestionably skinny, a trait made more prominent by the thick tufts of black hair that swallowed his head. Yolanda swathed him tight, held his contentedness to her face, nuzzling him. He instinctively suckled the finger that caressed the small pout of his lip and she wondered, as all mothers do in the face of such purity and innocence, what lay ahead for him. The future had never seemed bleaker for Colombian citizens, the distressful state of their country only increasing with time.

Diego and Fabian in Bogotá, Colombia

Jorge dropped off his children at an elite private school and the image of them made his eyes watery. It was the morning sun in his face and then it was joy, seeing them grasp so boldly at the opportunity. Fabian took Diego by the hand and the two of them marched confident, little gentlemen in navy blue blazers and grey wool trousers. Diego twirled back toward his father, once, waving to him with all his might. Fabian smiled broadly and then they were off, running to the building. Diego's feet on the pavement were haphazard in a child ever willing to go along.

Diego and Fabian in Bogotá, Colombia

He carried large bills, the conversion rate was abysmal, and still it was the largest sum of his life. He had sold his couch and his refrigerator and his suits; the Armani and Versace all gone. They had sold the dishes and Yolanda's wedding dress and managed to keep Mickey Mouse. It had amounted to $3,000 in U.S. currency—by the owner's estimation not enough for a mere vacation to Disneyland.

God will provide, Jorge. Yolanda in her faithfulness, Yolanda in her steadfast support.

THE PATRIOT

Diego in Conyers, Georgia

It was the gratitude that lay between them, the battles they'd fought together for one extraordinary chance. Maybe they had all had to band together so much that it seemed the clock had turned backward. A return to those old-fashioned family values, to the industry, the intimacy and the respect. They ate dinner together and they worked together and they prayed and played—together. Diego was a child from a farm in the 1930s. A "yes sir" and a poster boy. He'd known deprivation, and he'd known he had it in him to turn the thing around. He was like the kid who had been raised in the Depression who could rise to the occasion of World War II. It restored something in Yolanda to see the virtue, to see the All-American goodness that stood before her.

Diego, Fabian and George at Disneyland

They really hadn't planned to have more children, despite Diego's constant entreaties. "Kids are expensive," Fabian had lectured him. They had fast been approaching their teens then. Jorge's carpet cleaning business had suddenly turned a corner, and still Fabian had been consumed with the economy. They had reached profitability, and Diego had sighed and resorted to the bathroom where he'd stumbled onto that most interesting stash.

He had found his mother's birth control pills and then he had hid them—because God helped those who helped themselves, it seemed.

Diego and Stephanie in Conyers, Georgia

She had gone into labor with their fourth child on April 13, 1997 in an audacious move on her part. So far as the men knew, the Masters Tournament was won on the back nine, and always on a Sunday in April. She had paced the halls, and Diego had appeared torn as he had taken his turn beside her.

Tiger Woods was up. He had strained for a peek and had been thankfully relieved as Jorge had come toward them both, hedging.

Yolanda had taken Jorge's hand in hers. "Oh!" he had cried, losing her grip …

"Did you catch that, Yolanda?" *He's on his way to a tournament record, a 12-shot victory over Tom Kite.* "He's only been in the pros since you got pregnant. Can you believe that, baby?"

Yolanda hadn't believed it. She really hadn't. *Please, God, send me a girl.*

Diego in Conyers, Georgia

He was an immigrant and when he'd touched down on America, he'd offered it some sacred thing. That's what America was—even with all its imperfections—a melting pot of devotion. People still came to the United States after more than two centuries to dream and to build and to contribute. The devil couldn't do that and so he'd enlisted his legions to tear them all down in revolt. Well, the devil would care to step aside because in this one thing, Diego was right. To one end he'd been born and to one end his family had come, and God help the next terrorist who threatened it. He rose up in fury with such

unusual clarity because it took such great hold: he was a warrior at heart and the time had come again when the world was in need of a warrior.

Yolanda, Diego, Jorge and Stephanie at Ft. Benning

Willing and able. That was the trumpet that blared in the blaze of the June sun. Diego was headed to the famed Ft. Stewart, the 3rd Infantry Division (Mechanized), the "Rock of the Marne." His statuesque halt came suddenly to life as he was turned blue and his father stepped back. The richness of his heritage, the fortune of his future—he owed it all to a singular vision. He leaned toward Jorge with absolute spontaneity, the pleasure and the sacrifice and the hardship—he kissed his father on the cheek with what seemed like the last remnants of boyhood still apparent in his smile. It was his finest hour yet: he was a man and a soldier and he reassumed his ramrod position.

THE SOLDIER

PFC Diego Rincon at the "Rock of the Marne," Ft. Stewart

Diego stepped foot on the sprawling garrison with the hot July sun on his face. In the summer of 2002, it was easy to be egocentric, easy to believe that it all existed for him. He had inspired that respect among his family and friends, that public deference that came with the uniform. In Conyers, he had passed veterans whose faces bore the emotion, an unmistakable regard. Perhaps it was a realization their youth was expendable—that their most virulent days had come and gone; perhaps it was relief that the full weight of humankind lay on fresh, idealistic shoulders.

Or perhaps it was sadness, the weariness of battle, of man's inhumanity to man—only ten months had passed since the September 11 attacks and the pain still reeled in many eyes.

PFC Michael Creighton-Weldon and PFC Paolo Ronquillo, Operation Iraqi Freedom

There was a childhood echo of insecurity that generally plagued even soldiers. Like the first day of school, Diego was naturally curious but couldn't overtly display it. He shielded the pique with the fallback of duty, attentive, restrained, and stoic. The private next to him did the same—exceedingly terse and focused. It was a façade, of course, the aloof demeanors, the halting mannerisms, the detachment. It would be something casual, some unassuming moment, which would eventually cement them, brothers. The rigors of training and the strain and the sweat would peel back the layers of dissension. All their hopes and their dreams, all their vulnerabilities would be exposed in a prop field somewhere….

The funny thing about Creighton, not easily discernible, was the immensity and grace of his heart. If he was shown kindness once, he would never forget it—he would die for a touch of goodwill.

SPC Anthony Farina,
Operation Iraqi Freedom

Farina foresaw the impending crisis, Diego being a shade of himself. His was the guileless manner that had once been Farina's, before his four years in the Marines. They were both small town boys, some of Atlanta's suburbs almost as rural as Farina's hometown in the heartland. They had that hopefulness—that finely honed leadership that came from being big fishes in small ponds.

High school had granted them the repetitive exposure, the means to take risks and absorb the outcomes. It was the small town kid who, more often than most, got to succeed or fail so publicly.

PFC Robbie Brooks at a
tactical Alpha Alpha in
Kuwait

Brooks was a military brat and that brief introduction to Diego seemed to account for a lot. *How ya doin'…nice to meet you*—not one of those cordialities applied. A wide open stance and a slap on the back and a big grin were going to be slow coming. To meet Robbie Brooks was to be offhandedly observed, to be sized up in a most interesting way. There was something of detachment that was oddly reassuring because Brooks avoided the rush to rash judgments. He nodded his head in general acknowledgment, neither overextended nor rude.

CPL Michael Curtin at Camp Pennsylvania, Kuwait

There had come "the talk," the commander's encouragement that stemmed from an assessment of burnout. Curtin had come so far in such an elite undertaking—that had been the well-meaning rhetoric.

Despite his sociability, Curtin had said little; he wasn't one to bare his soul. He had responded in the impeccable, curt kind of language that had made him worthy of his beret.

"No sir," he had steeled. "I prefer the infantry, sir." *There's nothing you can say or do to change my mind, sir.*

That had been all; he'd been quietly dismissed with orders to go to the 2-7.

PFC Michael Creighton-Weldon and PFC Adrian Cavazos at a tactical Alpha Alpha, Kuwait

It had often been said that history turned on small hinges, and this was a hinge kind of night. A soldier, just returned from airborne school, approached the wood line in the damp and burden that Georgia forests exuded with rainfall. His boots made a sucking noise as he slopped through the field, pretending indifference the closer he came to the clusters of hooches. There was something brewing, the sky was bulging, and the air was tense and electrical.

Cavazos wore a white gold wedding band, one of those immediate distinctions that caught Creighton's eye as he unpacked. That he retained it in the field was a telling sign, a man who wore his heart on his sleeve. The ring was too shiny, too polished and unmarred to have been on his finger for long. Creighton never judged a man—not when he was married—until he had seen the wife.

SPC Patrick Sawicki, Operation Iraqi Freedom

The men were soaked on the outer limits of their makeshift shelter by the sheets of driving rain. The ponchos collapsed with so little flourish that a wonder settled over the group. Cavazos scrambled to salvage the essentials, but his rucksack was caught in the downpour.

Someone cursed the rain.

Someone cursed the infantry.

Someone cursed Sawicki for good measure.

They sat cross-legged and from his outside peer Sawicki saw three bumps of heads in the tarps. It was one of the moments they'd laugh about later—but Sawicki was amused right away. To be so wretched, freezing, and isolated, under a drenching cloak of their own making....

He left them to their whining, a familiar voice crying out, questioning why they had all joined the Army.

The Outlaw Platoon in Kuwait

Their skills were razor sharp; their heads were in the game when the game simulated life and death. He saw something special—what a commander could never really dictate—he saw that his soldiers had chemistry.

In the infantry, the proximity drew men together and the hardships forced them to get along. Somehow Johnson's platoon didn't have an air of being compelled, though—their unity in the mock battles seemed to come naturally. It was the commander's job to assess the flaws, to play off the strengths of each squad. There were only a couple of weak links and there came the exceptional character: the stronger ones carried them like rucksacks. There were no glaring breaks, no breakdowns in morale; they just quietly compensated where they had to. It was a beautiful sight, a well-oiled machine, and Johnson had never been more pleased.

*Naemi and PFC Adrian Cavazos
at Cottrell Field, Ft. Stewart*

The men of 2-7 marched to waiting buses in the early morning hours of January 23, 2003. The sun hid its face in a final show of respect, in the mournful sympathy of rain....

"Baby, you know—I probably won't see any action. We don't even know there'll be a war."

But if there is, I'll be here. I'll be right here, Adrian. I'll be the one holding down the fort.

It's what her father used to say: "You hold down the fort." And she would hold still and hold on and hold back. Adrian needed that assurance, that light in her eyes, that beacon that anchored him to shore. If when he crossed the ocean again, if he came home changed, if he came home with less than two legs—Naemi would be there; she would always just be there; she was his constant, his hope, and his whole world.

*Saddam's revenge outside
Camp Pennsylvania, Kuwait*

The troops landed on Mars, a red planet of swirling sand that riddled their skin like fire ants. It assaulted them first thing, a constant irritant in their eyes, their noses, and throats; the enemy they could not contain. They hadn't arrived in season—the storms were most prevalent from March until August—and still a fine mist shrouded their sleeping bags, even the underwear they wore. Kuwait just blinded a man; and, after the dust settled, what they saw they didn't believe.

PFC Diego Rincon in a Bradley fighting vehicle, headed to a tactical Alpha Alpha

Diego set up his cot with the rest of the company, row after row of camouflage sleeping bags and personal effects spilling out of their rucksacks. The first night was bitterly cold and the soldiers were plagued by mosquitoes, trying to draw small, shivering breaths. They suffocated themselves in the bags, trying to evade the malaria; by mid-day, the tent was oppressively hot. Their belongings were covered in flies and Diego felt like a pig, roasting on a spit. It was the beginning of a mindless routine of living like animals in their own mire, bunkered in the same slop and sameness of oversized tents, the grit, and the tedium.

Only forty-eight hours had passed and the 2-7 was ready, primed for war just to get out of Camp Pennsylvania.

1LT Brian Johnson and PFC Robbie Brooks, National Training Center outside Ft. Irwin

Lieutenant Johnson was lazed in his portable chair, absorbed in a copy of *Band of Brothers*. He sat outside with his bare head exposed to the wrath of the sun in its decline. He used a Bic razor, a manual stroke, to achieve the smooth baldness that branded him. He wore dark glasses, small, round lenses that reflected the brashness of the heat. He assumed the pose of Socrates that was his habit, his index finger thoughtful on his cheek. Brooks leaned over him with his chin on his fist, Auguste Rodin's renowned statue, "The Thinker."

"Hey, Lord of the Flies," Cavazos called to Johnson, "we found out Rincon here was a cheerleader."

"You'll get his attention if you yell 'bookmobile' real loud. He'll run after it—like a kid and an ice cream truck."

SPC Hyomin Chong and SPC Anthony Farina, Operation Iraqi Freedom

Diego took a seat on Farina's cot, and it was covered with letters from Indiana. The children from the school where his mother-in-law taught had written to express their support. Every once in a while the soldiers got shipments like that: drawings and misspellings and beginning grammar. And then some of the hometown kids who had written were in junior high and they had soul-searching praise for the troops. *Anthony Farina. You are my hero. I wouldn't have the courage to fight like you do.*

He had held that notebook sheet for a very long time, his chest tightening on the effect of the words. He ached to live to hear his baby's first sentence and that sparkle in the eyes of his four-year-old. Sometimes he didn't feel like such a hero; sometimes he didn't feel he could take one more step.

PFC Paolo Ronquillo and SPC Adrian Cavazos at Ft. Stewart following their first deployment to Iraq, February, 2004

Ronquillo was bright. Ronquillo was articulate. He marched to a different drum. His face was sincere, even when he wasn't, and so his expressions were always mixed. He had the markings of a bygone school president except for the sardonic humor—Ronquillo had a purity and a childlike trust to him and still somehow came off as jaded. It took exactly one beer to fuzz his world and so he rarely drank.

None for me, thanks. It's all in the moderation. You know how I get if I drink.

Really, they didn't. He never lost control, but there was no starting point, no convention to begin with.

PFC Robbie Brooks, CPL Michael Curtin, PFC Erwin Rendon outside Ft. Irwin.
PFC Michael Creighton-Weldon in background

He poured out his feelings and then he folded the papers, and he never sent the letters to his mother. She was having hard time, a seamstress in New York, afraid to answer the door. Rendon's younger brother had been deployed to the USNS Comfort—all of her boys in the waves of combat. She didn't leave the house for fear there might be news, and she didn't answer the door for the same reason. Rendon wrote her about their sandbox, all the pains and the humilities and he told her about each of the men. Diego was kind and Black was funny and Cavazos could never sit still. "Mike Creighton is a white guy but, Mom, you should meet him: he has a big, Hispanic heart..."

Curtin, too, was writing, making a plea for his family to send something overseas to Brooks. Brooks never received packages, rarely got letters and Curtin felt the sting of reproach. Brooks had family and he'd been known to drive home to Florida nearly every weekend to see them. It didn't make sense and Brooks never let on that he'd held to his own hard and fast rule: there would be no word until the fighting was over, until he'd made it out alive.

PFC Diego Rincon at a tactical Alpha Alpha in Kuwait

They gathered for another briefing on a critical mission, what the commanders referred to as the Karbala Gap. There was a natural depression, a previous sort of impasse, which made the desert concave. "The Outlaw Platoon will pass through the Gap between the town of Karbala and the reservoir on the way to Bagdad. There is a high probability of getting gassed at the Gap."

The chemicals were able to float above the basin and then seep into the depression on the men. It was the Devil's Playhouse with no escape hatches, no safety valves, and no cameras. No mere tests of endurance or cogent thoughts and no thumbs up at the end. Saddam Hussein was a madman, and he was going to get desperate as each day passed in the conflict.

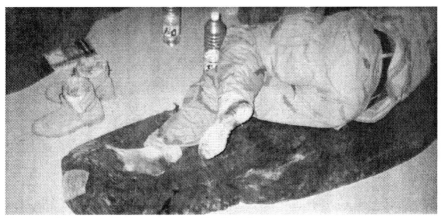

The feet of a fast and furious march to Baghdad

Creighton shifted again and stared at his feet, at the soiled sweat that would never wash out.

"It's hard enough over here. You need to have money."

"I'll pay you back. I swear it."

"Oh, you'll pay me back." He had to say it. Because he was frugal and he needed to ease things. There was clearly emotion, a touched kind of gratitude that just wasn't Creighton's style.

PFC Robbie Brooks, CPL Richard Snavely and CPL Michael Curtin in the barracks, Ft. Stewart

"Look guys, don't panic," Johnson tried to restore order among them. "There are going to be plenty of scuds...."

The men picked up where they'd left off in the game, Corporal Richard Snaveley with two balls and a strike. Snavely was half German and half Puerto Rican, which accounted for a lot in their interactions. The men called him Snuggles; he was the fabric softener bear and no one recalled who ordained him that. Snavely was just crazy enough to keep them all sane, the Hawkeye Pierce of their tent banter. He didn't wax as poetic as his alter ego of M*A*S*H, but he was spontaneous and comically warped. They figured someday Snavely would rise up and declare the war dead on account of his own lack of interest.

"Not even close Dogs. Not even close," Snavely pooh-poohed Saddam with disdain.

SGT Ronald Tolbert, Operation Iraqi Freedom

Johnson had the platoon sergeant gather the men and ask them to circle and take a knee. The finality of the moment was overwhelming and a relief; the men appeared to succumb gratefully. Black took Creighton's hand and Creighton took Diego's and so the chain of unity continued. With all of the earnestness his soul was known to afford, Sergeant Tolbert pleaded for them and pleaded for their great undertaking.

Diego felt himself repeating each phrase, a hallowed echo of feeling.

PFC Adrian Cavazos and PFC Allen Black, Operation Iraqi Freedom

It had been more than two days since they'd left Kuwait and every soldier was exhausted—the nerves had heightened the pain and malaise that came with traveling in such cramped quarters…They crawled into the Bradleys and were plunged into an abyss again of the unknown and the unseeing of their confines. The simple pattern they relied on, their only sure habit, resembled a kitchen table where every family member knew his place….

"Close your legs," Cavazos demanded of Black, who spread his legs wider to spite him. "I'm serious, man, you're in my space." Black became nearly spread-eagled.

"Ouch!"

"I told you man. My space. Your space. There's an imaginary line…right…here."

"If there's some kinda direction there…I…can't…see…you," Black's taunt was short-lived in his weariness.

SGT Todd Walker with an enemy weapons cache, Operation Iraqi Freedom

Sergeant Tolbert manned the main gun and Sergeant Todd Walker was the driver. Diego begged for a turn at the wheel. "Are we there yet?' he pestered from the minute they rolled out, offering his services to navigate. Johnson was amused by Diego's eagerness; at the same time it brought him up short. They were such little boys, still teenagers in some cases, and they carried the weight of humanity on their shoulders. For all of his ranting—or because of his ranting—Urquhart had trained them to be supreme and dependable. Johnson leaned to that notion, took solace in that notion, because even a commander experienced nerves.

SSG Chad Urquhart with newly liberated Iraqi children, Operation Iraqi Freedom

An Iraqi boy, five years old perhaps, appeared like an apparition, his face full of strange introspection. He hung back from the crowd a bit, mesmerized by the flurry and outpouring of those who surrounded him. He held out his hands, tiny and empty as if to demonstrate need. He took short, halting steps, something shy and remote and, in them, was an epic kind of progress. He wore the cropped haircut that had once been Diego's when he'd stepped onto American soil. His smile was engaging if not so broad as the Colombian child he mirrored. They were baby strides and the resilience to advance to the brink of something extraordinary for the first time.

It was simply promise: an ideal he could neither fully grasp, nor ever shrug off again.

The morning routine, L-R, in front: PFC Allen Black, PFC James Lane, PFC Adrian Cavazos, PFC Diego Rincon, PFC Michael Creighton-Weldon; SSG Chad Urquhart seated inside the Bradley and CPL Michael Curtin on top in the background

They were near the end of their morning routine; Johnson stirred his coffee slowly. They'd salvaged enough hot cocoa from their MREs to make his most exotic blend. He laid down his book and Tolbert took his position, the turret widening its arc. The car inched forward in a slink from the gunner and two civilians eased back to the farm. There were just the locals, the goats and the chickens, and Cavazos began to relax.

Someday, when they were old men, they would sit around a table and drink coffee and tell stories and laugh. A real table with real chairs and real cups and real food, and they would joke about using brown tees as toilet paper. For the moment, all they had was that morning routine, but there was a great deal of comfort in that shallow berm. Perhaps it was the predictability; perhaps it was the companionship; perhaps it was just the normalcy.

SGT Eugene Williams, PFC Allen Black & SPC Dustin Wheeland at a tactical Alpha Alpha in Kuwait

His voice drifted off and the last note, when it came, was melancholy, rich, and vibrant. It resembled the tones of the popular artist Usher and in its sophistication came a simple swan song—it was the summary of Williams' essence, nothing emanating from him that wasn't ultimately pleasurable and pure. There had been times when he'd ridden the men, when he'd had to reprimand them, when he'd been tough and exacting and unyielding. But admirable in Williams, Farina had always observed, was that he tried to do right by his men. If ever he came down on them, he sought each man out afterward, and made his peace with them right away. His high expectations were to be taken as a compliment, just like his music, the outreach of his soul.

PFC Paolo Ronquillo and PFC Erwin Rendon at Camp Pennsylvania, Kuwait

He was among the first to reach the safety net, and then he heard a familiar voice yelling.

"Friendly! Friendly! I'm making a move! Friendly at five o'clock!"

He shouldered his weapon, watching each back. There were more low crawls and approaches.

Friendly! They were moving in so fast and furious, it seemed he was surrounded on all sides.

They were gathered in like chicks under a hen's wing, except for one noticeable absence. He was poignantly missing, the last of their brood to be slow coming in and panic enveloped Rendon.

"Ronquillo!" he called. "Ronny Q, where are you??" A body lay motionless in the field. "Ronny Q! Is that you?" *C'mon, man please talk to me. Please get up off the ground!!!*

PFC Diego Rincon, Operation Iraqi Freedom

It looked on them curiously, strutted to the rise, and weaved in and out of the SAWs.

"What are *you* lookin' at?" Cavazos rolled sideways. "You got to get out of the rain, chicken."

Diego smiled wide, a sign of genuine pleasure he hadn't shown since Kuwait. The chicken hopped on his barrel, perched in front of the thermal and jutted its head in the inspection. "You see anything out there? I think we smoked 'em all." The chicken cocked its head as if contemplating....

"Let's eat that chicken."

Diego shook his head, rarely one to dissent, a softness overcoming his face.

"Leave it alone man. That chicken's doing nothing. That chicken isn't hurting anybody."

PFC Diego Rincon feeling "like Rambo" in Kuwait

The trickle of Brooks' clowning was already evaporating as Curtin made his move toward the car. Even when he wasn't marching, he looked like he was marching. Curtin in his undeviating stride. Farina picked out Diego, just by the graced assuredness of his walk, as the Bravo team edged out behind Curtin. He had flashed a large smile, too big for his face. *Okay, little bro.* Farina nodded. Somewhere in the universe there were onlookers, a crowd. Someone yelling to Diego, "No, no, no." He gripped his weapon in his Midas touch, the way he he had of turning tumbles into victories.

All roads lead to Baghdad, Operation Iraqi Freedom

Johnson sustained himself because he had to: each man had chosen his path. Each man had stood at a crossroads: *two roads diverged in a wood.* It was the "Road Not Taken," by Robert Frost, that had drawn their heartstrings to near breaking. And then it was those woods that beckoned from courage—all the longing and the sorrows of war....

Johnson himself could not succumb, so far from home, on the fringes of utter civility: the Karbala Gap loomed in all of its depravity; that symbol of their most sinister, earthly depression. If they could get the enemy on the run, they'd overcome it, roll all the way to Baghdad. If they could fight through their grief and wade through their grief, Saddam's statue would fall, in Firdous Square. They would stop and get shot at, stop and get shot at, but if they could just win every clay house, every raid....

Their training would kick in, it would pull the trigger, and their platoon would never lose another man.

THE CITIZEN

The Rincon family with select members of the Outlaw Platoon following Class A Inspections, February, 2004, Ft. Stewart

Cavazos stretched forth a somber hand to Jorge, and the pain in his eyes was unmistakable. He was a young man who desperately needed to face his demons and would rather have crawled into a thousand shell-shocked berms than face them in the grief of parents. Jorge pulled the young man to him, and it wasn't so much awkward at first as it was just plainly cruel. The resemblance to Diego was so remarkable, so uncanny, it took Yolanda's breath away. She felt her son in the surety of her embrace of him and the genuineness of his warmth. She clung to Cavazos at the same time she clenched her jaw in an iron will on her emotions. She couldn't squeeze the tears back hard enough and they fell on Cavazos' Class A uniform, the weeping of a mother who had just wanted one last touch, her son, her Diego.

Yolanda, Stephanie, Jorge and George at "The Healing Field" during America's Freedom Festival, July, 2004, Provo, Utah

He hoped he didn't have to explain that he knew what love and loyalty and liberty were all about because of what he had once lacked. He hoped he didn't have to describe his gratitude for light only because he had experienced the absence of light.

He rose to the full height of his stature and he tried to give voice again to the swelling that kept getting blocked in his throat. Perhaps it was that base humility; perhaps it was what the men sensed, not what they heard, but soldiers who had served with Diego and soldiers who had only known him by name began to cry with Jorge....

"Bad people killed my son, but they cannot kill my American dream. You are the reason I still have my American dream.

"You are my heroes," his voice broke again. "And you will always be my sons."

REFERENCES

3rd Infantry Division: About "Rocky," the Story of the Dog Face Soldier. 3rd ID theme song and history of Rocky, the bulldog. http://www.stewart.army.mil.

AC/DC. "Hell's Bells." Atlantic Records, 1980. Limited lyrics re-printed in accordance with "Fair Use" practices outlined in *The Chicago Manual of Style.*

Ackert, Lori Ann. Sister of Sergeant Eugene Williams, member of the 3rd Infantry Division's 2nd Battalion, 7th Infantry Regiment, United States Army, KIA, March 29, 2003. Two manuscript overviews, conducted August 22, 2004 and September 19, 2004.

Ault, R. & J. Reese. *Law Enforcement Bulletin.* "A Psychological Assessment of Crime Profiling. *FBI,* vol. 49, March, 1980.

Beatles, The. "Two of Us." *Let It Be.* Capitol Records, May 8, 1970. Limited lyrics re-printed in accordance with "Fair Use" practices outlined in *The Chicago Manual of Style.*

Birch, Glenn & Mary Lue. Respectively: the author's former high school English, Spanish and drama teacher; the author's former high school substitute teacher. Final proofreading of the manuscript, conducted October 4-11, 2004.

Bolívar, Simón. *An Address of Bolivar at the Congress of Angostura (February 15, 1819)*, Reprint Ed., Washington, D.C.: Press of B. S. Adams, 1919, *passim.* Scanned by J. S. Arkenberg, California State University, Fullerton. (Prof. Arkenberg has modernized the text.)

Brooks, Robbie. Specialist, member of the 3rd Infantry Division's 2nd Battalion, 7th Infantry Regiment, United States Army. Multiple personal interviews and manuscript overviews, conducted between March 10 and July 29, 2004.

Campaign Atlas to Wars of Napoleon, The American Civil War, and The Great War. United States Military Academy, Department of History. West Point, N.Y., 1983.

Cavazos, Adrian. Specialist, member of the 3rd Infantry Division's 2nd Battalion, 7th Infantry Regiment, United States Army. Multiple personal interviews and manuscript editing, conducted between March7 and September 18, 2004.

Cavazos, Naemi. Wife of Specialist Adrian Cavazos. Multiple personal interviews and manuscript overviews, conducted between March 10 and September 18, 2004.

Creighton, Russell. Father of Private First Class Michael Russell Creighton-Weldon, member of the 3rd Infantry Division's 2nd Battalion, 7th Infantry Regiment, United States Army, KIA, March 29, 2003. Personal interview, March 7, 2004. Manuscript overview, September 27, 2004.

Curtin, Joan. Mother of Corporal Michael Curtin, member of the 3rd Infantry Division's 2nd Battalion, 7th Infantry Regiment, United States Army, KIA, March 29, 2003. Personal interviews and manuscript overview on September 12, 2004.

Curtin, John. Uncle of Corporal Michael Curtin. Personal interviews and manuscript overview on September 12, 2004.

Curtin, Mike. Father of Corporal Michael Curtin. Personal interviews and manuscript overview on September 12, 2004.

Curtin, Michael. Family home videos. Review provided courtesy of surviving family members, September 12, 2004. VHS copy in possession of the Curtin family.

Curtin, Michael. Personal letters, January 26 to March 28, 2003. March 28, 2003 letter re-printed in its entirety in the book. Provided courtesy of surviving family members. Copies of correspondence in possession of A.E. Dimond.

Curtin, Michael. Video of Corporal Michael Curtin's funeral, April 11, 2003. Review of Karen Thompson's eulogy and concluding services provided courtesy of surviving family members, September 12, 2004. VHS copy in possession of the Curtin family.

Dave Matthews Band. "Where Are You Going?" *Busted Stuff.* RCA Records, July 16, 2002. Title re-printed in accordance with "Fair Use" practices outlined in *The Chicago Manual of Style.*

Dimond, A.E. "A Wave Goodbye." Personal collection of writings by A.E. Dimond. Original copyright, 1989. Edited by Cara Jean Means. Poetry appears untitled in chapter six of "The Immigrant." All rights reserved.

DropKick Murphys. "Faraway Coast." *Do or Die.* Epitaph Records, January 27, 1998. Tangential references written in accordance with "Fair Use" practices outlined in *The Chicago Manual of Style.*

Eagles. "Hotel California." *Hotel California.* Elektra/Asylum Records, 1976. Limited lyrics re-printed in accordance with "Fair Use" practices outlined in *The Chicago Manual of Style.*

Egan, Ferol. *The El Dorado Trail: The Story of the Gold Rush Routes across Mexico.* Lincoln: University of Nebraska Press, 1970.

Eldredge, John. *Wild at Heart: Discovering the Secret of a Man's Soul.* Nashville: Nelson Books, April 3, 2001. Limited quotation re-printed in accordance with "Fair Use" practices outlined in *The Chicago Manual of Style.*

Farina, Anthony. Sergeant, formerly of the 3rd Infantry Division's 2nd Battalion, 7th Infantry Regiment, member of Special Forces, United States Army. Multiple personal interviews in addition to manuscript editing, conducted between May 18 and September 15, 2004.

Farina, Anthony. Personal journals, January to August, 2003. Provided courtesy of the author. Copies of entries in possession of A.E. Dimond.

Fernandez-Armesto, Felipe. *The Times Atlas of World Exploration.* New York: Times Books/Harper Collins, 1991.

Fort Benning Basic Training Video. *United States Army F 2-58.* VHS copy highlighting Foxtrot 2-58, including video segments of then Private Diego Rincon during various exercises throughout BT, March to April, 2002. Provided courtesy of surviving family members. Copy in possession of the Rincon family.

Frost, Robert. "The Road Not Taken." *Collected Poems of Robert Frost,* p. 131. New York: Halcyon House Edition. March, 1939. Original publish date, 1916. Limited references written under the work's designation as "Public Domain."

Frost, Robert. "Stopping by Woods on a Snowy Evening." *Collected Poems of Robert Frost,* p. 275. New York: Halcyon House Edition. March, 1939. Copyright, 1930, by Henry Holt and Company, Inc. Copyright, 1936, by Robert Frost. Tangential references written in accordance with "Fair Use" practices outlined in *The Chicago Manual of Style.*

Geography and Population of Iraq.
http://www.cia.gov/cia/publications/factbook. Updated May 11, 2004.

History of the 3rd Infantry Division: World War I.
http://www.grunts.net/army/3rdid1.html

Home of the Infantry—A Proud Heritage. History of Benning.
http://www.benning.army.mil.

Iraq Country Handbook. Department of Defense. 2630-IRQ-037-02, Armed Forces. September, 2002.

Johnson, Brian. Captain, former platoon leader in the 3rd Infantry Division's 2nd Battalion, 7th Infantry Regiment, company commander at Fort Benning, United States Army. Multiple personal interviews and manuscript overviews, conducted between March 10 and September 27, 2004. Final editing, conducted between September 27 and 30, 2004.

Kauffman, Gregory. *Manuela.* Seattle: RLN & Company. October 9, 2000.

Khamphiphone, Kenneth. Friend of Diego Rincon. Personal interview conducted on August 21, 2004. Knowles, John. *A Separate Peace.* New York: Scribner, 1996.

Krulak, Charles. General and former Commander of the United States Marine Corps. *The Urban Operations Journal.* http://www.urbanoperations.com

Lauro, Shirley. *A Piece of My Heart.* Samuel French, Inc. As staged by the drama department of Salem High School, Conyers, Georgia. Tangential references written in accordance with "Fair Use" practices outlined in *The Chicago Manual of Style.*

Leno, Mike. Pastor of the Conyers Seventh-day Adventist Church, Conyers, Georgia. Multiple personal interviews and manuscript editing, conducted between February 5, 2004 and June 28, 2004.

Leno, Mike. "God and the Green Card Soldier." *Liberty Magazine*. Reflections of Pastor Mike Leno found in "The Citizen" were based on the original article and modified for use in the book with the author's permission. http://www.libertymagazine.org/article/articleview/364/1/68 Liberty Magazine. July/August, 2003 issue.

Light Infantry Platoon/Squad, FM 7-70. Department of the Army.

M16A2 5.56mm Semiautomatic Rifle, http://www.fas.org/man/dod-101/sys/land/m16.htm. Federation of American Scientists. pp. 1-5.

Military Operations on Urban Terrain (MOUT). FM 90-10. Department of the Army. http://www.globalsecurity.org/military.

Miller, Zell. United States Senator, Georgia. "Honoring Our Soldiers." *United States Congressional Record*. http://thomas.loc.gov/r108/r108.html. Senate archives. April 9, 2003.

Montemayor, Catherine. Diego's girlfriend prior to deployment. Personal interview conducted April 17, 2004.

Noonan, Peggy. *When Character Was King: A Story of Ronald Reagan*. New York: Penguin Books, 2002.

Norrman, Britt L. Linguist and international public relations consultant. Manuscript review of Spanish translations. September 23, 2004.

O' Donnell, Michael Davis. Major, listed as Killed in Action, February 7, 1978. Quote extracted from writings attributed, January 1, 1970, Dak To, Vietnam. http://www.thewall-usa.com. The Vietnam Veterans Memorial Wall Page is a non-profit endeavor maintained by veterans of the 4th Battalion 9th Infantry Regiment.

Operating from Key Locations. FM 19-4. Department of the Army. http://www.globalsecurity.org/military.

Pershing, John J. Former General and Commander-in-Chief of the American Expeditionary Force, World War I. Later served as United States Army Chief of Staff. Quote extracted from the *Rock of the Marne*. http://www.army.mil/cmh-pg/art/P-P/USAIA/Rock.htm

Reagan, Ronald. *Quotes*. http://www.reaganfoundation.com

Rendon, Erwin. Private First Class, member of the 3rd Infantry Division's 2nd Battalion, 7th Infantry Regiment, United States Army. Multiple personal interviews and manuscript editing, conducted between March 10 and September 18, 2004.

Rendon, Erwin. Personal correspondence. Various lines penned throughout combat in a single letter to his mother, January to August, 2003. Provided courtesy of the author. Original letter in possession of PFC Erwin Rendon.

Rincon, Adela. Mother of Jorge Rincon. Personal interview, conducted on March 5, 2004.

Rincon, Diego. Private First Class, member of the 3rd Infantry Division's 2nd Battalion, 7th Infantry Regiment, United States Army, KIA, March 29, 2003. Compilation video of childhood in Colombia, 1985–1989. Provided courtesy of surviving family members. VHS copy in possession of A.E. Dimond.

Rincon, Diego. Compilation video of high school activities, including cheerleading competitions, wrestling matches, and gymnastics, 1999–2001. Provided courtesy of surviving family members. VHS copy in possession of A.E. Dimond.

Rincon, Diego. High school journals, written throughout junior and senior high school years, 2000–2001. Provided courtesy of surviving family members. Copies of entries in possession of A.E. Dimond.

Rincon, Diego. Personal letters from BT and AIT, Fort Benning, February to May, 2002. Provided courtesy of surviving family members. Copies of correspondence in possession of A.E. Dimond.

Rincon, Diego. FTX journal, Fort Benning, May, 2002. Provided courtesy of surviving family members. Copies of entries in possession of A.E. Dimond.

Rincon, Diego. Video of family farewell at Fort Stewart, recorded hours before the Outlaw Platoon's deployment, January 22 to 23, 2003. Provided courtesy of surviving family members. VHS copy in possession of A.E. Dimond.

Rincon, Diego. Personal wartime letters, January 26 to March 28, 2003. Letters may not be reproduced or distributed without express written permission. Copyright, March 29, 2003. All rights reserved. Portions of the February 22, 2003 letter appearing in the April 9, 2003 Congressional Record have been modified slightly for length. Letters provided courtesy of surviving family members. Copies of correspondence in possession of A.E. Dimond.

Rincon, Diego. Video of PFC Diego Rincon's funeral, April 12, 2003. Provided courtesy of surviving family members. VHS copy in possession of A.E. Dimond.

Rincon, Fabian. Personal interviews and manuscript editing, conducted between January 28 and September 8, 2004.

Rincon, Fanny. Sister of Jorge Rincon. Personal interview, conducted on March 5, 2004.

Rincon, Jorge. Personal interviews and manuscript editing, conducted between January 28 and September 10, 2004.

Rincon, Yolanda. Personal interviews and manuscript editing, conducted between January 28 and September 15, 2004.

Ronald Reagan Legacy Project. Select speeches. http://www.reaganlegacy.org.

Ronquillo, Paolo. Private First Class, member of the 3rd Infantry Division's 2nd Battalion, 7th Infantry Regiment, United States Army. Multiple personal interviews, conducted between March 10 and September 5, 2004.

Sawicki, Patrick. Sergeant, formerly of the 3rd Infantry Division's 2nd Battalion, 7th Infantry Regiment, member of the CID, United States Army. Multiple personal interviews and manuscript overviews, conducted between May 18 and September 3, 2004.

Schmidt, Philip and Pamela. Friends of the Rincon family. Personal interviews, conducted between February 5 and September 11, 2004.

Simón Bolívar: Biography. "El Libertador." Biblioteca Virtual de Simón Bolívar. http://www.geocities.com/Athens/Acropolis/7609/eng/bio.html

Simón Bolívar. Encyclopedia article from *Encarta.* http://encarta.msn.com/encyclopedia_761569365/Bolvar_Simn.html. Sections I-IV.

Simón Bolívar, El Hombre. "Biografías y Cronología de Simón Bolívar." http://www.Simón-bolivar.org. Copyright Johannes W. de Wekker, June, 2004. Information updated June 14, 2004.

Smith, Jerry, Jr. English Department Chair and Director of Theatre, Salem High School, Conyers, Georgia. Personal interview, conducted May 4, 2004.

Soldier Training Publication, STP 21-1-SMCT. Department of the Army.

Stewart-Summer, Leslie. Former English teacher and Assistant Director of Theatre, Salem High School, Conyers, Georgia. Teacher of Eighth Grade Language Arts, Richard Hull Middle School, Duluth, Georgia. Personal interview, conducted May 4, 2004. Multiple manuscript overviews and editing, conducted between May 11 and September 10, 2004.

Support for Insurgency and Counterinsurgency. FM 7-98. Department of the Army. http://www.adtdl.army.mil. Editorial contributions by General Dennis J. Reimer Training & Doctrine Digital Library.

Thompson, Karen. Aunt of Corporal Michael Curtin. Personal interviews and manuscript overview on September 12, 2004.

Tiger Tracks into History—1997. http://sportsillustrated.cnn.com/augusta/history/1997. David Westin, Chronicle Staff. April 13, 1997.

Tolbert, Ronald. Bradley gunner and staff sergeant in the 3rd Infantry Division's 2nd Battalion, 7th Infantry Regiment, United States Army. Personal interview, conducted October 6, 2004.

Urquhart, Chad. Sergeant, squad leader in the 3rd Infantry Division's 2nd Battalion, 7th Infantry Regiment, United States Army. Personal interviews, conducted March 10 and October 14, 2004.

Walker, Keith. *A Piece of My Heart: The Stories of 26 American Women Who Served in Vietnam.* New York: Presidio Press. Re-print edition, January 1, 1997.

White, E.B. *Charlotte's Web.* New York: HarperTrophy, 1974.

Williams, Brandy. Wife of Sergeant Eugene Williams. Personal interview, September 27, 2004.

Author's Notes: In addition to personal interviews with the soldiers—as well as the numerous letters and journals referenced—facts have been verified by both declassified military and other public records wherever possible. In a handful of cases, some minor events in Kuwait have altered timelines for the sake of narration. In the event of very slight discrepancies between eyewitness accounts during combat, deference has been given to the ranking officer and/or the accounts of the majority of soldiers interviewed. Certain portions of the book have been reviewed by officers with covert operations experience and cultural expertise in Iraq. Due to the sensitivity of their continued military responsibilities, such editors have not been named in the back cover credits, or in the "References" section. Input from such sources includes the more correct transliterations of Arabic words which appear in English. Definite articles have been placed in such references as "Al-Najaf" to reflect a more appropriate spelling than "An Najaf."(The latter adaptation is a common Western practice owing to perceived pronunciation.)

Dialogue has been re-constructed, in some instances, to reflect both the prevailing natures of real life characters, and to reflect the sentiments that were expressed during the actual events depicted. The author has taken poetic license in the depiction of some minor details with the express permission of the characters involved. A. E. Dimond was personally present for the events described in the final chapter of "The Citizen." Due to the passing of the book's main character—and the continuation of the narration to that end—some noteworthy events of the Outlaw Platoon have gone unexplored. As noted briefly in the final chapter of "The Soldier," the Outlaws uncovered critical intelligence which helped support the theory that U.S. Navy Pilot Scott Speicher survived the crash of his F-18 during Operation Desert Storm. Despite the gruesome scene found in their SUV, described in chapter six of "The Soldier," the journalists who fell victim to the RPG attack survived.

Finally, Spanish references have been reviewed for grammatical and cultural accuracy. The translations provided best represent Latin American Spanish and, in some specific cases, local dialects in Colombia.

ABOUT
THE AUTHOR

A. E. Dimond is a Wyoming native with a distinguished career in sports marketing and corporate communications. A graduate of the University of Wyoming, she attended graduate school at Brigham Young University and received the Admiral Emory S. Land Award for her promotion of athletics in 1989. She has traveled to and worked in 32 countries, spending extensive time in Latin America. Her experience at the USS Arizona memorial at Pearl Harbor on September 10, 2001 deepened her concern for geopolitical affairs. Her media relations efforts during America's Freedom Festival in 2003 became the catalyst for writing patriotic non-fiction.

In addition to donating a portion of the proceeds of the book to Oliver North's Freedom Alliance, Dimond is working to honor coalition soldiers who have been permanently disabled in the line of duty in a series of written tributes. She has become a guest lecturer, helping youth groups document veterans' stories for the U.S. Library of Congress. Dimond speaks to various civic groups and religious denominations on "Liberty's Brave Defenders."

0-595-33484-9

Printed in the United States
24490LVS00003B/40-534

9 780595 334841